REYNER BANHAM
AND THE PARADOXES OF HIGH TECH

REYNER BANHAM

AND THE PARADOXES OF HIGH TECH

TODD GANNON
WITH AN UNPUBLISHED ESSAY BY
REYNER BANHAM

THE GETTY RESEARCH INSTITUTE | LOS ANGELES

In the practical, handy, inventive Englishman who rather makes a thing himself than relies on others to make it there is an anti-aesthetic streak, and design had to turn anti-aesthetic to evolve a technique rather than a style.
　—Nikolaus Pevsner,
　　The Englishness of English Art, 1956

CONTENTS

1   INTRODUCTION

15   CHAPTER 1
        IN SEARCH OF ALTERNATIVES:
        BANHAM, BRITAIN, AND THE NEW BRUTALISM

53   CHAPTER 2
        UNCONVENTIONAL COMBINATIONS:
        A CLIP-ON ARCHITECTURE

89   CHAPTER 3
        SAVAGE MINDS AND THE WELL-TEMPERED ENVIRONMENT

119   CHAPTER 4
        HIGH TECH AND THE PERSISTENCE OF MODERNISM

147   CHAPTER 5
        MAKING ARCHITECTURE: THE ETHICS OF HIGH TECH

173   CHAPTER 6
        ARCHITECTURE BEYOND BUILDING

199   CONCLUSION:
        BUILDING BEYOND ARCHITECTURE

209   PLATES

233   HIGH TECH AND ADVANCED ENGINEERING
            REYNER BANHAM

247   ACKNOWLEDGMENTS
249   ABOUT THE AUTHOR
250   ILLUSTRATION CREDITS
252   INDEX

INTRODUCTION

On 15 December 1987, the British architectural historian and critic Reyner Banham wrote to the publisher Axel Menges to provide an update on his latest book project. Two years earlier, Menges had suggested that Banham "write a book…that integrates today's High-tech architecture (Foster, Rogers, Piano, Mangiarotti, etc.) into a tradtion [sic] of almost 200 years of technologically-oriented architecture."[1] With *Making Architecture: The Paradoxes of High Tech,* Banham planned to answer Menges's request with a detailed account of the movement's defining characteristics, historical sources, main practitioners, and implications for late twentieth-century architectural culture. He included with his letter a summary of his argument, a draft outline of the book's contents, and an "extensively re-written introductory chapter," which, he claimed, "represent[ed] his current thinking on the subject."[2]

At the time, Banham was in the process of relocating from his home in Santa Cruz, California, to New York City, where he had been named the Sheldon H. Solow Professor of the History of Architecture at New York University's Institute of Fine Arts. The book, he explained, would have to be put on hold until he and his wife, Mary, had completed their move, and he was able "to get [himself] into a High Tech writing frame of mind."[3] Unfortunately, the following weeks did not go as planned. The cancer for which Banham had undergone surgery the previous summer had returned, and he relocated not to New York but rather to London, where he succumbed to the disease on 19 March 1988.

Banham's death at the age of sixty-six silenced one of architecture's most distinctive voices, and his unfinished project on High Tech points to lacunae in the history of late twentieth-century architecture that have persisted into the present. Though several publications have been devoted to the work of Norman Foster, Renzo Piano, Richard Rogers, and other architects associated with High Tech, only a few general treatments of the movement exist, and the topic remains largely

Piano + Rogers (Renzo Piano, Italian, b. 1937; Richard Rogers, British, b. Italy, 1933).
Centre Georges Pompidou (Paris, 1977). General view (detail). Photo by Michel Denancé. See p. 222, pl. 13.

unexplored by twenty-first-century scholars.[4] Similarly, Banham's late-career work on High Tech has been little discussed in the growing literature on his influential writing and thinking.

In the present book, I address these lacunae with a detailed examination of writings by Banham from the 1950s to the 1980s, a period that coincides with the prehistory and maturation of High Tech architecture. Chapters focus on key moments in Banham's early engagement with the New Brutalism of Alison and Peter Smithson; his measured enthusiasm for various "clip-on" approaches pursued by the Archigram group, Cedric Price, and others; his advocacy of "well-tempered environments" fostered by integrated mechanical and electrical systems; and his late-career assessments of Foster, Piano, Rogers, and other High Tech practitioners. I complement these textual analyses with close readings of salient architectural projects of the period, not to provide a comprehensive historical treatment of High Tech but rather to bring into sharper relief the relationship between Banham's argumentation and specific qualities of the buildings and projects he chose to examine and, in a few important cases, to avoid. In contrast to other studies that focus on Banham's early writings and many extradisciplinary interests, I devote significant attention to Banham's late writings on High Tech, including archival materials held at the Getty Research Institute related to his unfinished manuscript. Banham's previously unpublished draft introduction to *Making Architecture,* "High Tech and Advanced Engineering," has been included.

As Banham planned to demonstrate, High Tech was plagued by ambiguities. On one hand, it was seen as a visual style based on easily graspable tropes such as exposed structure and mechanical services. On the other, it was understood as an attitude toward building particularly attentive to social relations and functional performance. Critics of the period seized on these apparent antinomies to charge the movement—and often along with it modern architecture more generally—with crimes ranging from contextual insensitivity to capitulation to capitalism. Banham, by contrast, saw in High Tech a reinvigoration of the visual qualities and guiding principles upon which modern architecture had been founded. For him, High Tech represented the continuation of an "*other* modern architecture," one that developed alongside the canonical International Style of the 1920s and '30s and traced its genealogy through lesser-known constructivist sources to "les grands constructeurs" of nineteenth-century engineering.[5] This "alternative Modernism," Banham claimed, could counter not only what he viewed as the clichéd tropes of the International Style but also the anachronisms of the then ascendant idiom of postmodern architecture.[6]

As is well known, Banham often railed against entrenched conventions and dominant traditions in twentieth-century architecture, and several commentators have addressed the distinctly antiestablishment current that runs through his writings. In a 1999 treatment, Panayotis Tournikiotis concentrated almost exclusively on Banham's first book, *Theory and Design in the First Machine Age* (1960), in which, he argued, Banham "exposes the real modern movement in order to be able to reject it."[7] Anthony Vidler, in an excellent assessment, linked Banham closely to his mentor, Nikolaus Pevsner, and demonstrated important links between Banham's modernism and Pevsner's advocacy of the picturesque tradition. Vidler's Banham articulated a "Futurist Modernism," with a "call for a posttechnological, postacademic, even postarchitectural discourse" in his writings of the 1950s and '60s,[8] a call Banham answered with *Los Angeles: The Architecture of Four Ecologies* (1971), *Scenes in America Deserta* (1982), and other texts. Nigel Whiteley, in a comprehensive critical biography, ultimately conjured a pragmatist Banham. "Pragmatism and its associated values," he concluded, "underlay Banham's architectural thinking and freed his mind from the sort of dogma that had infiltrated much modernist thinking."[9]

Though I at times take issue with points made by my predecessors, I do not aim in the present book to contradict earlier interpretations. The Banham I present here exists alongside Tournikiotis's antiestablishment Banham, Vidler's futurist Banham, and Whiteley's pragmatist Banham. But where earlier narratives focus on Banham's well-known impatience with disciplinary conventions, I draw attention to his simultaneous and seemingly contradictory embrace of the traditional values inscribed in those very conventions. This somewhat paradoxical Banham was as prone to quip that "architects who genuinely see how narrow and restricting are the traditions of their profession normally get out of it," as he was, just a few lines later, to endorse "a world in which 'architect' is a meaningful and productive category of human being."[10] This Banham is possible not because he famously "changed his mind" over the course of his career,[11] but rather because he tended to structure his arguments around persistent antinomies — tradition versus technology, aesthetics versus ethics, style versus performance — that he saw as key features of modern architecture and central to his discussion of High Tech.[12]

Drawing attention to these dialectics, particularly as they played out in Banham's late writings, brings to light important aspects of his thinking that to date have gone unexamined. Few have noticed, for example, that the "*other* modern architecture" Banham outlined in later texts was not identical with his earlier idea of *une architecture autre*,[13] or that his late-career formulation of "making architecture," which involved "clarity and frugality in resolving functional problems *within* the canons of architecture," does not square easily with the antiestablishment agenda for which he is so often celebrated.[14] Revisiting earlier writings with the concept of "making architecture" in mind not only clarifies Banham's various postulations of otherness in architecture but also reveals an *other* Banham, one committed not only to discrediting entrenched conventions and dissolving disciplinary boundaries but also to maintaining and strengthening core traditions and values.

This more "practice-oriented" Banham provides a unique lens through which to reexamine High Tech architecture.[15] Banham's early writings on the modern movement and the New Brutalism, his midcareer advocacy of the Archigram group and various "clip-on" approaches, and his elevation of environmental technologies in *The Architecture of the Well-Tempered Environment* (1969) deal directly with the movement's primary antecedents, while his late writings on the work of Norman Foster, Renzo Piano, and Richard Rogers remain some of the most valuable treatments of High Tech and its main exponents. A reevaluation of Banham's engagement with High Tech not only unsettles prevailing opinions regarding one of the twentieth century's most influential architectural historians, but also sheds new light on an important movement in architecture that has received scant critical analysis.

Before proceeding, some ground-clearing of key terms is in order. Following Banham, I oscillate between using the term *High Tech* as a label specific to certain works of architecture dating primarily to the 1970s and '80s and as a more general description of any object that promises (whether or not it delivers) technological innovation or enhanced performance.[16] Though the literature is not always consistent in this regard, as far as possible, capitalization signals the former sense of the term.

Such consistency is more difficult to maintain with other important terms, including *modern, modernist, modernism,* the *modern movement,* and the *International Style.* Banham often used these terms interchangeably, as in the second edition of *Theory and Design in the First Machine Age,* which begins, "The 'Modern Movement' or 'The International Style' has had a long and productive life in architecture";[17] at the outset of *A Concrete Atlantis: U.S. Industrial Building and European Modern Architecture* (1986), where he discussed "the classic modernist architecture of the International Style in Europe";[18] and in the introduction to *Making Architecture,* where he referred to "the older Modernism of the International Style."[19] Given such usage, a full disambiguation of his terminology is not possible.

Nonetheless, it is important to approach the chapters that follow with an understanding of Banham's signal concern with questions of style, particularly the International Style, which he claimed in 1980 to be "the dominant style of our present century,"[20] and which he later noted had been his "prime subject of study" as a historian.[21] Alfred J. Barr, the first director of the Museum of Modern Art in New York, is usually credited with coining the term somewhere around 1930,[22] and it acquired its canonical air as the title of Henry-Russell Hitchcock and Philip Johnson's famous 1932 book of the same name.[23] The *modern movement,* on the other hand, is closely associated with *Pioneers of the Modern Movement,* the classic 1936 study written by Banham's dissertation adviser and mentor, Nikolaus Pevsner.[24]

In the present book, both *International Style* and *modern movement* usually refer to the ambiguous cluster of visual characteristics and sociopolitical values associated with the architecture of Walter Gropius, Le Corbusier, Ludwig Mies van der Rohe, and related figures dating primarily to the 1920s and '30s and occasionally stretching back into the late nineteenth century and forward into the postwar period.[25] As Banham used them, these terms typically retain a close association with Barr, Hitchcock, Johnson, Pevsner, and, for reasons that become clear below, Sigfried Giedion, and they often imply the shortcomings he found in those authors' formulations.

Modern architecture is best understood in this context as a broader term that encompasses the canonical work of the 1920s and '30s, as well as later developments, including the New Brutalism, clip-on architecture, and High Tech. This broadness greatly blunts the term's precision, as Banham acknowledged in his 1962 *Guide to Modern Architecture*. Given that modern architecture appeared to have "grown up" by midcentury, he explained, the term could no longer stand exclusively for the "bang-up-to-date, born-yesterday, as-of-now attributes" that characterized the major achievements of the interwar years.[26] It would be better, he surmised, to take it simply to mean "not old"[27] and to see the white-walled, flat-roofed, patent-glazed consistency of the International Style as representing the "teenage uniform of modern architecture."[28] Extending Banham's metaphor, one might usefully understand the New Brutalist, clip-on, and High Tech works discussed in this book as attempts to devise appropriate garments for a more mature phase of modern architecture in the latter half of the twentieth century.

It is also important to note Banham's tendency to see modern architecture not simply as a style within the even broader category of "architecture" but rather as constituting the whole of the field. "If it isn't modern nowadays," he wrote in 1962, "it isn't architecture anymore, but archaeology, cowardice, or fancy dress."[29] Banham's tendency to draw disciplinary boundaries by a process of exclusion figures strongly in my narrative, particularly in his late-career treatment of High Tech and what he saw as its main stylistic adversary, postmodern architecture.[30]

Of course, *modern* and its many variants carry implications well beyond issues of style. The modern *movement,* for example, baldly implies action and, as Pevsner used it, signifies not only a stylistic category but also a cultural impetus, the collective ambition of a group of people who had placed the machine in a privileged position within society and artistic production.[31] Banham certainly subscribed to this central place for mechanical technology in any conception of a modern movement, and maintained it in his own formulation of various "machine ages" throughout his career. Related and somewhat loftier terms such as *modernity* and *modernism,* while occasionally used by Banham in reference to style, more often imply a cultural condition associated with self-conscious innovation and distinct—if not always total—ruptures between the often anxious inhabitants of a turbulent present and the established traditions and conventions of the past.[32]

This extended explication of terminology has been made necessary by Banham's persistent use of finely tuned, often dialectically structured terminological distinctions throughout his writing. Consider, for example, his 1955 gloss on the two main types of "isms" associated with the modern movement: "One, like *Cubism,* is a label, a recognition tag, applied by critics and historians to a body of work which appears to have certain consistent principles running through it, whatever the relationship of the artists; the other, like *Futurism,* is a banner, a slogan, a policy consciously adopted by a group of artists, whatever the apparent similarity or dissimilarity of their products."[33] With this succinct partitioning of the modern movement's formal and ideological inflections, Banham set up his famous characterization of the New Brutalism as a contest between aesthetics and ethics.[34] A similar structure is apparent in his 1960 "stocktaking" of contemporary architecture, in which he opposed the "operational lore" of disciplinary tradition with the "apparent intelligence" of advanced technology,[35] and in his planned exegesis of High Tech according to a fundamental tension between visual style and functional performance.

A similar set of oppositional themes structures my narrative. First among them is Banham's commitment to architecture's accommodation of human subjects, a commitment that drove him to challenge core tenets of architectural humanism.[36] Second is Banham's repeated postulation of the fundamental necessity of a coherent visual image to any architecture. This allegiance to the image often put Banham at odds with the suspicion of architectural formalism he maintained throughout his career and tempered his brash antiestablishmentarianism with a conspicuous respect for certain of the field's long-standing habits and expectations. Finally, attention is paid to Banham's persistent evocation of the disappearance of architecture in the face of other modes of design. This enthusiastic promotion of visual dissipation stands in stark contrast to his commitment to bold architectural imagery and mirrors other thematic oppositions that charge his writings, as well as the architecture he wrote about, with a provocative tension that remained both productive and unresolved throughout his oeuvre.

Banham's engagement with these dialectics resonates with other oppositions he made thematic in his writing. In the 1960s and '70s, Banham proposed *Homo Ludens,* the theoretical "man at play" first conceived by Johan Huizinga,[37] as an alternative to the classical concept of the Vitruvian Man. Just as the Vitruvian Man stood for the idealized human subject addressed by classical and modern humanists, *Homo Ludens* provided a theoretical personification of the alternative audience Banham wished to engage with his technologically progressive agenda. Banham often invoked *Homo Ludens* while rhapsodizing the indeterminate programmatic accumulations made possible by new technologies and made popular by progressive youth culture. Yet while he tirelessly championed *Homo Ludens*'s distracted subjectivity, Banham cultivated in himself and encouraged in his contemporaries the keen eye and rapt attention of a humanist connoisseur. Further, though one might expect Banham's support of programmatic indeterminacy to extend to the objects from which it issued, visually inconsistent works—the fractured and disintegrated forms increasingly favored by the architects of his generation—found, at best, an ambivalent ally in Banham. The historian who introduced architecture to the formal juxtapositions of clip-on architecture routinely chose visually integrated works as models for the otherness he sought, articulating qualities such as "absolute consistency,"[38] "convincing unity of the total effect,"[39] and a "unified aesthetic for structure and services"[40] to describe them. If visual unity was not readily apparent, Banham responded at times with searing criticism, at others with conspicuous silence, and occasionally with cunning invocations of invisibility.

A survey of Banham's major books attests to the oscillating themes that pervade his writings. Banham's first and still widely read book, *Theory and Design in the First Machine Age* (1960), famously concludes by announcing the potential disappearance of architecture in the face of technology. His *Guide to Modern Architecture* (1962), by contrast, ends with a close reading of Mies van der Rohe's meticulous details. After *The New Brutalism: Ethic or Aesthetic?* (1966), his chronicle of the idiom for which he developed the idea of "building as an 'image,'"[41] Banham moved on to *The Architecture of the Well-Tempered Environment* (1969), *Los Angeles: The Architecture of Four Ecologies* (1971), and, later, *Scenes in America Deserta* (1982), books that draw attention to mechanical systems, urban structures, and natural phenomena that previously had been overlooked by the field. With *Age of the Masters: A Personal View of Modern Architecture* (1975), *Megastructure: Urban Futures of the Recent Past* (1976), *A Concrete Atlantis: U.S. Industrial Building and European Modern Architecture, 1900–1925* (1986), and *The Visions of Ron Herron* (completed 1988, published 1994), Banham turned his attention toward more specifically architectural (and imagistic) concerns before outlining a complex interplay of arresting imagery and a contrasting dissipation of visible form for the unfinished *Making Architecture: The Paradoxes of High Tech*.

Exactly how Banham intended to develop his notion of High Tech's "paradoxes" is difficult to discern. The archive holds nothing specific on the topic beyond a brief description of a planned closing chapter to *Making Architecture* titled "The Paradoxes of High Tech," which focused on the "extremes and limitations of High Tech as an architectural genre, [the] penalties of a maintainance-intensive [sic] architecture, the consequences of the information revolution, [and a] summing-up of [the] present position."[42] Nonetheless, Banham's attraction to paradoxical formulations is evident throughout his work,[43] and his persistent use of seeming contradictions aligns neatly with the philosopher Susanne K. Langer's description of the phenomenon: "An absurd term or self-contradictory proposition that continues to function in serious, systematic thought, although its logical scandal is patent, is paradoxical."[44]

Langer's formulation comes from her influential 1953 book, *Feeling and Form*, in which she laid out a theory aimed at resolving the antinomies she found to be both rife and debilitating in writings about art. While many authors postulated a simple polarity between opposed terms as sufficient to accommodate persistent contradictions, Langer insisted that such formulations be resolved. "The conception of polarity," she claimed, "intriguing though it be, is really an unfortunate metaphor whereby a logical muddle is raised to the dignity of a fundamental principle."[45] For Langer, the primary function of any art form was symbolic expression. In too many cases, she argued, a clear understanding of this fact was obscured by the tendency of writers (and artists) to incorrectly elevate an associated but ultimately irrelevant term in their formulations. "Each art," she wrote, "has its special incubus of natural misconceptions" that arises from poorly formulated polarities. She continued, "The affliction of literature is its relation to fact, propositional truth; of drama, its nearness to moral questions; of dance, the personal element, the sensual interest; of painting and sculpture, the pseudo-problem of 'imitation'; of architecture, the obvious fact of utility."[46] Langer proposed to resolve the paradoxical relation between utility and expression in architecture by exposing the irrelevance of the former term. "The created space of architecture," she wrote, "is a symbol of functional existence. This does not mean, however, that *signs* of important activities—hooks for implements, convenient benches, well-planned doors—play any part in its significance.... Symbolic expression is something miles removed from provident planning or good arrangement."[47]

Banham was certainly familiar with Langer's work; he even structured a 1964 lecture for the Association of Collegiate Schools of Architecture (ACSA) in direct response to the passage cited above. Admitting that "the obvious fact of utility has always been one of the stumbling blocks in the critical evaluation of architecture as an art,"[48] Banham went on to argue that Langer's attitude toward utility, though seductive as a general theory, was impossible to maintain in the criticism of individual buildings. Utility, Banham claimed, must remain a primary concern, and symbolic expression should arise naturally from functional necessity. As an example, he offered the highly ritualized collection of benches, hooks, and other functional elements in a traditional Norwegian farmhouse. In these, he argued, expression and utility collapse into one another and cannot be distinguished. Langer, he concluded, had gotten it backward: "Had Suzanne [sic] Langer been an architect rather than the inventor of a systematic study of visual symbols, she would probably have said that it was symbolic expression and not utility which was the affliction of architecture."[49]

But if, for Banham, symbolic expression was architecture's "affliction," it was a necessary one. Though he occasionally treated aesthetic issues with a degree of impatience, he scrupulously maintained them throughout his formulations. "Part of the business of being an architect and/or an architectural critic," he explained, "is that you are dealing among other things (and I insist on 'among other things')…with visual symbols which are acceptable or not acceptable, for fashionable reasons, for personal reasons, irrespective of the functions that the building has to serve."[50] Thus, for Banham, architecture's seemingly irreconcilable obligations to both aesthetics and ethics, to tradition and technology, to style and performance were not conceptual "muddles" to be resolved through the abstract logic of the philosopher but rather were part of the actual circumstances involved in the design of buildings and as such were to be accounted for through the descriptive methods of the architectural critic and historian.

While Banham was sensitive to the differences between the activities of a critic and those of a historian,[51] in his ACSA address, he closely linked the tasks of the two professions, casting them not in opposition to each other but rather joining them in their common concern for specificity and in contrast to theory's necessary tendency toward generalization. As he put it, "The production of a properly generalized theory of architecture really involves leaving out the particulars. If you are going to begin to generalize, then your final intellectual construct, document, or whatever which embodies the theory will have to leave out pretty well all the particulars in order to achieve a general rule. But, presented with a particular building on a particular site, criticism, evaluation, history cannot proceed in the absence of such particulars."[52] Thus linked to the specific qualities of the object of investigation, in Banham's view, both history and criticism required a primarily descriptive methodology, with the ultimate goal "to make clear how and why the building got to be the way it is."[53] He maintained this commitment to what he later termed "observational" history throughout his career.[54] And though he often assumed a highly polemical posture and proved to be a formidable influence on his contemporaries, Banham's principal focus was not to advocate a personal vision of how architects should conduct themselves (even if he occasionally gave this very impression) but rather to provide dispassionate documentation and evaluation of the actual circumstances in which they did so. If paradoxical formulations were among the hows and whys that brought a building into being, then they, and whatever "logical scandal" they carried with them, must necessarily find their place in the history of architecture.

Importantly, for Banham, the task of the historian extended beyond mere description and evaluation. "All major works of historical philosophy," he opined, "extrapolate present trends into the future condition of men."[55] A historian did not simply document the events of the past but also outlined what he termed the "History of the Immediate Future." At the outset of his career, Banham saw in the immediate future the impending maturation of a second machine age, an era of individually focused mechanical technology and truly progressive architecture that finally would bring about the unkept promises of the heroic modern pioneers. As he put it in 1980, "What had been promised by the First Machine Age, but never properly delivered, now [in 1960] seemed to be at hand."[56] Of course, Banham understood such predictions were fallible, noting in 1961 that current events are prone to "develop characteristics which you could hardly have expected from earlier results."[57] Banham grappled with unexpected developments in modern architecture throughout his career, and by the 1980s, a melancholic tone had entered his writings. A passage from his introduction to the second edition of *Theory and Design* attests: "Every now and again the Machine Aesthetic will produce a burst of creative speed, but in general this grand old vehicle is nowadays just sputtering its way to the junkyard."[58]

Yet, at the same time that Banham was lamenting the decline of modern architecture, Foster, Piano, Rogers, and other High Tech practitioners were putting up what he judged to be "the best buildings that are actually being built in Europe and North America," and they were doing so with all of modern architecture's "mythologies (social, economic, technological) still intact."[59] In buildings such as Foster's Willis Faber & Dumas Headquarters (completed 1974) in Ipswich, England, and Piano + Rogers's Centre Georges Pompidou (completed 1977) in Paris, Banham found a reinvigorated modern architecture, both technologically advanced and aesthetically persuasive, perfectly suited to address the challenges presented by everyday as well as monumental commissions.[60] Eschewing the often arcane rhetoric of postmodern architecture, High Tech architects, like Banham himself, wagered that the best strategy to produce a viable architecture for the late twentieth century was not to abandon modern architecture's founding principles but rather to stand firm in unwavering commitment to them.

This study begins with an overview of Banham's early career and the postwar context in which he matured, devoting significant attention to his promotion of the New Brutalism and his development of the concept of *une architecture autre*. Revisiting Banham's enthusiasm for early exponents of the clip-on approach and his curiously tepid response to later built works in that idiom reveal two important tensions: one between his advocacy of extreme programmatic diversity and his insistence on coherent visual unity in the works he supported, and another stemming from his simultaneous endorsement of the immersive experience of distracted building occupants and of the critical distance traditionally associated with attentive connoisseurs. An examination of *The Architecture of the Well-Tempered Environment*, Banham's most aggressive postulation of an architecture of technology, alongside competing theoretical agendas advanced by his talented pupil, Charles Jencks, foregrounds Banham's simultaneous commitment to the monumental imagery of traditional architecture and to the dissipation of visual form he so often found in progressive applications of technology to building. Later chapters devoted specifically to High Tech architecture examine Banham's early endorsement of projects by Foster, Piano, Rogers, and others and outline the development of his thinking in late writings including archival materials related to *Making Architecture: The Paradoxes of High Tech*. In these texts, Banham assumed a staunchly critical stance to postmodern architecture and labored to make a case for the continued validity of modern architecture. I continue with analyses of little-studied late works by Banham, including his posthumously published book on Archigram member Ron Herron, in which Banham suggests that architecture might productively be understood to exist independently of buildings. My narrative concludes with an investigation of an alternative trajectory outlined in Banham's late writings that points to the possibility of a mode of building unencumbered by architectural convention.

In the pages that follow, I devote significant attention to oft-overlooked themes such as formal organization, construction details, programmatic accommodation, and the role of disciplinary convention. While these themes carry my investigations deep into the realm of building construction, my aim is not to assert the primacy of traditional building in the history of late twentieth-century architecture or to twenty-first–century practice. Instead, I argue that it was exactly attempts to project architecture beyond building that led architects from the 1950s to the 1980s to reexamine—and ultimately to reinforce—traditional disciplinary values. And, in tracing a parallel commitment to rational, accommodative construction from the New Brutalism to High Tech, I demonstrate that a little-studied trajectory of seemingly orthodox works came much closer to Banham's call for viable alternatives to conventional practice by suggesting a paradoxical mode of building beyond architecture.

NOTES

1. Axel Menges to Reyner Banham, 7 December 1985, Reyner Banham papers, acc. no. 910009, box 8, folder 2, Getty Research Institute, Los Angeles. Hereafter cited as the Reyner Banham papers.
2. Reyner Banham to Axel Menges, 15 December 1987, p. 1, Reyner Banham papers, acc. no. 910009, box 8, folder 2. Though Banham mentions an earlier draft of his introduction here, there is no record of it in the Reyner Banham papers, and I have not been able to locate a copy elsewhere.
3. Banham to Menges, 15 December 1987, p. 1, Reyner Banham papers.
4. See "Making Architecture: The Ethics of High Tech," this volume, for a review of High Tech literature.
5. Reyner Banham, "High Tech and Advanced Engineering," ca. 1987, p. 17, Reyner Banham papers, acc. no. 910009, box 8, folder 3; and "High Tech and Advanced Engineering," this volume, p. 243. "Les Grands Constructeurs" is emphasized in the original.
6. Banham, "High Tech and Advanced Engineering," this volume, p. 245.
7. Panayotis Tournikiotis, *The Historiography of Modern Architecture* (Cambridge, MA: MIT Press, 1999), 151.
8. Anthony Vidler, *Histories of the Immediate Present: Inventing Architectural Modernism* (Cambridge, MA: MIT Press, 2008), 154.
9. Nigel Whiteley, *Reyner Banham: Historian of the Immediate Future* (Cambridge, MA: MIT Press, 2002), 410.

10. Reyner Banham, *The New Brutalism: Ethic or Aesthetic?* (New York: Reinhold, 1966), 135.
11. Reyner Banham, "Foreword," in *Design by Choice,* ed. Penny Sparke (New York: Rizzoli, 1981), 7.
12. See, for example, Reyner Banham, "1960—Stocktaking," *Architectural Review* 127 (1960): 43–48, Banham's famous two-column essay organized under the headings of "Tradition" and "Technology"; Banham, *The New Brutalism,* in which he outlined the eponymous movement according to a tension between the visual qualities pursued by and the motivating values adhered to by midcentury practitioners; and Banham, "High Tech and Advanced Engineering," in which he discusses High Tech architecture primarily through a distinction between visual style and functional performance.
13. Banham coined the term *une architecture autre* (an "other" architecture) in "The New Brutalism," *Architectural Review* 118 (1955): 354–61. For informative treatments of the concept, see Nigel Whiteley, "Banham and 'Otherness': Reyner Banham and His Quest for an Architecture Autre," *Architectural History* 33 (1990): 188–221; Whiteley, *Reyner Banham,* 117–33; and Vidler, *Histories of the Immediate Present,* 133–40. On the relationship of *une architecture autre* to Banham's "*other* modern architecture," see "Making Architecture: The Ethics of High Tech," this volume.
14. Reyner Banham, "Making Architecture: The High Craft of Renzo Piano," *Architecture + Urbanism,* extra edition no. 3 (March 1989): 154, Banham's emphasis.
15. I am indebted to one of the anonymous reviewers of an earlier draft of this book for the phrase "practice-oriented Banham."
16. Banham provided a useful gloss on the term in "High Tech and Advanced Engineering," 1–3, Reyner Banham papers; and this volume, pp. 233–34.
17. Reyner Banham, *Theory and Design in the First Machine Age,* 2nd ed. (Cambridge, MA: MIT Press, 1980), 9.
18. Reyner Banham, *A Concrete Atlantis: U.S. Industrial Building and European Modern Architecture* (Cambridge, MA: MIT Press, 1986), 1.
19. Banham, "High Tech and Advanced Engineering," 20, Reyner Banham papers; and this volume, p. 245.
20. Banham, *Theory and Design,* 2nd ed., 9.
21. Banham, *A Concrete Atlantis,* 242.
22. For a discussion, see Sybil Gordon Kantor, *Alfred H. Barr and the Intellectual Origins of the Museum of Modern Art* (Cambridge, MA: MIT Press, 2002), especially pp. 257–61; and Terence Riley, *The International Style: Exhibition 15 and the Museum of Modern Art* (New York: Rizzoli, 1992), 91.
23. Henry-Russell Hitchcock and Philip Johnson, *The International Style: Modern Architecture since 1922* (New York: W. W. Norton, 1932), for which Barr provided the preface, was released in conjunction with Hitchcock and Johnson's famous exhibition, *Modern Architecture: International Exhibition,* at the Museum of Modern Art. The exhibition catalog is credited to Hitchcock alone; see *Modern Architecture: International Exhibition* (New York: Museum of Modern Art, 1932).
24. Nikolaus Pevsner, *Pioneers of the Modern Movement: From William Morris to Walter Gropius* (London: Faber & Faber, 1936). The book was expanded and rereleased in 1949 by the Museum of Modern Art under the revised title *Pioneers of Modern Design: From William Morris to Walter Gropius* (New York: Museum of Modern Art, 1949). For an interesting discussion of the significance of the title change, see Irene Sunwoo, "Whose Design? MoMA and Pevsner's Pioneers," *Getty Research Journal* 2 (2010): 69–82.
25. In 1980, Banham set the relevant dates of the "'Modern Movement' or the 'International Style'" as 1925 to 1970 (Banham, *Theory and Design,* 2nd ed., 9). It is significant to note that the term *modern movement* does not appear in his draft introduction to *Making Architecture.*
26. Reyner Banham, *Guide to Modern Architecture* (Princeton, NJ: Van Nostrand, 1962), 13.
27. Banham, *Guide to Modern Architecture,* 13. "Not old" is emphasized in the original.
28. Banham, *Guide to Modern Architecture,* 18.
29. Banham, *Guide to Modern Architecture,* 17.
30. I discuss Banham's entanglements with postmodern architecture primarily in "Savage Minds and the Well-Tempered Environment," this volume.
31. Pevsner, *Pioneers of the Modern Movement,* 28.
32. A wealth of literature exists on modernism as a cultural condition. Gabriel Josipovici's *What Ever Happened to Modernism?* (New Haven, CT: Yale University Press, 2010) and Matei Calinescu's *Five Faces of Modernity: Modernism, Avant-Garde, Decadence, Kitsch, Postmodernism,* 2nd ed. (Durham, NC: Duke University Press, 1987), have been useful to my development of this book. For a particularly relevant collection of texts specific to architectural modernism in the postwar period, see Sarah Williams Goldhagen and Réjean Legault, eds., *Anxious Modernisms: Experimentation in Postwar Architectural Culture* (Cambridge, MA: MIT Press, 2000).

33 Banham, "The New Brutalism," 355.

34 Banham's 1966 distinction between aesthetics, which referred to the visual and stylistic characteristics of buildings, and ethics, which for him entailed the possibility of "making a moral stand about matters of design," echoed his 1955 comparison of cubism and futurism in "The New Brutalism" discussed above. See Banham, *The New Brutalism,* 134–35. Nine years prior to Banham's book, Alison and Peter Smithson linked aesthetics and ethics in the context of the New Brutalism. See Alison Smithson and Peter Smithson, "The New Brutalism," *Architectural Design* 27 (1957): 113.

35 Reyner Banham, "1960—Stocktaking," *Architectural Review* 127 (1960): 93–100.

36 For a discussion of humanism and the term's various inflections in 1950s architectural discourse, see "In Search of Alternatives: Banham, Britain, and the New Brutalism," this volume.

37 See Johan Huizinga, *Homo Ludens: A Study of the Play Element in Culture* [1938] (Boston: Beacon, 1955).

38 Banham, "The New Brutalism," 357.

39 Banham, "Design by Choice: 1951–1961," *Architectural Review* 130 (1961): 45–46.

40 Reyner Banham, "High Tech Architecture: The Beginning of an Argument," 15 December 1987, p. 3, Reyner Banham papers, acc. no. 910009, box 8, folder 3.

41 Banham, "The New Brutalism," 358.

42 Reyner Banham, "Draft Outline of Proposed Contents of: Making Architecture: The Paradoxes of High Tech," 15 December 1987, p. 4, Reyner Banham papers, acc. no. 910009, box 8, folder 3.

43 Alan Colquhoun drew early attention to Banham's tendency toward paradox in his widely read review of *Theory and Design in the First Machine Age.* See Alan Colquhoun, "The Modern Movement in Architecture," *British Journal of Aesthetics* 2, no. 1 (1962): 59–65, reprinted in Alan Colquhoun, *Essays in Architectural Criticism: Modern Architecture and Historical Change* (Cambridge, MA: MIT Press, 1985), 21–25.

44 Susanne K. Langer, *Feeling and Form: A Theory of Art* (New York: Scribner's, 1953), 16.

45 Langer, *Feeling and Form,* 17.

46 Langer, *Feeling and Form,* xi.

47 Langer, *Feeling and Form,* 98–99, Langer's emphasis.

48 Reyner Banham, "Convenient Benches and Handy Hooks: Functional Considerations in the Criticism of the Art of Architecture," in *The History, Theory, and Criticism of Architecture,* ed. Marcus Whiffen (Cambridge, MA: MIT Press, 1965), 91.

49 Banham, "Convenient Benches," 105.

50 Banham, "Convenient Benches," 91.

51 See Banham, "Foreword," in *Design by Choice,* 7. For a treatment of Banham's design criticism and its relation to history writing, see Naomi Stead, "The Rocket-Baroque Phase of Ice Cream Vernacular: On Reyner Banham's Criticism of Architecture and Other Things" (paper presented at "Techniques and Technologies: Transfer and Transformation," the fourth annual conference of the Association of Australasian School of Architecture, Sydney, September 2007). Whiteley provides another useful discussion in *Reyner Banham,* chap. 6, especially pp. 318–28, and in his conclusion, pp. 397–400.

52 Banham, "Convenient Benches," 92.

53 Banham, "Convenient Benches," 101.

54 On Banham's notion of "observational" history, see his "Actual Monuments," *Art in America* 76, no. 10 (1988): 173–77, 213, 215; and "Architecture beyond Building," this volume. In his ACSA address, he used the terms "existential" and "situationist" criticism to describe his method. See Banham, "Convenient Benches," 101.

55 Reyner Banham, "The History of the Immediate Future," *RIBA Journal* 68, no. 7 (1961): 252.

56 Banham, *Theory and Design,* 2nd ed., 10.

57 Banham, "The History of the Immediate Future," 252.

58 Banham, *Theory and Design,* 2nd ed., 10.

59 Reyner Banham, "Introduction," in *Foster Associates,* by Norman Foster (London: RIBA, 1979), 4.

60 On Banham's distinction between everyday "appropriate tech" and monumental High Tech, see "High Tech and the Persistence of Modernism," this volume.

CHAPTER 1

IN SEARCH OF ALTERNATIVES
BANHAM, BRITAIN, AND THE NEW BRUTALISM

Reyner Banham's entrée into British architectural circles in the 1950s coincided with a period of contentious debate regarding the future of modern architecture. Though as late as 1960 Nikolaus Pevsner would argue that the "style of the century" he described twenty-four years earlier in *Pioneers of the Modern Movement* was "still valid,"[1] the devastation of World War II led many to question the adequacy of prewar modernism to address the challenges of reconstruction. Such questions were particularly pressing in Great Britain. Modern architecture had arrived relatively late to the British context. Both before and after the war, its proponents, many of them (like Pevsner) émigrés from the Continent, had struggled against perceptions of elitism and an increasingly nationalistic political climate to win broad support from the architectural establishment, institutional clients, and the general public.[2] By the late 1940s, many British architects, critics, and historians had been experimenting with alternatives. For example, at the influential *Architectural Review,* where Pevsner served on the editorial board, a prewar editorial focus on modern architecture widened to allow for promiscuous affiliations ranging from popular art to the picturesque tradition. In private firms and municipal agencies, such as the Architect's Department of the London County Council (LCC), the so-called Contemporary style, redolent of vernacular precedents, was adopted by a generation of architects committed to "humanizing" the built environment. In academic circles, the writings of Rudolf Wittkower and others sparked a renewed enthusiasm for classical proportions. The fine arts witnessed a similar questioning of the tenets of modernism, as interest in the supposedly timeless and universal qualities of modern art gave way in many circles to nationalism and neo-romanticism.

Banham was part of a generation of young artists and architects, many of them combat veterans, dismayed by these events, which they viewed to be largely backward-looking, parochial, and sentimental. As Banham's widow, Mary, remembered,

Alison Smithson (British, 1938–93) and Peter Smithson (British, 1923–2003).
Hunstanton Secondary Modern School (Hunstanton, England, 1954). Interior view (detail).
See p. 25, fig. 1.11.

"We, and our friends, were far more interested in the work of European architects, Le Corbusier particularly, rather than what we considered somewhat 'tame' British work."[3] At the time, tempers ran hotter, particularly among artists in the Banhams' circle, such as Eduardo Paolozzi and William Turnbull, whom Reyner Banham recalled as aiming with their work "to kick Henry Moore in the teeth."[4] With similar venom directed at the establishment, Alison and Peter Smithson developed their own ruthless version of modern architecture, the New Brutalism, in the early 1950s. And it was by linking the New Brutalism tightly to the ambitions of artists such as Paolozzi and Turnbull that Banham would fashion his famous call for *une architecture autre*.

Both the New Brutalism and *une architecture autre* have received significant attention in recent scholarship.[5] In a 1990 study, Nigel Whiteley found the concept of *une architecture autre* to be central to Banham's writing. "Underlying all Banham's criticism," he wrote, "was a commitment not to form nor even a system of aesthetics, but to an *attitude*. And it was this attitude—derived from post-war *art autre* with its undercurrent of anti-traditionalism and anti-convention—which was manifest throughout Banham's quest for an *architecture autre*."[6] In a perceptive 2008 analysis, Anthony Vidler came to a somewhat different conclusion, noticing "Banham's insistence on the role of aesthetics—of the viewer and in experience—in the promulgation of a new architecture,"[7] and arguing that Banham's "real agenda with regard to 'une architecture autre'…[was] a call for an architecture that technologically overcomes all previous architectures, to possess an expressive form."[8] Thus, with one linking *une architecture autre* to an attitude and the other to a call for expressive form, Whiteley and Vidler together rehearsed exactly the tension Banham himself used to structure both *The New Brutalism: Ethic or Aesthetic?*, his 1966 book on the movement, and his initial formulations of *Making Architecture: The Paradoxes of High Tech,* which he left unfinished two decades later. Indeed, many of the dialectics Banham planned to investigate in the latter book—between style and performance, tradition and technology, architecture and the possibility of "other" alternatives—were present in his early work on the New Brutalism and find their roots in British architectural debates of the 1950s. And though a surfeit of literature on these debates as well as Banham's role in them exists,[9] their centrality to the formation of High Tech architecture necessitates a brief review of salient issues here.

Background

To begin, a few biographical notes offer some orientation.[10] Peter Reyner Banham was born in Norwich, England, in 1922. He began engineering training at Bristol Technical College in 1939, but his study was cut short by the outbreak of World War II. He spent the war years as an engine fitter in the Bristol Aeroplane Company, and then he began writing art reviews for the local paper in Norwich after the war. Following their marriage in 1946, he and his wife, Mary, relocated to London, where he undertook a course of study in art history at the Courtauld Institute of Art in 1949. Moving to Primrose Hill, London, in 1951 made the architect Colin St. John Wilson a neighbor and brought Banham into contact with a circle of ambitious young architects and artists, including Alan Colquhoun, Richard Hamilton, Nigel Henderson, Robert Maxwell, Eduardo Paolozzi, Alison and Peter Smithson, James Stirling, and William Turnbull, among others.[11] Sunday morning coffee at the Banhams' flat became something of a ritual for the group, what Banham later described as "an invisible college of a remarkable kind."[12] In 1952, he began doctoral studies at the Courtauld under the supervision of Nikolaus Pevsner. The following year, Pevsner invited him to join the staff of the *Architectural Review,* where Banham would remain until 1964.[13] Thus, by 1953, Banham had fallen into close contact with two groups that would constitute the opposing sides of a debate over the legacy of modern architecture in postwar Britain. On one hand, Banham was aligned with the young artists and architects who would form the core of the Independent Group and would author some of England's most progressive buildings throughout the 1950s and '60s.[14] On the other, he was employed at a prestigious establishment publication and was working both professionally and academically under Pevsner, arguably England's most venerated architectural historian.[15]

During his doctoral studies, Banham immersed himself in the literature of modern architecture. In addition to Pevsner's *Pioneers of the Modern Movement,* Banham identified Sigfried Giedion's *Bauen in Frankreich, Bauen in Eisen, Bauen in Eisenbeton* (1928) as a crucial text. Both authors located the sources of modern architecture in the nineteenth century, with the former crediting the English arts and crafts movement, art nouveau, and Victorian engineering as crucial antecedents and the latter offering technical advances in steel, reinforced concrete, and glass as seminal catalysts. Though one worked primarily through period styles and the other through building tectonics, both foregrounded historical continuities between the nineteenth and twentieth centuries and argued that the canonical modern style was well in place by the 1910s. In 1932, Henry-Russell Hitchcock and Philip Johnson provided a seminal catalog of works in the modern idiom in their famous exhibition at the Museum of Modern Art in New York and its attendant publications, including *The International Style: Architecture since 1922.*[16]

In examining these and other works, Banham noticed what he termed a "zone of silence, extending from about 1910 to 1926" in the historical literature.[17] Pevsner, he observed, concluded his study in 1914 with the Werkbund exhibition at Cologne, while Giedion effectively terminated his in the nineteenth century. The canonical works associated with the International Style—Le Corbusier's classic villas, Walter

Gropius's Bauhaus, Ludwig Mies van der Rohe's Barcelona Pavilion, and the modernist showcase at the Stuttgart Weißenhofsiedlung (in which all three architects participated)—date to the latter half of the 1920s. "In the process of creating this Zone of Silence," Banham wrote, "two alternative misconceptions were propagated—one, always in favour with some group or another, that there were scandals to be hidden; the other, the official line until fairly recently, that the Modern Movement is a direct continuation of the Rationalism and Functionalism of the nineteenth century."[18]

Banham turned his attention toward the "zone of silence" in his doctoral research, with a series of articles in the *Architectural Review* marking his progress.[19] He labored to explain "aberrations" such as Gropius's 1921 Sommerfeld House as part and parcel to the tumultuous aesthetic and political context of its day, and he was particularly attentive to the unacknowledged contribution of Italian futurists, German expressionists, Russian constructivists, and other groups in the formation of modern architecture.[20] After completing his dissertation in 1958, he appended a polemical introduction and conclusion and published the results two years later as *Theory and Design in the First Machine Age*.

If Banham's research into the misfit projects and personalities of modern architecture's early years demonstrated them to be lacking in scandal or embarrassment, his book exposed other questionable behavior in the period. In their propagandistic zeal to give the impression of a coherent, focused, and apparently inevitable movement, he argued, "modern architects decided to cut off half their grandparents without a farthing."[21] Major historical accounts of the period, he noted, tended to be "selective and classicizing,"[22] written "with all the Futurists, Romantics, Expressionists, Elementarists, and pure aesthetes omitted."[23] Further, continuities between modern architecture and nineteenth-century sources were not so much a continuation of the earlier century's rationalism and functionalism, as Giedion and Pevsner had written, but rather a continuation of the academic conventions codified in the supposedly antithetical École des Beaux-Arts. Finally, and perhaps most damningly, modern architecture's close links to technology, epitomized in Le Corbusier's famous manifesto, *Vers une architecture*,[24] proved upon examination literally to be whitewash, the plaster rendering concealing traditional blockwork at the Villa Savoye standing as an apt reification of Le Corbusier's overtures to technology, which Banham showed largely to be rhetorical veneer.[25]

Banham's book bolstered a younger generation whose interest in Continental modernism ran counter to mainstream developments in British architectural circles, which had taken a distinctly nationalistic turn during World War II.[26] By the mid-1940s, the *Architectural Review* had begun a rehabilitation of the English picturesque tradition with a series of articles on the topic by Pevsner and others.[27] This was a

significant move on the part of the *Review,* which, under the influence of its eccentric proprietor, Hugh de Cronin Hastings, had been a dependable proponent of modern architecture since the 1930s.[28] By the 1950s, the magazine had launched its promotion of Townscape, a mode of urban planning based on picturesque visual principles, the incorporation of existing vernacular construction, and an appeal to the inherent reasonableness of the English national character.[29]

The immediate postwar years in Great Britain also saw the victory of Clement Attlee's Labour party in the 1945 general election and with it a significant strengthening of the welfare state and a parallel institutionalization of the arts. Government agencies—including the Council of Industrial Design, founded in 1944, and the Arts Council, chartered in 1946—promoted a leavening of Continental modern art and design with elements of British tradition, which coalesced, in painting and sculpture, into a form of neo-romanticism based on nostalgic and often fictional portrayals of Britain's rural past and, in design and architecture, into the so-called Contemporary style.[30] Proponents of the Contemporary style drew inspiration from the socialist realism promoted in the Soviet Union since the 1930s by Andrei Zhdanov and from recent architecture in the established welfare state of Sweden. Prior to the war, modern architecture had had some success in Sweden, as evidenced by Sven Markelius's sober student union building at the Royal Institute of Technology in Stockholm of 1930 and Erik Gunnar Asplund's more playful buildings for the *Stockholmsutställningen* (Stockholm exhibition) of the same year (fig. 1.1). By the end of the decade, the supposed "objectivity" of modern architecture, which Asplund already had challenged with his exhibition buildings, was more specifically called into question as Swedish architects sought to reintroduce traditional aspects of coziness and informality.[31] In his 1937 Summer House at Stennäs (fig. 1.2), for example, Asplund employed a casual massing and a traditional, if somewhat stripped down, vocabulary of plastered walls, high chimneys, and pitched roofs, while in

FIG. 1.1 | **Erik Gunnar Asplund (Swedish, 1885–1940).**
Stockholmsutställningen (Stockholm exhibition), Entrance Pavilion (Stockholm, 1930). General view.

FIG. 1.2 | **Erik Gunnar Asplund (Swedish, 1885–1940).**
Summer House (Stennäs, Sweden, 1937). General view.

 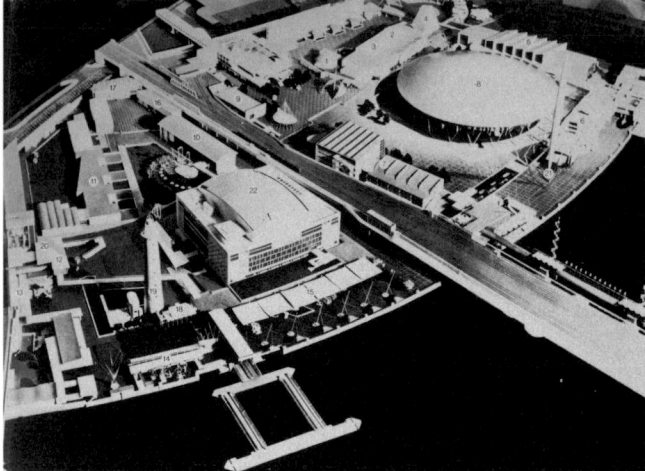

his celebrated buildings at the Woodland Cemetery in Stockholm, he combined aspects of modern and classical architecture in a bucolic setting. Asplund's later works became a model for younger Swedish architects such as Ralph Erskine and Sven Backström, whose projects neatly aligned with the ambitions of the burgeoning Townscape movement and were enthusiastically documented in the *Architectural Review* in the late 1940s under the banner of the New Empiricism.[32]

As *Review* editors developed these varied alternatives to prewar modern architecture, left-leaning British architects, including many associated with the Architect's Department of the London County Council (at the time, the main employer of younger architects in London), adopted the Contemporary style through the use of the "people's detailing," a vocabulary of pitched roofs, brick walls, small-paned windows, and other traditional elements strongly reminiscent of Swedish precedents and sometimes referred to as the New Humanism (fig. 1.3).[33] These new "isms" often were conflated with each other and with the Contemporary style in the literature of the period,[34] and they signaled—regional and temporal inflections notwithstanding—a desire across British architectural culture to provoke a "progressive humanization of the Modern Movement."[35]

In 1951, these various strands came together in the design of the Festival of Britain (fig. 1.4).[36] Frankly nationalistic in their ambitions, festival organizers excluded international participants and encouraged neoromanticism in the fine art they commissioned.[37] The buildings of the main exhibition on London's South Bank contrasted the more traditional manner that dominated other festival sites with a formal vocabulary somewhat reminiscent—particularly in the three-hundred-foot-tall cable-stayed Skylon—of Russian constructivism. The influence of Asplund's lighthearted interpretation of the International Style at the *Stockholmsutställningen* also was apparent, as was that of the proponents of Townscape.[38] Kenneth Frampton, at the time a first-year student at London's Architectural Association School,

FIG. 1.3 | **London County Council Architect's Department (Housing Division).**
Alton East Housing (London, 1953–56). View of terrace housing. Photo by London County Council Architect's Department Photographic Unit.

FIG. 1.4 | **Hugh Casson (British, 1910–84).**
The Festival of Britain, South Bank Exhibition (London, 1951). Model.

later remembered the South Bank festival site as "vaguely Swedish...in its overall tone."[39] The editors of the *Architectural Review* applauded the design for its resonance with the modern picturesque planning they advocated.[40]

Alongside the architects in his circle, Banham found little to celebrate in the Festival of Britain. While he later recalled an "observable internationalism" in the festival architecture, he noted that among architects of his generation, "the Festival style was anathema."[41] Colquhoun, the Smithsons, Stirling, Wilson, and other young architects bristled at the "humanized" and provincial modernism espoused by festival architects, practiced at the LCC, and promoted by the *Architectural Review*. In response, they turned their attention toward the work of canonically modern architects such as Mies van der Rohe and Le Corbusier, whose recent projects in steel and reinforced concrete (figs. 1.5, 1.6) seemed to offer more suitable models for their own work.[42]

The Independent Group and the Birth of the New Brutalism

Banham and his contemporaries found a similar taste for the conviction of Continental modernism at the Institute of Contemporary Arts (ICA), which had been founded in London in 1948 by the artists E. L. T. Mesens and Roland Penrose and the art historian Herbert Read.[43] In contrast to the populist trends promoted by official government agencies, the ICA advocated an elitist form of modern art with close ties to Mesens's and Penrose's roots in surrealism and to Read's purist, Neoplatonic aesthetic theories.[44] Though the ICA often received funding from the Arts Council and even staged an exhibition for the Festival of Britain, the institute operated largely outside the mainstream and quickly came to be seen as "the place to go for outrageous art."[45] Artists and architects of Banham's circle gravitated to the institute soon after its acquisition of a permanent headquarters in 1950.[46] In 1951, Richard Hamilton assembled the exhibition *Growth and Form* at the ICA to coincide with the eighth Congrès internationaux d'architecture moderne (CIAM) meeting,

FIG. 1.5 | **Ludwig Mies van der Rohe (German, 1886–1969).**
Illinois Institute of Technology (Chicago, 1945–47). View of (left to right) Alumni Memorial Hall, Metallurgy Building, and Chemistry Building.

FIG. 1.6 | **Le Corbusier (French, b. Switzerland, 1887–1965).**
Unité d'Habitation (Marseille, 1948–54). General view.
Photo by Lucien Hervé.

held at Hoddesdon, England.⁴⁷ The following year, the Independent Group began to meet at the institute, with Banham chairing the sessions that fall and through the spring of 1953.⁴⁸ The sessions built upon the interest in the sciences Hamilton had advanced in *Growth and Form,* with presentations on topics such as helicopter design, microbiology, and, by Banham, the "machine aesthetic."⁴⁹

Both *Growth and Form* and the 1952–53 Independent Group sessions exhibited a strong contrast not only to the populism of the Festival of Britain and the Arts Council but also, it is important to note, to the orthodox modernism espoused by the ICA leadership. Where Read "emphasized timelessness and everlasting qualities of beauty," Independent Group members were drawn to notions of the "ephemeral and accidental" that they had gleaned from their study of D'Arcy Thompson's classic 1917 work *On Growth and Form,* from which Hamilton had taken the title for his exhibition.⁵⁰ Thompson's outline of the development of biological forms offered group members a compelling model for the production of visual images that conformed to "very precise physical laws" but, they believed, were free of the "involved psychological processes" that permeated the art world in general and Herbert Read's writings in particular.⁵¹ In the eyes of the Independent Group, Thompson's visual materials, along with the materials gathered for the *Growth and Form* exhibition, possessed an air of empirical exactness as well as an immediacy and directness they found to be lacking in both the populist realism sponsored by government institutions and the orthodox modernism favored by the ICA.

In the fall of 1953, Henderson, Paolozzi, and the Smithsons pursued this interest in affective images in a small and now famous exhibition, *Parallel of Life and Art,* at

FIG. 1.7 | **Nigel Henderson (British, 1917–85), Eduardo Paolozzi (British, 1924–2005), Alison Smithson (British, 1938–93), and Peter Smithson (British, 1923–2003).** *Parallel of Life and Art* exhibition at the Institute of Contemporary Arts (London, 1953). Installation view. Photo by Nigel Henderson.

the ICA.⁵² One hundred twenty-two photographic prints—many of them reproductions of material from popular magazines and scientific journals—were hung at various angles from the walls and ceiling to create a visceral, immersive milieu (fig. 1.7). All of the prints, as Banham later observed, "had a coarse grainy texture which was clearly regarded by the collaborators as one of their main virtues."⁵³ This material sensibility was reminiscent of Paolozzi's recent sculptures and the texture of Henderson's own experimental photographs (fig. 1.8), and it resonated with topics frequently discussed among the Independent Group, including the rough concrete surfaces (*béton brut*) of Le Corbusier's recently completed Unité d'Habitation in Marseille (see fig. 1.6) and the coarse materiality of Jean Dubuffet's *art brut,* which Paolozzi had studied during a two-year stay in Paris in the late 1940s. Referring to themselves as "editors," the four organizers claimed to be guided largely by intuition, selecting images based on "what moved them."⁵⁴ As the Smithsons later explained,

FIG. 1.8 | Page featuring an image of *Parallel of Life and Art* (lower left) and works by Jackson Pollock, Alberto Burri, Nigel Henderson, Magda Cordell, Eduardo Paolozzi, and Alison and Peter Smithson. From Reyner Banham, "The New Brutalism," *Architectural Review* 118 (1955): 359.

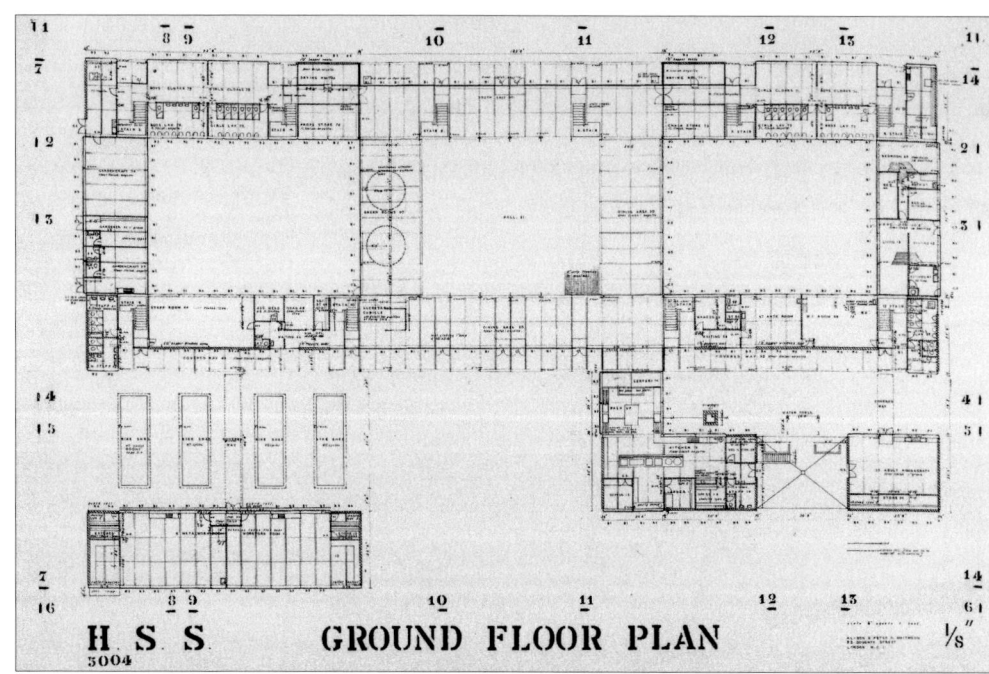

FIG. 1.9 | **Alison Smithson (British, 1938–93) and Peter Smithson (British, 1923–2003).** Hunstanton Secondary Modern School (Hunstanton, England, 1954). Ground-floor plan.

the aim of the exhibition "was to offer some evidence of a new attitude,"[55] which, as Alex Kitnick observed, had to do largely with "the effect that images had on human subjects."[56]

The Smithsons' desire to move past what they saw as the exhausted conventions of prewar modernism and to work instead with "what moved them" extended to their architectural practice. But where their curatorial interests took them well outside the ken of modern art, in their architecture of the period, they maintained close, if somewhat fickle, ties to the work of established modern masters. They outlined their position in a brief statement written shortly after the *Parallel of Life and Art* exhibition:

> With the completion of the Pavillon Suisse, modern architecture became academic.
> With the completion of the Unité, life has returned.
> In the *béton brut* of the Unité, a new human architecture has been born.
> Technique is seen once more as a tool: the machine as means.
> A new humanism has been born.
> The dead hand of De Stijl can be lifted from our backs.
> Cezanne [*sic*] can be seen as a boring painter of little importance.
> Perhaps even Pollock is more important. Who can say?
> All we know is what moves us now.
> This day.
> January 23, 1954.[57]

This short text appeared at a moment when the term *New Brutalism,* which for several years had circulated among younger London architects as a "mildly sarcastic" send-up of the various other new "isms" they derided, began to take on a more serious air.[58] From the start, the epithet was closely associated with the Smithsons, who adopted it as something of a personal battle cry that encapsulated their view of "architecture as a direct result of a way of life."[59] As they described it in 1955, that way of life involved "a sort of reverence for the natural world and, from that, for the materials of the built world." The latter, they claimed, would affect "a realization of the affinity which can be established between building and man."[60] Such relationships, they surmised, took on a deep resonance with human history: "In the Golden Age, the humblest swineherd between his doorposts was the image of humanity: deliberate, noble, and even elegant. The dream takes positive shape—a built domain where our everyday life will seem heroic."[61]

While the oft-cited importance of material choices and no-frills building construction should not be underestimated, it is important to underscore here the centrality of abstract, often classically inspired form to the Smithsons' early conception of the New Brutalism. In a 1953 text on their Hunstanton Secondary Modern School (figs. 1.9–1.11; see pl. 1), for example, they made their classical affiliations overt: "Plastically it achieves its ends through finite, locked, symmetrical relationships, a complex on a raised podium whose ancestor is the Sunion [sic] Temenos."[62] The following year, they implored their readers to notice an important duality in their understanding of the school:

> Consider, therefore, the Hunstanton School as having two lives: an everyday life of teaching, children, noise, furniture, and chalk dust, as equals with the building elements, all of which add up to the word, "School."
>
> And a secret life of pure space, the permanent built Form which will persist when School has given way to Museum or Warehouse, and which will continue

FIG. 1.10 | **Alison Smithson (British, 1938–93) and Peter Smithson (British, 1923–2003).** Hunstanton Secondary Modern School (Hunstanton, England, 1954). Exterior view.

FIG. 1.11 | **Alison Smithson (British, 1938–93) and Peter Smithson (British, 1923–2003).** Hunstanton Secondary Modern School (Hunstanton, England, 1954). Interior view.

to exist as idea even when the Built Form has long disappeared. It is through BUILT FORM that the inherent nobility of man finds release.[63]

In the Smithsons' conception of the New Brutalism, quotidian function, though a part of a building's "everyday life," was transient. Abstract form, by contrast, would persist even in the absence of the noble materials from which Brutalist buildings had been constructed, and was, ultimately, the guarantor of nobility.

In these early texts, the Smithsons' earnest solemnity with respect to abstract form is palpable. Read over half a century later, it is easy to miss that in the early 1950s, as Anthony Vidler pointed out, the movement also "carried all the overtones of an elaborate fiction, a style-hoax visited on the unsuspecting establishment of British left-wing modernism."[64] This sarcastic air, as well as the Smithsons' commitment to abstract form, has been obscured in recent scholarship, which tends to focus on the role of concrete materials, visceral images, and earnest rhetoric and to conflate the artistic ambitions of other Independent Group members with the architectural motivations of the Smithsons. In part, these tendencies stem from Banham's own famous 1955 essay on the New Brutalism, in which he introduced his complex notion of the "image" and named *Parallel of Life and Art* as "a *locus classicus* of the movement."[65] Yet, as Dirk van den Heuvel has pointed out, "the foursome responsible for the installation never explicitly conceived of the exhibition as a manifestation of the New Brutalism as such."[66] Indeed, while the influence of the young artists in their circle on the Smithsons is undeniable, the respective attitudes of the artists and architects toward the relevance of modern precedents to their own work were sharply divergent. As Banham explained in 1958, artists such as Paolozzi and Turnbull "resolutely rejected that aesthetic of pure form...and the theory of the Thirties; the Brutalists have rejected only the forms, on the ground that they are false to the theory; and the theory they accept in its full moralistic, functional, and rationalistic rigour, as it has been accepted, more or less, by progressive architects for over a century now."[67]

The forms in question here were those "rule-and-compass shapes" of the "white architecture of the Thirties,"[68] that is, of the International Style, whose compositional logic stemmed from exactly the classical sources that the Smithsons had held in high regard in the early 1950s. Banham, by contrast, saw such forms as impediments to technological progress, and they became important targets in his writing of the period. In "The New Brutalism," he crafted a delicate treatment of the movement that carefully isolated, neutered, and excised classical associations as it nudged the Smithsons away from conventional formalism and closer to the artistic ambitions of Henderson, Paolozzi, and Turnbull. A key component of his argument was the Smithsons' apparent abandonment in the early 1950s of the "formal" and classically inspired planning of the Hunstanton School for the "aformal" organization of their competition design for an extension to Sheffield University (see figs. 1.15, 1.20, 1.21). This move, Banham surmised, represented a crucial break with conventional modern architecture and could be understood as a signal of the Smithsons' commitment to producing "*une Architecture Autre*…which fully matches up to the threat and promise of *Parallel of Life and Art*."[69]

Banham's Brutalism

Nevertheless, in his 1955 text, Banham cited the Hunstanton School and the small house the Smithsons designed for themselves at Colville Place in Soho, London, in 1953, as "the points of architectural reference by which the New Brutalism in architecture may be defined."[70] Curiously, Banham had little else to say about the Soho House. It is not mentioned again in his 1955 essay, and it is entirely left out of his 1966 book. Similarly, the project largely has been overlooked in the historical literature on the New Brutalism.[71] This lack of attention presumably owes to the fact that the house was never built and that published drawings of it are limited to a spare collection of plans, sections, and elevations (fig. 1.12). Yet, with its brash combination of straightforward construction, sensible functionality, and often witty nods to classical convention, the Soho House serves as a telling encapsulation of the formal and historical tensions that would prove central to the New Brutalism and with which Banham would grapple throughout his career.

Planned for an infill site that had been bombed during the war, the Soho House comprised four floors measuring fifteen by twenty feet that were joined by a compact stair. The uppermost and ground floors were left undivided but for the stair and were to accommodate living space and a studio, respectively. The remaining floors were divided equally by a single partition to define spaces for sleeping and cooking on the first floor and bathing and storage in the basement. According to the architects, this curious organization of program was determined not in deference to the prevailing conventions of the project's Georgian context but rather by a sober consideration of environmental conditions. "The air and sunlight of the attics in the daytime," they surmised, "suggests that living quarters should be up top, with the bathroom in the cool dim basement."[72] Entry from the street was located at the northeast corner, with a small garden accessed over a concrete bench that spanned the south facade and cleverly allowed natural light to enter the bathroom below.[73] In anticipation of neighboring row houses to the east and west, uninterrupted brick bearing walls were planned to sandwich the interior spaces. Concrete lintels spanning between them capped large strips of windows (patio doors at the garden) at the north and south facades. The lintels would have been left exposed on the two visible facades and, along with a corresponding concrete beam at the center of the

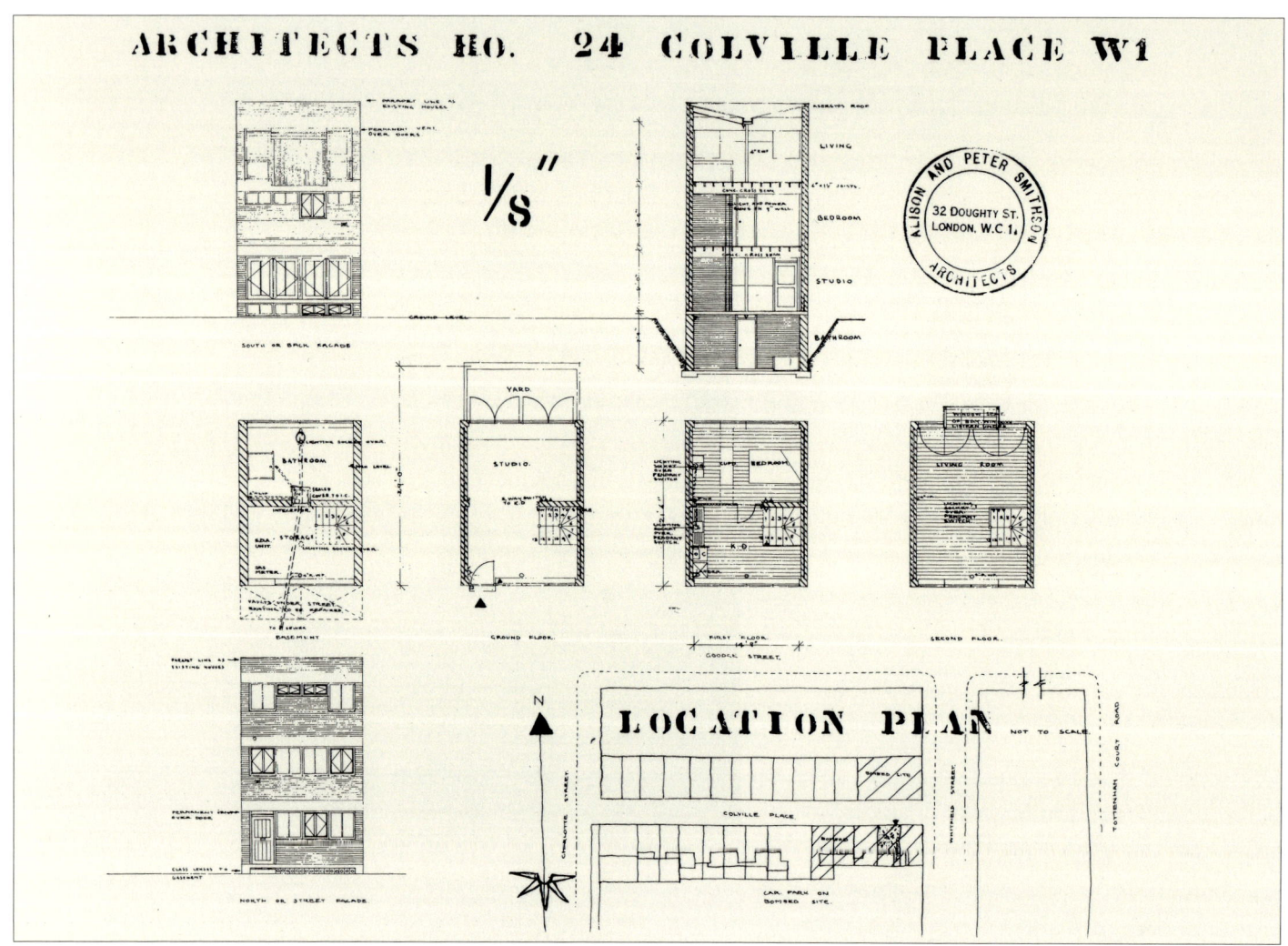

FIG. 1.12 | **Alison Smithson (British, 1938–93) and Peter Smithson (British, 1923–2003).** House at Colville Place (Soho, London, 1952). Plans, sections, elevations.

space, on the interior. Wood floor joists and tongue-and-groove decking also would have been exposed, though the clinker brick of the central partition and surrounding the windows to the north and south was to have been plastered. At the upper level, the wooden roof would have sloped in from the party walls to a single gutter that bisected the space lengthwise and joined a cast-iron drain pipe ceremoniously located at the center of the north facade.

The overall effect is curious, at once strangely formal and casually ad hoc. On one hand, the patchwork of bare brick, plaster, wood, and concrete on the interiors, in concert with what undoubtedly would have been a spartan collection of furnishings, would have given the impression of an austere yet comfortable environment free of the anachronistic conceits of its Georgian neighbors. Exposed plumbing and electrical equipment would have added to the frankness of the endeavor. On the other hand, conspicuously clever details (such as the glass blocks at the base of the bench at the back of the studio) and the project's insistent symmetries, proportional rigor, and cheeky axial relationships appear to have been devised with a mischievous wink in the direction of those who were paying attention. The axial comedy is best observed in the basement, where the toilet, lit from above by the south-facing bench-cum-clerestory, is honorifically aligned with both the bathroom door and the prominently placed drain pipe centered on the opposite wall.

Further pretensions, if less outright wit, were to be found in the dimensions governing the plan. The stair, for example, occupies a five-foot square module of a grid that extends over the entire plan of the building. Its corner position subdivides the front room into two additional squares, one five by five feet and the other ten by ten feet.[74] Each of the smaller rooms measures fifteen by ten feet and the larger ones twenty by fifteen feet. These proportions, 3:2 (musically, a perfect fifth) and 4:3 (a perfect fourth), were among those discussed by Rudolf Wittkower in his influential *Architectural Principles in the Age of Humanism* (1949), in which he described a preference among Renaissance architects for "an easily perceptible ratio between the length, height, and depth of a building."[75]

Alongside many in their generation, the Smithsons enthusiastically read Wittkower's book in the late 1940s and early '50s.[76] *Architectural Principles* contributed not only to the increased interest in rigorously applied geometric and proportional systems by the Smithsons and their contemporaries but also, particularly as interpreted and built upon by Wittkower's student Colin Rowe, to bridging the gap between modern architecture and the historical past.[77] Though most contemporary commentators (including Banham) focused on the discussions of abstract geometric matrices that formed the core of *Architectural Principles,* Wittkower devoted considerable attention in the book to "societal meaning" and tightly linked form, function, and symbolism in his interpretations.[78] These tendencies undoubtedly contributed to the book's influence on contemporary architects, who found in it an antidote to the prevailing tendencies of mainstream practice. As Peter Smithson put it, Wittkower's book had given his generation "something to believe in."[79]

Equally important to the reception of *Architectural Principles,* as Alina Payne has shown in a perceptive essay, was the book's echo of Sigfried Giedion's writings, particularly *Space, Time, and Architecture* (1941), in which he closely linked science with the arts and favored objectivity and rationalism over subjectivity and expressionism in modern architecture.[80] This desire to link art and science was a common theme among the Independent Group and many postwar practitioners of the Smithsons' generation, and it was adopted with well-known zeal by Banham, who would argue for a "scientific aesthetic" in his famous "Architecture after 1960" series in the *Architectural Review.*[81]

If Wittkower's book squared neatly with Giedion and the modernist establishment, it also diverged sharply from the status quo in Renaissance studies. Prominent earlier accounts of the period—such as those of John Ruskin, Geoffrey Scott, and Heinrich Wölfflin—privileged Renaissance architecture's sensuous aspects and its emotional impact on human subjects, and they showed little connection between the arts and science.[82] According to one reviewer, Wittkower's book fully eclipsed such interpretations and "dispose[d], once and for all, of the hedonistic, or purely aesthetic, theory of Renaissance architecture."[83] Taking specific aim at the sensuous humanism Scott advanced in his influential *Architecture of Humanism* of 1914, Wittkower proposed instead a humanism in which abstract geometries (primarily those inscribed in two-dimensional plans and elevations) took precedence over sculpture and ornament.[84] If, for Scott, humanism had to do primarily with the body, for Wittkower, it had to do with the mind.

This privileging of intellection over perception also put Wittkower at some remove from the visual bias of Nikolaus Pevsner and other editors of the *Architectural Review,* who had professed in a 1947 statement to be committed "to re-establish the supremacy of the eye."[85] Like Wittkower's, the *Review*'s position was bound up with the question of humanism, but their call for a "new humanism"[86] had less to do with Renaissance historiography than with an attempt to humanize contemporary architecture by intersecting it with the planning principles of the English picturesque tradition under the banner of Townscape. A key component of this process was "the recovery of ornament, color, texture, and a specific consciousness of history in relation to place."[87] Often, these qualities were sought by drawing attention to the "submerged third" of town planning, elements such as power lines, advertising, paving surfaces, and other everyday items deemed by the *Review*'s editors to have been left out in the division of professional responsibilities that characterized modernist planning.[88]

As mentioned above, the younger generation hotly disputed the *Review*'s promotion of Townscape through the early 1950s, and the Smithsons, who would later declare to have positioned their early work in direct contrast to the "going literary style of the *Architectural Review,*"[89] soon also distanced themselves from Wittkower's thinking. In April 1957, they summed up the formal development of the New Brutalism as a search for a holistic approach to problems of human inhabitation that of necessity moved beyond Wittkower's abstract geometries: "From individual buildings, disciplined on the whole by classical aesthetic techniques, we moved on to an examination of the *whole* problem of human associations and the relationship that building and community has to them. From this study has grown a completely new attitude and non-classical aesthetic."[90]

Banham's skepticism of Wittkower-inspired neoclassicism, as well as of the neo-picturesque position of his employers at the *Architectural Review,* is well known. Yet, in his famous three-part formulation of the New Brutalism's main characteristics as "1, Memorability as an Image; 2, Clear exhibition of Structure; and 3, Valuation of Materials 'as found,'"[91] one finds traces not only of Wittkower's intellectual humanism but also of the picturesque humanism of Pevsner and the *Review* and even of the earlier hedonistic humanism of Scott.

Banham's valorization of as-found materials, for example, calls to mind not only the rough concrete surfaces of Le Corbusier's Unité d'Habitation and the unvarnished interiors of the Smithsons' Soho House but also the quotidian bric-a-brac of the "submerged third" that drew the attention of the *Architectural Review*'s editors. Advocates of Townscape and the New Brutalism alike shared a keen attentiveness to architectural surfaces, particularly to the textures and colors of common building materials, and architects associated with both camps exhibited a tendency to work with, as opposed to against, the limitations of existing conditions. Indeed, Banham's valorization of materials "as found" lies as close to the Smithsons' aim to "drag a rough poetry out of the confused and powerful forces which are at work"[92] in society as it does to the *Review* editors' desire, through the incorporation of everyday materials into new work, "to invoke the messy vitality of the urban condition."[93]

Banham's requirement of "Clear exhibition of Structure," though obviously associated with visibly exposed structural assemblies in buildings, also had broader implications. As he clarified toward the end of his 1955 essay, "structure, in its fullest sense, is the relationship of parts" in a building.[94] With this expanded definition, Banham amplified an echo of Wittkower in his own formulation — both historians stressed the clear presentation of abstract organizational systems and integrated part-to-whole relationships that gave buildings their convincing sense of unity.

Also like Wittkower, Banham sought in architecture a legible reflection of the contemporary moment and even linked his idea of "Memorability as an Image" to the centralized church of Santa Maria della Consolazione (begun 1508) in Todi, Italy, the first realized building illustrated in *Architectural Principles*.[95] And though he noted that image-making was "conceptual,"[96] for Banham, memorability as an image had little to do with Wittkower's cool mathematical logic.[97] As he put it in an oft-quoted paraphrase of Thomas Aquinas in the 1955 essay, "Image may be defined as *quod visum perturbat* — that which seen, affects the emotions."[98] In this, Banham aligned his concept not only with Le Corbusier's definition of architecture as "the use of raw materials to establish stirring emotions"[99] but also with the hedonistic humanism advocated by Scott and others. But where Scott's hedonism cleaved closely with the ancient pleasures of Vitruvian delight, the emotions that interested Banham were of a more forceful sort.

Indeed, it was another quality of the Smithsons' work, its "*je-m'en-foutisme*, its bloodymindedness," that, for Banham, set the Smithsons apart from other

architects, such as Louis Kahn, whose 1953 Yale University Art Gallery (fig. 1.13) superficially aligned with New Brutalist visual qualities but fell short of the movement's aggressive stance due to "arty" details and movable display screens that threatened the building's formal clarity.[100] The Smithsons' frankly exposed structure, piping, and ductwork, however, delivered what Banham felt was a more unified and impactful coherence (see pl. 1). Just as importantly, the Smithsons' "abstemious under-designing of the details" resulted in "ineloquence, but absolute consistency" and carried the project's unvarnished conception through to all aspects of the visual field. For Banham, this ruthless consonance between concept and percept, planning and execution, and fact and appearance engendered an architectural object of singular, unmitigated coherence and formed the core of his concept of "building as 'an image.'"[101]

FIG. 1.13 | **Louis Kahn (American, b. Russia, 1901–74).**
Yale University Art Gallery (New Haven, Connecticut, 1953). View of gallery.
Photo by Lionel Freedman. Philadelphia, Louis I. Kahn Collection, University of Pennsylvania and Pennsylvania Historical and Museum Commission.

The term *image* held special significance in Banham's circles and has been much discussed in recent literature.[102] The affective quality Banham described was clearly similar to the images Independent Group members found "moving"—such as the paintings of Jean Dubuffet and Jackson Pollock reproduced in *Growth and Form* and *Parallel of Life and Art*—and sought to achieve in their own work. And though Banham suggested the term's "special use" at the time had been coined by Henderson,[103] this specifically affective sense resonates with a range of other sources. As

Alex Kitnick has pointed out, Banham's usage recalls the writings of André Breton, who claimed in his *Manifeste du surréalisme* (1924) that "the will is powerless...and no longer controls the faculties" when faced with surrealist images.[104] Anthony Vidler noticed a similar sense of the term in the writing of the art historian Ernst Gombrich, who in the 1950s was a lecturer at the Warburg Institute in London.[105] In a widely read 1951 essay, Gombrich discussed images not in familiar terms having to do with the imitation of form but rather as visual stimuli that provoke specific reactions in a perceiving subject. Drawing on biological research into animal behavior, Gombrich hypothesized that a viewer's response to certain images had less to do with the recognition of a represented object than with more primal aspects of human perception. As he put it: "We know that there are certain privileged motifs in our world to which we respond almost too easily....Our automatic response is stronger than our visual awareness."[106]

Concurrent writings by the philosopher Susanne Langer also resonate with Banham's usage. For Banham, the possibility of architectural objects being understood as viscerally affective images was a crucial step toward the achievement of *une architecture autre*. Langer, too, closely linked the idea of an image with otherness. In her widely read 1953 text, *Feeling and Form,* she wrote:

> The work of art...if it is successful, detaches itself from the rest of the world.
>
> Every real work of art has a tendency to appear thus dissociated from its mundane environment. The most immediate impression it creates is one of "otherness" from reality—the impression of an illusion enfolding the thing, action, statement, or flow of sound that constitutes the work. Even where the element of representation is absent, where nothing is imitated or feigned—in a lovely textile, a pot, a building, a sonata—this air of illusion, of being a sheer image, exists as forcibly as in the most deceptive picture or the most plausible narrative.[107]

For Langer, an object "becomes an image when it presents itself purely to our vision, i.e. as a sheer visual form instead of a locally and practically related object."[108] Langer's notion of an artwork's striking alterity aligned closely with the effects Banham praised in the work of Alberto Burri, Magda Cordell, Henderson, Paolozzi, and Pollock that he used to illustrate "The New Brutalism" (see fig. 1.8), while her description of an "impression of illusion" predicted Banham's insistence that image-making was "conceptual."[109]

Despite these alignments, Banham made no mention of these sources in his 1955 essay nor in his 1966 book on the New Brutalism. Though unlikely, the possibility remains that he was unfamiliar with Langer's book at the time,[110] but her absence, as well as that of Gombrich and surrealism, might better be attributed to

the close ties all three sources maintained with the establishment positions Banham resisted. Gombrich was associated with Banham's formal education at the Courtauld, while surrealism, through Mesens and Penrose, was part of the legacy of the ICA leadership. And even if, as Mark Jarzombek noted, Langer's writings were "*eagerly* consumed by a young generation of artists, architects, and architectural theorists uncomfortable with the strictures of formalist analyses of the modernist style that had so dominated aesthetic discourses in the 1950s,"[111] Langer had also exerted a strong influence on Herbert Read's art criticism and, on those grounds, presumably was best left out of the discussion.[112]

In the end, the main target of Banham's argumentation was the classically inspired formalism to which all these sources were in some way linked. He stressed in his 1955 essay that the concept of the image was not beholden to the "standards of classical aesthetics," and even, in its affective influence on the emotions, "could subsume the pleasure caused by beauty."[113] To bolster his case for an architecture conceived not so much against as beyond classical ideals, Banham invoked two unbuilt projects by the Smithsons that moved well away from conventional formalism. Their 1952 scheme for the Golden Lane Estate (fig. 1.14), he argued, was notable for "its determination to create a coherent visual image by non-formal means," while their proposal for Sheffield University (fig. 1.15; see also figs. 1.20, 1.21) moved further into nonformalist territory, with an "intuitive sense of topology" replacing conventional architectural composition.[114] At the outset of his essay, Banham had summarized the Hunstanton School's salient qualities as "1, formal legibility of plan; 2, clear exhibition of structure; and 3, valuation of materials for their inherent quality 'as found.'"[115] To underline the significance of the shift from formal planning to alternative organizational schemata, Banham concluded by revising his initial triad of principles and nominating a new project as the flagship example of New Brutalist architecture. Having demonstrated it to be extraneous to the New Brutalism's logic, Banham

FIG. 1.14 | **Alison Smithson (British, 1938–93) and Peter Smithson (British, 1923–2003).** Golden Lane Estate (Hunstanton, England, 1952). Photomontage of street deck.

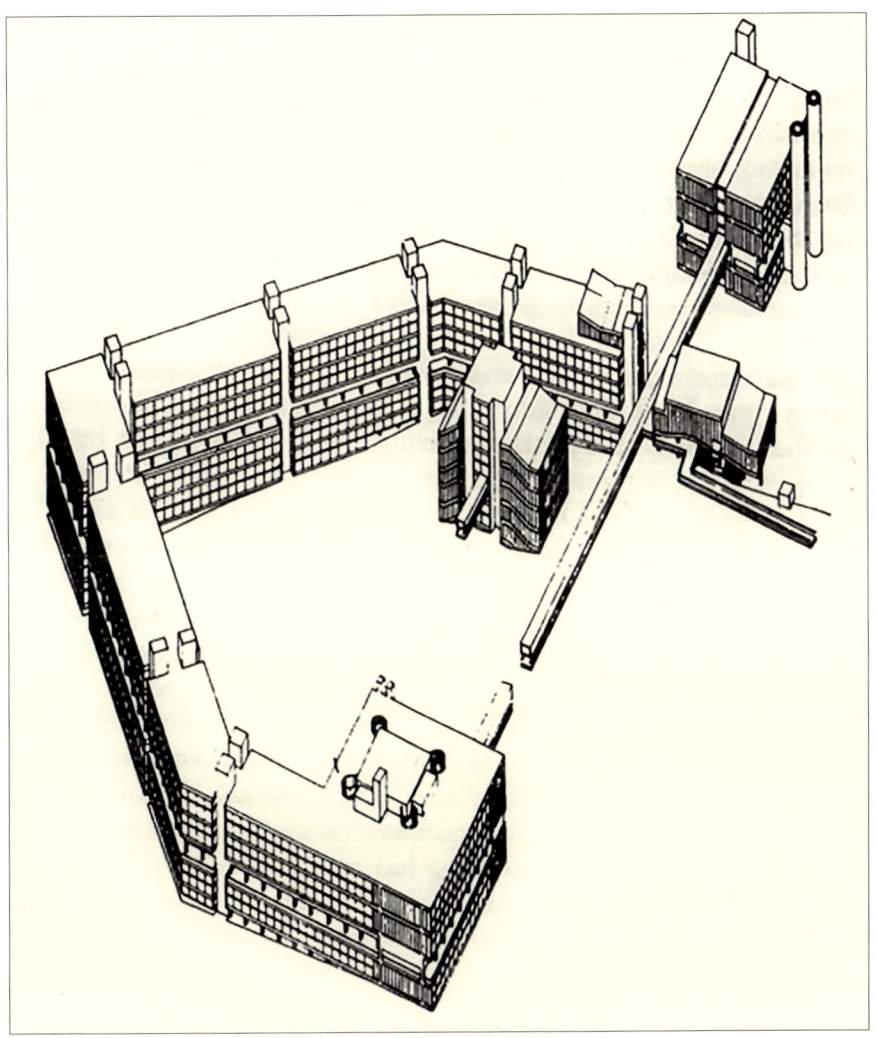

dropped "formal legibility of plan" from his list of core qualities, "Memorability as an Image" took its place alongside "Clear exhibition of Structure" and "Valuation of Materials 'as found,'" and the Sheffield University scheme, uncompromised by formal axiality, superseded the Hunstanton School as "the most extreme point reached by any Brutalists in their search for *Une Architecture Autre*."[116]

Une Architecture Autre

In contrast to his concise three-part encapsulation of the New Brutalism, Banham's initial definition of *une architecture autre* was vague. In his 1955 essay, he relied primarily on analogies to the art world. In addition to *Parallel of Life and Art,* the French art critic Michel Tapié's 1952 book, *Un art autre* (in which Paolozzi appeared alongside other "anti-artists" such as Dubuffet and Pollock), provided a crucial source.[117] In his 1966 book, Banham provided a more specific description. *Une architecture autre,* he claimed, "was intended to stand for something equally radical" to Tapié's concept.[118] It represented "an architecture whose vehemence

FIG. 1.15 | **Alison Smithson (British, 1938–93) and Peter Smithson (British, 1923–2003).** Sheffield University Extension (Sheffield, England, 1954). Axonometric.

FIG. 1.16 | **Frederick Kiesler (American, b. Austria, 1890–1965).** Endless House project (1950–60). Exterior view of the model (1958). Photo by George Barrows. New York, Architecture & Design Study Center, The Museum of Modern Art.

FIG. 1.17 | **Alison Smithson (British, 1938–93) and Peter Smithson (British, 1923–2003).** Sugden House (Hertfordshire, England, 1956). View of south facade.

transcended the norms of architectural expression as violently as the paintings of Dubuffet transcended the norms of pictorial art; an architecture whose concepts of order were as far removed from those of 'architectural composition' as those of Pollock were removed from the routines of painterly composition."[119] He went on to foreground the core formal issues involved: "'Une architecture autre' could be expected to abandon the concepts of composition, symmetry, order, module, proportion, 'literacy in plan, construction, and appearance' in the sense accepted in the theory of architecture as taught in the Ecoles [sic] des Beaux-Arts, and piously preserved in the Modern Architecture of the International Style and its postwar successors."[120] Importantly, *une architecture autre* signaled a move not only beyond the formal planning of projects like the Hunstanton School but also beyond the informality of picturesque composition. Instead of these established approaches, Banham argued, *une architecture autre* had to do with an "a-formal" approach to the organization of built form "unconcerned with geometrical or visual compositional techniques of any preconceived type."[121] Aformalism in this sense was not to be confused with the "formlessness" of projects such as Frederick Kiesler's 1950s Endless House (fig. 1.16), which, though reminiscent of Paolozzi's visual language, "only superficially fulfil[led] this concept of 'other.'"[122] Something closer to the concept could be found in the Smithsons' 1956 Sugden House (fig. 1.17), in which the architects, while maintaining the everyday materials and methods of suburban prototypes, discarded the conventional grammar by which those materials usually were arranged to develop instead "another language" with which they produced a "subtly subversive building."[123]

Banham saw another promising alternative to conventional approaches in the Smithsons' House of the Future (figs. 1.18, 1.19), a prototype of which was built for

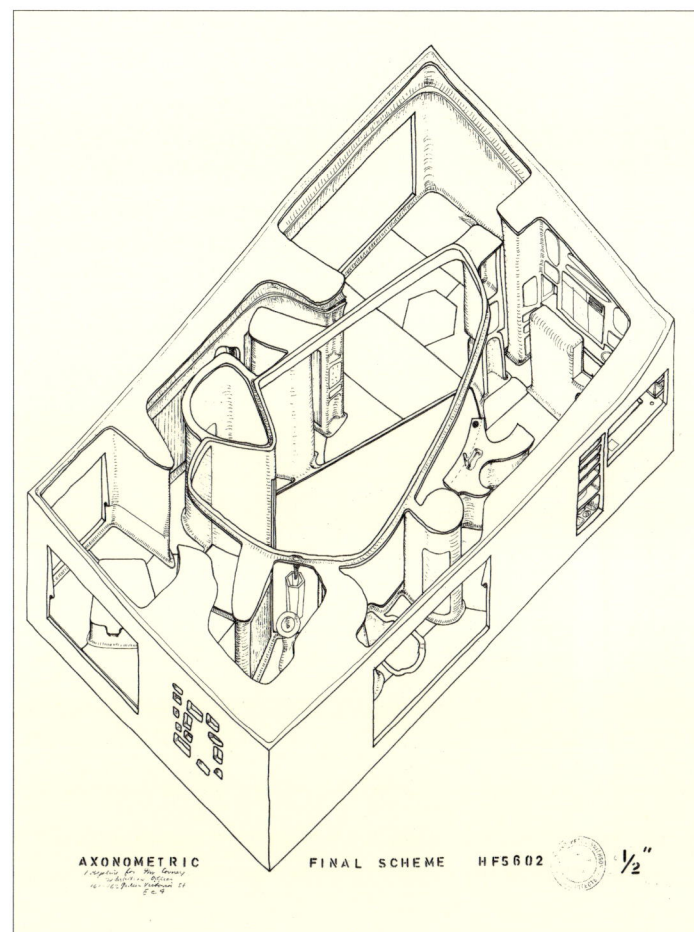

the 1956 Ideal Home exhibition, staged by the London *Daily Mail.* Unlike previous Smithsons projects that had employed conventional architectural materials, the House of the Future called for molded "plastic-impregnated fibrous plaster" panels joined by synthetic gaskets.[124] Individual programmatic volumes rose seamlessly from the plastic floor, took asymmetrical, somewhat expressionistic shapes, and were loosely arranged around a central ovoid courtyard. The house was outfitted with a full battery of modern technical gadgetry, including stereo, television, and short-wave radio. At the exhibition, futuristically clad models (women in nylon dresses and tightly curled, frosted hair; men in snug wool leggings with integrated shoes) completed the scene. Banham saw alterity not only in the house's futurist "styling" but also in its detailing, which the Smithsons developed from their study of American automobile design. Unlike British car manufacturers, which according to Banham accommodated accessories and components by "sticking them in as afterthoughts," American designers "exhibited a dazzling command of details, joints, and connections."[125] Likewise, the Smithsons offered a "complete aesthetic of panels and joints" and a convincing sense of unity that, because it issued primarily from its detailing, owed no allegiance to traditional architectural conventions.

FIG. 1.18 | **Alison Smithson (British, 1938–93) and Peter Smithson (British, 1923–2003).**
House of the Future (London, 1956). Axonometric.

FIG. 1.19 | **Alison Smithson (British, 1938–93) and Peter Smithson (British, 1923–2003).**
House of the Future (London, 1956). Interior view.

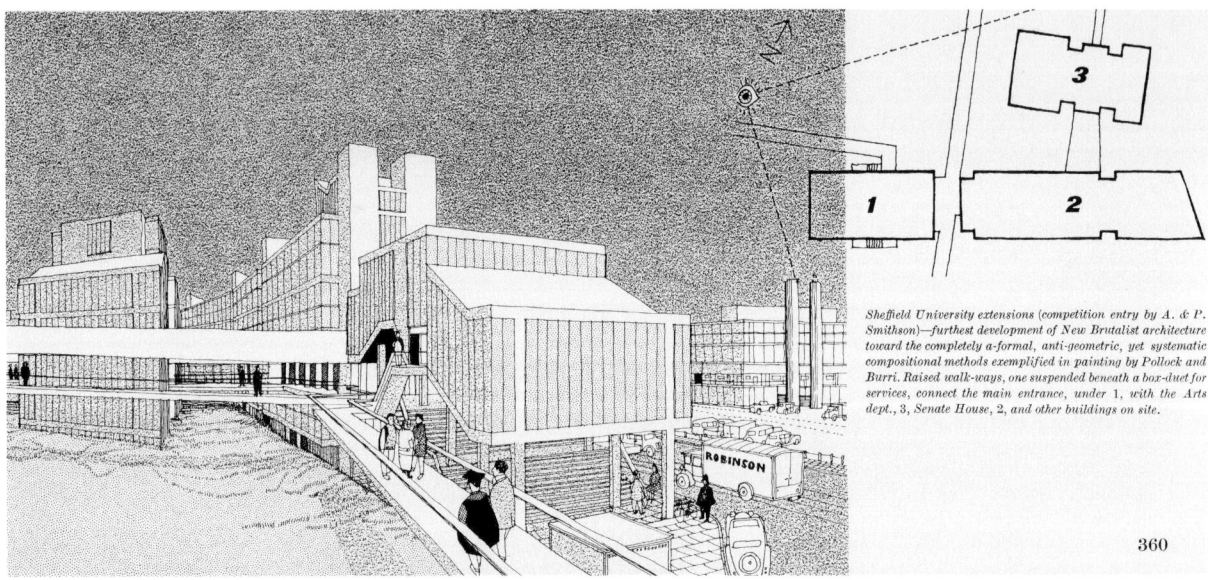

FIG. 1.20 | Alison Smithson (British, 1938–93) and Peter Smithson (British, 1923–2003). Sheffield University Extension (Sheffield, England, 1953). Perspective and partial site plan. Detail from Reyner Banham, "The New Brutalism," *Architectural Review* 118 (1955): 360.

But even with these later works, the Sheffield University scheme remained the Smithsons' most promising postulation of an "other" architecture. In his 1955 essay, Banham described the scheme as one in which "aformalism becomes a positive force in its composition as it does in a painting by Burri or Pollock."[126] Yet, this was a composition "based not on the elementary rule-and-compass geometry which underlies most architectural composition, so much as an intuitive sense of topology."[127] As Banham used it here, *topology* stood for a sort of unity derived not from geometric integration of building forms but rather from the unifying connective tissue of circulation systems.[128] Banham's use of *topology*, like his use of *image*, was closely related to his ambition to develop a discourse for architecture more in line with scientific culture than with traditional aesthetics, as Laurent Stalder described in a perceptive essay.[129] The term, which Banham borrowed from D'Arcy Thompson, gave his argumentation a quasi-scientific air and underwrote a desire to move architecture away from "unitary, simple, and elementary" forms toward more open systems and a rigorous, analysis-driven approach to the solution of architectural problems.[130] In Stalder's reading, Banham saw topology as a method. Image, by contrast, was the expression of that method.

Yet, as Banham admitted in his 1966 book, the Smithsons' arrangement of buildings at Sheffield gave the impression, at least superficially, of informal picturesque planning. But, he continued, "whereas Picturesque compositional techniques were normally used to build up images of rich and confusing abundance, the effect of the arrangement offered by the Smithsons appears in the drawing to be aloof, rebarbative, and deliberately anti-graceful, replacing the sweetness and sentimentality of the Picturesque with a blunt and uncompromising statement of structure and function in every part."[131] Indeed, at Sheffield, expedient function appears to trump the

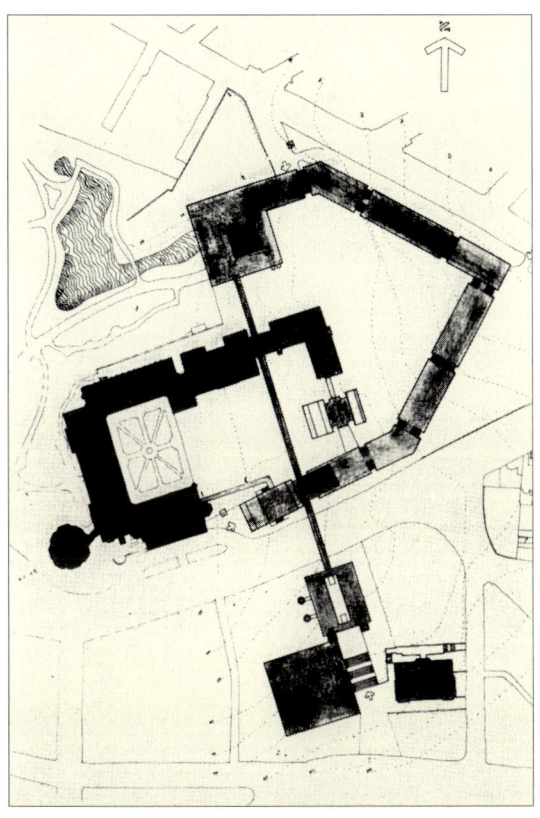

niceties of picturesque planning. In the plan, the project snakes around the perimeter of the site to define a loose, pentagonal courtyard, its disparate ends linked to each other and to existing buildings on the site by linear catwalks (see fig. 1.21). In line with Banham's New Brutalist checklist, the Smithsons depicted a building in which materials (bare concrete and glass) were deployed "as found" and the structural system was frankly displayed. With its exterior expression derived entirely from the even rhythm of the concrete frame and glazing joints, the building—particularly in a much-reproduced axonometric drawing (see fig. 1.15)—exhibited an uncompromising and distinctly memorable image.

An altogether different impression is given by the perspective view Banham included with his 1955 essay (fig. 1.20). Here, a loose, asymmetrical group of building elements of varying heights reminds one less of the aggressive aformalism of Pollock than the crenellated silhouettes of the picturesque tradition. Though less apparent in the published images of the Sheffield scheme, further associations with that tradition—as well as with the neo-picturesque of Townscape—stem from the planned juxtaposition of the Smithsons' addition to the existing Victorian buildings on the project site. While this might indicate the dictates of function taking precedence over the niceties of form, it seriously erodes Banham's insistence on a unified visual image. Had Sheffield been built, nearly any vantage point would have revealed not just the "bloodyminded" rigor of the Smithsons' concrete-and-glass

FIG. 1.21 | **Alison Smithson (British, 1938–93) and Peter Smithson (British, 1923–2003).** Sheffield University Extension (Sheffield, England, 1953). Site plan.

intervention but also the intervention's complex compositional dialogue with surrounding buildings (fig. 1.21). The design proposed elevated concrete walkways and mechanical conduits that mercilessly skewer polite nineteenth-century facades. To the east, the Smithsons' Brutalist perimeter focuses attention on the Victorian tail of the existing linear building. The older elevation assumes an honorific central position, while the new intervention offers a neutral backdrop. To the south, roles are reversed, as the Smithsons' Senate House forms a centralized modern pavilion within the existing building's Victorian perimeter. The visitor would be subjected to brash juxtapositions of Brutalist and Victorian elements everywhere, with careful formal relationships locking new and old into a dynamic composition. Far from visually unified, Sheffield's dissonant assemblage of elements achieves Banham's "absolute consistency" as an image only when existing buildings, so carefully grafted into the Smithsons' proposal, are cropped out of view, as they are in both the perspective and the partial site plan that illustrate "The New Brutalism" (see fig. 1.20).[132] It is tempting to speculate that these views were chosen for publication precisely because they occlude the existing buildings at Sheffield, thus exaggerating the project's visual unity.[133] Whether or not Banham was slanting the evidence to make his case, his commitment to ruthless visual consistency would soon come into conflict with his similarly vocal insistence on facile programmatic accommodation and drive him in later writing to develop an increasingly complex position with respect to dissonant architectural imagery.

Accommodating Dissonance

A trio of well-known essays illustrate the point. Banham's famous two-column analysis of the state of the discipline at the close of the 1950s, "1960—Stocktaking," appeared in a series of articles he assembled for the *Review* that addressed emerging technological opportunities for the field.[134] Many of the themes Banham traced in "The New Brutalism" are in evidence here, from attacks on Wittkowerian humanism and axial planning to a delicate treatment of the role of history in contemporary practice. Beyond the obvious tactic of composing the essay itself as a juxtaposition of two opposing viewpoints, Banham's short concluding section, "The Gap—Town Planning," warrants attention. Here, he argued that prevailing ideas concerning the city, like much of the "operational lore" he disparaged under the heading "Tradition," are debilitating presuppositions to be overcome. While he admitted that most people—designers as well as the broader public—assume that cities ought to be compact, each group also "expect[s] to be able to drive straight down an Autoroute de l'Ouest, straight through the Arc de Triomphe, and into a Champs Elysées that still has the urbanity of a sequence from *Gigi*. They demand suburban expansiveness, and urban compactness, ancient monuments and tomorrow's mechanical aids simultaneously and in the same place."[135] For Banham, the contradictory demands placed on the contemporary city called neither for a consistent expression nor for a ruthless adherence to a singular mode of organization, but rather for a dissonant accretion of multiple experiential possibilities and, by implication, their inevitable juxtaposition within the visual field.

Banham soon extended his accretive vision to architectural practice in a 1961 address to the Royal Institute of British Architects (RIBA). Railing against the field's tendencies toward "architecture for architecture's sake," Banham insisted on the necessity of direct engagement with life. Again, he proposed the New Brutalists as examples: "If Brutalists reached different and more radical judgments than other architects, it was not because of the cases with which they have asked to judge, but because the standards they have taken in passing judgment are different and, doubtless, more radical. And those standards have come from outside architecture, and what drives people mad about the Smithsons is that the standards are apt to be different from one building to the next."[136] Here, six years after the publication of "The New Brutalism," consistency of approach, characterized now as the "pure formalism of architects' architecture,"[137] has become a detriment; and an agile, ad hoc, and expedient incorporation of outside influences—from science, technology, programmatic concerns, and elsewhere—signifies a progressive mode of operation.

Notice the abrupt shift in Banham's argumentation. In 1955, he wrote, "One thing of which the Smithsons have never been accused is a lack of logic or consistency in thinking through a design."[138] In 1961, one finds that the "attempt to design by the light of a pure theory of architecture…has resulted in much of the most vacuous architecture we have."[139] Consistency of approach now signified the "architects' architecture" of an aloof and disconnected establishment, and it failed to deliver anything beyond "empty expertise."[140] By contrast, "positive manifestations of architecture gaining strength, or conviction, from its non-architecture content" were readily available to be pressed into service as counter proposals.[141] Banham's indictment against the establishment was sweeping, and his remarks prompted this stinging reply from an audience member: "Dr. Banham has suggested that the human sciences are gathering momentum and that they should be our inspiration for the future.… While we are doing our best to use the human sciences will he not be standing-by looking pontifical (rather like a younger G. K. Chesterton) and, when we have done our best and the buildings are complete, will he not come along and pass judgment on them in *aesthetic* terms?"[142] The criticism was valid, and Banham struggled, both in this talk and elsewhere, to strike a balance between an aesthetic agenda and the functionalist ethic he was advancing alongside. In his eyes, the New Brutalism offered a visual expression that did not fall into the nostalgic traps of "the

FIG. 1.22 | **BBPR (Gianluigi Banfi, Italian, 1910–45; Lodovico Barbiano di Belgiojoso, Italian, 1909–2004; Enrico Peressutti, Italian, 1908–76; Ernesto Nathan Rogers, Italian, 1909–69).**
Pirelli Tower (Milan, 1958).
General view.
Photo by Paolo Monti.

FIG. 1.23 | **Vittoriano Viganò (Italian, 1919–96).**
Istituto Marchiondi Spagliardi (Milan, 1959). View of dormitory block.

so-called New Humanism of the early '50s, and the endless guff we used to hear in those days about the need for human scale, etc. etc."[143] By demonstrating a rigorous concern for building occupants and incorporating expertise from outside the discipline in the process, the New Brutalists, in Banham's estimation, had proven more humane than any New Humanists, and, just as importantly, they had not compromised the aesthetic quality of their architecture in the process.

But the New Brutalism's visual expression was prone to take any number of forms and could lead as easily to the relentless visual consistency of Hunstanton as to the visual dissonance of Sheffield. In his RIBA address, Banham seemed resistant to giving credence to the latter result. The Milanese examples with which he illustrated his talk, BBPR's 1958 Pirelli Tower (fig. 1.22) and Vittoriano Viganò's 1959 Istituto Marchiondi Spagliardi (fig. 1.23), conveniently displayed a visual consistency in concert with the ruthless attitudes he had applauded in the New Brutalism, even if he was reluctant to bestow the label on either building. In stark contrast to the city of discordant experiences he had described in "Stocktaking," individual buildings in Banham's writings of the late 1950s and early '60s were valorized for consistent and integrated visual expression.

Consider "Design by Choice," his celebrated text of July 1961.[144] Here, Banham's observations about the multivalent design criteria of city planning in "Stocktaking" resonate at the scale of an interior. And, just as the prospect of "handing over responsibility [for the design of cities] to the will of a dictator—Le Corbusier at Chandigarh, Lucio Costa at Brasilia"[145]—failed to deliver sufficiently flexible urban experiences, so too was an architect's tendency to design stylized built-in containers around new technological elements such as televisions "little more than an attempt to impose a veneer of totalitarian order in a situation where something like democratic give and take may have been more to the point."[146] Visual consistency was strained by the demands of experiential diversity (not to mention vilified by unsavory political associations), and the disciplinary status quo again was found ill-equipped to deliver a solution. But all was not lost, and it was Le Corbusier himself who offered a way out:

> It is possible to abandon the position of autocratic dominance implicit in Bauhaus theory without losing control of the over-all design. Very small powers of accommodation enable the architect to do what Le Corbusier anticipated as long ago as 1925, that is, to exercise creative choice. His Pavillon de l'Esprit Nouveau was entirely furnished with equipment from manufacturer's catalogues, without the architect himself having to design a thing. Although the convincing unity of the total effect was doubtless helped by the fact that the rooms themselves had been designed in what he conceived to be the style of the objects that were to furnish them (and in this there is a lesson to be pondered), the whole operation was a triumph of disciplined and adventurous selection from what was at hand.[147]

As Sylvia Lavin noticed, Banham's recalibration of the architect's responsibilities shifted focus away from the visual attributes of individual objects toward their interactive contributions to the overall affective milieu.[148] And while this recalibration might have lessened "the architect's claim to be the absolute master of the visual environment," it was also a signal that "there may be more useful work done and better service rendered to the public."[149]

"Design by Choice" stands as an important refinement of Banham's rhetoric in "The New Brutalism." With no direct link to a particular architectural practice or style, the concept was insulated from the aesthetic criticism that plagued the New Brutalism while remaining true to the three tenets he offered as its definition. The incorporation of manufactured objects "off-the-peg," an idea that would gain currency in Banham's writings throughout the 1960s, was but a small step beyond using materials "as found." The resistance to homogenizing architectural millwork used to conceal dissonant technological accoutrements was similarly a refinement of his 1955 call to clearly exhibit the structure, and it foreshadowed his later writings that would work aggressively to put mechanical services on par with structure as legitimate objects of architectural expression.[150] Banham's final requirement, that architecture should be memorable as an image, was rendered here as "convincing unity of the total effect" and would remain a crucial factor in his later writings.

Texts such as these reveal a subtle shift in Banham's writing of the mid-1960s away from analogies to contemporary art toward more direct links to function and technology. They also indicate an important decoupling of the concept of *une architecture autre* from the New Brutalism. By 1966, the promise of the New Brutalism had faded in Banham's eyes. Its foremost practitioners, he argued, turned out to be "committed in the last resort to the classical tradition," while their promising ethical stance had "never broken out of the aesthetic frame of reference" and proved, ultimately, to be "backward-looking."[151] The concept of *une architecture autre*, by contrast, had come to represent the possibility of an "utterly uninhibited functionalism"[152] with "no cultural preconceptions." It implied an architecture that "ought to abandon the dominance of the idea that the prime function of an architect is to employ structure to make spaces."[153] And though, Banham admitted, "many would agree that to abandon this space/structure synthesis is to abandon architecture altogether,... all that is really abandoned is the notion of the art of architecture that has been current since the Renaissance."[154] For Banham, this was little cause for concern, as "society at large has never shown much interest in this notion, because it has nothing to do with the architect's function in relation to society," which primarily had to do with providing "environments for human activities and symbols of society's cultural objectives."[155] Thus liberated from conventional obligations, "an 'other architecture' might well employ structure merely as a way of holding up environmental controls, without endowing it with the monumental significance it enjoyed when massive construction was almost the only environmental control mankind possessed."[156] In *The New Brutalism,* Banham invoked recent projects by Cedric Price, whose Fun Palace (see fig. 2.7, pl. 2) design he judged to be "one of the most complete 'anti'-buildings ever projected in Europe,"[157] and R. Buckminster Fuller, who appeared to have abandoned traditional notions of architecture as involving the synthesis of structure and space in favor of a "quest for ever-higher environmental performance in some more 'other' way,"[158] as representative of the radicalism he envisioned. Yet these projects, Banham admitted, did not represent "the direction the New Brutalism as an international movement was headed."[159] Such a radical break with architecture's traditions was not to be found in the work of the Smithsons or any other Brutalists, and, indeed, Fuller's radical experiments often were met with "an attitude of extreme hostility" from more conventional architects. Worse, according to Banham, "The Smithsons are to be included among those who have adopted this attitude to Fuller, so are practically all others who could carry the name Brutalist. In the last resort they are dedicated to the traditions of architecture as the world has come to know them: their aim is not 'une architecture autre' but as ever, 'vers une architecture.'"[160]

If the New Brutalism had thus devolved from a "promising ethic" to a traditional aesthetic, in the concept of *une architecture autre,* Banham attempted to hold in suspension both an ethic of "uninhibited functionalism" and a progressive aesthetic of unmitigated visual coherence. And if, by the mid-1960s, the Smithsons had failed to deliver on that promise, Fuller, Price, and a new generation of young architects experimenting with what Banham had christened a year earlier a "clip-on" approach[161] had already begun to exhibit signs of a more promising agenda.

NOTES

1. Nikolaus Pevsner, foreword to the 1960 Pelican edition of *Pioneers of Modern Design* [1936], reprinted in Pevsner, *Pioneers of Modern Design: From William Morris to Walter Gropius,* 4th ed. (New York: Penguin, 1991), 17–18.
2. A wealth of scholarship exists on modern architecture in Britain in the wake of World War II. For two particularly pertinent collections, see Mark Crinson and Claire Zimmerman, eds., *Neo-Avant-Garde and Postmodern: Postwar Architecture in Britain and Beyond* (New Haven, CT: Yale University Press, 2010); and Lisa Tickner and David Peters Corbett, eds., *British Art in the Cultural Field, 1939–69* (London: Wiley, 2012). On the role played by émigrés in British modern architecture, see Charlotte Benton, *A Different World: Émigré Architects in Britain, 1928–1958* (London: Routledge, 2007).
3. Mary Banham, foreword to *The Festival of Britain: A Land and Its People,* by Harriet Atkinson (New York: I. B. Tauris, 2012), xvii.
4. Reyner Banham, "Machine Aesthetes," *New Statesman,* 16 August 1958, 192.
5. The literature on the New Brutalism is vast. In addition to Banham's famous text "The New Brutalism," *Architectural Review* 118 (1955): 354–61, and his later book *The New Brutalism: Ethic or Aesthetic?* (New York: Reinhold, 1966), other short texts by the same title are important primary sources; see Theo Crosby, "The New Brutalism," *Architectural Design* 25 (1955): 1; and Alison Smithson and Peter Smithson, "The New Brutalism," *Architectural Design* 27 (1957): 113. These and other essays from the 1950s were assembled alongside twenty-first-century interpretations by Hal Foster, Alex Kitnick, Hadas Steiner, Anthony Vidler, and others in "New Brutalism," ed. Alex Kitnick and Hal Foster, special issue, *October* 136 (Spring 2011). Dirk van den Heuvel's "Alison and Peter Smithson: A Brutalist Story" (PhD diss., Technische Universiteit Delft, 2013) is an excellent recent study. Editors Claude Lichtenstein and Thomas Schregenberger assembled a well-illustrated compendium of New Brutalist architecture and related developments in the fine arts in *As Found: The Discovery of the Ordinary* (Baden, Switzerland: Lars Müller, 2001).

    Banham first used the phrase "une architecture autre" in "The New Brutalism," and the concept has received significant treatments by Nigel Whiteley and Anthony Vidler. See Nigel Whiteley, "Banham and 'Otherness': Reyner Banham (1922–1988) and His Quest for an *Architecture Autre,*" *Architectural History* 33 (1990): 188–221; Nigel Whiteley, *Reyner Banham: Historian of the Immediate Future* (Cambridge, MA: MIT Press, 2002), 117–33; and Anthony Vidler, *Histories of the Immediate Present: Inventing Architectural Modernism* (Cambridge, MA: MIT Press, 2008), 133–40.
6. Whiteley, "Banham and 'Otherness,'" 219, emphasis in the original.
7. Vidler, *Histories of the Immediate Present,* 139.
8. Vidler, *Histories of the Immediate Present,* 134.
9. Vidler's chapter on Banham in *Histories of the Immediate Present* remains the strongest treatment of Banham's early career to date. Banham's own, slightly sarcastic version of events is also excellent. See Reyner Banham, "Revenge of the Picturesque: English Architectural Polemics, 1945–65," in *Concerning Architecture: Essays on Architectural Writing Presented to Nikolaus Pevsner,* ed. John Summerson (Baltimore: Penguin, 1968), 265–73.
10. To date, Whiteley has offered the most thorough account of Banham's life in *Reyner Banham,* 4–29. John Maule McKean's two-part interview—"The Last of England? Part 1," *Building Design,* 13 August 1976, 8–9; and "The Last of England? Part 2," *Building Design,* 27 August 1976, 26–27—also provides a useful biographical sketch, as do interviews by Martin Pawley, "The Last of the Piston-Engine Men," *Building Design,* 1 October

1971, 6–7; Charles Jencks, "In Undisguised Taste," *Building Design,* 16 May 1975, 12–13; and Penny Sparke, "The Machine Stops," *Design* 384 (1980): 31. Additional glosses are provided in Sparke's introduction to Reyner Banham, *Design by Choice* (New York: Rizzoli, 1981), 8–18; in Mary Banham's biographical notes in Reyner Banham, *A Critic Writes: Essays by Reyner Banham,* ed. Mary Banham (Berkeley: University of California Press, 1996), 1, 47, 149, 235; and in Thomas Hines's review of Whiteley's book, "Knock Down, Throw Away: Reyner Banham and the Expendable Building," *Times Literary Supplement,* 5 April 2002, 3–4. Banham offers a personal recollection in "The Atavism of the Short-Distance Mini-Cyclist," *Living Arts* 3 (1964): 91–97. The following biographical notes were gleaned from these sources.

11   A decade later, in another accident of proximity, Banham would find himself living across the street from Archigram founder Peter Cook on Aberdare Gardens in South Hampstead, London.

12   McKean, "The Last of England? Part 1," 8.

13   Banham served as assistant literary editor from 1953 to 1959 and as assistant executive editor from 1959 to 1964. For an informative treatment of Banham's years at the *Review,* see Erdem Erten, "Shaping 'The Second Half Century': *Architectural Review,* 1947–1971" (PhD diss., Massachusetts Institute of Technology, 2004), 264–78, 321–27.

14   The Independent Group was a loose collection of young artists, architects, and writers active at the newly formed Institute of Contemporary Arts (ICA) in London from 1952 to 1956. Banham chaired the meetings of the group's first sessions in 1952 and 1953. For an informative account of the group and its activities, see Anne Massey, *The Independent Group: Modernism and Mass Culture in Britain, 1949–59* (Manchester: Manchester University Press, 1995). Other important studies include David Robbins, ed., *The Independent Group: Postwar Britain and the Aesthetics of Plenty* (Cambridge, MA: MIT Press, 1990); and Anne Massey, *Out of the Ivory Tower: The Independent Group and Popular Culture* (Manchester: Manchester University Press, 2014). Whiteley provides extensive commentary on Banham's involvement with the Independent Group in *Reyner Banham,* 82–139.

15   For an informative treatment of Banham's relationship with Pevsner, see Nigel Whiteley, "The Puzzled *Lieber Meister*: Pevsner and Reyner Banham," in *Reassessing Nikolaus Pevsner,* ed. Peter Draper (London: Ashgate, 2004), 213–26.

16   Though neither Giedion nor Pevsner employed the term *International Style,* each advocated the visual style associated with the canonical works of Le Corbusier, Walter Gropius, and Ludwig Mies van der Rohe of the 1920s that Hitchcock and Johnson outlined in their exhibition and book. See Henry-Russell Hitchcock, *Modern Architecture: International Exhibition* (New York: Museum of Modern Art, 1932) and Henry-Russell Hitchcock and Philip Johnson, *The International Style: Architecture since 1922* (New York: W.W. Norton, 1932).

17   Reyner Banham, "History under Revision," *Architectural Review* 127 (1960): 326.

18   Banham, "History under Revision," 326.

19   Important examples among these *Architectural Review* essays include Reyner Banham's "Mendelsohn," vol. 116 (1954): 84–93; "Sant'Elia," vol. 117 (1955): 295–301; "Footnotes to Sant'Elia," vol. 119 (1956): 343–44; "Ornament and Crime: The Decisive Contribution of Adolf Loos," vol. 121 (1957): 85–88; "The Glass Paradise," vol. 125 (1959): 87–89; and "Futurist Manifesto," vol. 126 (1959): 77–80.

20   On the Sommerfeld House, see Banham, "History under Revision," 330–31.

21   Banham, "The Glass Paradise," 89.

22   Reyner Banham, "The Machine Aesthetic," *Architectural Review* 117 (1955): 225.

23   Banham, "The Glass Paradise," 89.

24   Le Corbusier, *Vers une architecture* (Paris: G. Crès, 1923), translated by Frederick Etchells as *Towards a New Architecture* (London: John Rodker, 1931). A newer translation by John Goodman—*Toward an Architecture* (Los Angeles: Getty Research Institute, 2007)—corrects certain infelicities in Etchells's translation. Nonetheless, given its influence over the architects examined in this study, citations will usually be drawn from the earlier version.

25   Reyner Banham, *Theory and Design in the First Machine Age* (London: Architectural Press, 1960), 220–46.

26   For useful overviews of postwar architecture in Britain, see the following chapters: Kenneth Frampton, "New Brutalism and the Architecture of the Welfare State, 1949–59," in idem, *Modern Architecture: A Critical History,* 4th ed. (London: Thames & Hudson, 2007), 262–68; Anne Massey, "Welfare State Culture," in idem, *The Independent Group,* 4–18; Hadas Steiner, "Modern Architecture in England," in idem, *Beyond Archigram: The Structure of Circulation* (London: Routledge, 2009), 38–69; and Dirk van den Heuvel, "Competing Traditions: Englishness and the Post-War Debate on Modern Architecture," in idem, "Alison and Peter Smithson," 105–55. For further reading into many of the topics sketched below, see the essays collected in Crinson and

Zimmerman, eds., *Neo-Avant-Garde and Postmodern;* and in Tickner and Corbett, eds., *British Art in the Cultural Field.*

27 Important titles in the literature include Nikolaus Pevsner, "Heritage of Compromise, A Note on Sir Joshua Reynolds Who Died One Hundred Fifty Years Ago," *Architectural Review* 91 (1942): 37–38; Nikolaus Pevsner, "The Genesis of the Picturesque," *Architectural Review* 96 (1944): 139–46; and Nikolaus Pevsner, "Sir William Temple and Sharawaggi," *Architectural Review* 106 (1949): 391–94.

28 "If anyone asks me who invented modern architecture," wrote John Betjeman, who worked alongside Hastings as a *Review* editor from 1930 to 1935, "I answer, 'Obscurity Hastings.'" A. N. Wilson, *Betjeman: A Life* (New York: Farrar, Straus, & Giroux, 2006), 85. "Obscurity" was among a number of nicknames and pseudonyms attached to Hastings, who in the 1920s inherited the magazine from his father, Percy Hastings, who had founded it as the *Architectural Review for the Artist and Craftsman* in 1896. The younger Hastings's role began as assistant editor in 1927, shifted to executive editor in 1935, and extended to his retirement in 1973.

29 See I. de Wolfe (pseudonym of Hugh de Cronin Hastings), "Townscape: A Plea for an English Visual Philosophy Founded on the True Rock of Sir Uvedale Price," *Architectural Review* 106 (1949): 354–62. Gordon Cullen, a frequent *Review* contributor and illustrator, later produced two books on the movement. See Gordon Cullen, *Townscape* (London: Architectural Press, 1961); and Gordon Cullen, *The Concise Townscape* (London: Architectural Press, 1971). For an informative collection of essays on the Townscape movement, see the *Journal of Architecture* 17, no. 5 (2012).

30 For a discussion, see Massey, *The Independent Group,* 4–11. For Banham's version of these developments, see the section "Polemic before Khrushchev," in Banham, *The New Brutalism,* 11–15.

31 Sven Backström, "A Swede Looks at Sweden," *Architectural Review* 94 (1943): 80.

32 See J. M. Richards, "The New Empiricism: Sweden's Latest Style," *Architectural Review* 101 (1947): 199–204; and Eric de Maré, "The New Empiricism: Antecedents and Origins of Sweden's Latest Style," *Architectural Review* 103 (1948): 9–11.

33 For a discussion, see Kenneth Frampton, "The English Crucible," in *CIAM Team 10: The English Context,* ed. D'Laine Camp, Dirk van den Heuvel, and Gijs de Waal (Delft: TU Delft, 2002), 113–29. Banham discusses the people's detailing in "The New Brutalism," 356, and, more expansively, in Banham, *The New Brutalism,* 10–12.

34 They remain so in many secondary sources. For a useful disambiguation, see Joan Ockman, "New Empiricism and New Humanism," *Design Book Review* 41/42 (2000): 18–21.

35 De Maré, "The New Empiricism," 10. While "The New Humanism" was a recurrent heading for editorials in the *Architectural Review* throughout the 1950s, the notion of a "New Architecture of Humanism" had been raised as early as a 1944 meeting of the Modern Architectural Research (MARS) group, the British wing of the Congrès internationaux d'architecture moderne (CIAM). See M. Hartland Thomas, "Report of the Discussion of 13th December: What Is Modern Architecture," *MARS Report* 1 (1945): 32. For a brief discussion, see Steiner, *Beyond Archigram,* 49.

36 On the Festival of Britain, see Atkinson, *The Festival of Britain;* Mary Banham and Bevis Hillier, eds., *A Tonic to the Nation: Festival of Britain, 1951* (London: Thames & Hudson, 1976); and Becky Conekin, *The Autobiography of a Nation: The 1951 Festival of Britain* (Manchester: Manchester University Press, 2003).

37 Massey, *The Independent Group,* 12–17.

38 *Review* editor J. M. Richards was part of an advisory council assembled to provide guidance to the festival architects. For a discussion, see Erten, "Shaping 'The Second Half Century,'" 86–90.

39 Frampton, "The English Crucible," 115.

40 "The Exhibition as Landscape," *Architectural Review* 110 (1951): 80.

41 Reyner Banham, "The Style: 'Flimsy…Effeminate?,'" in M. Banham and Hillier, *A Tonic to the Nation,* 191–94.

42 For an informative portrait of the conflict between "Swedish empiricists" and "Corbusian rationalists" within the LCC in the 1950s, see Stephen Kite, "Softs and Hards: Colin St. John Wilson and the Contested Visions of 1950s London," in Crinson and Zimmerman, eds., *Neo-Avant-Garde,* 55–77.

43 For an overview of the ICA's early years, see Massey, *The Independent Group,* 19–32. For a collection of essays on the institute's first decades, see Anne Massey and Gregor Muir, eds., *Institute of Contemporary Arts: 1946–1968* (London: Institute of Contemporary Arts, 2012).

44 Massey, *The Independent Group,* 19. See also Herbert Read, *Art Now: An Introduction to the Theory of Modern Painting and Sculpture* (London: Faber & Faber, 1933); and Herbert Read, *Art and Industry: The Principles of Industrial Design* (London: Faber & Faber, 1934).

45 Massey, *The Independent Group,* 28.

46 Hamilton and Henderson assisted with the 1950 exhibition *James Joyce: His Life and Work,* while Paolozzi

collaborated on the institute's interior renovation and provided custom furniture and decoration for its bar area. See Massey, *The Independent Group,* 39–40.

47 For a discussion of the exhibition, see Isabelle Moffat, "'A Horror of Abstract Thought': Postwar Britain and Hamilton's 1951 *Growth and Form* Exhibition," *October* 94 (2000): 89–112. On CIAM 8, see Eric Paul Mumford, *The CIAM Discourse on Urbanism, 1928–1960* (Cambridge, MA: MIT Press, 2001), 201–15.

48 For an outline of Independent Group (IG) activities throughout the 1950s, see Graham Whitham, "Chronology," in Robbins, *The Independent Group,* 12–48. For a discussion of the first IG sessions, see Massey, *The Independent Group,* 45–53.

49 Whitham, "Chronology," 22.

50 Massey, *The Independent Group,* 44–45.

51 Richard Hamilton, "Growth and Form Exhibition, First Draft Schedule," undated, ca. 1950, ICA Papers, TGA 955.1.12.26, Tate Gallery Archive, London, quoted in Moffat, "A Horror of Abstract Thought," 100. Per Moffat's note 21 in "A Horror…," "The pages have no date but the cover page preceding the text in the file reads '20 December 1950.'"

52 For a discussion, see Massey, *The Independent Group,* 54–61. For a well-illustrated overview, see Graham Whitham, "Exhibitions," in Robbins, *The Independent Group,* 124–30. For Banham's review of the exhibition, see "Parallel of Life and Art," *Architectural Review* 114 (1953): 259–61, reprinted in *October* 136 (2011): 9–10.

53 Banham, *The New Brutalism,* 41.

54 Alex Kitnick, "The Brutalism of Life and Art," *October* 136 (2011): 70.

55 Alison Smithson and Peter Smithson, *The Charged Void: Architecture* (New York: Monacelli, 2001), 118.

56 Kitnick, "The Brutalism of Life and Art," 72.

57 Alison Smithson and Peter Smithson, "Some Notes on Architecture," *244: Journal of the University of Manchester Architecture and Planning Society* 1 (1954): 4, reprinted in *October* 136 (2011): 13.

58 Banham discusses the term's etiology in "The New Brutalism," 355–56; and, in greater detail, in *The New Brutalism,* 10. For an extensive analysis of the term's development and varied associations, see Van den Heuvel, "Alison and Peter Smithson," 161–93.

59 See Crosby, "The New Brutalism," 1, which includes a long statement from the Smithsons from which this quote has been taken.

60 Crosby, "The New Brutalism," 1.

61 Peter Smithson, "Reflections on Hunstanton Becoming a School" [7 Sept 1954], in A. Smithson and P. Smithson, *The Charged Void,* 42.

62 A. Smithson and P. Smithson, *The Charged Void,* 42, which reprints a text written in February 1953.

63 Peter Smithson, "Reflections on Hunstanton," 42. Capitalization in the original.

64 Anthony Vidler, "Another Brick in the Wall," *October* 136 (2011): 115.

65 Banham, "The New Brutalism," 356.

66 Van den Heuvel, "Alison and Peter Smithson," 181.

67 Banham, "Machine Aesthetes," 192.

68 Banham, "Machine Aesthetes," 192.

69 Banham, "The New Brutalism," 361.

70 Banham, "The New Brutalism," 357.

71 Anthony Vidler provides a notable exception that highlights the more humorous aspects of the New Brutalism in "Another Brick in the Wall," 108–12.

72 Alison Smithson and Peter Smithson, "House in Soho, London," *Architectural Design* 23 (1953): 342.

73 The bench, set roughly fourteen inches above the ground floor level, provided a window seat at the back of the ground-floor studio and would have been stepped over to access the garden beyond. The gap between the bottom of the bench and the top of the foundation wall provided space for operable windows in the bathroom below, while the gap between the front of the bench and the first-floor slab was sealed with glass bricks. At night, this arrangement would have guaranteed a subtle glow beneath the bench when the bathroom light was turned on.

74 These opposed squares reverse position in the bedroom, where a built-in cabinet was centered on the edge of the ten-by-ten-foot square of the sleeping space. In the published drawings, even the bed participates in these geometric games. At about nine by five feet, it was drawn conspicuously longer than any standard size of that era, and the conventional diagonal drawn across it to represent the top sheet quite unconventionally spans from one corner to a point on the opposite edge that defines yet another five-by-five-foot square, this one slipped half a module off the grid in both directions.

75 Rudolf Wittkower, *Architectural Principles in the Age of Humanism* [1949], 3rd ed. (New York: W. W. Norton, 1971), 74.

76 For an informative discussion of the influence of Wittkower on midcentury developments, see Henry Millon, "Rudolf Wittkower, *Architectural Principles in the Age of Humanism*: Its Influence on the Development and Interpretation of Modern Architecture," *Journal of the Society of Architectural Historians* 31 (1972): 83–91.

77 Banham, *The New Brutalism*, 15. See also Millon, "Rudolf Wittkower," 85–91. Anthony Vidler has provided useful analyses of Rowe's influence at the time in *Histories of the Immediate Present*, 61–104; and Anthony Vidler, "Reckoning with Art History: Colin Rowe's Critical Vision," in *Reckoning with Colin Rowe: Ten Architects Take Position*, ed. Emmanuel Petit (London: Routledge, 2015), 41–55.

78 Millon, "Rudolf Wittkower," 85.

79 "Report of a Debate on the Notion 'That Systems of Proportion Make Good Design Easier and Bad Design More Difficult,'" *RIBA Journal* 64 (1957): 460–61, cited in Millon, "Rudolf Wittkower," 86.

80 Alina Payne, "Rudolf Wittkower and Architectural Principles in the Age of Modernism," *Journal of the Society of Architectural Historians* 53 (1994): 322–42.

81 See Banham's marginal comments to Nikolaus Pevsner et al., "Propositions," *Architectural Review* 127 (1960): 386–87. For a lucid discussion of the "Architecture after 1960" articles, which ran in the *Review* from January to June of that year, see Vidler, *Histories of the Immediate Present*, 125–33.

82 Payne, "Rudolf Wittkower," 332.

83 Kenneth Clark, "Humanism and Architecture," *Architectural Review* 109 (1951): 65–69. Wittkower agreed with Clark's sentiments, stating in the introduction to the 1971 edition of *Architectural Principles* that "this defines my intention in a nutshell." Wittkower, *Architectural Principles*, i.

84 Payne, "Rudolf Wittkower," 325. For a good discussion of the relationship between Scott's book and Wittkower's, see Paul Barolsky, "The Aesthetic Criticism of Geoffrey Scott," in *The Architecture of Humanism: A Study in the History of Taste* [1914], by Geoffrey Scott (New York: W. W. Norton, 1999), xv–xx.

85 See James Richards et al., "The Second Half Century," *Architectural Review* 101 (1947): 21. Erdem Erten has provided a thorough treatment of the *Architectural Review* during this period in "Shaping 'The Second Half Century.'"

86 Richards et al., "The Second Half Century," 36.

87 Erten, "Shaping 'The Second Half Century,'" 24.

88 The editor, "The Submerged Third," *Architectural Review* 104 (1948): 50. For a discussion, see Mathew Aitchison, "Townscape: Scope, Scale, and Extent," *Journal of Architecture* 17 (2012): 621–42.

89 Alison Smithson and Peter Smithson, *Without Rhetoric: An Architectural Aesthetic, 1955–72* [1973] (Cambridge, MA: MIT Press, 1974), 2.

90 A. Smithson and P. Smithson, "The New Brutalism," 113, emphasis in the original.

91 Banham, "The New Brutalism," 357.

92 A. Smithson and P. Smithson, "The New Brutalism," 113.

93 Aitchison, "Townscape," 633.

94 Banham, "The New Brutalism," 357.

95 Banham, "The New Brutalism," 358; and Wittkower, *Architectural Principles*, 18. For a good discussion of Banham, Wittkower, and the Todi church, see Laurent Stalder, "'New Brutalism,' 'Topology,' and 'Image': Some Remarks on the Architectural Debates in England around 1950," *Journal of Architecture* 13 (2008): 263–81.

96 "All great architecture has been 'conceptual,' has been image-making." See Banham, "The New Brutalism," 358.

97 For an informative contrast of Banham's method and Wittkower's approach, see Claire Zimmerman, "From Legible Form to Memorable Image: Architectural Knowledge from Rudolf Wittkower to Reyner Banham," *Candide* 5 (2012): 93–108. Additional discussions may be found in Stalder, "New Brutalism"; and John Macarthur, "Brutalism, Ugliness, and the Picturesque Object," *Formulation Fabrication—The Architecture of History: The Proceedings of the Seventeenth Annual Conference of the Society of Architectural Historians, Australia and New Zealand* ([Australia]: Society of Architectural Historians, Australia and New Zealand, 2005), 259–66.

98 Banham, "The New Brutalism," 358.

99 This translation, by John Goodman (see Le Corbusier, *Toward an Architecture*, 194), is more felicitous to Le Corbusier's original French than Frederick Etchells's influential 1931 translation, which would have been in circulation among English-speaking architects in the mid-1950s. Banham used the original French ("L'architecture, c'est avec des matières bruts, établir des rapports émouvants") as the epigraph of "The New Brutalism." Etchells rendered this as "The business of Architecture is to establish emotional relationships by means of raw materials." See Le Corbusier, *Towards a New Architecture*, 151.

100 Banham, "The New Brutalism," 358.

101 Banham, "The New Brutalism," 358.

102 See, for example, Kitnick, "The Brutalism of Life and Art," 80–82; Stalder, "New Brutalism"; and Zimmerman, "From Legible Form to Memorable Image."

103 Banham, *The New Brutalism,* 61.

104 André Breton, "Manifesto of Surrealism" [1924], quoted in Kitnick, "The Brutalism of Life and Art," 81.

105 Vidler, *Histories of the Immediate Present,* 135. The Warburg Institute was (and remains) closely related to the Courtauld, where Banham was studying at the time, both through mutual affiliation with the University of London and through their collaborative publication of the annual *Journal of the Warburg and Courtauld Institutes.*

106 Ernst Gombrich, "Meditations on a Hobby Horse" [1951], in idem, *Meditations on a Hobby Horse and Other Essays on the Theory of Art,* 4th ed. (London: Phaidon, 1985), 6.

107 Susanne K. Langer, *Feeling and Form* (New York: Scribner's, 1953), 45.

108 Langer, *Feeling and Form,* 47.

109 Banham, "The New Brutalism," 358. Vidler succinctly described Banham's notion of "conceptual" as "more an idea of the relation of form to function than a reality." See Vidler, *Histories of the Immediate Present,* 135.

110 Banham's earliest mention of Langer in print is in "Convenient Benches and Handy Hooks: Functional Considerations in the Criticism of the Art of Architecture," in *The History, Theory, and Criticism of Architecture,* ed. Marcus Whiffen (Cambridge, MA: MIT Press, 1965), 91–105. For a discussion, see the introduction, 13–14.

111 Mark Jarzombek, *The Psychologizing of Modernity: Art, Architecture, and History* (Cambridge: Cambridge University Press, 2000), 201, emphasis in the original.

112 David Goodway, ed., *Herbert Read Reassessed* (Liverpool: Liverpool University Press, 1998), 4.

113 Banham, "The New Brutalism," 358.

114 Banham, "The New Brutalism," 361.

115 Banham, "The New Brutalism," 357.

116 Banham, "The New Brutalism," 361.

117 Michel Tapié, *Un art autre; où, Il s'agit de nouveaux dévidages du réel* (Paris: Gabriel Giraud & Fils, 1952). For Banham's discussions of this book, see "The New Brutalism," 358; and *The New Brutalism,* 61. For a thorough treatment, see Whiteley, "Banham and 'Otherness.'"

118 Banham, *The New Brutalism,* 68.

119 Banham, *The New Brutalism,* 68.

120 Banham, *The New Brutalism,* 68.

121 Banham, *The New Brutalism,* 41.

122 Banham, *The New Brutalism,* 69.

123 Banham, *The New Brutalism,* 67–68. Banham noticed a similar alterity in the "enigmatic" brickwork of Sigurd Lewerentz's Markuskyrka in Stockholm, Sweden, of 1960. See Banham, *The New Brutalism,* 125.

124 The mock-up at the exhibition was constructed in painted plywood over timber forms with colored tape standing in for the gaskets. For a discussion and a thorough graphic presentation, see A. Smithson and P. Smithson, *The Charged Void,* 162–77. For a collection of essays on the Smithsons' domestic architecture, see Dirk van den Heuvel and Max Risselada, eds., *Alison and Peter Smithson: From the House of the Future to the House of Today* (Rotterdam: 010 Publishers, 2004).

125 Banham, *The New Brutalism,* 63.

126 Banham, "The New Brutalism," 361.

127 Banham, "The New Brutalism," 361.

128 Banham, *The New Brutalism,* 43.

129 See Stalder, "New Brutalism."

130 Stalder, "New Brutalism," 273.

131 Banham, *The New Brutalism,* 43.

132 See Banham, "The New Brutalism," 360.

133 The editors at the *Review* may not have had much choice. A survey of the Smithsons' publications of the project reveals a conspicuous lack of information regarding existing buildings on the site. The most frequently published image, an axonometric overview (Banham included this image, along with a complete site plan, in *The New Brutalism,* 52 [see fig. 1.15]), indicates the presence of the existing building only by its absence—in the gap left in the north-south elevated walkway/mechanical conduit and the untethered projection poking mysteriously from the Senate House.

134 Reyner Banham, "1960—Stocktaking," *Architectural Review* 127 (1960): 93–100. The other articles in the *Architectural Review* 127 series are as follows: Banham, "Architecture after 1960," 9–10; A. C. Brothers, M. E. Drummond, and Richard Llewelyn-Davies, "The Science Side: Weapons Systems, Computers, Human Sciences" (1960): 183–90; "The Future of *Universal Man* Symposium, with Anthony Cox, Gordon Graham, John Page, and Lawrence Alloway" (1960): 253–60; Banham, ed., "History under Revision," with Banham, "History and Psychiatry" and "Questionnaire, Masterpieces of the Modern Movement" (1960): 325–32; and "Propositions," with J. M. Richards, Nikolaus Pevsner, Hugh Casson, and H. de C. Hastings, sidebar notes by Banham (1960): 381–88. Vidler discusses these essays at length in *Histories of the Immediate Present,* 125–33.

135 Banham, "1960—Stocktaking," 100.

136 Reyner Banham, "The History of the Immediate Future," *RIBA Journal* 68 (May 1961): 253.

137 Banham, "The History of the Immediate Future," 253.

138 Banham, "The New Brutalism," 358.

139 Banham, "The History of the Immediate Future," 252.

140 Banham, "The History of the Immediate Future," 253.

141 Banham, "The History of the Immediate Future," 253.

142 Roger T. Walters, "Vote of Thanks," *RIBA Journal* 68 (May 1961): 259, emphasis in the original.

143 Banham, "The History of the Immediate Future," 256.

144 Reyner Banham, "Design by Choice: 1951–1961," *Architectural Review* 130 (1961): 43–48.

145 Banham, "1960—Stocktaking," 100.

146 Banham, "Design by Choice," 45.

147 Banham, "Design by Choice," 45–46.

148 See Sylvia Lavin, *Form Follows Libido: Architecture and Richard Neutra in a Psychoanalytic Culture* (Cambridge, MA: MIT Press, 2004), 6–9.

149 Banham, "Design by Choice," 47.

150 See Reyner Banham, *The Architecture of the Well-Tempered Environment* (London: Architectural Press, 1969).

151 Banham, *The New Brutalism,* 134–35.

152 Banham, *The New Brutalism,* 135.

153 Banham, *The New Brutalism,* 68.

154 Banham, *The New Brutalism,* 68.

155 Banham, *The New Brutalism,* 68.

156 Banham, *The New Brutalism,* 68. Banham did not elaborate on how legible cultural symbols might be achieved through such an approach, and as will be demonstrated in the next chapter, the provision of meaningful visual symbols in the absence of "monumental significance" would prove difficult.

157 Banham, *The New Brutalism,* 43.

158 Banham, *The New Brutalism,* 69.

159 Banham, *The New Brutalism,* 43.

160 Banham, *The New Brutalism,* 69.

161 Reyner Banham, "A Clip-On Architecture," *Design Quarterly* 63 (1965): entire issue.

CHAPTER 2

UNCONVENTIONAL COMBINATIONS
A CLIP-ON ARCHITECTURE

A year before completing his book on the New Brutalism, Reyner Banham offered an in-depth portrait of an alternative agenda being outlined by a younger generation of London-based architects. "A Clip-On Architecture" first appeared as a full issue of the American journal *Design Quarterly,* in mid-1965, and was reprinted in the London-based *Architectural Design* that November.[1] In it, Banham developed his interest in compositional strategies that avoided the classicizing tendencies, which, in his view, had compromised the New Brutalism. Drawing inspiration from midcentury American practitioners as diverse as R. Buckminster Fuller and Eero Saarinen, architects such as Cedric Price and the Archigram group offered what Banham viewed as convincing forms of compositional coherence built up from the combination of dissonant elements. Shades of this approach had been apparent in New Brutalist projects such as Alison and Peter Smithson's 1952 Sheffield University extension (see figs. 1.15, 1.20, 1.21), which proposed the juxtaposition of a rough concrete and glass structure with an existing Victorian campus building in brick.[2] Nonetheless, Banham did not mention the New Brutalism in his 1965 essay. Instead, he concentrated on extradisciplinary influences, including outboard boat motors and camping trailers, on works such as Price's Fun Palace (1963–66) (see pl. 2) and Archigram cofounder Peter Cook's Plug-In City (1964) (see pl. 3). Though never constructed, these brash, technologically inspired projects would provide crucial inspiration for later built works in the clip-on idiom and other early examples of High Tech architecture.

Banham was among the first to use the phrase "clip-on architecture" in print, and he remained a vocal proponent of both Price and the Archigram group from the mid-1960s forward. Yet he was curiously quiet as the earliest examples of the clip-on approach were built in London in the late 1960s. When he did choose to write about constructed clip-on projects, he was surprisingly critical. At first blush, these

Cedric Price (British, 1934–2003).
Fun Palace for Joan Littlewood Project (1963–66). Perspective (detail). New York, The Museum of Modern Art. See p. 211, pl. 2.

FIG. 2.1 | **Alison Smithson (British, 1938–93) and Peter Smithson (British, 1923–2003).** Upper Lawn Pavilion, Fonthill Estate (Tisbury, Wiltshire, England, 1959–82). Exterior view.

FIG. 2.2 | **Alison Smithson (British, 1938–93) and Peter Smithson (British, 1923–2003).** The *Economist* building (London, 1964). View from St. James Street. Photo by William J. Toomey.

responses seem to contradict his professed enthusiasm for clip-on, but as outlined in the previous chapter, Banham had already proven himself to be somewhat skeptical of discordant compositions. In both his 1955 essay and 1966 book on the New Brutalism, he downplayed the brash juxtapositions of the Smithsons' Sheffield University scheme, and he did not mention other proto–clip-on projects by the pair, such as their Wayland Young Pavilion (begun 1959), in which they attached a spare modern block to an existing nineteenth-century house, or their own weekend house at the Fonthill Estate in Tisbury, Wiltshire, where they added a small wood-framed structure to the remnants of a stone cottage and garden wall (fig. 2.1).[3] When Banham did treat such schemes directly, he tended to cast them in a negative light, at least in terms of his own agenda. Of the Smithsons' acclaimed 1964 *Economist* building in London (fig. 2.2), which deftly incorporated the existing eighteenth-century Boodles Club building into its four-square composition, he wrote, "Far from being an example of an 'other' architecture, this is a craftsmanly exercise in the great tradition."[4]

In their easy alignment with either the "formal" sensibility of the classical tradition or the informality of the picturesque, these Brutalist projects fell short of the aformalism Banham saw as a key feature of an "other" architecture. And though later clip-on projects by the Farrell/Grimshaw Partnership, Richard and Su Rogers, James Stirling, and others evinced the "uninhibited functionalism" that characterized Banham's later formulations of *une architecture autre,* in their juxtaposition of technological prostheses with traditional construction, these too apparently failed to exude the uncompromising visual unity he saw in the relentlessly consistent concrete frames of the Smithsons' Sheffield scheme, Vittoriano Viganò's 1959 Istituto Marchiondi Spagliardi (see fig. 1.23), and Jack Lynn and Ivor Smith's Park Hill Flats in Sheffield of 1957–61 (fig. 2.3).[5] In Banham's assessment, a lack of coherent imagery also counted as a strike against Price's Fun Palace, which, in its radical privileging of functional accommodation over monumental form, seemed to risk yet another pitfall of technologically advanced architecture—not the loose informality of picturesque composition but rather a distinct loss of visual impact that resulted, as discussed below, from mechanical technology's tendency to dissipate the visual coherence of architectural form.

I begin this chapter with an examination of "A Clip-On Architecture" that highlights the tension in Banham's text between impactful visual imagery and the threat of technologically induced invisibility. I pursue this and other tensions with analyses of early built works in the clip-on idiom, including James Stirling's Olivetti Training Center in Haslemere, England, completed in 1974. This famous project, alongside a lesser-known renovation at the Olivetti site by Edward Cullinan, illustrates another important tension in Banham's writing, this time between his advocacy of architecture's typically distracted public audience and the careful attention to detail he himself paid the buildings he examined. Taken together, these seminal clip-on projects introduce important achievements in this nascent phase of High Tech architecture and reveal the early stirrings of conceptual paradoxes that would prove central to Banham's later formulation of High Tech.

Beyond Brutalism

Though Banham did not focus on the juxtaposition of discordant architectural elements in his writings on the New Brutalism, Robin Middleton, his close contemporary, brought this aspect to light in a 1967 review of Banham's book on the topic.[6] In his review, Middleton offered a careful modification of Banham's formulations that provided an alternative genealogy for the New Brutalism (reaching back to the Smithsons' school days in Newcastle), and he outlined architectural qualities that did not rely on structural legibility and the use of materials such as rough concrete. Instead, he proposed a New Brutalism derived from the Smithsons' attitudes toward building organization and their ambitions to reconnect with disciplinary first principles. A key passage addressed the Hunstanton School:

> [Ludwig] Mies van der Rohe's beautifully articulated buildings for the Illinois Institute of Technology suggested a point of departure—these buildings were reticent, clean, and easily apprehended. They provided a ready-made aesthetic. But the Smithson's [sic] real discovery of how to purify architecture and return

FIG. 2.3 | **Ivor Smith (British, b. 1926) and Jack Lynn (British, 1926–2013).**
Park Hill Flats (Sheffield, England, 1957–61). Aerial view.

to the fundamentals of design was more personal in inspiration. *They realized that they would have to build up their architecture from whatever fragments were available. They would have to use 'objects as found' as the basis of their architecture.... Such fragments took on for them a magical quality; they became cult-objects, to be conspicuously displayed.*[7]

To complete their formulation, the Smithsons borrowed a method for arranging these fragments from another American source, Charles and Ray Eames's recently completed house in Pacific Palisades, California. There, the Smithsons discovered that "objects could be arranged, apparently casually, against a neutral background to forceful resultant effect. The combination of the Mies aesthetic with the Eameses' concept of arrangement proved electrifying when interpreted by the Smithsons. The wash-handbasins and kitchen stoves at Hunstanton seen against walls of glass convey still the strongest impression of the Brutalist image" (see pl. 1).[8] According to Middleton, as the Smithsons gained confidence in using this hybrid of Miesian aesthetics and Eamesian curation, they advanced more complex architectural proposals. Unsatisfied to simply collage elements into new combinations, they experimented with and quickly abandoned Palladian geometry before arriving at a more useful organizing logic in Louis Kahn's notion of "the link."[9] As Middleton described, "The link and the route soon became all important for the Smithson's [sic] concept of an organic architecture, in which individual homes or buildings were all slotted into the town as a whole."[10] Middleton then recounted precedents (including Alvar

Aalto's 1948 Baker House at the Massachusetts Institute of Technology) and early projects (such as Smith and Lynn's Park Hill Flats [see fig. 2.3]) that subscribed to this logic and led in a clear progression from Hunstanton to the *Economist* building. Contrasting Banham's disappointed assessment in *The New Brutalism,* Middleton argued that the *Economist* building demonstrated not the Smithsons' abdication of but rather their deep commitment to the ethical mission of the New Brutalism.

Some of Middleton's arguments resonated with Banham's. But where Middleton, like the Smithsons, was content to see new techniques and as-found components distilled into polished solutions such as the *Economist* building, Banham remained committed to an alternative aesthetic to be coupled with alternative principles. A year prior to the release of *The New Brutalism,* Banham published "A Clip-On Architecture." Sidestepping Brutalism altogether, in the text he located clip-on's roots in the emergence of "endless and indeterminate" projects, such as Eero Saarinen's General Motors Technical Center in Warren, Michigan (1948–55) (fig. 2.4), and in accompanying midcentury rhetoric. Gerhard Kallman's suggestion that traditional modes of centralized compositional unity were threatened with obsolescence by new techniques involving indeterminate extension was crucial: "The question of whether—with emerging new realities of the anonymous, of endlessly linked chains, of fugal and progressional rhythms—all centristic concepts, be they geometrical or irregular, will give way to new concepts, is now becoming a very burning one."[11] Certainly an advocate of such noncentristic approaches, Banham noted that Kallman's query fell on deaf ears in America: "Subsequent history shows that the

FIG. 2.4 | **Eero Saarinen (American, 1910–61).**
General Motors Technical Center (Warren, Michigan, 1948–55).
General view.
Photo by William J. Toomey.

FIG. 2.5 | Alison Smithson (British, 1938–93) and Peter Smithson (British, 1923–2003). House of the Future (London, 1956). Sketch of unit aggregation.

question burned nobody in the United States—where a generation of architects, genially misled by Philip Johnson, turned to old-world centristic concepts to solve their problems of architectural composition."[12]

England provided a more suitable context. The nonhierarchical, additive approach enabled architects to be "cautiously noncommittal among the uncertainties of postwar reconstruction."[13] Though some commentators, such as Richard Llewelyn Davies, associated the approach with Mies van der Rohe's work at the Illinois Institute of Technology,[14] Banham found that project's classical associations too overt and offered instead anticlassical examples such as Emile Aillaud's housing blocks near Paris and Lynn and Smith's Park Hill Flats (see fig. 2.3). Such projects, Banham observed, represented "an architecture whose form was not defined by the accepted rules of architecture—symmetry, unity, coherence, balance, and all those."[15] Instead, these projects were provided with a sense of unity through the organization of circulation systems. Each featured pedestrian walkways and bridges that linked the various housing blocks together in a manner akin to the elevated circulation routes the Smithsons had used in their Golden Lane Estate (see fig. 1.14).

Rehearsing his arguments in *The New Brutalism,* Banham associated these aformal innovations with parallel developments in contemporary art, including the nonhierarchical qualities of Jackson Pollock's paintings, which, he noted, had been introduced to British architectural audiences by Philip Johnson in a 1951 lecture at the Royal Institute of British Architects (RIBA).[16] These varied sources led British architects to seek "a kind of building design which was not only endless, indeterminate, and a-formal, but in which every bit was as good as another and could be replaced by any other."[17] In Banham's view, they did not find such a method. Indeed, Banham did not see nonhierarchical interchangeability, as Middleton did, in the New Brutalism. Rather, in the Smithsons' urban schemes of the period and even in the Park Hill Flats, which, he admitted, came "pretty close to 'an other architecture,'"[18] Banham saw a distinct "re-appearance of the Picturesque method,"[19] which precluded the possibility of the otherness he sought. Nevertheless, it was the Smithsons themselves who provided a seminal counterexample.

The Smithsons' 1956 House of the Future (see figs. 1.18, 1.19) offered what Banham saw as a new approach to producing endlessness in architecture. Yet what set it apart from contemporary examples was not its seamless integration of technology but rather its clever aggregation of housing units. With its monolithic exterior interrupted by just a single door and interior light provided by the central open court (and ample artificial lighting), multiple houses could be arranged in side-to-side and back-to-back rows, producing an extendable urban system of repeated living units (fig. 2.5). Banham saw this innovation as crucial:

Where Davies had identified repeating structural units that could be added up into a useable volume, the Smithsons were offering usable volumes that could be added up to something more complex. The concept was less intellectually pellucid, but emotionally more appealing—it is difficult to identify oneself with a pair of vertical mullions, an underwindow air-conditioner, and an area of tinted glass, but easy to identify with a room you can stand up and walk around in.[20]

Such an arrangement bolstered Banham's argument against the formalism associated with traditional architectural humanism (by offering endlessness as an alternative to "centristic" concepts) and simultaneously appealed to its audience by offering an architecture that, while unusual, remained open to empathetic engagement by human subjects.[21]

While the House of the Future was an anomaly that would not be revisited in the Smithsons' oeuvre, clip-together plastic components were studied further by the Belgian architect Jacques Baudon, whose Clip-On House (1959) joined prefabricated kitchens, baths, and bedrooms to an ambiguously constructed "free-form" living space via repeatable sections of plastic corridor elements. Despite their innovative approach, Banham noted a severe limitation in these early clip-together proposals:

> Services, communication, and other manifestations of interdependency will have to be consciously designed at the same time as the units themselves—the result of not doing so can be seen in the overhead jungle of wires and marginal slummery of so many American trailer camps. If the units are simply spread on the ground, then the circulation of men and vehicles among them will become a determinant of the layout—as with the corridors of Baudon's house, or even with the way the Smithson houses stack with their doors outwards, thus fixing the lines of communication along the sides of the super-blocks into which they aggregate. If the units are stacked vertically, then some form of external structure will be needed to take up their cumulative weight; and if any substantial number are to be serviced with water, air, gas, piped music or you-name-it, then those services are going to thicken up into some pretty impressive ducts and trunking-in places.[22]

Notice here Banham's dismissal not only of the ad hoc accretion of mechanical servicing but also of circulation design as methods for coordinating the aggregated system. The repeated living blocks of the House of the Future as well as the end-on-end corridor elements of Baudon's Clip-On House could produce only more or less orthogonal streets and hallways around which living spaces would be organized.

The more units joined in this manner, the more the projects would resonate with traditional axial organizations and familiar street grids. While one easily can imagine modifications that would elicit more complex plan shapes for either scheme, both remain limited to single-story aggregations. Once again, a promising advance seemed to elicit disappointingly traditional results. As if predicting Middleton's 1967 assessment of the New Brutalism, Banham dismissed the implicit traditionalism of the "link and route" approach as an insufficiently robust vehicle for an "other" architecture of clip-on components.

Playgrounds for *Homo Ludens*

The Archigram group, especially in Peter Cook's famous Plug-In City (fig. 2.6), offered bolder solutions. Reversing the idea of repeated standard units containing building services such as plumbing and cooking equipment, as well as that of technological enhancements added like outboard motors to existing spatial enclosures, Cook provided a fixed structural and mechanical armature into which individual living pods—for the most part devoid of mechanical encumbrances—could be plugged as needed. Though Banham downplayed them in his essay, the aesthetic implications of this reversal were profound.[23] While the outboard approach promoted ad hoc assemblages in the manner of the Smithsons' Sheffield proposal, schemes such as Plug-In City, Ron Herron's Capsule House, and Price's Fun Palace—though unconventionally articulated and designed to engender buildings in states of perpetual and indeterminate flux—were nonetheless composed through the accumulation of near-granular individual elements, resulting in surprisingly integrated visual compositions (see pl. 3). Unencumbered by the formal dissonance of earlier combinatorial works, these newer projects could project something akin to "absolute consistency" and, despite their complexity, could be "grasped as a totality" in the manner of the New Brutalist works Banham had praised in 1955.

Another major innovation was the younger architects' incorporation of play into the realm of advanced technology. Where the "inhuman" endlessness of a Saarinen automotive plant might also satisfy Banham's earlier call for visual consistency, the inability of such works to resonate with their human audiences remained a concern. Endlessness alone was unlikely to deliver an architecture that adequately engaged its human occupants. In a 1961 address to the RIBA, Banham had argued for the incorporation of "non-architectural content" to generate an "other kind of humanism" as an antidote to the formulaic conventions of the New Humanism.[24] In Price's and the Archigram group's proposals, that outside content came in the concerted accommodation of unscripted human activity, programmatic improvisation, and play.

Price's Fun Palace of 1963–66 (fig. 2.7; see pl. 2) was conceived as an indeterminate space aimed at exactly these ends.[25] Banham described it as "a mechanized

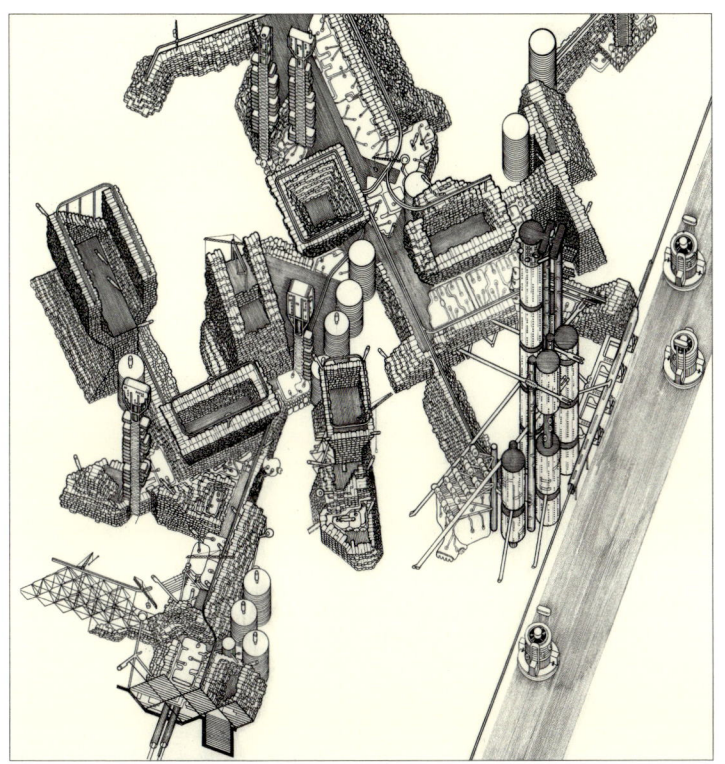 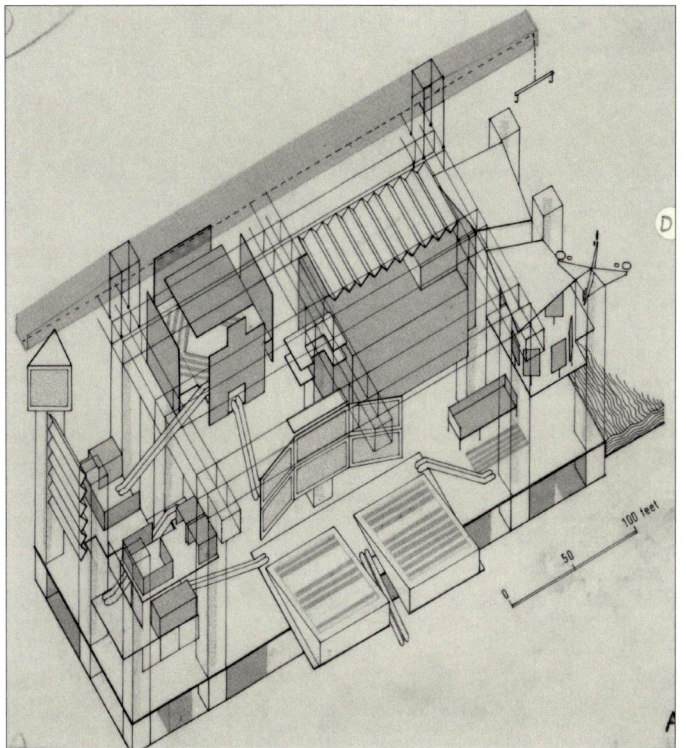

shrine to *Homo Ludens*…a zone of total probability in which the possibility of participating in practically everything could be caused to exist, from political rallies to Greco-Roman wrestling, table tennis and choral song, dervish-dancing, model drag-racing or just goofing and falling about, where even the simple business of walking about or finding where to go next would be rewarding and stimulating."[26] Banham would invoke *Homo Ludens,* the theoretical "man at play" theorized by Johan Huizinga in 1938, repeatedly in the 1960s and '70s as an alternative to the classical concept of the Vitruvian Man.[27] It was a useful substitution—just as the Vitruvian Man stood for the idealized human subject addressed by classical and modern humanists, *Homo Ludens* provided a theoretical personification of the alternative audience Banham wished to engage with his technologically progressive agenda.

Further, as in the conclusion of "Stocktaking,"[28] one finds Banham rhapsodizing the sort of dissonant programmatic juxtapositions accommodated by Price's scheme. But where Banham previously had been reluctant to embrace the formal indeterminacy such operational flexibility might imply, here he altered his stance. The Fun Palace, with its array of movable, reconfigurable parts, was, for Banham, "indeterminacy raised to a new power."[29] In 1955, Banham had seen Louis Kahn's movable partitions at the Yale University Art Gallery as undermining the formal conviction of the design (see fig. 1.13); at the Fun Palace, such flexible indeterminacy was a primary asset. And while the Fun Palace undoubtedly would have struck a commanding profile within the urban milieu, Banham chose to highlight instead the

FIG. 2.6 | **Peter Cook (British, b. 1936).**
Plug-In City (1964). Overhead view, axonometric.

FIG. 2.7 | **Cedric Price (British, 1934–2003).**
Fun Palace (1963–66). Axonometric.

building's more ephemeral qualities: "No permanent monumental interior space or heroic silhouette against the sky will survive for posterity.... If it is going to be a monument to anything, it will be a monument to architecture's silent partners, the invisible and long-suffering mechanical servitors who keep most buildings going, but never receive thanks or acknowledgement for it."[30]

Later in the text, Banham further intimated the dissipation of monumental architecture into an unrecognizable collection of equipment: "One of the most frustrating things to the arty old Adam in most of us is that the wonders of technology have a habit of going invisible on us. It is no use cyberneticists and Organization-and-Research men telling us that a computerized city might look like anything and nothing: most of us want it to look like something; we don't want form to follow function into oblivion."[31] Given this risk, it was not the fleeting imagery of the Fun Palace that would carry the day but rather the pop excesses of the Archigram group. Where Price's attenuated line drawings seemed on the verge of invisibility (see fig. 3.2), Archigram offered exuberant, brightly colored images (see pl. 3). Price's reticent drawings—though impressive in their technical detail—failed to have a compelling emotional impact on the various constituencies to which they were addressed.[32] Archigram offered far less technical clarity but made up for it with striking imagery. It was with a celebration of the imagistic qualities that Banham would conclude his essay. Underlining the compositional themes with which he organized the essay, his oft-quoted final prognosis focused on the project's "formal lessons": "A Plug-In City must look like a Plug-In City. If people are to enjoy manipulating this kind of adaptable mechanical environment (and if they don't enjoy it, we have gained nothing over previous environments) then they will have to be able to recognize its parts and function, so that they can understand what it is doing to them, and what they are doing to it."[33] In this, technical legibility couples with active performance while emotional enjoyment amplifies conventional empathy.[34] As Banham saw it, Archigram had turned the tables on the entire discussion: "We started with Kallman making cautious predictions about what technology might do to aesthetics, we finish with aesthetics offering to give technology its marching orders."[35] In these fantastical urban proposals, the hierarchical stasis of modern classicism was replaced by the loose flexibility of a Pollock canvas. At the same time, architecture's time-honored ideal subject, the geometrically stable Vitruvian Man, was rejected in favor of the fun-seeking *Homo Ludens*. This new architectural subject was not the wellspring of geometric hierarchies and proportional certainties to be reflected in architectural form but rather a fickle and active occupant whose pursuit of a good time reigned supreme. The New Brutalism, from the start committed to disciplinary first principles, had in Banham's assessment begun its inexorable decline into classicism almost as soon as it began. The clip-on approach swore no such allegiance to classical convention and, bolstered by the unlikely celebrity of the Archigram group and the impending construction of the Fun Palace, appeared in 1965 to have an extremely promising future.

As is well known, very few "highly mechanized future environments" on the order of Plug-In City came to pass, and the Fun Palace soon succumbed to the crushing bureaucracies of the English building and planning authorities.[36] Nonetheless, a collection of small-scale built works appeared in London through the second half of the 1960s that stayed true to the ambitions of clip-on. Early built projects are notable for their pragmatic approach. Where a Plug-In City would require significant capital investment as well as a wholesale reconsideration of existing building codes, construction techniques, leasing agreements, and lifestyle habits, these more modest proposals could capitalize on the delivery of increased functional efficacy from an economically priced and easily constructed add-on element. The remainder of this chapter presents three of these projects in detail: Farrell/Grimshaw Partnership's Student Hostel Service Tower for the International Students Club (1967, commonly known as the Bathroom Tower), Richard + Su Rogers's Conversion and Roof Extension for the Design Research Unit (1969–71, the DRU Conversion), and James Stirling and Edward Cullinan's work at the Olivetti Training Center in Haslemere (1969–74). Each comprised a renovation of and addition to an existing nineteenth-century structure, and all three were designed with forms, materials, and programmatic elements in stark contrast to existing conditions. Though these early examples of High Tech architecture reflected exactly the tactics he had outlined in "A Clip-On Architecture," Banham had curiously little to say about them. He never published a word on the Bathroom Tower or the DRU Conversion, and, in his published comments on the Olivetti Training Center, he was surprisingly critical of his friend Stirling's work. His position on these projects ultimately proved consistent with his preference for visual coherence over dissonant juxtaposition, and his comments on Olivetti introduce a telling development in his thinking regarding human subjects, particularly the varying levels of attention afforded buildings by distracted inhabitants and attentive critics alike.

The Bathroom Tower

With the Bathroom Tower (figs. 2.8–2.10; see pl. 4), the Farrell/Grimshaw Partnership converted six nineteenth-century terrace houses in London's Paddington district into a dormitory facility for 190 mostly international university students. Beyond this, the clients requested that the buildings be "united" both horizontally and vertically.[37] While ample volume for sleeping, dining, and study spaces could be accommodated in the existing buildings, retrofitting these masonry structures with sufficient plumbing facilities was deemed too costly. Further, the structural

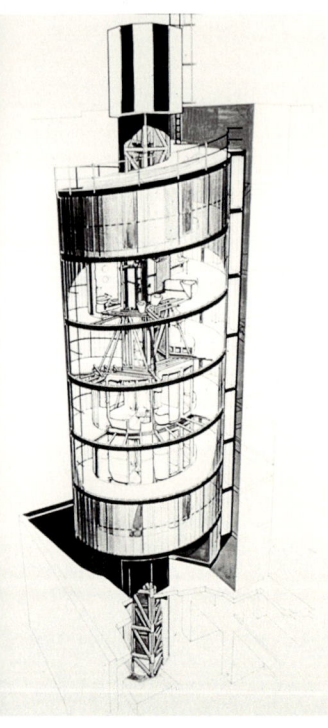

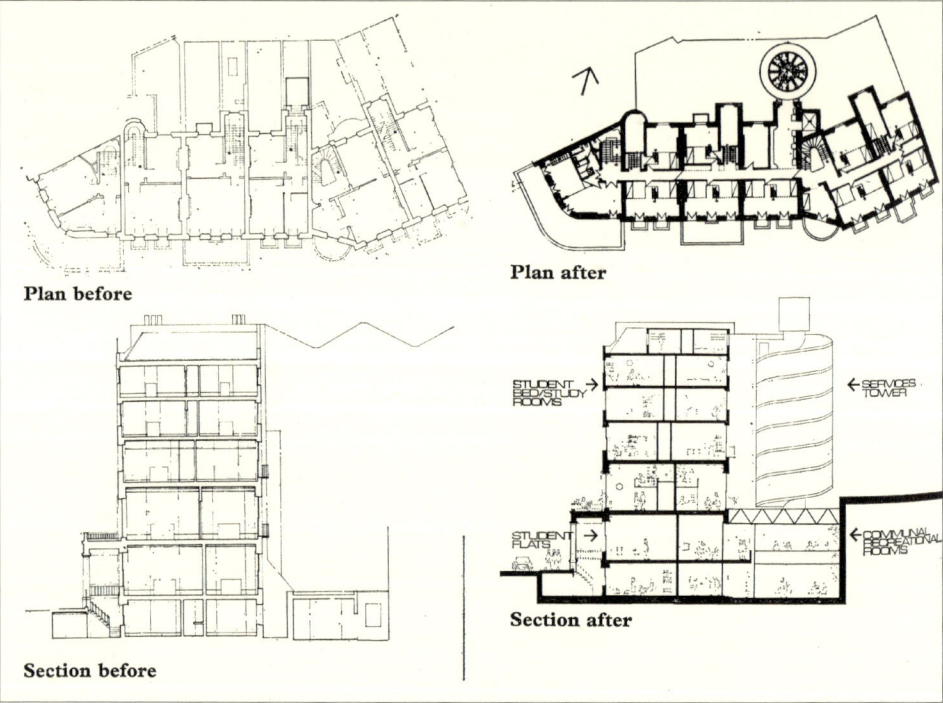

FIG. 2.8 | Farrell/Grimshaw Partnership (Terry Farrell, British, b. 1938; Nicholas Grimshaw, British, b. 1939). Student Hostel Service Tower (London, 1967). Cutaway perspective. Photo by Nicholas Grimshaw.

FIG. 2.9 | Farrell/Grimshaw Partnership (Terry Farrell, British, b. 1938; Nicholas Grimshaw, British, b. 1939). Student Hostel Service Tower (London, 1967). Nicholas Grimshaw and R. Buckminster Fuller at the tower. Photo by Tessa Traeger.

FIG. 2.10 | Farrell/Grimshaw Partnership (Terry Farrell, British, b. 1938; Nicholas Grimshaw, British, b. 1939). Student Hostel Service Tower (London, 1967). Plan and section (detail). From "Conversion: The Farrell/Grimshaw Partnership's Bathroom Tower," *Architectural Design* (October 1968): 491.

requirements of a necessary 3,600-gallon water tank exceeded the bearing capacity of the existing masonry, and site access precluded the use of a crane for construction. Farrell/Grimshaw's solution offered a freestanding steel-frame mast that was six feet across its hexagonal plan. The mast, located at the rear of the site, was crowned with a water tower and skewered communal recreational rooms and dining halls below. The mast, which carried a crane during construction, also supported thirty-five prefabricated bathroom pods in glass-reinforced polyester (GRP). These were hung outboard of the hexagonal superstructure and were accessed by a continuous helical ramp, also cantilevered from the central mast, which cleverly negotiated the varying floor-to-floor heights of the existing buildings. Students would enter the ramp from their respective floors, continuing up or down until they encountered a vacant cell. Translucent glass panels spanned vertically between the ramp's levels to provide enclosure. Within the existing town houses, central corridors ran the length of the block, puncturing party walls to access a variety of room types. Double-height lofts cleverly colonized the space above corridors on the first floor, while more perfunctory "study bedrooms" filled in the upper levels.

In their solution, Farrell/Grimshaw drew heavily on the excitement over clip-on architecture that swept through London student circles in the mid-1960s. Nicholas Grimshaw had come under the sway of Archigram member Peter Cook while studying at the Architectural Association School from 1962 to 1965. In 1966, his student work had even been featured in *Archigram* 6.[38] The Bathroom Tower undeniably resonated with Archigram projects of the period, especially Warren Chalk's famous

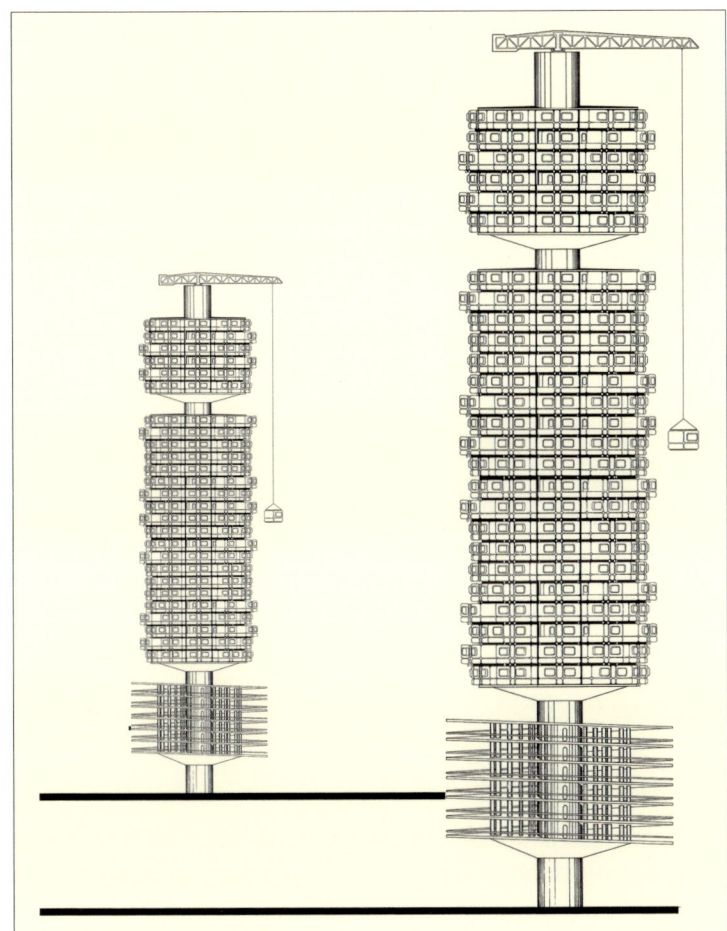
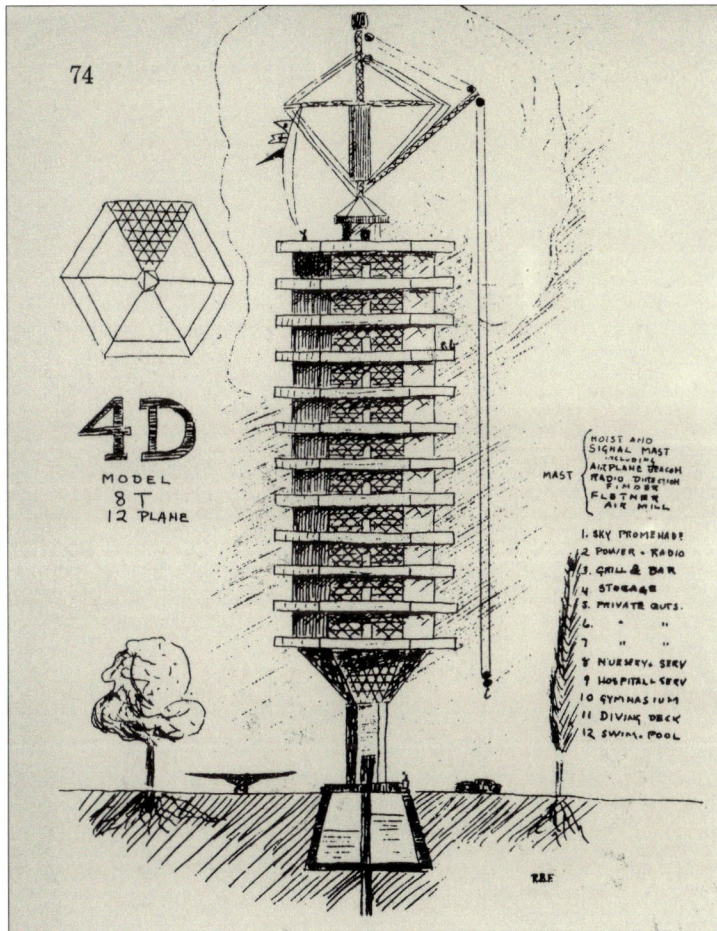

Capsule Homes Tower of 1964 (fig. 2.11). In Chalk's proposal, individual plastic elements could be plugged into a central structural and mechanical mast, while car parking was provided at the base of the tower on a helical ramp. The central mast supported a rooftop crane used to maneuver the prefabricated pods into and out of the matrix. Chalk's project owed much to earlier precedents. It bore more than a passing resemblance to Bertrand Goldberg's Marina City Towers in Chicago (1959–65), but it was Buckminster Fuller, who by the mid-1960s had achieved guru status among London's young architects, who provided the strongest inspiration.

Fuller's rise to disciplinary notoriety came in the wake of commentaries by British authors.[39] John McHale, an influential member of the Independent Group, published an important article in the *Architectural Review* in 1956, while Banham famously cast Fuller into a messianic role in the conclusion of *Theory and Design in the First Machine Age* (1960).[40] Fuller's work regularly turned up in the *Archigram* pamphlets,[41] and it occasionally even appeared in Archigram projects, as evidenced in the accretion of geodesic domes in Peter Cook's Entertainments Tower for Expo '67 in Montreal (unbuilt, designed while Cook was employed at Taylor Woodrow Design Group, 1963) (see pl. 5).

FIG. 2.11 | **Warren Chalk (British, 1927–87).**
Capsule Homes Tower (1964). Elevation.

FIG. 2.12 | **R. Buckminster Fuller (American, 1895–1983).**
4D Tower (1929). Elevation.

A comparison of early Fuller projects with later proposals by Archigram members and Farrell/Grimshaw demonstrates the depth of influence. Fuller's first publication, *4D Time Lock* (1929), features a trove of salient precedents.[42] The work's title project, the 4D Tower, a hexagonal structure supported on a central tower and capped by a crane, was to be delivered and installed by a zeppelin (fig. 2.12).[43] Fuller elucidated the project in unorthodox drawings, including a six-frame comic strip. It is a clear antecedent to Herron's Capsule Tower and Cook's later Instant City (1968), which was similarly to be delivered to the site by dirigible. While it is unlikely that Fuller's text would have been available to the Archigram group in the early 1960s,[44] the comic strip was reproduced in Ulrich Conrads's influential *Architecture of Fantasy* (1962), as well as in the widely read *Dymaxion World of Buckminster Fuller* (1960), which featured a chapter-length treatment of the project.[45] Cook included the latter book in an "infectious" bibliography in his book *Architecture: Action and Plan* (1967).[46] Centrally supported, hexagonal structures would also serve as the key device of Fuller's Dymaxion house studies (1927–45), in which he again exploited the structural efficiency of such configurations. Subdivided into equilateral triangles and warped over a sphere, the hexagon also features prominently in Fuller's most famous work, the geodesic dome.[47] Further offering cues to later capsule projects, Fuller designed (and later patented) his famous self-contained Dymaxion bathroom unit in 1937; and, in an apparently irresistible provocation to Farrell/Grimshaw, he illustrated an earlier "unitary bathroom" being hoisted into a hexagonally structured steel tower in 1927.[48]

The hexagonal form throws all of these works into a difficult relationship with calls for a renewed humanism pursued by various strains of midcentury modern architects.[49] In the opening pages of *Architectural Principles in the Age of Humanism* (1949), Rudolf Wittkower outlined Leon Battista Alberti's preference for centralized churches, and he illustrated the hexagon among a series of geometric constructions derived from circles that Alberti listed as suitable for church plans in *De re aedificatoria* (written ca. 1450, first printed 1486).[50] In Book IV of his treatise, Alberti noted that "nature also delights in the hexagon. For bees, hornets, and insects of every kind have learned to build the cells of their hives entirely out of hexagons."[51] Taken at face value, these passages threaten to open Fuller, Archigram, Farrell/Grimshaw, and other iconoclastic practices to alignment with classical paradigms and suggest yet another impending slide into neoclassicism. Yet Manfredo Tafuri suggested Alberti delivered his lines with a high degree of sarcasm and that they signaled his "aversion to Neo-platonism [*sic*]." Tafuri continued: "The tone he adopts when listing the orifices of animals as guide to the number of openings that a building should have leaves us with little doubt as to the pervasive irony of his intentions."[52] In Tafuri's revisionist reading, even a humanist of Alberti's caliber approached ideal geometries with a degree of skepticism and indeed worked toward a "desacrilization of any possible transcendent principle."[53] As Robin Middleton had described the Brutalists as working with "whatever fragments were available,"[54] Tafuri depicted an Alberti that operated through the expedient deployment of fragments within the urban milieu.[55] For Tafuri, the efficacy of Alberti's humanism resided not in ideal architectural configurations (and certainly not in hexagonal, insect-related ones[56]) or in "inane forms of curiosity regarding first principles" but rather in "action" and "the deeds of mortals." He concluded in an echo of New Brutalist rhetoric: "Architecture is, therefore, a manifestation of ethics."[57]

Regardless of the hexagon's level of humanist pedigree (or, for that matter, of Alberti's proto-Brutalism), Fuller's unusual forms and pervasive disinterest in disciplinary convention were certainly factors in Philip Johnson's assertion that "Bucky Fuller was no architect,"[58] as well as in other midcentury architects' "attitude of extreme hostility" toward Fuller, which Banham noted in *The New Brutalism*.[59] In his influential lecture, "The Seven Crutches of Architecture," Johnson paid homage to Fuller's legendary energy while rejecting his output:

> It's like a hurricane, you can't miss it if it's coming: he [Fuller] talks, you know, for five or six hours, and he ends up that all architecture is nonsense, and you have to build something like discontinuous domes. The arguments are beautiful. I have nothing against discontinuous domes, but for goodness sake, let's not call it architecture. Have you ever seen Bucky trying to put a door into one of his domed buildings? He's never succeeded, and wisely, when he does them, he doesn't put any covering over them, so they are magnificent pieces of pure sculpture. Sculpture also cannot result in architecture because architecture has problems that Bucky Fuller has not faced, like how do you get in and out.[60]

If Fuller's work did not resonate with the establishment, his influence over later generations was profound. The debt owed Fuller by young practitioners has been well documented, and the relationship between Fuller and his fans quickly became reciprocal. By the mid-1960s, the American inventor was speculating on large-scale proposals with clear Archigram overtones, and he developed many ideas from the late 1960s onward in concert with Norman Foster, John McHale, and others.[61]

Of all these connections and sources, Fuller's modest Mechanical Wing (1940), which Banham presented as a seminal antecedent in "A Clip-On Architecture," warrants attention. The project—a small, self-contained, trailer-borne unit containing a bathroom, kitchen, and mechanical equipment that could be attached to an existing structure—had been featured in the October 1940 issue of *Architectural Forum,* where, alongside a cutaway perspective view, it was sketched in combination with a tent, a small cottage, and a modern ranch home. Like early 4D and Dymaxion studies, these illustrations admit no reservations about dissonant compositional juxtapositions. An outboard motor for domestic enclosures, the Mechanical Wing offered enhanced mechanical performance with little regard for the aesthetic integration of a traditional architectural body into its technological prostheses.

Farrell/Grimshaw's similarly pragmatic attitude with the Bathroom Tower sets their project apart from concurrent clip-on experiments. Where the Fun Palace, Plug-In City, the Capsule Homes Tower, and other Archigram projects offered the clip-on sensibility as stand-alone projects, Farrell/Grimshaw took the additional step of clipping their clip-together unit to a conventional masonry structure. Not satisfied to leave this upgraded object "as found," the architects aggressively transformed the internal spaces as well, stripping out elegant (though dilapidated) conventional rooms in pursuit of the expedient satisfaction of immediate programmatic necessity. Where the preexisting townhouses offered a familiar hierarchy of served and servant spaces, Farrell/Grimshaw's renovation followed both Tafuri's Alberti and Johnson's Pollock,[62] "desacrilizing" a traditional diagram to elicit a series of spaces in which "every bit was as good as another and could be replaced by any other."[63] Tall-ceilinged parlors and cramped attics alike were converted into livable dormitory spaces, while neglected basement rooms and "every odd kink" were elevated to the role of communal gathering space.[64] With a shared technological apparatus appended to this matrix and accessible at all levels, individual living functions were disengaged from their conventional spatial containers to be distributed evenly across an energized, expedient, and indeterminate architectural milieu.

Yet, for all this, Banham had no comment on the project. The omission is curious, in terms of the project's close resonance with his own interests at the time as well as his prolific output as a critic. Part of the reason may be personal—Banham rarely mentioned Farrell or Grimshaw in his writings, and when he did, he tended to adopt a negative tone. But the omission likely had more to do with compositional concerns. Like the Smithsons' Sheffield proposal, the Bathroom Tower was locked in close compositional dialogue with an existing Victorian structure. Despite Banham's allegiance to clip-on expediency in theory, his silence here points again to his aversion to its compositional implications in practice.

The DRU Extension

Banham's similar silence with respect to Richard + Su Rogers's DRU Conversion (figs. 2.13, 2.14; see pl. 6) reinforces the point. The project came at a difficult time for the Rogerses, who had recently dissolved Team 4, their earlier partnership with Norman and Wendy Foster.[65] After the split, the two formed their own practice, initially as an independent subsidiary of the Design Research Unit. The DRU had

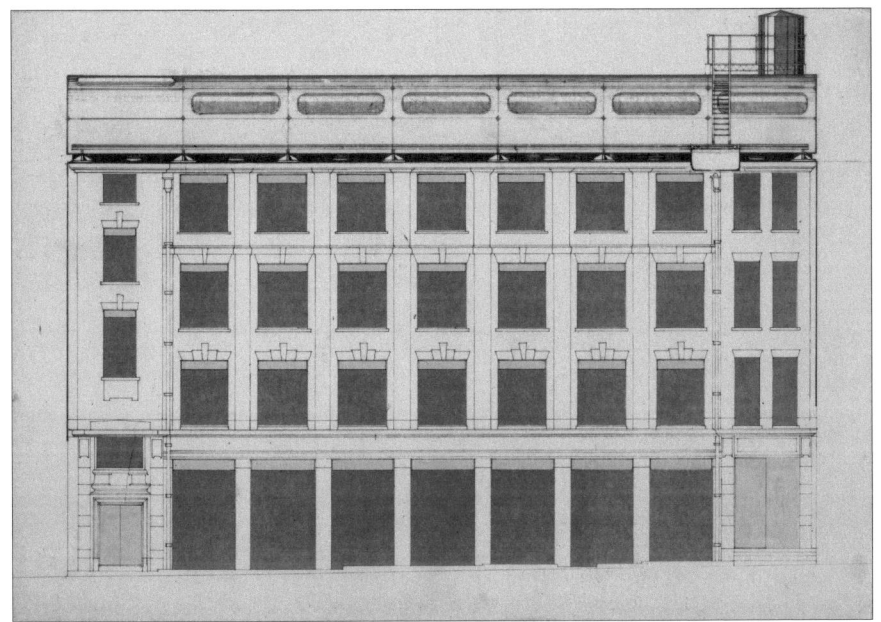 

been conceived in 1942 as a multidisciplinary design consultancy by Marcus Brumwell, Su Rogers's stepfather, in consultation with Herbert Read, and it began operating the following year.[66] Though it had enjoyed a high degree of success in the postwar period,[67] by the late 1960s, the firm seemed to Misha Black, its managing architect, to be somewhat behind the curve of contemporary British design. Black felt the Rogerses' presence might improve the firm's overall working atmosphere.[68] Their first commission was a study in which the young architects were highly critical of the aging institution's organization and methods. Despite this alienating report, the Rogerses were commissioned to design the new DRU offices in London in 1969, with their fledgling practice taking up residence in a rooftop extension of their own design in 1971.

In designing the interior fit-out for the DRU's new office space, the Rogerses struggled to replace the cellular plan of the firm's previous offices with an open, flexible system better attuned to the indeterminate nature of the practice. As in Farrell/Grimshaw's dormitory conversion, traditional interiors were rejected in favor of open, nonhierarchical arrangements. Conceiving every occupant "as good as any other" (at least in spatial terms), all office employees regardless of rank were allotted a similar amount of workspace within the open milieu.[69] The Rogerses outfitted these new floor plans with vibrantly colored mobile furniture of their own design. Framed with off-the-shelf metal sections supporting plastic laminate work surfaces, the furniture pieces were seen by one commentator to "assault or delight the visitor depending on his or her ability to gulp down colour by the gallon."[70]

The 1971 rooftop extension drew on earlier research the architects had conducted into prefabricated clip-together constructions for their Zip-Up Enclosure

FIG. 2.13 | **Richard + Su Rogers (Richard Rogers, British, b. Italy, 1933; Su Rogers [née Brumwell], British, b. 1939).**
Conversion and Roof Extension for the Design Research Unit (London, 1969–71). Intermediate scheme elevation.
Photo by Richard + Su Rogers.

FIG. 2.14 | **Richard + Su Rogers (Richard Rogers, British, b. Italy, 1933; Su Rogers [née Brumwell], British, b. 1939).**
Conversion and Roof Extension for the Design Research Unit (London, 1969–71). View of the street facade (detail).
Photo by Richard Einzig.

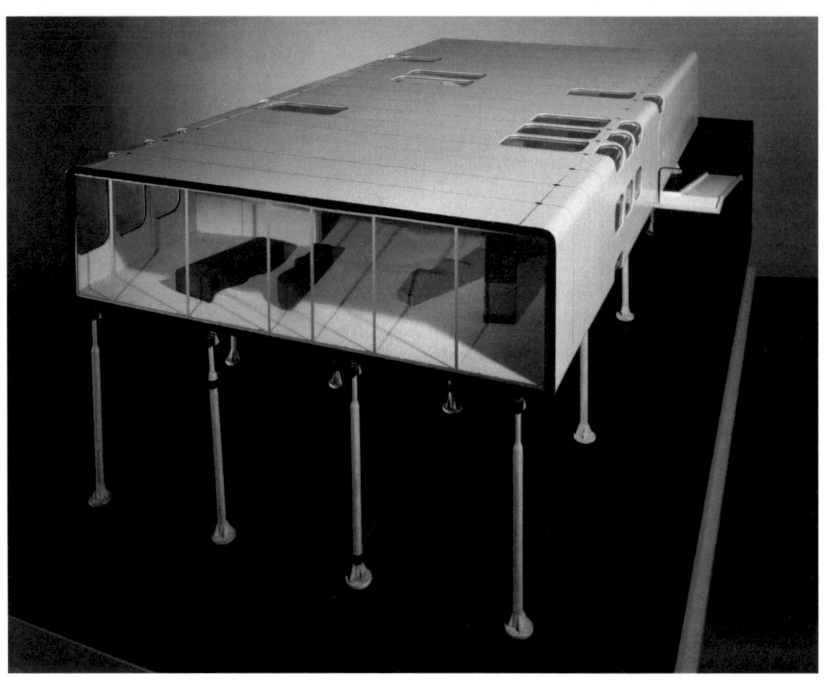

No. 1 of 1969 (fig. 2.15). The *Architectural Review* was quick to point out project's affiliations with Fuller: "Richard and Su Rogers, following in the footsteps of master Bucky with his attempt to use aeroplane technology for his Dymaxion house, are experimenting with a nouvelle vague technology of highly insulated lightweight panels and neoprene gasketry."[71] The house took its name from the neoprene gaskets employed to zip together the prefabricated structural sandwich panels from which the house was constructed. The panels—aluminum skins over an insulating PVC core—formed rectangular "rings" that merged walls, floors, and ceilings into a single continuous loop. Intended to be available for purchase at local stores, the rings were zipped together end-to-end to enclose an indeterminate space of any length. End elevations were to be fully glazed, while openings in the rings were cut at the discretion of the owner. As individual needs changed over time, additional rings easily could be added to the system, and non-load-bearing interior partitions and even plumbing locations could be adjusted as desired.[72] The project was supported on a grid of adjustable steel jacks able to negotiate variable terrain and enabling easy relocation to other sites if the need or opportunity should arise.

While the Zip-Up concept had been met with significant resistance as a stand-alone proposal in a variety of sites,[73] the specific constraints of a nineteenth-century rooftop were well suited to the Rogerses' unconventional system. The DRU had secured planning approval for an additional floor to be added to the existing four-story structure when the firm took ownership in 1969, but when the extension design was undertaken in 1971, it was discovered that the existing foundations could

FIG. 2.15 | **Richard + Su Rogers (Richard Rogers, British, b. Italy, 1933; Su Rogers [née Brumwell], British, b. 1939).**
Zip-Up Enclosure No. 1 (1969). Detail color presentation competition model, scale 1:20.
Photo by Eamonn O'Mahony.

not support an additional story of conventional masonry.[74] The Rogerses' lightweight Zip-Up system was a perfect match.

From the start, the Rogers office, now expanded to include architects Jan Kaplický and Renzo Piano, intended a bold juxtaposition of old and new. Kaplický's tongue-in-cheek photo-collage of the brick warehouse capped by an oversize Volkswagen Beetle—the car rendered in bright green and plugged into the existing roof by what appears to be a pneumatic hose—set the tone (see pl. 6). The firm's original scheme brashly proposed an external truss frame to span twenty-seven meters longitudinally between the building's party walls. Arched sandwich panels, this time with skins of GRP over a phenolic resin core, were to be affixed to the existing front and back facades and suspended from the truss frame, with a longitudinal skylight running the length of the scheme. Adding to the dissonance between old and new systems, the Rogerses designed the three-by-nine-meter panels to be cranked askew of the existing building's orthogonal grid.[75] In keeping with the Zip-Up concept, the new office floor was raised off the existing roof on adjustable jacks, while electronics, computer equipment, and HVAC took their places in the plenum created between new floor and existing roof. The scheme's bright yellow finish was carried through the existing facade at new window heads and door panels in the openings below.

Like previous Zip-Up schemes, the proposal was not approved by London planning officials. The revisions the project went through to achieve approval unfolded from Kaplický's original image to the final built work in a clear trajectory of domestication, as dissonant juxtaposition gave way to clear, if slightly begrudged, conformance. The final scheme dispensed with the external truss frame and proposed a series of three-meter-wide sandwich panels. In lieu of the GRP cladding rejected by the Greater London Council, the Rogerses offered an aluminum skin. The panels were supported internally on aluminum arched portals that spanned twelve meters orthogonally from front to back. An intermediate scheme showed seven equal bays in the extension, causing a disjunction with the rhythm of the existing facade's nine structural bays below (see fig. 2.13). In the final, realized scheme, nine aluminum bays march in lockstep with the existing masonry frame. The seven-bay scheme boasted asymmetrical windows, a cylindrical water tank to the north, industrial access ladders with exaggerated railings wrapping from front to back, and frankly exposed leveling jacks perched on an existing cornice. The constructed scheme offers unabashed symmetry in panels and fenestration, while a continuous ribbon of steel (mounted to support window-washing equipment) screens the previously exposed leveling jacks and reinforces the existing cornice line with a deep shadow (see fig. 2.14). Roof access via spiral stair, the industrial railings, and the water tank also were eliminated, leaving behind a minimal access ladder at the south end as the lone asymmetrical feature.

The Olivetti Training Center

Working in a highly visible site in central London, the young Rogers office struggled with a conservative planning commission and a client steeped in the conventions of postwar modern architecture. In suburban Haslemere, James Stirling's far more established firm enjoyed a secluded site and a progressive client eager to embrace innovative design ideas for the Olivetti Training Center (see figs. 2.16–2.23, pls. 7, 8). Nine years Richard Rogers's senior, Stirling was a celebrated personality in the British architectural scene, having made a resounding entrance with his famous Leicester University Engineering Building (with James Gowan, 1959–63) and the Cambridge History Faculty Building (1964–67). Like the Rogerses and Farrell/Grimshaw, Stirling was charged with the expansion of an existing structure. In this case, Branksome Hilders (1900–1905), an Edwardian country estate by E. J. May, was to be transformed into a training facility for the growing Italian industrial-design powerhouse. And like the Rogerses, Stirling offered a dissonant counterpoint to the existing vernacular in brightly colored GRP. But where the younger architects found themselves tracing a series of domesticating revisions that ultimately diluted the radicalism of their initial studies, Stirling, with a carefully choreographed assemblage of disparate elements and discordant spaces, advanced the dissonant qualities of the clip-on approach to unprecedented heights.

The project entailed the conversion of the existing house (which previously had functioned as a secondary school) to accommodate approximately one hundred trainee-residents and the addition of a new wing for training rooms and meeting spaces (fig. 2.16). Stirling enlisted Edward Cullinan, a talented London architect five years his junior, to design the renovation, freeing himself to concentrate on a new structure to accommodate the education facilities. Though both architects contributed greatly to the final product, credit routinely goes to Stirling alone, despite Banham's efforts to correct prevailing lopsided attributions.[76] Indeed, Banham's presentation in the *Architectural Review* remains the only published documentation of Cullinan's contribution (see figs. 2.17, 2.18, pl. 7).

Cullinan inherited a rambling, vaguely U-shaped plan set upon a high ridge, its central service court open to the north. The western arm of the U stretched north of its eastern counterpart and cranked to the west; a front door with gabled porch occupied the joint in the dogleg. The cranked portion of the house conformed to an orthogonal arrangement of outbuildings to the west. Three gabled bay windows at the southern facade faced a broad meadow and swimming pool beyond. At the eastern wing of the house, a loosely cruciform annex building extended the eastern wing's axis roughly parallel to a steep drop into the adjacent woods (fig. 2.17).

Cullinan's intervention kept much of the existing construction intact, but, as Farrell/Grimshaw had done at the International Students Club, he bore little

FIG. 2.16 | James Stirling (British, 1926–92) with Edward Cullinan (British, b. 1931).
Olivetti Training Center (Haslemere, England, 1969–74). Aerial view.

FIG. 2.17 | Edward Cullinan (British, b. 1931).
Olivetti Training Center residential wing (Haslemere, England, 1969–74). Floor plans.
From Reyner Banham, "Problem × 3 = Olivetti," *Architectural Review* 155 (1974): 192.

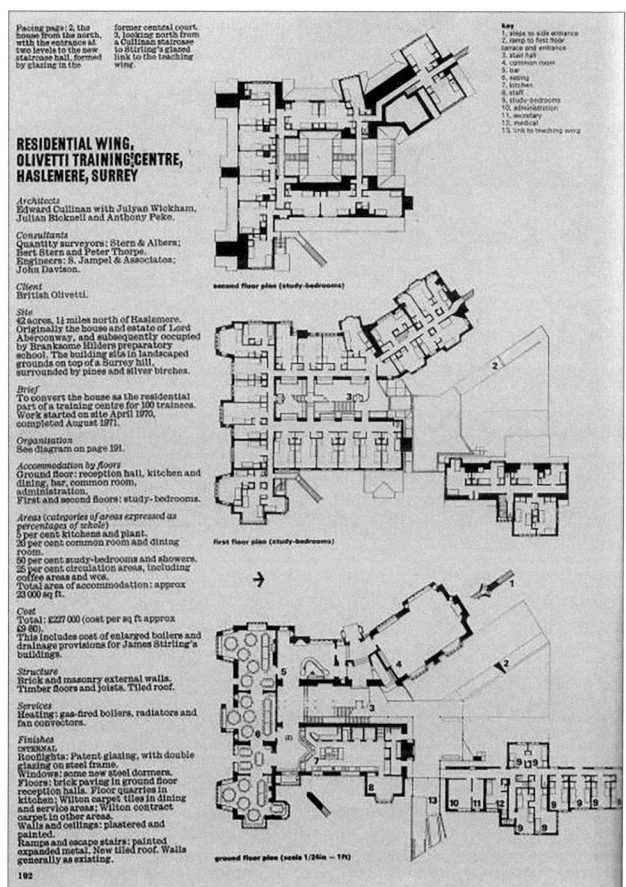

sentimentality for the previous organization. Rather than attempt to correct existing anomalies, Cullinan added a collection of dissonant elements to the mix. A glazed steel canopy was inserted to connect the annex with the existing building, the space between them becoming the link with Stirling's new structure to the east. The glazed element became the new entry to the complex, with the existing annex and cranked wing appearing to focus attention on the entry. Exterior stairs and ramps were added throughout to join the ground plane directly to new residential quarters above, a move that undercut the hierarchical formality of the existing building with an array of expedient and informal connections (fig. 2.18). The canopy opens onto a double-height hall occupying the former service yard (see pl. 7). Open stairs link the ground-floor common areas to a dense collection of dormitory rooms jigsawed into the irregular plan above.

Cullinan's white steel rails and ad hoc stairs, ramps, and gangways gave his intervention a distinctly nautical air in stark contrast to the polite eccentricities of May's existing brick-and-shingle manse. As Banham noted, the architect justified the approach with deadpan rationality: "Cullinan himself explains it in terms of the need to find a mode of design that could bridge the gap between his (and his office's) own attitudes and those expressed by the house, and the only real point of

FIG. 2.18 | **Edward Cullinan (British, b. 1931).**
Olivetti Training Center residential wing (Haslemere, England, 1969–74). Exterior views.
From Reyner Banham, "Problem × 3 = Olivetti," *Architectural Review* 155 (1974): 193.

contact they could find was the functional/romantic style of Edwardian riverside boathouses and the like."⁷⁷

But the scheme was far more than a stylistic compromise. As Banham pointed out, Olivetti's program required "radical reworking" of the existing building to provide additional fire exits, mechanical services, and other infrastructural updates. Cullinan's approach enabled a particularly cost-effective design. Aside from the removal of several unnecessary chimneys and external buttresses, the architect left the majority of May's work intact, casting the existing house as host for a set of delicate prostheses. Through the shingled roofs, Cullinan punched gabled dormers to bring light into new attic-level study-bedrooms. These dissonant elements—framed in white steel and constructed entirely of glass—mimic forms appropriate to May's original but are rendered in materials that have no place in the otherwise nineteenth-century vocabulary. Easily mistaken for original by approaching visitors (and viewers of published photographs), these subtle clues are the only indication from the south and west that something out of the ordinary is afoot.

Cullinan's most transformative intervention inhabits the interstitial space of the former service court. The bright lobby was articulated with lightweight steel connectors in an abstract composition that linked the dormitory rooms above to one another and to the common spaces below (see pl. 7). The geometries and colors recall at once constructivist sources, industrial scaffolds, and children's toys. While Cullinan largely restricted his elemental exuberance to the new stair hall, he affected a significant transformation of the entire structure. Within this new enclosure, Cullinan supplied necessary plumbing, electrical, and HVAC without expensive manipulation of the existing building. A new basement below provided space for mechanical services for both the original house and Stirling's addition. Thus, Cullinan's central hall offered an expedient solution to the infrastructural and circulatory problems and provided a concentrated source from which both necessary environmental services and a contemporary sensibility emanated. Banham's assessment is noteworthy: "The result is not in any sense an unified style; it is a converter's idiom, which exists in its pure form in the center of the plan, and dilutes itself as it spreads outward and penetrates the older building."[78] Working with "whatever fragments were available,"[79] Cullinan marshaled the scattered picturesque elements of May's scheme into a new, complex coherence.

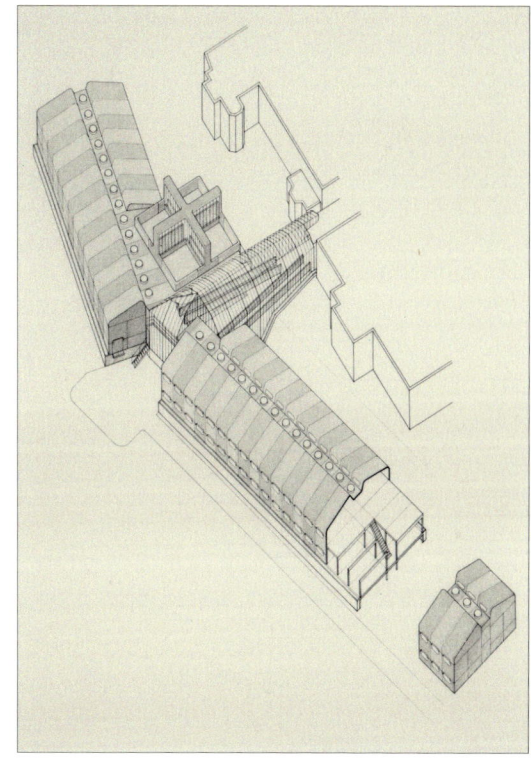

FIG. 2.19 | **James Stirling (British, 1926–92).**
Olivetti Training Center (Haslemere, England, 1969–74). Axonometric.

Stirling's contribution exhibits a similar blend of deadpan efficiency and brash dissonance (see figs. 2.19–2.23, pl. 8). The bulk of the scheme comprises double-loaded classroom wings clad in GRP that extend roughly parallel to the east facade of the existing house. With rounded rectangular windows and gasketed connections between the GRP bays, the project bears more than a passing resemblance to the Rogerses' Zip-Up prototypes, though, here, the younger architect's svelte rectangular section was stretched vertically along its central axis to suggest a gable. Countering the upward thrust of the roof slopes, depressed ridges punctured with a row of circular skylights run the length of the wings. The rounded corners, alternating colors, bucolic site, and clearly secondary status with respect to the original house all conspire to make the project resemble an inflatable tent for a garden party, its internal pressure somewhere short of snapping the ridge into its full upright position (fig. 2.19).

In his characteristic style, Stirling explained his formal complexities as the result of no-nonsense efficiency. To "avoid colliding with groups of very large specimen trees" and to occupy "level ground to permit linear expansion" along the top of the ridge, the classroom wings were cranked inward toward the house.[80] Though the building has not been extended since completion, the ambition to produce the possibility of repeatable elements distinctly aligns the work with the "endless and indeterminate" projects Banham examined in "A Clip-On Architecture." The idiosyncratic central area, however, gives rise to contrasting readings of insistent specificity. The plan renders the scheme an asymmetrically broken bar—its two ends nudged inward to cradle the existing house while the glass membrane provides visual access to the splintered middle section.[81] Here, the GRP bars were tethered to the renovated facility by a glass link containing skewed ramps negotiating both the slope of the site and the geometries of the glass enclosure. Adding further complexity to the scene, a square "multispace" was planted resolutely within

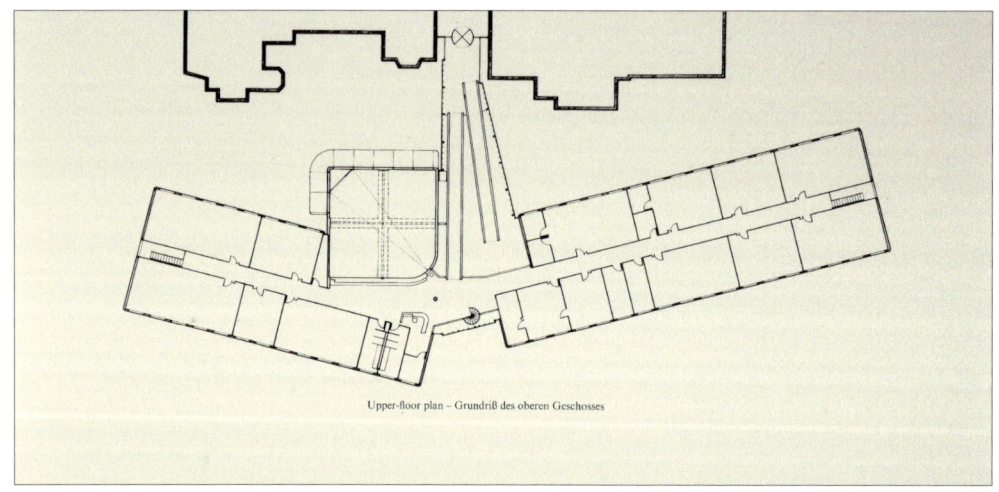

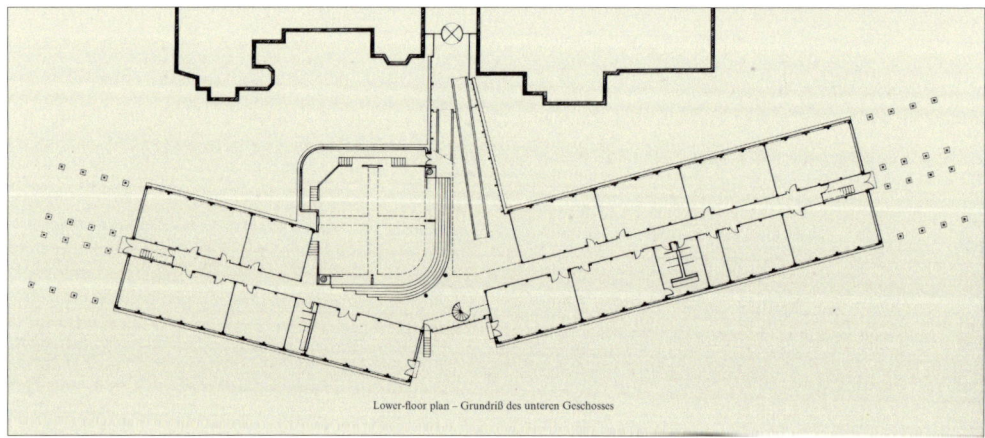

this central zone (fig. 2.20). Crowned with a protruding cruciform roof, this element rests unperturbed by the adjacent formal commotion.

The project's spatial and elemental complexity is manifest most forcefully in the glazed central zone (fig. 2.21). The multispace was set orthogonal to the main house, as was the southern edge of the glazed link. The northern edge of the link adheres to the grid of the north teaching wing, resulting in a splayed triangular space that Stirling capped with a glass gambrel roof and tipped toward the existing building to produce a spatial funnel back toward the entry. Two ramps connect the upper and lower floors of the addition to Cullinan's new entry. The southern ramp accesses the upper level and aligns with the orthogonal south wall, while the northern ramp splays roughly eleven degrees to split the angle between the southern ramp and the north wall. This directs the visitor's view not out the glazed eastern wall to the woods beyond, nor directly at the blank interior face of the classroom wall but instead, curiously, at an interior corner. The obvious visual conclusion of the woods is neither fully acknowledged nor denied; rather, one's view is deflected off an interior angle, and the climax is left jarringly unresolved (see pl. 8). Choosing the upper ramp similarly frustrates the viewer's visual access to the woods, as the

FIG. 2.20 | **James Stirling (British, 1926–92).**

Olivetti Training Center (Haslemere, England, 1969–74). Floor plans.

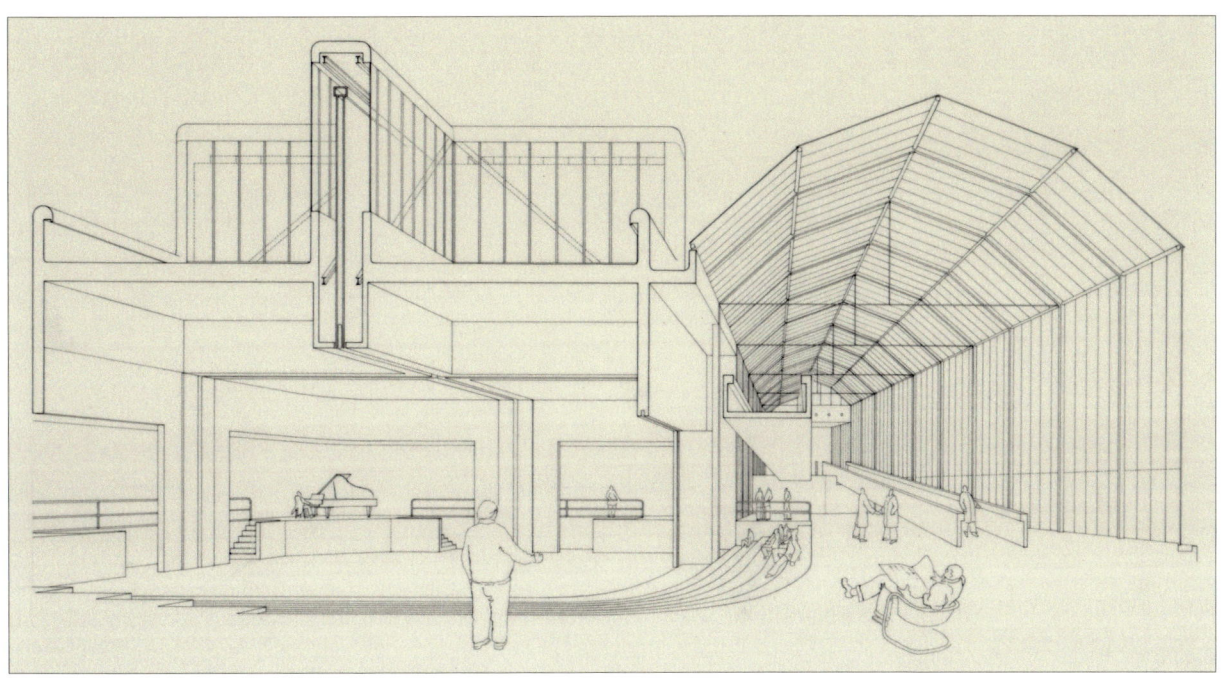

ramp aligns on one of two double-height, brightly colored radiator grills positioned in front of the glass wall to the east. From the ramps, space spills into the multispace, eddies into the classroom corridors, and unceremoniously leaks past a spiral staircase into the adjacent woods through the glazing beyond.

Complex mechanical apparatuses further add to the complexity. The multispace can be subdivided into smaller areas by lowering wall partitions (and a stabilizing central column) from a cruciform protrusion in the roof. Full enclosure can be achieved by deploying retractable walls that scroll away into the northeast and southwest corners. Doing so results not only in the various room configurations Stirling's office carefully studied in their trademark axonometric drawings but also in a disturbing leftover gulley between the base of the access stairs and the flexible wall. This odd space leaves the remaining area of the link abruptly cropped, and it cleverly reiterates a similarly discomforting confrontation between the lawn's downward slope and the encroaching vertical wall in the space between the teaching wings and the existing house. The space is peppered with additional mechanical elements: Two-story radiators frame the view to the woods to the east (off-center to the roof overhead but symmetrical within the wall glazing) and, to the west, march in step with the structure of the glazed link. Air supply and return ducts punctuate interior surfaces as exaggerated nozzles and grommets. Two bulbous mushroom columns at the corner of the multispace suggest pistons lifting the upper-floor slab, while a spiral stair just beyond recalls a spring under compressive load. These elements reinforce a diagonal axis across the multispace, with a corner stage, the paired columns, and the spiral stair all carefully aligned, befuddlingly, on

FIG. 2.21 | **James Stirling (British, 1926–92).**
Olivetti Training Center (Haslemere, England, 1969–74). Interior perspective of multispace and glazed link.

the southernmost corner of the north teaching wing. Literally crowning this bizarre scene, a mechanized window-cleaning apparatus, featuring a clever double-hinged mechanism to negotiate the telescoping geometry of the link, periodically lumbers across the glass roof above.

In a perceptive formal analysis, Joseph Rykwert further enumerated the project's discordant effects and linked them to previous Stirling efforts: "A spiral staircase to focus an unresolved climax has been used by Stirling elsewhere: most conspicuously at Leicester. The gawky effect is of course part of the mannerist intention."[82] Deploying exuberant metaphorical rhetoric, Charles Jencks highlighted the varied references embedded in the project. He likened the plastic wings to "railroad cars or Greyhound buses" and even "stacked waste-bins" before describing the central space as a promiscuous mash-up of historical sources: "The Spada Gallery of Borromini with scissor ramp of Le Corbusier and glazing by Paxton—a kind of greenhouse ship's deck where grey flannel technicians can meet quietly and converse." While accumulating these metaphors was his primary concern in the text, Jencks perceptively outlined the project's clear inheritance of the historical trajectory being traced in the present book:

> The plan is similar to the informal topological planning of the Brutalist movement for which growth was a primary consideration. But beyond this is Stirling's particular brandmark, a quality (that can be found in all his buildings) of dynamic dissonance. A comparable feeling in music would be the suspensions and tensions of Stravinsky; in painting, the distortions of Francis Bacon. The effect is tense, elastic, and frightening. Perhaps also it communicates the moral commitment of functionalism: a stern asceticism and a preference for truth over beauty.[83]

Here, Jencks tightly linked the dissonant assemblages of the clip-on approach to the legacy of Brutalism. In adhering to a moral stance of "truth over beauty," Stirling sacrificed "elegance" in favor of "a toughness and uncompromising quality."[84] Yet while Stirling's (and Cullinan's) deadpan rhetoric and efficiently attached clip-on prosthetics might signify a "moral commitment of functionalism," their mischievous relish in the aggressive (and functionally unnecessary) subversion of traditional formal and programmatic configurations belies any "stern asceticism." The unconventional techniques evidenced at Haslemere move well beyond functional propriety or clip-on expediency. They mark a sustained effort to wittily undermine (or in Tafuri's term, to "desacrilize") established conventions in order to meditate on alternative forms of architectural coherence.

Strangely, Stirling's efforts drew a cool assessment from Banham. In contrast to the brash alterity suggested by Rykwert and Jencks, Banham found in Haslemere a

FIG. 2.22 | **James Stirling (British, 1926–92).**
Olivetti Training Center (Haslemere, England, 1969–74). View from the south.
Photo by Richard Einzig.

restrained, almost conventional contribution to the lineage of plastic-shell construction. Turning his attention to the interior, he complained of questionable acoustics and inadequate environmental control in the teaching rooms and dismissed the central multispace and glazed link as "curiously under-organized" and "uncomfortable." He was similarly unimpressed by the proliferation (and performance) of mechanical gadgets, and he struggled with Stirling's unconventional tactics for achieving coherence within the complex. In describing the central space, he noticed that

> what holds it together are not the surfaces that bound the space, but the things in it—the mushroom columns, the enormous vertical radiators, the elaborately sculptured staircase, and the powerful colors. In strong sunlight, when external objects are seen through the glass, the effect of all this is liberating, if disorienting, so that there can be a faint feeling of insecurity as one perambulates the sloping surfaces of the ramps (a domestic version of the perilous spaces of the Eiffel Tower), but when it is dark outside and most of the light comes from the link's own internal sources, the whole scene goes out of focus somehow.

He found a more convincing coherence on the exterior, where a view from the south between Stirling's wing and May's original "galvanizes the whole plastic panel system into architectural life" (fig. 2.22). This, he argued, "is perhaps the most telling view of the whole ensemble; the multispace sitting as mute and as smug as an electronic installation on the one side, and the house, fussy and eloquent with false but familiar 'historical' values on the other. And between them, once again, the glazed and problematical link-block. To this, it seems we must always come back if the center is to be understood as an architectural whole."[85] Banham repeated this concern for a holistic understanding throughout his essay. Where Olivetti had "presented and promoted" the "center *as a whole*"[86] while advancing only Stirling as its architect, Banham emphasized Cullinan's crucial contribution to the overall project. Foreshadowing his strangely conventionalizing conclusion, Banham alluded to the decentralizing tendencies of Stirling's partitioning of the project, noting that the division of labor "emphasizes the *distacco* (appropriately Wittkowerian word) between Stirling's work and the old house and makes him look as if he is designing sheds at the bottom of the back garden. Not least of the successes of the combined design has been to retrieve that situation."[87] Returning to themes of centrality and wholeness, Banham concluded his assessment with a rumination on "the center of the Center." He noticed that the provision of the glazed link was not required functionally, but having made the choice to provide it, Stirling appeared committed to a specific (and starkly conventional) resolution: "The logic of the situation appears to demand at least the diagram of a monumental solution.... Once the commitment to a closed and formal link is made, however, it brings with it an important consequence: at the end it must, in physical detail, resolve the differences between the two kinds of architecture."[88]

In 1955, Banham had praised the Smithsons for their "abstemious under-designing of the details" at Hunstanton and denigrated Louis Kahn's details at the Yale University Art Gallery as "arty."[89] Here, Stirling's parallel candor met with disapproval. While he found Stirling's joints between the glass wall and adjacent GRP panels at the east side of the central hall to be "nice, open, and more-or-less rectangular,"

> where the situation changes the solution can be much less happy, as at the interface (I'm sure that's the appropriate word!) between the flank of the multi-space and the glazed side on the link, the joint over the fire-escape is a real brute visually. That is the more astonishing because it is Stirling joining to Stirling, whereas where Stirling joins Cullinan at the point where the link meets the house, everything is carried off so neatly you don't even notice it at first.[90]

To underline his point, Banham illustrated the inelegant Stirling-to-Stirling connection with what is likely his own photograph (fig. 2.23).[91] The link was handled with a raised brake-metal lap splice over an expansion joint that accommodates differential movement between the concrete structure of the GRP wings and steel frame of the multispace. The splice flashing was soldered to a metal infill panel that closed

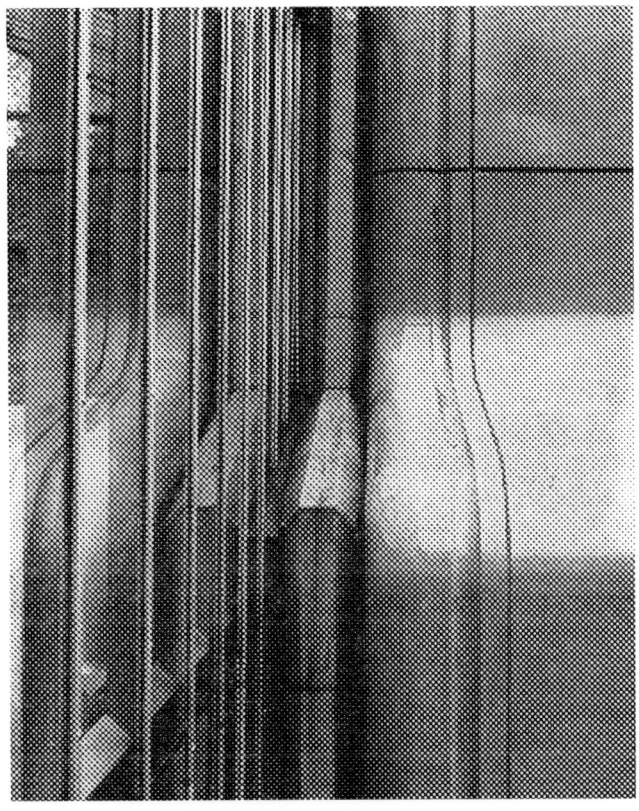

the odd-shaped gap left between it and the glazing system. At the GRP side, a bead of sealant closed the gap.[92] A common solution to conceal expansion joints, this ad hoc approach signals the laboring hand of an on-site craftsperson and undermines the clip-together image of the rest of the complex.[93]

If this intra-Stirling interface suffered for being overly visible and underdistilled, it was the apparent seamlessness of the Cullinan-to-Stirling connection that, for Banham, maintained the integrity of the overall scheme. Though the two offices employed different framing details in their adjoining glazed elements, "the continuity of the glass itself prevails over the discontinuity of the detail." In the end, it was a "similarity in mood" between the two architects that "pervades the architecture of all public spaces of the center" and tied the disparate elements of the training center into an integrated whole. Banham continued:

> It would be possible to enter under Cullinan's external ramp, pass through the entrance hall, up Stirling's ascending ramp in the link to a class-room on the upper level; or go from the multispace through the link into the stairhall and up to one of the study bedrooms, experiencing only changes of emphasis in an architectural mood that was consistent and... *festive?*
>
> It is difficult to find the exact word... but I remember Rudolf Wittkower using the word "festive" to describe the swags of carved greenery between

FIG. 2.23 | **James Stirling (British, 1926–92).**
Olivetti Training Center (Haslemere, England, 1969–74). Joint between glazed link and GRP panels.
From Reyner Banham, "Problem × 3 = Olivetti," *Architectural Review* 155 (1974): 199.

the capitals of Inigo Jones's Banqueting House in Whitehall—"as if hung there for a festival." Something of that quality comes from the clear bright colors of Haslemere.[94]

This closing assessment marks an unexpected turn in Banham's writing. Invoking Wittkower for a second time in the text, Banham coupled him with the historical concept of mood (famously developed by Wittkower's onetime teacher Heinrich Wölfflin[95]) to synthesize the complex dissonances between the work of three architects (May, Cullinan, and Stirling) into a clear, coherent whole that cleaved exactly to the "centristic" concepts to which he appeared so allergic in his earlier writings. Adding to the conventional complexion of his assessment, Banham admonished an expedient detail at a rarely seen corner for failing to live up to the restrained elegance of a properly articulated architectural connection. Indeed, Banham here seems on the verge of full apostasy of his iconoclastic position. Coupling his quest to elucidate the "center of the Center" and his implied desire for elegant detailing, he appeared to embrace exactly those classical conventions of "symmetry, unity, coherence, balance, and all those" he had lampooned in "A Clip-On Architecture."[96]

Given the trajectory of Banham's writings, one might have expected him to praise Stirling's clunky detail as an admirably unvarnished solution chosen from well-known sources—something akin to the "abstemiously under-designed details" he had praised at the Hunstanton School.[97] In its awkward expedience, the perfunctory seam underlines the dissonant themes so perceptively noted by Jencks and Rykwert and so consistently championed by Banham throughout the 1950s and '60s. Yet in these early writings, Banham repeatedly backpedaled in the face of visually dissonant architectural compositions. From his advocacy of the Smithsons in "The New Brutalism" to his choice of Cook's Plug-In City as the high point of "A Clip-On Architecture," Banham consistently favored visually integrated architectures as illustrations of the otherness he sought.

Faced with Stirling's and Cullinan's brashly incongruous elements, Banham took a surprising tack. True to his impatience with disorderly objects, he found Stirling's spaces at Haslemere "under-organized," his mechanical contraptions "ponderous," and his detailing brutish. He barely concerned himself with the formal intricacies that so perplexed Rykwert and Jencks and appealed instead to a traditional notion of centrality. Notice that his clue to the holistic centeredness of the Training Center was found when he initially failed to notice an architectural detail, at the point where mismatched glazing elements disappear into the reflective twinkle of adjacent glass planes. Unmolested by tectonic assemblies demanding scrutiny, the visitor glides happily past this irrelevant deficiency and on through the facility. At Olivetti, Banham exchanged the connoisseur's rapt attention for the distracted immersion of the flâneur, advancing exactly the shift in subjectivity suggested earlier in the replacement of the Vitruvian Man with *Homo Ludens* at the Fun Palace.

Though the Olivetti complex was densely populated with playful architecture devices that offered sufficient diversion to entertain less-aggressive critics, for Banham, Olivetti's "festive mood" was produced neither through conventional ornamentation (Inigo Jones's lively swags at the Banqueting House) nor through look-at-me compositional devices (Stirling's rooftop robots, giant radiators, clumsy details, and frustrated axes). Indeed, such elements—and the scrutiny they demand—keep the subject-object relation of traditional architecture firmly intact. While "Stirlingologists" and other initiates into what Banham would later refer to as "the arcane and privileged aesthetic code"[98] of the discipline might enjoy the witty subversions deployed throughout the space, such pleasures, and the subjectivities they sanction, remain, like the New Brutalism, firmly within the realm of Le Corbusier's *Vers une architecture* (1923). In the end, Stirling and Cullinan's clip-on conversion exceeded Farrell/Grimshaw's functional iconoclasm at the Bathroom Tower while avoiding the Rogerses' capitulation to convention at the DRU Conversion. In doing so, Olivetti advanced bold new forms of compositional coherence to stand as an unparalleled achievement in the clip-on idiom. But such compositional advances were of little interest to Banham. For him, it was in the work's contributions beyond the visual register—its suggestion of a subjectivity unencumbered by the visual strictures of conventional formalism and its provocation of alternative modes of immersive experience—that marked Olivetti's most productive swerve toward an "other" architecture.

NOTES

1. Reyner Banham, "A Clip-On Architecture," *Design Quarterly* 63 (1965): entire issue. The essay was reprinted in *Architectural Design* 35 (1965): 534–35; and, in German translation, in *Bauen und Wohnen* 22, no. 5 (1967): 66–73. For discussions of this text in relation to Banham's ideas of "une architecture autre" and his advocacy of popular science, respectively, see Anthony Vidler, *Histories of the Immediate Present: Inventing Architectural Modernism* (Cambridge, MA: MIT Press, 2008), 133–40; and Nigel Whiteley, *Reyner Banham: Historian of the Immediate Future* (Cambridge, MA: MIT Press, 2002), 171–78.
2. For a discussion of the dissonant compositional characteristics of the Sheffield University scheme, see "In Search of Alternatives: Banham, Britain, and the New Brutalism," this volume.
3. For documentation of these schemes, see Alison Smithson and Peter Smithson, *The Charged Void: Architecture* (New York: Monacelli, 1999), 102, 224–47.
4. Reyner Banham, *The New Brutalism: Ethic or Aesthetic?* (New York: Reinhold, 1966), 134.
5. For Banham's discussion of the Sheffield University scheme, see Banham, "The New Brutalism," *Architectural Review* 118 (1955): 361; and Banham, *The New Brutalism*, 42–43. On the Istituto Marchiondi Spagliardi, see Banham, "The History of the Immediate Future," *RIBA Journal* 68 (May 1961): 253; and Banham, *The New Brutalism*, 127–29. On the Park Hill Flats, see Banham, *The New Brutalism*, 131–33.
6. Eleven years Banham's junior, Middleton also completed his dissertation in 1958 under Nikolaus Pevsner's supervision. Like Banham, he held an influential role at a major London architectural publication, in his case, as technical editor of *Architectural Design*. In contrast to the *Architectural Review*, which, in spite of Banham's presence, maintained a proestablishment point of view throughout the 1950s and '60s, AD, under the

editorial leadership of Monica Pidgeon and through the significant influence of its technical editors (Theo Crosby from 1953 to 1962, Kenneth Frampton from 1962 to 1964, and Middleton from 1964 to 1972), was a dependable mouthpiece for progressive practices such as the Smithsons and, later, the Archigram group. For an informative comparison of the editorial practices of these two publications in the 1950s and '60s, see Steve Parnell, "*AR*'s and *AD*'s Post-War Editorial Policies: The Making of Modern Architecture in Britain," *Journal of Architecture* 17 (2012): 763–75.

7   Robin Middleton, "The New Brutalism; or, A Clean, Well-Lighted Place," *Architectural Design* 37 (1967): 7, emphasis added. Middleton's use of the term *fragment* here implies both a part separated from an original whole as well as an element that operates with a certain level of autonomy within an architectural composition. For a useful treatment of the term's long history in architecture, see Dalibor Vesely, "The Nature of the Modern Fragment and the Sense of Wholeness," in *Fragments: Architecture and the Unfinished, Essays presented to Robin Middleton,* ed. Barry Bergdoll and Werner Oechslin (London: Thames and Hudson, 2006), 43–56.

8   Middleton, "The New Brutalism," 7–8.

9   See Louis Kahn, "Toward a Plan for Midtown Philadelphia," *Perspecta* 2 (1953): 11–27.

10 Middleton, "The New Brutalism," 8.

11 Gerhard Kallman, "The Way through Technology: America's Unrealized Potential," *Architectural Review* 108 (1950): 414. Quoted in Banham, "A Clip-On Architecture," 4.

12 Banham, "A Clip-On Architecture," 4.

13 Banham, "A Clip-On Architecture," 5.

14 See Richard Llewelyn Davies, "Endless Architecture," *Architectural Association Journal* 67 (1951): 106–12. Cited in Banham, "A Clip-On Architecture," 4.

15 Banham, "A Clip-On Architecture," 7.

16 Banham, "A Clip-On Architecture," 7.

17 Banham, "A Clip-On Architecture," 7–8.

18 Banham, *The New Brutalism,* 132.

19 Banham, *The New Brutalism,* 74.

20 Banham, "A Clip-On Architecture," 9.

21 In this context, *empathy* implies what David Morgan has described as "the attempt to construct a theory of perception in which human feeling is projected into forms through the eye's constructive acts of visual interpretation." It was a key component in the Wittkowerian humanism Banham resisted. See David Morgan, "The Enchantment of Art: Abstraction and Empathy from German Romanticism to Expressionism," *Journal of the History of Ideas* 57, no. 2 (1996): 317. The concept was articulated by Heinrich Wölfflin, among others, in the nineteenth century. For a useful collection on the topic, see Harry Francis Mallgrave and Eleftherios Ikonomou, eds., *Empathy, Form, and Space: Problems in German Aesthetics, 1873–1893* (Santa Monica, CA: Getty Center, 1993), which features key texts by Conrad Fielder, Adolf Göller, Adolf von Hildebrand, August Shmarsow, Robert Vischer, and Wölfflin. William Worringer's *Abstraction and Empathy: A Contribution to the Psychology of Style* [1906] (New York: International Universities Press, 1967) also is a seminal text in this regard. For a discussion of empathy theory in relation to the context of midcentury English architecture, see Christopher Hight, *Architectural Principles in the Age of Cybernetics* (London: Routledge, 2008), 103–8.

22 Banham, "A Clip-On Architecture," 11.

23 "Too much should not be made of this distinction between extreme forms of the two concepts [clip-on and plug-in]: technically they are often intimately fused in a single project, and the aesthetic tradition overruns niceties of mechanical discrimination." Banham, "A Clip-On Architecture," 11.

24 Reyner Banham, "The History of the Immediate Future," 256.

25 For an account of the project from the period of its conception, see Cedric Price, "Fun Palace, Camden, London," *Architectural Design* 139 (1967): 522–25. For an excellent recent treatment, see Stanley Mathews, *From Agit-Prop to Free Space: The Architecture of Cedric Price* (London: Black Dog, 2007), especially pp. 44–191.

26 Banham, "A Clip-On Architecture," 13.

27 See Johan Huizinga, *Homo Ludens: A Study of the Play Element in Culture* [1938] (Boston: Beacon, 1955).

28 Reyner Banham, "1960—Stocktaking," *Architectural Review* 127 (1960): 93–100.

29 Banham, "A Clip-On Architecture," 15.

30 Banham, "A Clip-On Architecture," 15.

31 Banham, "A Clip-On Architecture," 30.

32 Price's spare drawings have been suggested as one of the causes for the ultimate failure of the Fun Palace to

gain a wide audience and to be seen successfully through to approval and construction. See Mathews, *From Agit-Prop to Free Space,* 173.

33   Banham, "A Clip-On Architecture," 30.
34   On the concept of empathy in architecture, see note 21.
35   Banham, "A Clip-On Architecture," 30.
36   For a full account, see Mathews, *From Agit-Prop to Free Space,* 170–91.
37   See "Conversion: The Farrell/Grimshaw Partnership's Bathroom Tower," *Architectural Design* 38 (1968): 491.
38   See Nicholas Grimshaw, "University," in *Archigram* 6 (1966): n.p.
39   See K. Michael Hays, "Fuller's Geological Engagements with Architecture," in *Buckminster Fuller: Starting with the Universe,* ed. K. Michael Hays and Dana Miller (New York: Whitney Museum of Art, 2008), 6–7.
40   John McHale, "Buckminster Fuller," *Architectural Review* 120 (1956): 13–20; and Reyner Banham, *Theory and Design in the First Machine Age* (London: Architectural Press, 1960), 325–30.
41   See *Archigram* 3 (1963): n.p., which featured the Dymaxion bathroom, Dymaxion car, and the 1948 Wichita House; and *Archigram* 5 (1964): n.p., which featured the Underwater Island.
42   See R. Buckminster Fuller, *4D Time Lock* [1929] (Albuquerque: Biotechnic, 1970).
43   Fuller proposed to excavate a foundation by dropping a bomb from the blimp, then lowering the preassembled tower into the crater. For Fuller, the process was akin to "planting a tree." See R. Buckminster Fuller and Robert Marks, *The Dymaxion World of Buckminster Fuller* (Carbondale: Southern Illinois University Press, 1960), 74–75.
44   Fuller's book was not professionally published until 1970. Fuller self-published the work in 1929, sending two hundred copies unsolicited to distinguished thinkers throughout the world. The second edition, cited above, reproduces excerpts of Fuller's cover letters as well as a selection of return correspondence he received.
45   See Ulrich Conrads, *The Architecture of Fantasy: Utopian Building and Planning in Modern Times* (New York: Praeger, 1962), 19; and Fuller and Marks, *The Dymaxion World,* 74–85.
46   Peter Cook, *Architecture: Action and Plan* (London: Studio Vista, 1967), 96.
47   For a useful summary of the dome's development, see Michael John Gorman, *Buckminster Fuller: Designing for Mobility* (Milan: Skira, 2005), 85–176.
48   Grimshaw undoubtedly would have been familiar with this image, originally produced for *4D Time Lock,* from Fuller and Marks's *The Dymaxion World,* 94.
49   For a discussion, see "In Search of Alternatives: Banham, Britain, and the New Brutalism," this volume.
50   Rudolf Wittkower, *Architectural Principles in the Age of Humanism* [1949], 4th ed. (New York: W. W. Norton, 1972), 4.
51   Leon Battista Alberti, *On the Art of Building in Ten Books* [1486], trans. Joseph Rykwert, Neal Leach, and Robert Tavernor (Cambridge, MA: MIT Press, 1988), 196.
52   Manfredo Tafuri, *Interpreting the Renaissance: Princes, Cities, Architects* [1992] (New Haven, CT: Yale University Press, 2006), 47.
53   Tafuri, *Interpreting the Renaissance,* 51.
54   Middleton, "The New Brutalism," 7.
55   Tafuri describes "Alberti's poetics" as "one composed of proud and desperate fragments of rationality that are nonetheless "satisfied" with their own peculiar sense of *finitio*." See Tafuri, *Interpreting the Renaissance,* 53.
56   Building his case for an anti-Neoplatonic Alberti, Tafuri pointed out Alberti's punning connection between the origin of music and the common fly (in the original Latin, *musica* and *musca,* respectively): "Alberti, employing a sarcastic pun, insists that 'Pythagorici a musca musica nuncupavere.'" He continued:

  > The origin of music is, then, to be found in the sounds produced by flies: from the world of insects—the same world Alberti teaches us to protect ourselves from in Book X of his treatise—would derive the art that is closest to the sublime—at least according to the Neoplatonists. Inevitably, one senses the close affinity between this kind of literary joke and the passage in which recourse to hexagonal forms is modeled after the nests created by bees and *crabone*.

  Tafuri, *Interpreting the Renaissance,* 47.
57   Tafuri, *Interpreting the Renaissance,* 51.
58   Karen Goodman and Kirk Simon, *Buckminster Fuller: Thinking Out Loud,* American Masters series, PBS, April 1996, http://www.thirteen.org/bucky/johnson.html, cited in Hays, "Fuller's Geological Engagements," 2.
59   Banham, *The New Brutalism,* 69.
60   Philip Johnson, "The Seven Crutches of Architecture," *Perspecta* 3 (1955): 43.
61   See *ANY* 17 (1997) for an excellent compilation of writings on Fuller by Sanford Kwinter, Reinhold Martin, Antoine

Picon, Mark Wigley, and others. For Fuller's own assessment of his sources, see R. Buckminster Fuller, "Influences on My Work" [1955], in *The Buckminster Fuller Reader,* ed. James Meller (London: Pelican, 1972), 44–68.

62   Banham discussed Johnson's description of Jackson Pollock in "A Clip-On Architecture," 8.
63   Banham, "A Clip-On Architecture," 7–8.
64   "Conversion," 491.
65   Early Team 4 projects are considered in "Making Architecture: The Ethics of High Tech," this volume. For a treatment of the firm's breakup and the founding of Richard + Su Rogers, see Bryan Appleyard, *Richard Rogers—A Biography* (London: Faber & Faber, 1986), 132–41.
66   For a discussion of the DRU's founding, see David Goodway, *Herbert Read Reassessed* (Liverpool: Liverpool University Press, 1998), 151–52.
67   The DRU played an important role in the design of the Festival of Britain. For a discussion, see Goodway, *Herbert Read Reassessed;* and Harriet Atkinson, *The Festival of Britain: A Land and Its People* (New York: I. B. Tauris, 2012), 41–46.
68   Appleyard, *Richard Rogers,* 134.
69   "Designers' Offices, Marylebone, London," *Architectural Review* 150 (1971): 100.
70   "Designers' Offices," 100.
71   "Short Life, Long Life," *Architectural Review* 148 (1970): 194. Though this piece was published without a byline, its rhetorical structure and vocabulary suggest the anonymous pen of Reyner Banham at work.
72   Kenneth Powell, ed., *Richard Rogers: Complete Works,* vol. 1 (London: Phaidon, 1999), 82.
73   The Rogerses devised a two-story Zip-Up scheme for their own residence in London in 1971, inserting a lightweight steel frame within the panel thickness to take up increased structural loads. The strategy was advanced at a much larger scale for the Universal Oil Products (UOP) Factory in Kent (1969–72). Neither was realized. A similar project for UOP was later built by Piano + Rogers at Tadworth, Surrey, in 1974. See "Piano + Rogers," *Architectural Design* 45 (1975): 297; and Powell, *Richard Rogers,* 146–51.
74   Richard Rogers, *Richard Rogers + Architects* (London: Academy, 1985), 75.
75   See "Sopralzo a Londra," *Domus* 570 (1977), 17; and "Piano + Rogers," 293.
76   This imbalance largely was the result of the Olivetti marketing machine, which trumpeted their association with the internationally renowned Stirling while giving short shrift (though plenty of subsequent projects) to the lesser known Cullinan. Reyner Banham, "Problem × 3 = Olivetti," *Architectural Review* 155 (1974): 197–200.
77   Banham, "Problem × 3," 198.
78   Banham, "Problem × 3," 198.
79   Middleton, "The New Brutalism," 7.
80   James Stirling, *James Stirling: Buildings and Projects, 1950–1974* (London: Thames & Hudson, 1975), 144.
81   In a clever piece of writing, Douglas Graf argued that the "broken bar" diagram at Haslemere ironically gives rise to serial postulations of ideality and centrality. See Douglas Graf, "Diagrams," *Perspecta* 22 (1986): 64.
82   Joseph Rykwert, "Lo spazio policromo: Olivetti Training Center," *Domus* 530 (1974): 42.
83   Charles Jencks, "Haslemere: James Stirling's Corporate Culture Machine," *Architecture Plus* 2, no. 2 (1974): 81–83. Jencks more systematically tallied the metaphorical associations at Haslemere in "A Semantic Analysis of Stirling's Olivetti Center Wing," *Architectural Association Quarterly* 6, no. 2 (1974): 13–15.
84   Jencks, "Haslemere," 81.
85   Banham, "Problem × 3," 199.
86   Banham, "Problem × 3," 197, Banham's emphasis.
87   Banham, "Problem × 3," 198.
88   Banham, "Problem × 3," 199.
89   Banham, "The New Brutalism," 357.
90   Banham, "Problem × 3," 200.
91   See Banham, "Problem × 3," 199, for the unattributed photograph of the joint.
92   This description is based on my interpretation of very few available photographs. While they appear to support my description, I have not yet had the opportunity to examine Stirling's construction documents or the detail in situ.
93   Panel-to-panel joints elsewhere were handled with a vacuum tube gasket not unlike the neoprene "zippers" imagined by the Rogerses for the Zip-Up projects. As Jencks pointed out, the process was not as smooth as it might appear to have been: "The panels, although prefabricated for ease of assembly, had in fact to be knocked into place by hand since the technology was relatively new to England." See Jencks, "Haslemere," 82.
94   Banham, "Problem x 3," 200. The first ellipsis is Banham's.

95 See Heinrich Wölfflin, *Renaissance and Baroque* [1888] (Ithaca, NY: Cornell University Press, 1967).

96 Banham, "A Clip-On Architecture," 7.

97 Banham, "The New Brutalism," 357.

98 See Reyner Banham, "A Black Box: The Secret Profession of Architecture" [written 1988], *New Statesman and Society,* 12 October 1990, reprinted in Reyner Banham, *A Critic Writes: Essays by Reyner Banham,* ed. Mary Banham (Berkeley: University of California Press, 1996), 297.

CHAPTER 3

SAVAGE MINDS AND THE WELL-TEMPERED ENVIRONMENT

In the late 1960s, Reyner Banham produced some of his most polemical essays and perhaps his most radical book, *The Architecture of the Well-Tempered Environment* (1969).[1] In these texts, one finds not just an interrogation of key canonical buildings and a showcase of unsung examples from outside the disciplinary ken but also a persistent critique of modernist heroes such as Le Corbusier, an elevation of important outsiders such as Willis Carrier, and, as shown below in the case of Philip Johnson's Glass House, a cunning confiscation of works typically associated with orthodox modern architecture for the cause of "other" possibilities. At the same time, theoretical debates with his contemporaries revealed Banham's staunch commitment to core modern movement values and his ongoing struggle between the promotion of appropriate visual images for contemporary architecture and an allegiance to the technological forces that seem to guarantee the field's inexorable slide into invisibility.

Technology versus Meaning in Architecture

The buildings and writings examined in this chapter were developed at a time when both orthodox modern architecture and the science-minded functionalism of Banham's generation were coming under increasing scrutiny by a younger generation of critics and intellectuals. *Meaning in Architecture* (1969), edited by Banham's pupil Charles Jencks and the Canadian architect and critic George Baird, provides an important portrait of the burgeoning debate. As the editors opined, the book was an attempt to address what they saw as current crises in architecture: "On the one hand, there is a general crisis over such issues as revolution and change within architecture (some authors wishing to jettison 'architecture' altogether) and on the other hand there is a specific crisis over what 'meaning in architecture' (or, rather, 'meanings') is relevant."[2] To account for the various positions at play, the editors included

Philip Johnson (American, 1906–2005).
Glass House (New Canaan, Connecticut, 1949). General view (detail). Photo by Steven Brooke. See p. 219, pl. 10.

FIG. 3.1 | **Eero Saarinen (American, 1910–61).**
CBS Building (New York, 1965).

FIG. 3.2 | **Cedric Price (British, 1934–2003).**
Potteries Thinkbelt Project (1964–66). Perspective of Madeley Transfer Area. New York, The Museum of Modern Art.

essays by authors harboring diametrically opposed viewpoints and allowed themselves as well as each contributor to add marginal comments to one another's texts.

For the most part, the contributors to *Meaning in Architecture* examined these crises through a specifically structuralist lens. The writings of Claude Lévi-Strauss resonate through nearly all the collected essays, and while Gillo Dorfles and Geoffrey Broadbent each raised concerns about the importation of his and other extra-disciplinary theoretical frameworks into architecture, the structuralist position of seeing architecture as a mode of communication was generally adopted throughout, as evidenced by a pervasive engagement of themes such as language, primitivism, essential patterns, and historical continuity.[3] Banham provided a glaring exception with his offerings, which specifically opposed Baird's contribution, "'La Dimension Amoureuse' in Architecture," with invocations of technology, futurism, innovation, and historical rupture.

In his text, Baird attempted to demonstrate the bankruptcy of prevailing modes of architectural design by attacking two representative projects, Eero Saarinen's CBS Building in New York (1965) (fig. 3.1) and Cedric Price's Potteries Thinkbelt proposed for Staffordshire, England (1964–66) (fig. 3.2).[4] The former project stood for the "total design" tactics typical of the modernist establishment, while the latter, with its ruthless functionalism and open scorn for traditional aesthetics, represented the "empirical method" adopted by many of the younger generation. Despite these differences, Baird saw the two works as more similar than different, with both finding their ideological roots in the distant past. In his view, "the concept of 'total design' underlying CBS, like Walter Gropius' ideas of 'total theatre' and 'total architecture,' was nothing more nor less than a Wagnerian *Gesamtkunstwerk*.

And Price's idea of architecture as 'life-conditioning' rested on essentially the same view of human experience as Jeremy Bentham's Panopticon."[5] Both projects, he continued, derived from a nineteenth-century "loss of faith in rhetoric" that had caused their architects to misconstrue architecture's communicative role in society, which Baird portrayed as fundamental.[6]

In Baird's view, human society was structured as a communication network, and architecture's role in society had primarily to do with the production and transmission of meaning. With CBS and the Thinkbelt, he argued, both Saarinen and Price naively attempted to hold "privileged positions" within society's communication network by attempting to exert rigid control over the way their respective projects produced legible meaning through architectural form. Saarinen, he claimed, worked to "heighten [the] experience" of the occupants of his building through a careful and elegant coordination of all elements in the environment. Price, by contrast, attempted to dissipate the architectural object into a functionalist milieu unencumbered by outmoded aesthetic or symbolic conventions. Both architects, Baird reasoned, eliminated the possibility of ambiguity and irony to register in their work and ultimately impoverished communication. Saarinen, he claimed, treated his audience like children, Price, like objects. Richer modes of architectural communication were available by taking cues from Lévi-Strauss's anthropological research, through which an architect would learn to understand the relationship between architecture's *langue* (codes) and *parole* (individual works); would learn to take seriously into account the impact of both present and historical contexts; and would learn to "design *in* his fellows' experience, rather than above it, or outside it."[7] To do so would be to offer the possibility of a truly meaningful architecture (as opposed to Saarinen's empty symbolism or Price's vapid utility), to regain the power of rhetoric in architecture, and to trade in the responsibility and tolerance he associated, in an echo of Roland Barthes, with architecture's "amorous dimension."[8]

Banham saw things differently and cleaved to a distinctly more pragmatic position. In Baird's attempt to recalibrate architecture as a mechanism of meaningful communication, Banham found little more than a conservative appeal to tradition, habit, and convention. With respect to the Thinkbelt, where Baird saw either meaningless utility or, worse, Benthamesque "conditioning," Banham saw a "nearly value-free" environment devoid of "other people's values left over from the past." Such an environment might be "capable of generating new values symbiotically with its inhabitants," but Baird and his "apologists," he reasoned, were wary of such projects because they appeared to sanction the formation of subject positions different from those one would expect from traditional campus architecture.[9] Banham was unperturbed by this move away from the status quo. For him, the Thinkbelt signaled a powerful alternative future for the field.

Such "almost value-free" environments were the focus of Banham's two other texts reprinted in *Meaning in Architecture,* "Flatscape with Containers" and "A Home Is Not a House."[10] Both focused on environments that evaded the conventions of traditional architecture to produce an alternative spatial and social milieu. Banham's position in both essays was decidedly antimonumental, with the former examining the architectural effects of the so-called container revolution in shipping and the latter waxing poetic on the near-future possibilities of inflatable construction and mechanical environmental control systems.

The constructions of "flatscapes" moved architecture well beyond both the conventional monumental patterns Banham saw as limiting the potential of contemporary architecture and the timeless ritual patterns that could be gleaned from the anthropological study of primitive cultures. Where Lévi-Strauss's writings might suggest compelling continuities between then and now, Banham saw in new projects, such as the docklands at Tilbury outside London, nothing but jarring ruptures between now and then. No longer serviced by a landscape of monumental warehouse buildings in picturesque brick, Banham pointed out that contemporary goods transportation was carried out in weather-tight containers that needed no buildings at all. And despite the protestations of critics such as Baird, he reasoned that architects sooner or later would have to deal with these new antimonumental landscapes — landscapes not only bereft of traditional values but often also devoid of buildings — if they were to keep pace with the relentless march of technology.

Banham outlined one possible future in "A Home Is Not a House." Here, he combined the increasing presence of mechanical equipment in contemporary construction with a somewhat cheeky line of argumentation that foregrounded a tradition in American culture to eschew monumentality in favor of the "great outdoors."[11] Such tendencies, he reasoned, worked against conventional architecture and, taken together, might catalyze a radically alternative vision of human habitation. In Banham's view, America's architectural development was one of inexorable dissipation into nature: "If dirty old Nature could be kept under the proper degree of control (sex left in, streptococci taken out) by other means, the United States would be happy to dispense with architecture and buildings altogether."[12] With a typical nod to Buckminster Fuller, he arrived at a possible vehicle of a habitation revolution: "A standard-of-living package (the phrase and the concept are both Bucky Fuller's) that really worked might, like so many sophisticated inventions, return Man nearer to a natural state in spite of his complex culture." In an ironic play on contemporary invocations of Lévi-Strauss, the technology-minded Banham offered his own link to humanity's "natural state." He continued with mythical rumination on humanity's primal modes of inhabitation: "Man started with two basic ways of controlling environment: one by avoiding the issue and hiding under a rock, tree, tent, or roof

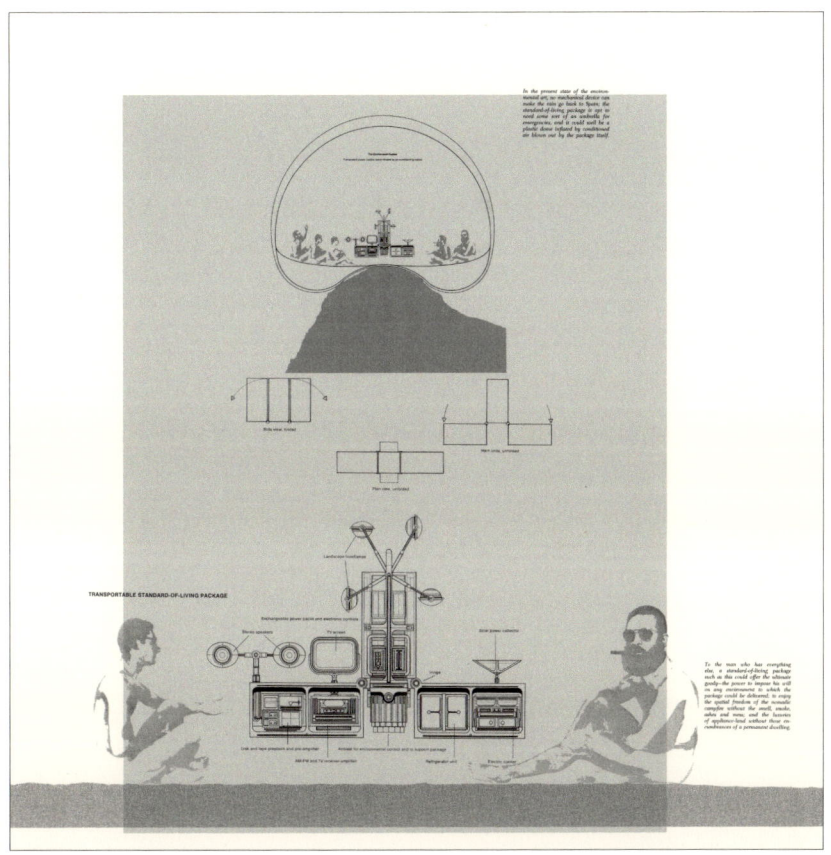

(this led ultimately to architecture as we know it) and the other by actually interfering with the local meteorology, usually by means of a campfire, which, in a more polished form, might lead to the kind of situation now under discussion." In contrast to the massive and static nature of traditional enclosures, the campfire offers an environment characterized by "freedom and variability." Defined not by walls and roofs but rather by emitted light and heat, the habitable zone around the campfire accommodates activities more loosely and embraces, rather than evicts, its natural surroundings. Banham's "standard-of-living package" operated along similar lines. But rather than support the primitive fireside activities he mockingly cited ("shrinking a human head," "the floating knuckle-bones game"), new technology offered a decidedly more contemporary scene. An oft-quoted passage described "a properly set-up standard-of-living package, breathing out warm air along the ground (instead of sucking in cold air like a campfire), radiating soft light and Dionne Warwick in heart-warming stereo, with well-aged protein turning in an infra-red glow in the rotisserie, and the ice-maker discreetly coughing cubes into glasses on the swing-out bar."

Completing this portrait of a technologically enhanced return to a primitive state were François Dallegret's famous accompanying drawings (see pl. 9). In one, a naked and gesticulating Banham, his woolly beard contrasted by aviator sunglasses,

FIG. 3.3 | **François Dallegret (French, b. 1937).**
Un-house. Transportable Standard-of-Living Package / The Environment-Bubble.
Top: The Environment-Bubble, section.
Middle: Transportable Standard-of-Living Package, plan and elevations of different configurations.
Bottom: Transportable Standard-of-Living Package, elevation.
From Reyner Banham, "A Home Is Not a House," *Art in America* 53, no. 2 (1965): 74–75, 77.

reclines in the primal comfort of an "Environment-Bubble" (fig. 3.3). Over the ensuing pages, Banham went on, in a predictive reverie reminiscent of Paul Scheerbart's 1914 *Glasarchitektur,* to offer a lavish depiction of new lifestyle possibilities interspersed with plausible technical solutions for their delivery.[13] Thus, while appearing to proceed with tongue firmly in cheek, Banham offered a seriously considered alternative to the growing interest in low-tech primitivism that was sweeping through architectural culture in the mid-1960s. Where the structuralist approach embraced in *Meaning in Architecture* led many to treat building as a primal mode of communication evidenced in the humblest ancient human shelters, Banham's technological take on the theme projected humanity to a time before constructed shelter altogether to identify a fork in the mythical road of architectural history. One path ("hiding under a rock") led inexorably to the conventions of traditional architecture. The other ("interfering with the local meteorology") charted a radically alternative trajectory.

Engineer versus *Bricoleur*

Alongside the interest in primal patterns of culture and communication already mentioned, Levi-Strauss introduced the notion of *bricolage,* an important theme that would be addressed by several architects throughout the 1960s and '70s. The anthropologist introduced the term in the first chapter of his influential book *La pensée sauvage* (1962; *The Savage Mind,* 1966), where he deployed it as an analogy for the "mythical thought" of so-called primitive cultures.[14] His aim was to demonstrate the intellectual efficacy of such cultures by comparing the language patterns and conceptual foundations of non-Western tribes with modern scientific thought. Scientific thought, he explained, dealt primarily in abstract concepts while mythical thought relied largely on direct observation of concrete reality. The seeming absence of abstraction from mythical thought, however, did not entail an absence of conceptual thinking, but rather it represented a different approach to the more fundamental problem of finding order in the sensible world. Where science advanced by means of verifiable knowledge alone, he argued, it must pay for its rigorous defensibility by allowing a degree of uncertainty and openness (for example, unproven hypotheses and other conceptual lacunae) to remain in the system. Mythical thought tolerated no such uncertainty; it filled in the gaps between observable facts with unverifiable concepts (such as magic and witchcraft) to maintain a closed system. While such closure came at a price too dear for science and thus typically was dismissed as irrational, mythical thought's fundamental expediency, Lévi-Strauss concluded, offered nonscientific cultures discernible advantages, and it often was able to beat science to the punch, sometimes leading to "brilliant unforeseen results" independent (and often well in advance) of scientific cultures.[15]

Lévi-Strauss clarified the relationship between these two modes of thought with his famous comparison of allegorical figures associated with each mode—the engineer and the *bricoleur.* An oft-quoted passage warrants full citation here:

> The "bricoleur" is still someone who works with his hands and uses devious means compared to those of the craftsman.... The "bricoleur" is adept at performing a large number of diverse tasks; but, unlike the engineer, he does not subordinate each of them to the availability of raw materials and tools conceived and procured for the purpose of the project. His universe of instruments is closed and the rules of his game are always to make do with "whatever is at hand," that is to say with a set of tools and materials which is always finite and is also heterogeneous because what it contains bears no relationship to the current project, or indeed to any particular project, but is the contingent result of all the occasions there have been to renew or enrich the stock or to maintain it with the remains of previous constructions or destructions. The set of the "bricoleur's" means cannot therefore be defined in terms of a project (which would presuppose besides, that, as in the case of the engineer, there were, at least in theory, as many sets of tools and materials or "instrumental sets," as there are different kinds of projects). It is to be defined only by its potential use or, putting this another way in the language of the "bricoleur" himself, because the elements are collected or retained on the principle that "they may always come in handy."[16]

In other words, the *bricoleur* works with "whatever fragments were available."[17] Indeed, Lévi-Strauss's *bricoleur* resonates distinctly with Robin Middleton's 1967 description of Alison and Peter Smithson. Middleton did not cite Lévi-Strauss in his text, but the *bricoleur* analogy would prove irresistible to many of his contemporaries. Alan Colquhoun, who appealed to Lévi-Strauss's *Anthropologie structurale* (1958; *Structural Anthropology,* 1963) in his contribution to *Meaning in Architecture,* engaged Lévi-Strauss's ideas throughout his oeuvre and specifically deployed both myth and *bricolage* to structure a 1978 discussion of the work of Michael Graves.[18] That same year saw the publication of Colin Rowe and Fred Koetter's influential book *Collage City,* in which they reproduced almost exactly the passage from *The Savage Mind* cited above.[19] Here, reiterating Baird's arguments in "'La Dimension Amoureuse' in Architecture," Rowe and Koetter seized upon the concept of *bricolage* to counter Gropius's idea of total architecture and what they described as "the still shining afterglow of a unitary and holistic utopian faith."[20]

The year 1978 also saw an important publication in English of Jacques Derrida's famous 1966 lecture, "La structure, le signe et le jeu dans le discours des sciences humaines" ("Structure, Sign, and Play in the Discourse of the Human Sciences").[21]

This text would receive significant attention during architecture's flirtations with deconstruction in the 1980s, but it found little traction in architectural circles in the wake of its initial presentation.[22] In it, as Rowe and Koetter would do in *Collage City*, Derrida aligned Lévi-Strauss's work with a critique of prevailing notions of stability and centrality: "It is here that we rediscover the mythopoetical virtue of *bricolage*. In effect, what appears most fascinating in this critical search for a new status of discourse is the stated abandonment of all reference to a *center,* to a *subject,* to a privileged *reference,* to an origin, or to an absolute *archia*."[23] The crucial term here is *appears*. In typical fashion, Derrida quickly turned the observation back on itself:

> If Lévi-Strauss, better than any other, has brought to light the play of repetition and the repetition of play, one no less perceives in his work a sort of ethic of presence, an ethic of nostalgia for origins, an ethic of archaic and natural innocence, of a purity of presence and self-presence in speech—an ethic, nostalgia, and even remorse, which he often presents as the motivation of the ethnological project when he moves toward the archaic societies which are exemplary societies in his eyes.[24]

By the 1980s, Derrida's critical domestication of Lévi-Strauss largely would be accepted across the cultural landscape.[25] But if architectural culture remained unperturbed by Derrida's arguments into the mid-1970s, its exponents had become comfortably familiar with the general content of the Lévi-Strauss's work. Robert Maxwell, in a 1976 text, offered a typical demonstration of the attitude while conveniently summarizing its distinctly English resonances: "Long before Claude Lévi-Strauss's bricolage was proposed as an alternative to engineering, [Ivor] de Wolfe was on to the art of bric-a-brac assembly as the only way to put visual coherence into our 'brickish-a-brackish mid-century world of barbed wire…' Because our landscape was the product of unhappy accident, the happy accident had to be cultivated."[26]

In this, Maxwell illustrated (but was careful not to subscribe to) a pervasive misreading of Lévi-Strauss's analysis in English architectural circles. Lévi-Strauss did not offer *bricolage* as an alternative to engineering; rather, he used the term as a metaphor for how mythical thought operated. In a treatment of art practices that immediately followed the section on *bricolage,* Lévi-Strauss clearly indicated his view that "art lies half-way between scientific knowledge and mythical or magical thought. It is common knowledge that the artist is both something of a scientist and of a 'bricoleur.'"[27] Rowe and Koetter recognized this distinction. They argued not for "the architect as 'bricoleur'" but rather enthusiastically promoted a synthetic position similar to Lévi-Strauss's characterization of the artist: "The artist (architect) as both something of a bricoleur and something of a scientist!" Such a combination, they surmised, could produce "a truly useful dialectic" elicited from "reestablishing 'bricolage' alongside science" as a corrective to contemporary urban planning.[28]

Charles Jencks, writing in 1972, advanced a far more partisan position in *Adhocism: The Case for Improvisation*. At the outset of his section of the book, Jencks reproduced the lines from *The Savage Mind* cited by Rowe and Koetter (and above). But where Rowe and Koetter used the quotation to sanction a dialectical synthesis of engineering and *bricolage,* Jencks used it to propose a shift in sensibility from the methods of the former to those of the latter. Though he noted that "the distinction between bricolage and engineering of science is one of degree and intention rather than kind or quality," his preference was clear: "The scientist is intent on using the tools and hypothesis appropriate to his job, whereas the bricoleur or adhocist is intent on undertaking his job immediately, with whatever resources are available."[29] Throughout, Jencks attacked both totalizing and empirical design methods and demonized modern architecture. Adhocism, he argued, offered a means to overcome the stultifying bureaucracies and oppressive theories that had come to overshadow individual needs in the late twentieth century. Further, the adhocist/*bricoleur* apparently offered the chance to reclaim theoretical territory ceded to the engineer by Le Corbusier in *Vers une architecture*. Jencks challenged mainstream modern architecture by invoking such varied developments as electronic communication, cybernetics, hippie culture, the do-it-yourself movement, and the space program. He ultimately proposed an alternative mode of design that proceeded not toward the mechanized standards of engineered mass production but rather toward the expedient combination of preexisting and readily available parts into heterogeneous new wholes.

Jencks would harden his position against modern architecture in later writings. In his influential *Language of Post-Modern Architecture* (1977), he further articulated the pluralistic agenda he had first set down in the dissertation he completed at London University under Banham's supervision in 1970.[30] Beyond its usefulness in resisting modern architecture's status quo, Lévi-Strauss's formulation of *bricolage,* along with Jencks's own compositional proclivities, breathed new life into particularly English modes of architectural composition that had seen both enthusiastic reception and vehement rejection in the 1950s, '60s, and '70s. Proponents of the nostalgic proposals of Townscape, the brash juxtapositions of clip-on, and Jencks's postmodern pluralism each could find a convenient theoretical alibi in Lévi-Strauss's notion of *bricolage.*

Unlike his ambitious pupil, Banham would remain committed to modern architecture's core values and resistant to any potential resonance with the picturesque (and what he saw as its inherent provincialism) throughout his career. Even as he advanced the technological expediency of clip-on architecture, he was careful not to embrace fully its visual character and compositional implications. And if he made his initial ambivalence about clip-on known largely through insinuation, his resistance to adhocism and the mythology of the *bricoleur* was vocal and emphatic.

For Banham, the engineer, the *bricoleur,* and the methodological distinction from which they were produced were pure myth, the product of a generation of "academics bricolating theories out of other people's books." *Bricolage,* in his view, did not represent an alternative to engineering but rather "the way the world has always worked."[31] He cited an array of examples from engineering—from space capsules to Ferrari race cars—that demonstrated that engineers tend not to "conceiv[e] and procur[e] everything specially for the project," but rather, because they are driven for the most part by profit, that they work primarily with components "off-the-peg" and "ex-catalogue."[32] He continued, "Even if, as Jencks sagely observes, the difference between Bricoleur and Engineer is one of degree, then on an evenly graded scale from the one to the other, practically everybody, *including* the engineers, is going to be up the brico end."[33] In this, Banham reached a conclusion nearly identical to the one Derrida arrived at over a decade earlier: "As soon as we admit that every finite discourse is bound by a certain *bricolage* and that the engineer and the scientist are also species of *bricoleurs,* then the very idea of *bricolage* is menaced and the difference in which it took on its meaning breaks down."[34] And while the farcical portrayal of the engineer as "Satan" in this new "bricosmology" might offend Banham the engineer, it was the widespread acceptance of this "trifling metaphor" that more deeply troubled Banham the scholar. He found the idea "worrying in that it is only a symptom of a general ignorance about engineering among those who profess to tell us what's wrong and what's right with western culture, and—above all—what's wrong with engineering as a part of that culture."[35] Of course, Banham was not simply defending engineering as a profession; he was at the same time defending modern architecture as a discipline.

This marks an important turn in Banham's writing. Throughout the 1960s, Banham had maintained the position of the *enfant terrible* of architectural discourse.[36] His early writing set out to correct interpretations of modern architecture that had misconstrued the relationship between modern aesthetics and the functional principles on which they were based. Banham had placed much of the blame at the feet of his dissertation adviser, Nikolaus Pevsner, which added a personal, Oedipal component to his labors. But in the mid-1970s, Banham faced a modern movement suffering not from internal contradictions—the promotion of a puritanical style often at odds with that movement's underlying functional principles—but rather from external attacks that fundamentally opposed both modern architecture's appearance *and* its principles. Worse, those attacks emanated from a talented scholar whom Banham himself had trained. Jencks offered his polemic writings not to correct the modern movement but rather to advocate for its replacement. And if, as Nigel Whiteley has pointed out, Jencks appeared to have mastered many of his mentor's rhetorical techniques, it was the younger historian's adoption of Pevsner's approach—his concentration on outward appearance, attentiveness to stylistic labels, and predilection for picturesque massing—that gave his writing much of the force necessary to challenge Banham's compelling arguments and formidable reputation.[37]

An assessment of Jencks's writings demonstrates that it was not toward the *bricoleur*'s tactics but rather toward the visual character of an architect's output that he directed the bulk of his attention. This marks an important distinction from other appeals to Lévi-Strauss encountered previously. Jencks, like Baird, was committed to shifting architecture away from the technologically focused modern movement toward an understanding of architecture that saw legible meaning (as communicated through constructed form) as a primary motivating factor. Of course, modern architecture, and indeed its foremost manifesto, *Vers une architecture,* also had been concerned with formal legibility, as evidenced by Le Corbusier's careful graphic design and famous visual comparisons of Greek temples and contemporary automobiles.[38] But in Jencks's Post-Modern turn,[39] the name of the game was no longer the suggestion of idealized perfection through the use of Euclidean forms but rather polyvalent meanings that spoke at once to expert audiences within the discourse as well as to popular audiences at large.[40] George Baird and other advocates of what would soon mature into architectural postmodernism similarly were concerned with a broader understanding of architectural communication and the necessary grappling with attendant ambiguities such an understanding would entail, but Jencks's innovation was to offer a catalog of new visual examples—and a growing vocabulary of equally new stylistic labels—for the buildings he hoped would emerge from this new idiom.[41] His gambit would pay off handsomely. Where *Adhocism* offered precious few contemporary buildings that embodied its compositional ambitions (by necessity given its early date of publication), *The Language of Post-Modern Architecture* was full of them. Indeed, the page count of later editions ballooned as Jencks quickly collected, identified, and classified new built work and stylistic trends in his popular and ever-expanding catalog.[42] At the same time, his initial position that "accept[ed] everyone as an architect" slackened somewhat as he sanctioned not a wider array of design practitioners but rather a wider popular audience to be addressed by the architectural establishment.[43] While *bricolage* might have been suggested to Jencks by the DIY craftsmen and hippie dropouts in the late 1960s and early '70s, by the 1980s, he was advocating the approach in order to influence established professionals at the center rather than precocious amateurs at the fringe.

Thus, as for Lévi-Strauss before him, the *bricoleur* was for Jencks not the crux of a theory but an expedient means to an end. The character was not mentioned again after the opening pages of *Adhocism* and would not return in Jencks's later writings, in which the visual character of architectural form remained the primary concern.[44] Ironically, and despite his condescending attacks, Banham would embrace certain qualities associated with the concept throughout his career. Jencks's argumentation from the late 1960s would move the younger critic toward a careful taxonomy of architectural imagery. Banham, by contrast, would move increasingly to engage architecture's technological drive toward invisibility.

Boffins and the Well-Tempered Environment

Banham saw the myth of the *bricoleur* as little more than an attempt to expand architectural discourse in order to engage the "operational lore" of Continental academe. And as a "purely academic construct,"[45] Lévi-Strauss's portrayal of the engineer displayed little of the "apparent intelligence" Banham routinely celebrated in figures such as Buckminster Fuller. Nonetheless, Fuller embodied many of the qualities that popular architectural opinion had enshrined in the figure of the *bricoleur*. Of course, Fuller also displayed a deep commitment to "the dreaded technostructure" Jencks railed against[46] and easily could be characterized as a Lévi-Straussian engineer "always trying to make his way out of and go beyond the constraints imposed by a particular state of civilization."[47]

A better label for the kind of designer Banham celebrated is the British term *boffin*. Though its etymology is uncertain, the designation has been linked to radar scientists associated with the Royal Air Force during World War II.[48] *Boffin* quickly entered into popular usage throughout Great Britain and its former territories as an endearing description of a clever tinkerer/scientist typically working in secret or obscurity and often possessing marginal social skills. Q, the quirky inventor featured in Ian Fleming's James Bond novels of the 1950s and '60s and, more substantially, in their subsequent film adaptations from 1962, is a prototypical boffin. The term quickly found its way into English architectural conversation. Banham would praise Independent Group member Frank Cordell as "Top Pop Boffin" in 1958,[49] and, as Simon Sadler pointed out, "Archigram's self-styled eccentricity shared affinities with the boffin subculture of systems design."[50] By 1970, Peter Cook would invoke the "'boffin'-designer" as an alternative to the "'artist'-designer."[51] Cook later expanded on his formulation, linking the idea directly to High Tech architects:

> There are two traditions of good English architects. Those who are basically artists, and for whom, the natural eccentricity and episodicness [sic] of our culture has led to an occasional series of quaint distortions of the European traditions.

> The others are boffins—or mechanics. There is that stream of English fiddlers-with-cars, builders-of-boats, cannibalisers and people who always seem to have another way of using a working part from the one that you expect. In recent years, the originality of the Smithsons, Cedric Price, Norman Foster, and the Rogers team seem to have had far more to do with the latter instinct.[52]

Banham always had been drawn to such fringe personalities, as evidenced by the attention he directed at Pierre Chareau, Buckminster Fuller, and Jean Prouvé, among others. A decade before Cook's comments on the boffin tradition, Banham set down similar sentiments in "1960—Stocktaking": "The service that architects propose to perform for society can often be accomplished without calling in an architect in the sense discussed in the article that runs parallel to this, and the increasing range of technological alternatives to bricks and mortar may yet set a term to the custom-sanctioned monopoly of architects as environment-purveyors to the human race."[53] These alternatives often were developed by "peripheral radicals" such as Fuller, "whose ideas call the whole professional apparatus into question."[54] Banham frequently returned to Fuller's boffinesque tendencies as indications of an alternative way of working that operated alongside architecture's mainstream rather than within it. His praise of Fuller's 1927 Dymaxion House in *Theory and Design in the First Machine Age* (1960) provides a telling example:

> The Dymaxion concept was entirely radical, a hexagonal ring of dwelling-space, walled in double skins of plastic in different transparencies according to lighting needs, and hung by wires from the apex of a central duralumin mast which also housed all the mechanical services. The formal qualities of this design are not remarkable, except in combination with the structural and planning methods involved. The structure does not derive from the imposition of a Perretesque or Elementarist aesthetic on a material that has been elevated to the level of a symbol for "the machine," but is an adaptation of light-metal methods employed in aircraft construction at the time. The planning derives from a liberated attitude to those mechanical services that had precipitated the whole Modern adventure by their invasion of homes and streets before 1914.[55]

The passage neatly encapsulates many of the themes Banham pursued in his writings through the 1960s: an embrace of new structural and organizational principles, an interest in new materials (particularly translucent, lightweight skins), a disregard of academic compositional methods and expressive ambitions (accompanied by thinly veiled jabs at Le Corbusier), the adaptation of extradisciplinary technology to architectural uses, and, significantly, "a liberated attitude to…mechanical services."

Banham investigated each of these themes and the boffin-designers that embraced them in *The Architecture of the Well-Tempered Environment* of 1969.

In his famous history of environmental technology in architecture, Banham attempted to unseat the primary role given to structure and style in traditional histories by offering an unprecedented account of the role of mechanical services and environmental performance. As *Theory and Design* presented Fuller as a hero from the fringe whose bold experimentation offers technological salvation to the field, *The Architecture of the Well-Tempered Environment* reserved pride of place for other peripheral figures that comfortably fit the boffin mold. As Banham put it, "The history of the mechanization of environmental management is a history of extremists, otherwise most of it would never have happened. The fact that many of these extremists were not registered, or otherwise recognized as architects, in no way alters the magnitude of the contribution they have made to the architecture of our time." Underlining the practical applications of documenting these achievements, he continued, "Perhaps finding such men a place in the *history* of architecture will be some help in resolving the vexing problems of finding their proper place in the *practice* of architecture."[56]

In many ways, the book was an elaboration of "A Home Is Not a House." Once again, a parable about humankind's prehistoric condition was deployed to introduce two fundamental modes of dealing with the problem of environmental control—one focused on massive structure and the other on applied power, with the former leading to architecture as we know it. Banham went on to chronicle humankind's exponentially increased ability to control its environment with applied power (primarily electricity) throughout the nineteenth century and to lament the bias toward massive structure and outward appearance generally maintained by architectural historians. Attempting to correct this bias, Banham set out to write what he called "a purely architectural history."[57]

Banham also documented a number of little-known nineteenth-century works with which boffinesque designers attempted to mitigate the foul atmospheric conditions brought on by rapid urbanization, such as John Hayward's 1867 house for himself, the Octagon, in Liverpool, which deployed a clever plan arrangement to provide an early version of what are now referred to as "air changes."[58] Later, Banham examined Thomas Edison's groundbreaking work on electricity, noting that Edison's true import "has less to do with the practicable lamp bulb…than with his invention and assembly of the complete system to supply that lamp with commercially profitable electricity."[59] Importantly, in each of these cases, the innovations were largely invisible. Hayward's plan arrangement (central lobbies at each floor) was not uncommon, and the openings that allowed air to travel between floors were discretely screened with decorative metalwork. Edison's power network, while having a visible trace in the urban milieu, had little visible impact on inhabited interiors—wiring from the first was concealed within walls.[60] The actual light sources that Edison's innovations made possible, however, introduced unprecedented problems for design professionals. A survey of early modern experiments with lighting design afforded Banham the opportunity to celebrate some lesser figures (Paul Scheerbart, Bruno Taut), to castigate some accepted masters (Walter Gropius, Le Corbusier), and to extol achievements in America (by Richard Neutra, Rudolf Schindler, and Frank Lloyd Wright), all common tactics—and targets—encountered throughout his writings.

There is a decidedly American slant to *The Architecture of the Well-Tempered Environment*. While European innovators (and fringe modernists) such as Pierre Chareau garnered positive treatment, Banham largely maintained a position that had European architects perfecting a dogmatic style while American designers busied themselves with the more pragmatic task of inventing workable technical solutions to the challenges presented by new technology. The development of air conditioning offered a compelling case. After a withering treatment of Le Corbusier's technical failures in that arena, Banham discussed the architect's fascination with American air conditioning.[61] His remarks set up one of the book's central provocations:

> While European modern architects had been trying to devise a style that would "civilize technology," US engineers had devised a technology that would make the modern style of architecture habitable by human beings. In the process they had come within an ace of producing a workable alternative to buildings as the unique means of managing the environment, and had thus come within an ace of making architecture culturally obsolete, at least in the sense in which "architecture" had been traditionally understood, the sense in which Le Corbusier had written *Vers une architecture*.[62]

As in "A Home Is Not a House," American technical innovation appeared poised to render architecture in the Western tradition obsolete. And it was in an arena largely outside the purview of traditional architectural histories that Banham found a quintessential boffin-hero, Willis Carrier, the inventor of air conditioning.[63] In the early years of the twentieth century, Carrier's pragmatic, profit-driven approach had him applying his system of "man-made weather" first in factories, where economic justifications for the application of this new and expensive technology could be made. Later, assisted by low-heat fluorescent light fixtures, office buildings could adopt the technology. The combination of air conditioning and electric lighting made possible the replacement of the involuted and inefficient floor plans of traditional office buildings (which were driven by a dependence on operable windows) with the sleek, cubic, and far more profitable deep floor plates of the burgeoning International Style. A similar formal freedom was soon afforded to domestic architecture, as packaged air-conditioning units allowed builders to eschew conservative approaches to environmental management and to make any configuration habitable in any climate with the adequate provision of Carrier's technology. For Banham, Willis Carrier had spearheaded a momentous architectural revolution. With his invention, "all precepts for climate compensation through structure and form are rendered obsolete."[64]

Ironically, the lack of visual expression for these technical innovations necessitated the commissioning of a large number of illustrations for the book. Beautiful and informative cutaway axonometric diagrams by Mary Banham, the author's wife and an accomplished draftsperson, are masterful achievements in architectural representation that reveal not the visual appearance but rather the technical functioning of the buildings discussed (see figs. 3.5, 3.7). Like François Dallegret's drawings for "A Home Is Not a House" (see fig. 3.3), they provided a compelling visual complement to Banham's forceful prose. But where Dallegret's images lent an air of conventional monumentality to Banham's futuristic reverie and thus undercut his arguments,[65] Mary Banham's crisp, clinical drawings amplified the technical veracity of the historian's endeavor.

Maintaining Modern Architecture

Though Banham was highly critical of many architects and historians of the modern movement (including his mentor, Nikolaus Pevsner) in *The Architecture of the Well-Tempered Environment,* the underdog did not always triumph, as an early example makes clear. Both Frank Lloyd Wright's Larkin Building (1903–6) in Buffalo (figs. 3.4, 3.5) and Henman and Cooper's Royal Victoria Hospital (1903) in Belfast (figs. 3.6, 3.7) made significant advances in environmental control. And though the Royal Victoria Hospital provided true air conditioning and the Larkin Building did not,[66] it was Wright's building that ultimately came out ahead. The Larkin Building, Banham explained, combined its technical achievement with a progressive visual expression that engaged the stylistic development of modern architecture. The Royal Victoria Hospital, by contrast, was "thoroughly discounted and out of fashion among consciously progressive architects of 1900."[67] Had Banham's ambition been simply to reject aesthetics in favor of environmental performance, the Royal Victoria Hospital would have made the case handily. But Banham's book was not a history of environmental controls—it was an *architectural* history that took environmental controls into account. As such, a conscious engagement of prevailing aesthetic sensibilities remained an integral part of the equation.

FIG. 3.4 | Frank Lloyd Wright (American, 1867–1959).
Larkin Building (Buffalo, New York, 1903–6). General view.
Photo by Henry-Russell Hitchcock.

FIG. 3.5 | Frank Lloyd Wright (American, 1867–1959).
Larkin Building (Buffalo, New York, 1903–6).
Cutaway axonometric by Mary Banham. From Reyner Banham, *The Architecture of the Well-Tempered Environment* (London: Architectural Press, 1969), 87.

FIG. 3.6 | Henman and Cooper (William Henman, British, 1846–1917; Thomas Cooper, British, 1847–1912).
Royal Victoria Hospital (Belfast, 1903). General view.

FIG. 3.7 | Henman and Cooper (William Henman, British, 1846–1917; Thomas Cooper, British, 1847–1912).
Royal Victoria Hospital (Belfast, 1903).
Cutaway axonometric by Mary Banham. From Reyner Banham, *The Architecture of the Well-Tempered Environment* (London: Architectural Press, 1969), 79.

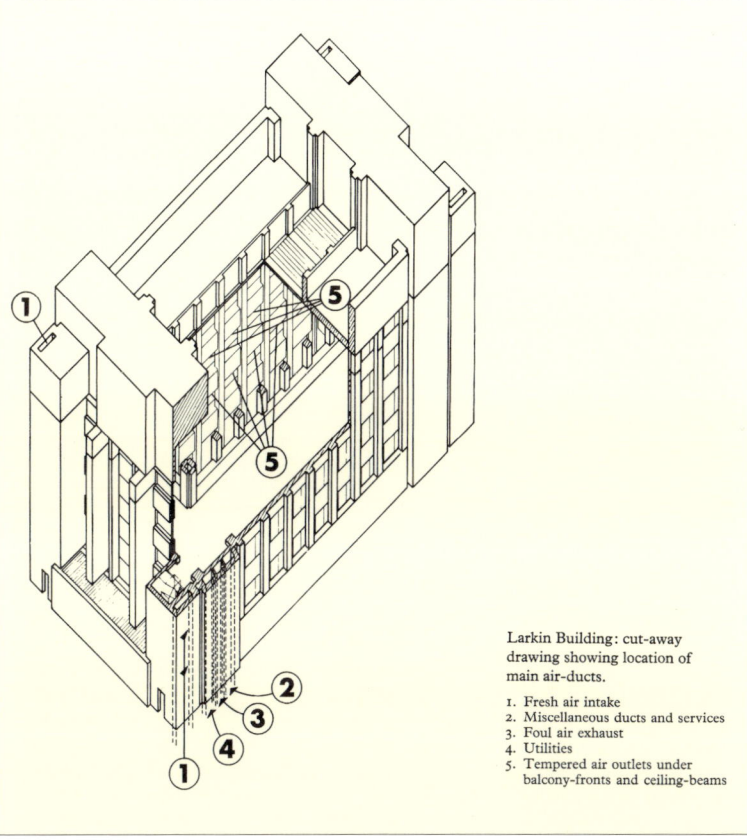

Larkin Building: cut-away drawing showing location of main air-ducts.

1. Fresh air intake
2. Miscellaneous ducts and services
3. Foul air exhaust
4. Utilities
5. Tempered air outlets under balcony-fronts and ceiling-beams

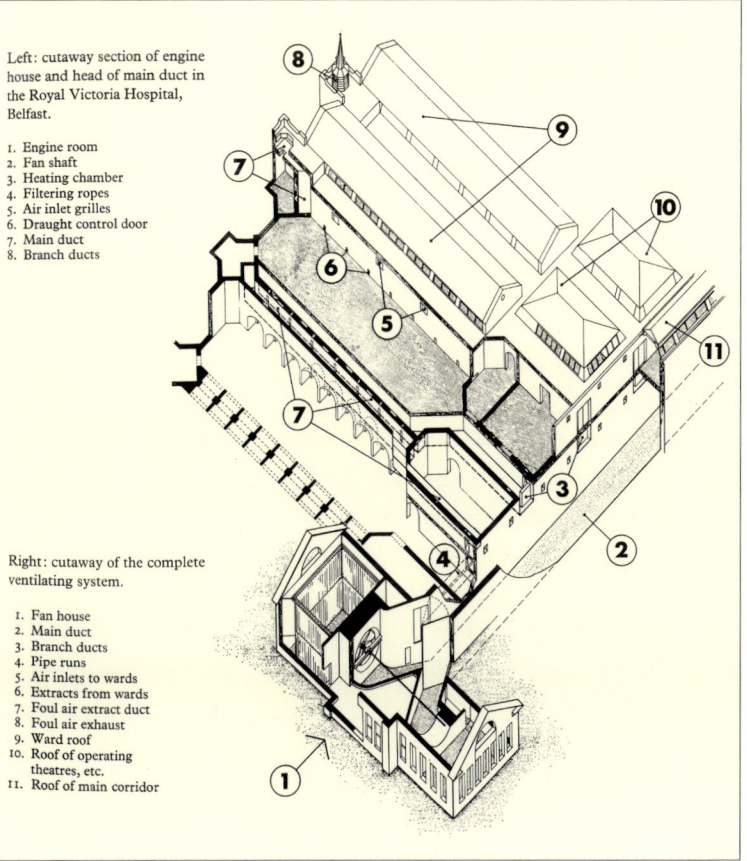

Left: cutaway section of engine house and head of main duct in the Royal Victoria Hospital, Belfast.

1. Engine room
2. Fan shaft
3. Heating chamber
4. Filtering ropes
5. Air inlet grilles
6. Draught control door
7. Main duct
8. Branch ducts

Right: cutaway of the complete ventilating system.

1. Fan house
2. Main duct
3. Branch ducts
4. Pipe runs
5. Air inlets to wards
6. Extracts from wards
7. Foul air extract duct
8. Foul air exhaust
9. Ward roof
10. Roof of operating theatres, etc.
11. Roof of main corridor

105

SAVAGE MINDS AND THE WELL-TEMPERED ENVIRONMENT

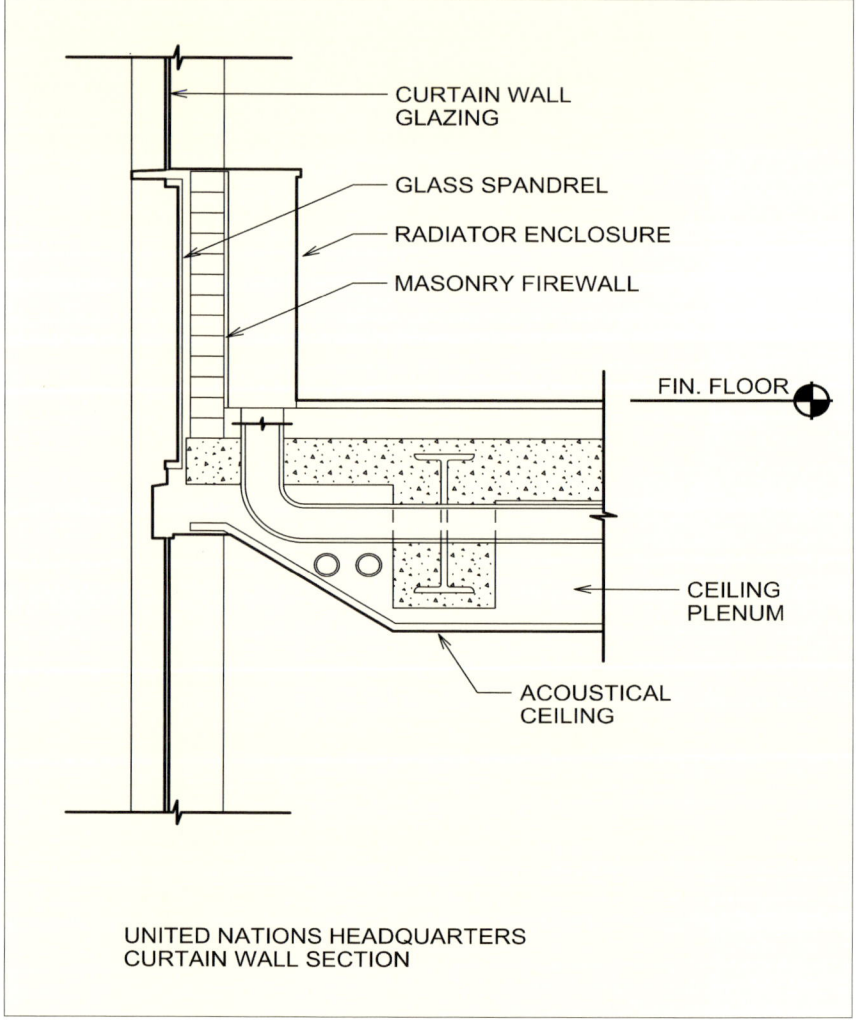

FIG. 3.8 | Harrison & Abramovitz, with Oscar Neimeyer and Le Corbusier (Wallace K. Harrison, American, 1895–1981; Oscar Neimeyer, Brazilian, 1907–2012; Le Corbusier, French, b. Switzerland, 1887–1965). United Nations Headquarters (New York, 1950). General view.

FIG. 3.9 | Harrison & Abramovitz, with Oscar Neimeyer and Le Corbusier (Wallace K. Harrison, American, 1895–1981; Oscar Neimeyer, Brazilian, 1907–2012; Le Corbusier, French, b. Switzerland, 1887–1965). United Nations Headquarters (New York, 1950). Curtain wall detail.

If Banham's preference for the Larkin Building illustrated his commitment to modern architecture, his comparison of details at Wallace Harrison's United Nations Headquarters Building (1950) and Gordon Bunshaft's Lever House (1951) (figs. 3.8–3.11), both in New York City, reinforced his disdain for ad hoc compositions. The two buildings were provided with required masonry firewalls at the slab edge, projecting up two feet six inches from the floor level. These masonry elements were masked in each case with an opaque glass spandrel panel on the facade and a radiator enclosure on the interior. At Lever House, Bunshaft mirrored the upstand firewall/spandrel on the facade with a similar downstand element, providing a clean stop to the plenum space above the suspended ceilings at each floor that was duly marked on the facade. At the UN, Harrison chamfered the plenum space to a minimal dimension at the facade, leaving just enough room for a heating duct to feed the radiator above and allowing the vision glass at each floor to rise nearly all the way to the upper-floor slab, which afforded no visual index of the plenum space on the facade. For Banham, the latter detail "may be ingenious, but

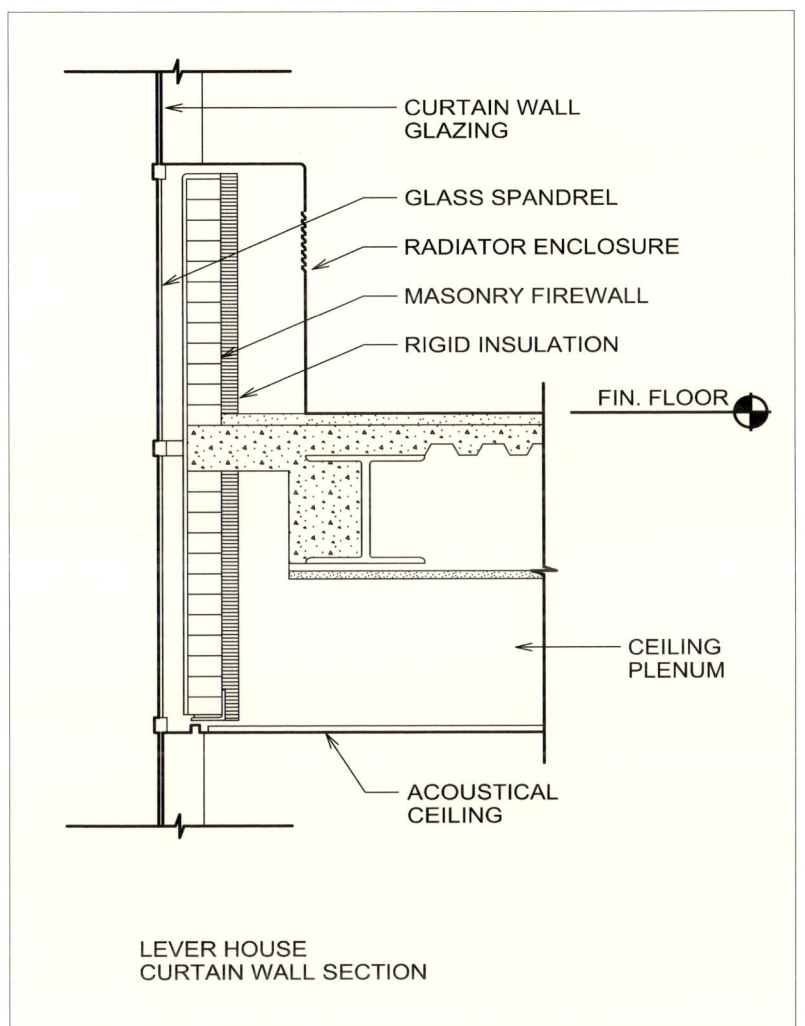

it is hardly an elegant solution." The former, however, "provides an excellent mask for the end of a suspended ceiling space amply deep for a full array of services; and the binary nature of this upstand-downstand solution is acknowledged with due honesty on the exterior."[68] As he had done in his exchange with Jencks over *Adhocism,* Banham displayed an unflinching commitment to legible, elegant, and honest visual coherence.

This attitude is consistent throughout the book. Examples as diverse as drive-in movie theaters, inflatable structures, and Emslie Morgan's St. George's School (Wallasey, Cheshire, 1961)—a work that employed heavy masonry construction and passive-solar techniques—derived their expressive effects from the thoughtful solution of environmental challenges with what Banham would later term "appropriate technology."[69] Some examples, such as the Las Vegas Strip, swerved daringly far from established architectural norms. Others, such as Victor Lundy's United States Atomic Energy Commission Pavilion (erected at various locations from 1959), merged familiar elements with cutting-edge technology. Others still, such as

FIG. 3.10 | **Gordon Bunshaft of Skidmore, Owings, and Merrill (Gordon Bunshaft, American, 1909–90).**
Lever House (New York, 1951). Curtain wall detail.

FIG. 3.11 | **Gordon Bunshaft of Skidmore, Owings, and Merrill (Gordon Bunshaft, American, 1909–90).**
Lever House (New York, 1951). General view.

Morgan's St. George's School, found both environmental performance and cogent expression in traditional forms. In each case, the expression derived directly from the technology employed.

At times, these forms coincided with the formal preferences (though not the mainstream rhetoric) of the modern movement. To illustrate, Banham included cunning treatments of Philip Johnson's Glass House (1949) at New Canaan (figs. 3.12, 3.13; see pl. 10) in both "A Home Is Not a House" and *The Architecture of the Well-Tempered Environment.* In the earlier text, he detached the house from its well-known European roots and recast it as typically American:

> So much has been misleadingly said (by Philip Johnson himself, as well as others) to prove this a work of architecture in the European tradition, that its many intensely American aspects are usually missed. Yet when you have dug through all the erudition about Ledoux and Malevitsch and Palladio and stuff that has been published, one very suggestive source or prototype remains less easily explained away—the admitted persistence in Johnson's mind of the visual image of a burned-out New England township, the insubstantial shells of the houses consumed by fire, leaving the brick floor slabs and standing chimneys.[70]

Lacking a visual enclosure in the traditional sense, the house was dissolved, like the inflatable un-house Banham described earlier in the text, to a collection of interior furnishings assembled in the landscape (see fig. 3.12).[71] In *The Architecture of*

FIG. 3.12 | **Philip Johnson (American, 1906–2005).**
Glass House (New Canaan, Connecticut, 1949). General view. Washington, D.C., Library of Congress Prints and Photographs Division. Carol M. Highsmith Archive.

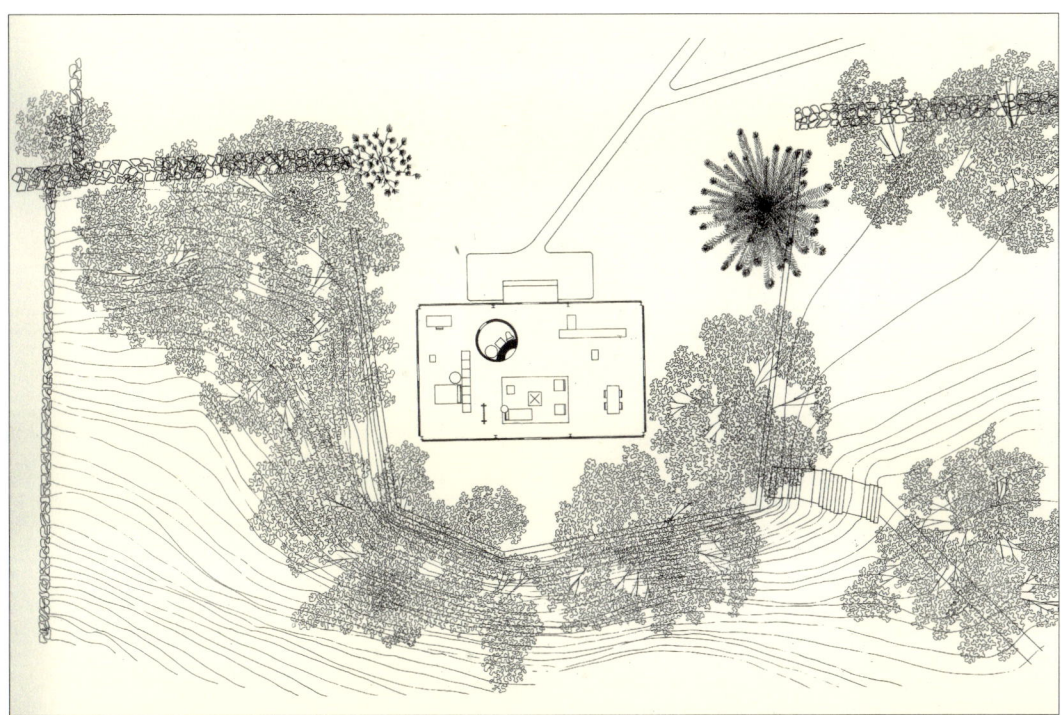

the Well-Tempered Environment, Banham elucidated the technical elements Johnson deployed to achieve his radical dissolution of architecture. Like Wright before him, Johnson used a hot-water heating system (here fully invisible in the radiant brick-clad floor slab) to render the space habitable in the winter. His monumental fireplace works "at the mainly ceremonial level of most of Wright's spectacular hearths."[72] In the summer, the glass shell marshals elements from well beyond the constructed perimeter of the building to boost its environmental performance. As the house is oriented with its long axis parallel to a steep bluff to the west, a stand of trees planted on this ridge at an elevation well below that of the house's floor level places the trees' thick deciduous canopy between the house and the oppressive afternoon summer sun. In winter, the bare branches admit the low winter sun to warm the interior (see fig. 3.13). In devising this vegetal *brise-soleil,* Johnson predicted the crafty dissipations of architecture into its neighbor disciplines of landscape and interior design that would be performed two decades later by the Archigram group[73] and, as shown below, would become an important ambition among High Tech architects.

The Crisis of Invisibility

Fifteen years after the initial appearance of *The Architecture of the Well-Tempered Environment,* Banham released a second edition. In it, he substantially revised his earlier conclusions regarding a proper mode of expression arising from appropriate technologies. Consider his treatment of a 1982 house in Santa Cruz, California,

FIG. 3.13 | **Philip Johnson (American, 1906–2005).**
Glass House (New Canaan, Connecticut, 1949). Site plan.

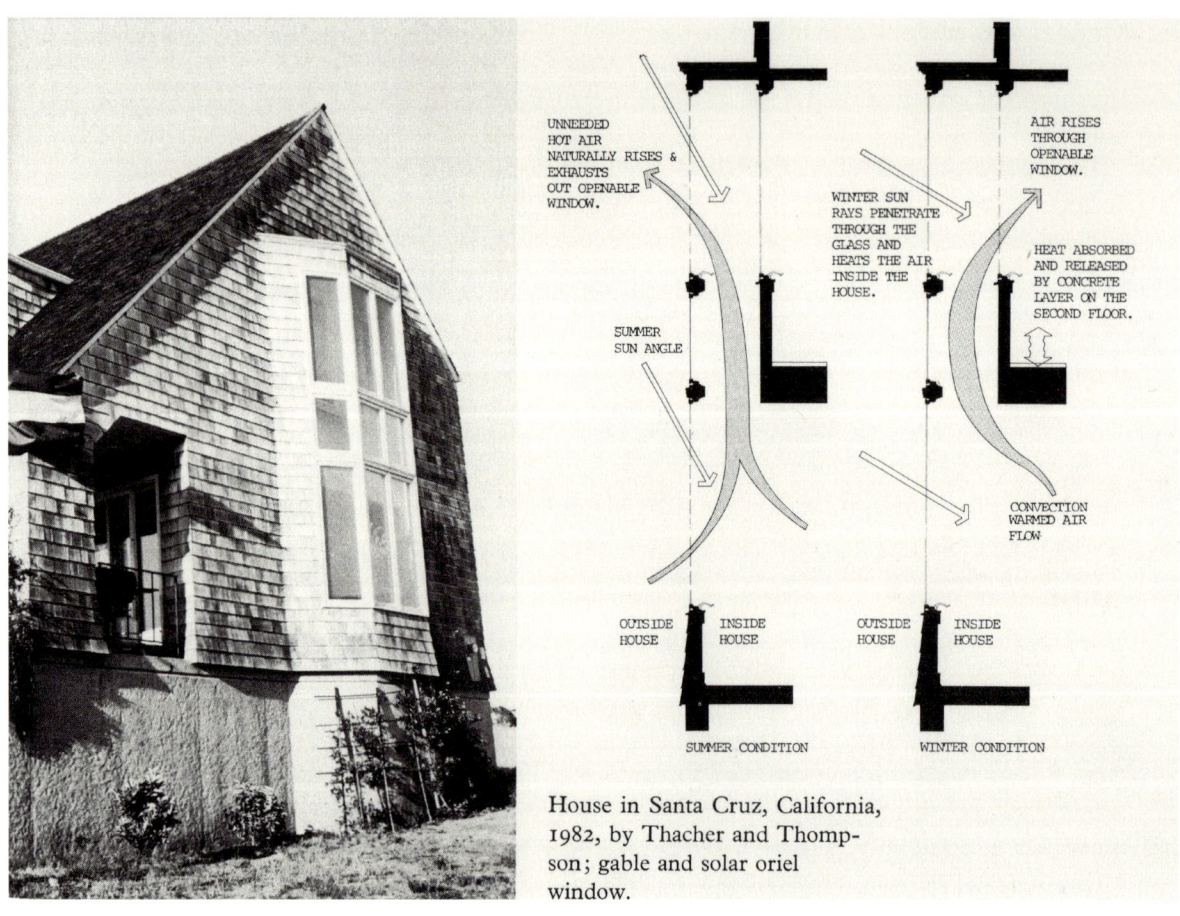

House in Santa Cruz, California, 1982, by Thacher and Thompson; gable and solar oriel window.

FIG. 3.14 | **Thacher and Thompson (Tom Thacher, American, b. 1947; Matthew Thompson, American, b. 1948).**
House (Santa Cruz, California, 1982). *Left:* View of oriel window. *Right:* Section of oriel window.
From Reyner Banham, *The Architecture of the Well-Tempered Environment* (London: Architectural Press, 1969), 309 (detail).

by the firm of Thacher and Thompson. A cedar-clad cottage with no pretensions to progressive aesthetics, the house deftly incorporated passive environmental solutions. Concrete floor slabs act as heat sinks in winter, while double layers of glass with operable panes in each layer allow the tuning of air-convection patterns based on the season (fig. 3.14). All this was invisibly accommodated within a traditional two-story oriel window unashamedly centered under the house's gable roof. For Banham, the radicalism of such works lay not in its outward appearance but rather in the far more subversive liberation of *"expected* performance" from "conventional form" that can come from "the application of radical intelligence and organized knowledge to the ancient craft of building."[74] When faced with the problem of mechanical systems, most of the architects featured in Banham's book tended toward clever camouflage or blatant exaggeration. Such tactics led nearly every building toward a traditional form of monumentality. The Larkin Building, Centre Georges Pompidou, and even Dallegret's drawings for "A Home Is Not a House" exhibit this tendency. And though Banham might have managed to squint through the traditional disciplinarity of Johnson's Glass House to glean indication of an "other" agenda at work, Thacher and Thompson's understated "neither-nor" approach signaled a more radical possibility. "Architecturally," Banham opined, this may leave us with a curious and almost unprecedented problem—that of the building that is perfectly honest about its functioning, but offers no clues as to what that functioning might be. This may only be seen as a problem in the aftermath of the International Style and Functionalism, when buildings were supposed to advertise their functions and exhibit their technical innovations, but we have to accept that we are still inhabiting that aftermath and are a long way from formulating appropriate alternative approaches.[75]

As he moved toward his conclusion, his tone grew increasingly melancholic: "Architecture, as commonly taught, practiced, and understood in the West, is still little more than a peasant vernacular, whatever the triumphs of art it has bequeathed to the human race," and the cultural force of the "hallowed forms" of tradition, he reasoned, long since had begun to wane. In the first edition, Banham saw hope that new forms soon would be constructed out of the stuff of environmental control. By 1984, this hope had dimmed significantly. "Perhaps," he concluded,

among the buildings discussed and illustrated in these pages, the outlines of a new and relevant language of symbolic forms may be discerned, but one must beg leave doubt it—yet. Such a development is not in the contract, so to speak. It is probably true that only when the architecture of the well-tempered environment disposes of a language of symbolic forms as entrenched in our culture as are those of the older dispensation will it be able to hope for equal conviction and monumental authority, but that possibility seems to be excluded by the very nature of the operation which has been chronicled here. The essence of what has been done to temper the environment has been—at every single stage—the displacement of habit by experiment, and of accepted custom by informed innovation. The greatest of all environmental powers is thought, and the usefulness of thought, the very reason for applying radical intelligence to our problems, is precisely that it dissolves what architecture has been made of to date: customary forms.[76]

This polemical opposition of traditional forms and innovative technology distinctly echoes argumentation employed by Le Corbusier in *Vers une architecture*. In his closing chapter, Le Corbusier issued the famous challenge: "Architecture or Revolution."[77] His method for avoiding that revolution, outlined in preceding chapters, was to fabricate the illusion that architecture's core principles, its "operational lore," were aligned with the forces of a technological society. But as was pointed out by Banham and countless critics in his wake, Le Corbusier's *machines à habiter* were in fact little more than primal geometries in contemporary costume, cunning attempts to stave off a societal revolution by galvanizing traditional form against the corrosive effects of technology.

It is tempting to read Banham's challenge differently—Revolution or Architecture—with the attendant corollary that architecture, not revolution, can be avoided. As he had argued in "A Home Is Not a House," human beings (at least Americans) equipped with adequate technology were likely to dissolve architecture in the Western tradition if presented the opportunity. In the fanciful un-house, Banham offered an extreme version of this scenario, while at Johnson's Glass House, he found evidence of immanent dissipation at the very heart of orthodox production. The revolution, it seems, had already occurred.

When *The Architecture of the Well-Tempered Environment* appeared in 1969, Banham already had immersed himself in research on the United States, the country to which he would relocate permanently in 1976. Judging by later titles such as *Los Angeles: The Architecture of Four Ecologies* (1971) and *Scenes in America Deserta* (1982), books committed to the automotive flux of an unruly metropolis and the sublime beauty of an alien landscape,[78] Banham apparently had beaten a westerly retreat from the Western tradition. Yet throughout his American sojourn, Banham kept a watchful eye on architectural activities across the Atlantic. And while he might have reveled in the freedoms and opportunities afforded by the dissolution of buildings and the triumph of the automobile, he would continue to bristle at the careless adoption of Continental thought by Jencks and others of the younger generation. In the end, it was to the tenets of modern architecture that Banham remained committed as a historian.

Like Le Corbusier, Banham's ambition was more corrective than revolutionary. The call was still "Architecture or Revolution," though the revolution to be avoided was not that of technology, which already had occurred, but rather that of postmodernism. Banham could celebrate an un-house, a Glass House, and even the anonymous vernaculars of the American Northeast and Southwest, but he could not stomach the backward-looking antics of contemporary postmodernists. Banham was deeply dismayed by the ascendancy of postmodern architecture, and, as the later edition of *The Architecture of the Well-Tempered Environment* made clear, he found little comfort in the largely irrelevant vernaculars of Emslie Morgan or Thacher and Thompson, however much "apparent intelligence" those works might display.

In the years that passed between the first appearance of his book and the end of his life, Banham devoted considerable attention not only to the American frontier but also to a group of talented British architects who appeared to agree with his Marxist assertion that if postmodernism represented "the time when history repeats itself as farce, then it is architecture which is offering to become farcical, not the technologies that have displaced it from its ancient role." Displaying equal parts boffinesque expedience and traditional elegance, Norman Foster, Renzo Piano, Richard Rogers, and other High Tech practitioners were (and remain) committed, as was Banham, to technology's "claim to be a permanent part of the craft of architecture."[79] Though a far cry from the radical examples he extolled in Los Angeles and the American desert, High Tech, with its paradoxical and distinctly English fusion of tradition and technology, appeared, to Banham, better equipped than any alternative to fend off the rising tide of postmodern architecture.

NOTES

1. These include Reyner Banham, "A Home Is Not a House," *Art in America* 53, no. 2 (1965): 70–79; Banham, "Flatscapes with Containers," *New Society* 10, no. 255 (1967): 231–32; and the four BBC radio talks published in *The Listener* that formed the basis for his book *Los Angeles: The Architecture of Four Ecologies* (1971). See "Encounter with Sunset Boulevard," *The Listener,* 22 August 1968, 235–36; "Roadscapes with Rusting Rails," *The Listener* 80 (29 August 1968): 267–68; "Beverly Hills, Too, Is a Ghetto," *The Listener* 80 (5 September 1968): 296–98; and "The Art of Doing Your Thing," *The Listener* 80 (12 September 1968): 330–31. For a discussion of the Los Angeles texts, see Anthony Vidler, *Histories of the Immediate Present: Inventing Architectural Modernism* (Cambridge, MA: MIT Press, 2008), 140–47.
2. Charles Jencks and George Baird, eds., *Meaning in Architecture* (New York: George Braziller, 1969), 7.
3. On the intersection of architecture and language in the 1960s, see Gillo Dorfles, "Structuralism and Semiology in Architecture," in Jencks and Baird, *Meaning in Architecture,* 39–49. K. Michael Hays provides another useful treatment in his introduction to idem, ed., *Architecture Theory since 1968* (Cambridge, MA: MIT Press, 1998), x–xv, and, more directly related to the present chapter, in his gloss on George Baird's writing in same volume, pp. 36–38.
4. George Baird, "'La Dimension Amoureuse' in Architecture," in Jencks and Baird, *Meaning in Architecture,* 79–99. The essay is revised from a paper that appeared in *Arena:* George Baird, "'La Dimension Amoureuse' in Architecture," *Arena: The Journal of the Architectural Association* 83 (1967); alongside other essays by Joseph Rykwert and Alan Colquhoun reprinted in *Meaning in Architecture.* More recently, the text has been reissued in Hays, *Architecture Theory since 1968,* 40–55.
5. Baird, "La Dimension Amoureuse," 79. See Walter Gropius, *The Scope of Total Architecture* (New York: Harper, 1955); and Jeremy Bentham, *The Panopticon Writings* (London: Verso, 1995), which gathers Bentham's late eighteenth-century writings on the subject. Cedric Price outlines his position in "Life-Conditioning: The Potteries Thinkbelt; A Plan for an Advanced Education Industry in North Staffordshire," *Architectural Design* 36 (1966): 483–97.
6. Baird, "La Dimension Amoureuse," 79.
7. Baird, "La Dimension Amoureuse," 97–98, Baird's emphasis.
8. "At the intersection of these two postulates [responsibility and tolerance] lies the role of the architect who attempts to take the measure of '*la dimension amoureuse.*'" Baird, "La Dimension Amoureuse," 97. The title of Baird's essay refers to a passage from Barthes that Baird also included as an epigraph: "La rhétorique, qui n'est rien d'autre que la technique de l'information exacte, est liée non seulement à toute littérature, mais encore à toute communication, dès lors qu'elle veut faire entendre à l'autre que nous le reconnaissons; la rhétorique est la dimension amoureuse de l'ecriture." ("Rhetoric, which is nothing but the technique of exact information, is linked not only to all literature but even to all communication, once it seeks to make others understand that we acknowledge them: rhetoric is the amorous dimension of writing." Roland Barthes, *Critical Essays,* trans. Richard Howard [Evanston, IL: Northwestern University Press, 1972], xvi.) K. Michael Hays provides a useful gloss on Baird's terminology and its implications for architecture: "In semiotic terms…architecture becomes a readable text, and the parameters of legibility are what we mean by rhetoric. Rhetoric operates within the structure of shared expectations and demands an ethical, even erotic relationship with the reader, an 'amorous dimension.'" Hays, *Architecture Theory since 1968,* 37.
9. Reyner Banham, "The Architecture of Wampanoag," in Jencks and Baird, *Meaning in Architecture,* 102.
10. See Jencks and Baird, *Meaning in Architecture,* 103–8 and 109–18, respectively. Banham's "Flatscapes with

Containers" originally appeared in *New Society,* 17 August 1967, 231–32. His "A Home Is Not a House" was reprinted from *Art in America* 53, no. 5 (1965): 70–79.

11   "Left to their own devices, Americans do not monumentalize or make architecture. From the Cape Cod cottage, through the balloon frame to the perfection of permanently pleated aluminum siding with embossed wood graining, they have tended to build a brick chimney and lean a collection of shacks against it." Banham, "A Home Is Not a House," 109.

12   Banham, "A Home Is Not a House," 111. Subsequent quotations in this paragraph are drawn from pp. 112–13 of this essay.

13   See Paul Scheerbart, *Glasarchitektur* [1914] (Munich: Rogner & Bernhard, 1971). An English translation is available in Paul Scheerbart and Bruno Taut, *Glass Architecture and Alpine Architecture,* ed. Dennis Sharp (New York: Praeger, 1972); and, more recently, in Todd Gannon, ed., *The Light Construction Reader* (New York: Monacelli, 2002), 345–68. Scheerbart (1863–1915) was a highly celebrated and oft-revisited character in Banham's writings, from his early introduction of the German writer to English-speaking audiences in Banham, "The Glass Paradise," *Architectural Review* 125 (1959): 87–89, to later invocations in Banham, *Theory and Design in the First Machine Age* (London: Architectural Press, 1960), 266–68; and Banham, *The Architecture of the Well-Tempered Environment,* 1st ed. (London: Architectural Press, 1969), 125–29.

14   Claude Lévi-Strauss, *The Savage Mind* [1962] (Chicago: University of Chicago Press, 1966), 1–33.

15   Lévi-Strauss, *The Savage Mind,* 17.

16   Lévi-Strauss, *The Savage Mind,* 16–17.

17   Robin Middleton, "The New Brutalism; or, A Clean, Well-Lighted Place," *Architectural Design* 37 (1967): 7. See "Unconventional Combinations: A Clip-On Architecture," this volume.

18   See Alan Colquhoun, "Typology and Design Method," in Jencks and Baird, *Meaning in Architecture,* 267–77; and Alan Colquhoun, "From Bricolage to Myth; or, How to Put Humpty-Dumpty Together Again," *Oppositions* 12 (1978): 1–19.

19   Colin Rowe and Fred Koetter, *Collage City* (Cambridge, MA: MIT Press, 1978), 102–3. The crux of its argument was published as Colin Rowe and Fred Koetter, "Collage City," *Architectural Review,* no. 952 (1975): 66–91; manuscript copies of the text were in circulation from 1973. For a useful gloss, see Hays's commentary in *Architecture Theory since 1968,* 88–91.

20   Rowe and Koetter, *Collage City,* 87.

21   Jacques Derrida, "La structure, le signe et le jeu dans le discours des sciences humaines" (lecture given at the conference "The Language of Criticism and the Sciences of Man" [convened by Richard Macksey and Eugenio Donato], Johns Hopkins University, 18–21 October 1966). The English translation, "Structure, Sign, and Play in the Discourse of the Human Sciences," was released as chapter 10 in Jacques Derrida's *Writing and Difference* (Chicago: University of Chicago Press, 1978), 278–93, but it was first published in 1970 in Richard Macksey and Eugenio Donato, eds., *The Structuralist Controversy: The Language of Criticism and the Sciences of Man* (Baltimore: Johns Hopkins Press, 1970), 247–65. For a discussion of the conference and its implications, see François Cusset, *French Theory: How Foucault, Derrida, Deleuze, and Co. Transformed the Intellectual Life of the United States* [2003] (Minneapolis: University of Minnesota Press, 2008), 28–32.

22   For a lucid treatment of architecture's difficult entanglements with Derrida and deconstruction, see Mark Wigley, *The Architecture of Deconstruction: Derrida's Haunt* (Cambridge, MA: MIT Press, 1993).

23   Derrida, *Writing and Difference,* 286, Derrida's emphases.

24   Derrida, *Writing and Difference,* 292.

25   See the comments of former Museum of Modern Art director Kirk Varnedoe in the context of the 1984 exhibition *Primitivism*: "Claude Lévi-Strauss's view of tribal society, so influential in the 1960s…regarded in its day as an assault on Western humanism, is lately painted as the established seat of all that tradition's logocentric evils." See Kirk Varnedoe, "On the Claims and Critics of the 'Primitivism' Show," *Art in America* 73, no. 5 (1985): 11–21, reprinted in Bill Beckley, ed., *Uncontrollable Beauty: Toward a New Aesthetics* (New York: Allworth, 1998), 250.

26   Robert Maxwell, "An Eye for an I: Failure of the Townscape Tradition," *Architectural Design* 46 (1976): 534–36, reprinted as Robert Maxwell, "The Failure of Townscape," in idem, *Sweet Disorder and the Carefully Careless* (New York: Princeton Architectural, 1993), 128. As noted in "In Search of Alternatives: Banham, Britain, and the New Brutalism," this volume, Ivor de Wolfe was a nom de plume adopted by the *Architectural Review* editor Hugh de Cronin Hastings in the late 1940s.

27   Lévi-Strauss, *The Savage Mind,* 22.

28   Rowe and Koetter, *Collage City,* 104–5.

29 Charles Jencks and Nathan Silver, *Adhocism: The Case for Improvisation* (New York: Doubleday, 1972), 17. Jencks and Silver structured the book in two parts, with part 1 (pp. 13–101) credited to Jencks and part 2 (pp. 103–98) to Silver.

30 A revised version of Jencks's dissertation was published as Charles Jencks, *Modern Movements in Architecture* (London: Pelican, 1973).

31 Reyner Banham, "Bricologues à la Lanterne," *New Society*, 1 July 1976, 25–26, reprinted in Reyner Banham, *A Critic Writes: Essays by Reyner Banham,* ed. Mary Banham (Berkeley: University of California Press, 1996), 198–99.

32 Banham, "Bricologues," 198.

33 Banham, "Bricologues," 197–98, Banham's emphasis.

34 Derrida, "Structure, Sign, and Play," in idem, *Writing and Difference,* 285.

35 Banham, "Bricologues," 199.

36 Banham discusses both his and Jencks's adoption of this role in a review of the second edition of Jencks's *Language of Post-Modern Architecture.* See Reyner Banham, "Two by Jencks: The Tough Life of the *Enfant Terrible,*" *AIA Journal* 69 (1980): 50. For a good treatment of Banham's relationship with Jencks, see Nigel Whiteley, *Reyner Banham: Historian of the Immediate Future* (Cambridge, MA: MIT Press, 2003), 373–77.

37 In recounting an exchange of letters between Banham and Jencks that followed the publication of "Bricologues," Whiteley argued that "Banham was being beaten at his own game in his own style" (Whiteley, *Reyner Banham,* 375). The letters appeared in *New Society,* 15, 22, and 29 July 1976, pp. 141, 195, and 251, respectively. While this exchange coincided with the ascendancy of Jencks in the architectural spotlight and a concurrent fading of influence for Banham, I do not agree with Whiteley's assessment. In these letters, Jencks maintained an extreme position with regard to engineering practice that discounted the importance of the ad hoc methods Banham described. While Whiteley attempted to align Jencks's position with the "macro scale" of the "technostructure" (Whiteley, *Reyner Banham,* 375), Derrida's critique cited above offers a formidable counterpoint. Not only did Banham's nuanced analysis reiterate Derrida's position in theory, it was also far more convincing in practice.

38 See Le Corbusier, *Towards a New Architecture* [1923], trans. Frederick Etchells (London: John Rodker, 1931), 134–35.

39 Following Jencks's usage, I retain his capitalization and pubescent hyphen, which helps to differentiate his version of the term from later manifestations of postmodernism in architecture, which I discuss below.

40 "A Post-Modern building is, if a short definition is needed, one which speaks on at least two levels at once: to other architects and a concerned minority who care about specifically architectural meanings, and to the public at large, or the local inhabitants, who care about other issues concerned with comfort, traditional building and a way of life." Jencks, *The Language of Post-Modern Architecture,* revised and enlarged edition (New York: Rizzoli, 1977), 6.

41 Jencks's *Language of Post-Modern Architecture* was a crucial text in the establishment of postmodern architecture. In it, Jencks described "Post-Modern" architecture primarily in terms of style, but as the term caught on and the discourse around it developed in architectural circles, the term lost its hyphen and took on implications that resonated with the cultural criticism of such thinkers as Jean-François Lyotard and Frederic Jameson. See, for example, Lyotard, *La condition postmoderne: rapport sur le savoir* (Paris: Les Editions Minuit, 1979); English translation by Geoff Bennington and Brian Massumi, *The Postmodern Condition: A Report on Knowledge* (Minneapolis: University of Minnesota, 1984); and Jameson, "Postmodernism, or, The Cultural Logic of Late Capitalism," *New Left Review* 146 (July–August 1984): 59–92. For an extremely useful presentation of the varied inflections of the term *postmodern* in architectural discourse and their gradual adoption by the field in the 1970s and '80s, see Mary McLeod, "The End of Innocence: From Political Activism to Postmodernism," in Joan Ockman, ed., *Architecture School: Three Centuries of Educating Architects in North America* (Cambridge, MA: MIT Press, 2012), 161–201.

42 Expanded editions of *The Language of Post-Modern Architecture* appeared in 1978, 1980, 1984, 1988, and 1991. A seventh edition appeared under the revised title *The New Paradigm in Architecture* in 2003. The first edition comprised a svelte 104 pages; *The New Paradigm,* even with a slightly larger trim size, required 288.

43 Jencks and Silver, *Adhocism,* 73.

44 Similarly, the topic drops out of *The Savage Mind* soon after the first chapter.

45 Banham, "Bricologues," 198.

46 Banham, "Bricologues," 199.

47 Lévi-Strauss, *The Savage Mind,* 19.

48 The *Oxford English Dictionary* puts the first use of the term, referring to aging naval officers, at 1941. See *Oxford English Dictionary,* s.v. "boffin," http://dictionary.oed.com. Wikipedia offers a list of possible etymologies, including a plausible derivation from "**B**ack **OFF**ice **IN**telligence." See "Boffin," *Wikipedia,* http://en.wikipedia.org/wiki/Boffin. For a worthwhile treatment of boffin culture, see Francis Spufford, *Backroom Boys: The Secret Return of the British Boffin* (London: Faber & Faber, 2003).

49 See Reyner Banham, "Top Pop Boffin," *Architects' Journal,* 20 February 1958, 269–71.

50 Simon Sadler, *Archigram: Architecture without Architecture* (Cambridge, MA: MIT Press, 2005), 118.

51 Peter Cook, *Experimental Architecture* (New York: Universe, 1970), 11–12.

52 Peter Cook, "Richard Rogers + Architects," in *Richard Rogers + Architects,* ed. Frank Russell (London: Academy, 1985), 5.

53 Reyner Banham, "1960—Stocktaking," *Architectural Review* 127 (1960): 94.

54 Banham, "1960—Stocktaking," 94.

55 Banham, *Theory and Design in the First Machine Age* (London: Architectural Press, 1960), 326.

56 Banham, *Well-Tempered Environment,* 1st ed., 17, Banham's emphases.

57 Banham, *Well-Tempered Environment,* 1st ed., 13.

58 Hayward's design used natural convection to draw fresh air through a heated chamber in the basement, which then rose through a series of grilles and louvers cleverly arranged in stacked lobbies provided at each floor to supply heated fresh air to each living space. Foul air was extracted via a series of ducts that connected in the attic to an exhaust flue. Banham, *Well-Tempered Environment,* 1st ed., 35–38.

59 Banham, *Well-Tempered Environment,* 1st ed., 60.

60 Banham noted Edison's dissatisfaction with exposed power lines in cities (Edison: "You don't lift waterpipes and gas-pipes up on stilts") and the inventor's early suggestion that they be buried. Banham, *Well-Tempered Environment,* 1st ed., 61.

61 Banham, *Well-Tempered Environment,* 1st ed., 155–63.

62 Banham, *Well-Tempered Environment,* 1st ed., 162–63.

63 Carrier (1876–1950) was granted a United States patent for his "Apparatus for Treating Air" in 1906. On Carrier's life and work, see Margaret Ingels, *Willis Haviland Carrier: Father of Air Conditioning* (Garden City, NY: Country Life Press, 1952).

64 Banham, *Well-Tempered Environment,* 1st ed., 187.

65 Banham acknowledged as much after the fact: "Dallegret's drawings evoke those values so effectively that it is clear that any fetishist of the *Dimension Amoureuse* who wants to keep up that particular ritual has room to do so in at least the static equipment, if not the enclosing membranes, of inflatable architecture." Banham, "The Architecture of Wampanoag," 102.

66 Banham pointed out that air conditioning, technically defined, requires the provision of cleaned, temperature-corrected, and humidity-controlled air. The Larkin Building failed to provide the last element. Banham, *Well-Tempered Environment,* 1st ed., 86–92.

67 Banham, *Well-Tempered Environment,* 1st ed., 84.

68 Banham, *Well-Tempered Environment,* 1st ed., 226.

69 Reyner Banham, "Introduction," in *Foster Associates,* by Norman Foster (London: RIBA, 1979), 5. The phrase also would appear in the second edition of *The Architecture of the Well-Tempered Environment* and is examined in detail in the next chapter.

70 Banham, "A Home Is Not a House," 117. Banham seems to have imagined that the village Johnson described was in New England. Johnson merely described "a burnt village I saw once" in his remarks on the house in Philip Johnson, "House at New Canaan, Connecticut," *Architectural Review* 108 (1950): 152–59. Both Peter Eisenman and Kenneth Frampton have associated this imagery with the devastation of Europe during World War II. See Eisenman's introduction to Philip Johnson, *Writings* (New York: Oxford University Press, 1979): 22–23; and Kenneth Frampton, "The Glass House Revisited," *Catalogue* 9 (1978): 39–59. Marc Wortman recently provided an analysis of Johnson's complex relationship to Nazism and his travels in Germany and Poland at the outset of World War II in *1941: Fighting the Shadow War: A Divided America in a World at War* (New York: Atlantic Monthly, 2016).

71 "As many pilgrims to the site have noticed, the house does not stop at the glass, and the terrace, and even the trees beyond, are visually part of the living space in winter, physically and operationally so in summer when the four doors are open." Banham, "A Home Is Not a House," 117.

72 Banham, *Well-Tempered Environment,* 1st ed., 231.

73 See *Archigram* 9, *Fruitiest Yet* (1970): entire issue; and "Architecture beyond Building," this volume.

74 Reyner Banham, *The Architecture of the Well-Tempered Environment,* 2nd ed. (Chicago: University of Chicago Press, 1984), 310, Banham's emphasis.
75 Banham, *Well-Tempered Environment,* 2nd ed., 308.
76 Banham, *Well-Tempered Environment,* 2nd ed., 311–12.
77 Le Corbusier, *Towards a New Architecture,* 267–89.
78 For a useful discussion of these books, see Vidler, *Histories of the Immediate Present,* 140–55.
79 Banham, *Well-Tempered Environment,* 2nd ed., 312.

CHAPTER 4

HIGH TECH AND THE PERSISTENCE OF MODERNISM

High Tech architecture, by most accounts, was born in London in 1967, though its formal and ideological antecedents stretch back into the nineteenth century, and its most important buildings—Piano + Rogers's Centre Georges Pompidou (1977; see pl. 13) and Norman Foster's Hong Kong and Shanghai Bank Headquarters (1986; see pl. 14)—would not begin to appear until at least a decade later. In 1967, the local architectural community quietly welcomed two modest buildings designed by two like-minded and ambitious young firms, Team 4's Reliance Controls Building (see figs. 4.3, 4.4, 4.6–4.9, pl. 11) in outlying Swindon and the Farrell/Grimshaw Partnership's Bathroom Tower in the Paddington district of London (see figs. 2.8–2.10, pl. 4).[1] Though not technically twins, the buildings share distinctive stylistic and technological affinities. Both were constructed of repetitive steel-and-glass components and, in their organizational schemata (the former a simple shed designed for axial extension in plan, the latter a rising helix suggesting a similarly extensible section), both adhered to the "endless and indeterminate" strain of postwar modern architecture.[2] Despite these and other similarities, the two buildings also display what might be construed as a form of sibling rivalry. Their contrasting characteristics—one, an elegant assembly of carefully coordinated components, the other, an expedient juxtaposition of ad hoc elements—exemplify the divergent tendencies that constitute High Tech architecture.

The movement developed smoothly from the historical trajectory traced in preceding chapters. From the New Brutalism, High Tech inherited an ethical commitment to function and a predilection for "bloodyminded" consistency. From clip-on, it took an opportunistic flair for ad hoc expediency and a stylistic affinity for elemental accretion. Many of High Tech's foremost practitioners (for example, Nicholas Grimshaw, Michael Hopkins, and Richard Rogers) trained at London's Architectural Association School of Architecture and were early under the sway of Reyner

Foster Associates (Norman Foster, British, b. 1935).
Hong Kong and Shanghai Bank Headquarters (Hong Kong, 1986). General view (detail).
Photo by Ian Lambot.
See p. 223, pl. 14.

Banham, Cedric Price, and Peter Smithson. Most were present to witness the early musings of the Archigram group, and they displayed a similar commitment to arresting imagery constructed of equal parts space-age appropriation and time-honored convention.[3] And, like Banham, these ambitious young practitioners were as enamored with the no-nonsense rationalism of outsiders such as Buckminster Fuller as with the tendency of properly deployed mechanical equipment to vaporize architecture's traditional monumentality into a nearly invisible environmental milieu.

Absorbing opposing tendencies such as these—often within single buildings—High Tech was plagued by the contradictions encountered in preceding chapters. Like the New Brutalism, the movement showcased dueling ethical and aesthetic ambitions. Like clip-on, its buildings appeared to be driven as much toward symbolic monumentality as toward subservient anonymity. And, like Banham, its main exponents generally exhibited a simultaneous desire for both programmatic freedom and formal control. Above all else, High Tech is an architecture of oppositional forces—at once conventional and cutting-edge, integrated and ad hoc, style-obsessed and socially conscious, immersed in "operational lore" and deploying "apparent intelligence." And it was to the movement's concerted attempts to reconcile such seemingly irreconcilable qualities that Banham devoted much of his attention in his final years.

Important differences between High Tech and the architecture examined in previous chapters also can be discerned. Alison and Peter Smithson frankly associated themselves with the New Brutalism as a specifically defined movement. The Archigram group similarly trumpeted their stylistic aims under broadly disseminated banners such as "Plug-in" and "Zoom." By contrast, Foster, Rogers, Renzo Piano, and other architects associated with High Tech uniformly disdained the label, proclaiming allegiance not to a High Tech (or any other) aesthetic but rather to a properly modern ethic committed to the social lives of their buildings' inhabitants.[4] The architecture advanced by these architects was a far cry from the burgeoning critical culture of postmodernism. As young pundits such as George Baird rejected prevailing notions of both "total architecture" and "life-conditioning" in the late 1960s,[5] High Tech architects appeared wholeheartedly to embrace both concepts and committed themselves not to theoretical posturing but rather to pragmatic issues of building organization and construction.

Alison and Peter Smithson built only sporadically after 1970, and Archigram Architects did not complete a single building during their official association as a practice from 1970 to 1975. High Tech practitioners such as Foster and Rogers (at first together and later independently) and the Farrell/Grimshaw Partnership, by contrast, saw buildings completed at a steady clip from the late 1960s. Even as the worldwide economic slump of the early 1970s had many architects seeking solace in academia and "paper architecture," High Tech architects remained doggedly committed to building. They managed to stay active by aligning with industrial clients and global corporations—Herman Miller, IBM, Olivetti, and, later, international financial institutions such as Lloyd's of London and the Hong Kong and Shanghai Bank—that were reviled by many as the very objects of the resurgent Marxist critique of capital that swept through architectural culture after 1968.[6]

Despite many of its architects' stated aversions to matters of style, High Tech sustained often harsh criticism for its alignment with modernist stylistic tropes, primarily from left-leaning advocates of postmodern architecture.[7] At the same time, conservative critics, including the Prince of Wales, railed against High Tech architects for what they saw as a lack of concern for building inhabitants and a lack of respect for historical contexts.[8] And though Banham had forsaken the New Brutalism for its ultimate alignment with conventional aesthetics and had refrained from fully endorsing early clip-on works such as the Farrell/Grimshaw Partnership's Bathroom Tower and Stirling's Olivetti Training Center,[9] he offered unwavering support to mature High Tech. To the end of his career, he maintained a commitment to High Tech's persistent modernism, which he saw as a potent alternative to rampant postmodernism. At the same time, he saw through High Tech's more conventional aspects to discern not the radical alterity he had previously sought in *une architecture autre* but rather the more nuanced qualities of an "other" tradition of modern architecture.

The Roots of High Tech: Foster and Rogers
Though its impact was global, High Tech was a particularly English innovation. Many of its early proponents were educated at the Architectural Association (AA) in the late 1950s and early '60s, when Banham, Price, and the Smithsons loomed large. Unlike their mentors, Norman Foster and Richard Rogers—High Tech's two most significant English practitioners—also enjoyed early firsthand exposure to American architecture. In 1961, Foster and Richard and Su Rogers left England to study at Yale University.[10] There, under the tutelage of the demanding American dean Paul Rudolph, both were exposed to a brand of modern architecture less specifically functionalist than their AA training had been. Yale, at that time, was an incubator of the sort of postwar monumentality advanced by Sigfried Giedion and others in the 1940s,[11] promoted in the pages of *Perspecta: The Yale Architectural Journal* in the 1950s, and found in built works by Rudolph, Eero Saarinen, and Louis Kahn in New Haven, Connecticut, and elsewhere from the 1940s into the 1970s. While Rudolph's Art and Architecture building would not be completed until 1963, after Foster and Rogers had departed, they enjoyed intimate contact with Kahn's work, as their studios were housed on the top floor of his University Art Gallery. Rogers's biographer,

recounting an exchange between Rudolph and Rogers over the optimal depth of a sunken parking garage, elucidated the change in ideological tenor between London and New Haven. When Rogers "argued from the standard AA position" that "functional requirements of the circulation of cars and pedestrians" should determine the depth of the garage, Rudolph countered with his opinion that "car roofs looked pretty from above *en masse,*" and that the correct depth would be determined by discerning how to afford pedestrians the best view.[12] Such unashamedly visual criteria, as well as the grueling all-night demands of Yale's studio culture, were anathema to the young Brits. As Rogers recounted, "We certainly learned to work extremely hard and to use our eyes, not an English tradition."[13]

At Yale, Foster and Rogers grew close to James Stirling, by then a regular visiting professor with whom they made frequent weekend trips to New York. They also studied with Serge Chermayeff, another European, who would take over Rudolph's role as dean of the school in 1962,[14] and they met Craig Ellwood, one of the Case Study architects, who opened their eyes to architectural developments in California. After extensive travels across the United States to see the work of Frank Lloyd Wright and Ludwig Mies van der Rohe, Foster and the Rogerses found work in San Francisco—Foster at the firm of Anshen and Allen; Richard Rogers at Skidmore, Owings, and Merrill; and Su Rogers at the Federal Housing Authority.[15] While on the West Coast, they traveled to Los Angeles to see the work of Richard Neutra, Rudolph Schindler, and Wright, as well as that of Charles and Ray Eames, Ellwood, and other Case Study architects.

In a posthumously published essay, Banham outlined the depth of influence of the Case Study program on the development of High Tech.[16] Known through John Entenza's *Arts and Architecture* magazine from the late 1940s, the work of Case Study architects, particularly that of the Eameses, was widely admired in England. "The appeal of the Case Study houses," Banham argued in an echo of his earlier characterizations of the New Brutalism, "lay in the way they reinforced the dogmas of honesty, clarity, and unity, the exposure of structure, the use of certifiably modern materials, and the absence of ornament," qualities Banham cited as "the moral truths" of modern architecture.[17] In the previous paragraph, Banham incorrectly derived "honesty, clarity, and unity" from an unsigned text likely written by Richard Lohse.[18] The German original, as Banham noted, read "Klarheit, Ehrlichkeit, Einfachkeit," which should have led him to "clarity, honesty, and *simplicity,*" not "unity" (*Einheit*). Though Banham would make other errors in his late-career translations from German, this substitution may have been intentional, as the valuation of unity over mere simplicity would prove crucial in his late writings.

Beyond these orthodox characteristics, the new work in California also displayed "open-minded, experimental, hands-on, improvisatory, quirky" characteristics—in

short, "wit"—that offered "a much needed antidote to the cut-and-dried recipes of routine modernism being taught in the schools."[19] This unique ability to both maintain and challenge the status quo of European modernism caught the attention of London journals such as *Architectural Design* and the *Architectural Review* from the mid-1950s and, importantly, of Alison and Peter Smithson.

While Foster was training at the much more traditional Manchester University, Richard Rogers was developing a close rapport with Peter Smithson at the AA. The older architect undoubtedly directed his student's attention to the Eameses' work. A few years later in California, Foster and Rogers were able to examine the Eames house in situ. Strongly contrasting the pristine details (and expense) of Mies van der Rohe's canonical projects in Chicago, the Eames House was straightforwardly assembled from low-cost, off-the-shelf components such as industrial sash windows and standard steel sections (fig. 4.1). The house became something of a model for young English architects, and by the early 1960s, students at the AA were scouring the pages of Esther McCoy's *Modern California Houses*,[20] paying particular attention to the work of the Eameses, Ellwood, and Raphael Soriano, architects whose "relaxed alternative usage" of the modern vocabulary they found to be "a liberating revelation."[21]

Much of that relaxed usage was to be found in the detailing, particularly in welded steel connections. The possibilities of welded joints were well known to midcentury architects worldwide through Mies van der Rohe's famous Farnsworth House (1951) (fig. 4.2). There, Mies erased all trace of assembly by specifying plug welds, a meticulous and expensive process that belies the painstaking handicraft

FIG. 4.1 | Charles Eames (American, 1907–78) and Ray Eames (American, 1912–88).
Case Study #9 (Pacific Palisades, California, 1949). General view.
Photo by Julius Shulman.
Los Angeles, Getty Research Institute.

FIG. 4.2 | Ludwig Mies van der Rohe (German, 1886–1969).
Farnsworth House (Plano, Illinois, 1951). View of entry.
Photo by Victor Grigas.

involved (joints must be temporarily bolted together, then welded, then ground smooth). Michael Cadwell described the implications of the process: "Each operation disappears with the next. The mechanical craft of the seated connection disappears with the industrial craft of welding, the industrial craft of welding disappears with the handicraft of sanding, and the handicraft of sanding disappears with its own operation. There is no glorification of technology in this curious sequence, just as there is no remnant of craft."[22] Such elegant erasures, though essential to the ethereal abstraction of Mies's domestic masterpiece, were far too expensive for more quotidian applications. Bolted connections, which frankly display the mechanical processes of their assembly, remain the norm, and welds, when employed, usually remain visible as the welder left them.

Of course, connections of any sort, while necessary, are expensive; limiting their number and complexity is essential to cost-effective building. In the 1950s, English architects had approached the problem with prefabricated building systems such as the one developed by the Consortium of Local Authorities Special Programme (CLASP). From 1957, the consortium elaborated a system for steel-frame buildings constructed using standard details and components assembled according to a preestablished dimensional system. The results were at least superficially convincing—a CLASP school was premiated at the 1960 Milan Triennale—but, as Banham pointed out in 1962, the system met with harsh criticism from the architectural community in its early years. Its details were assumed, often sight-unseen, to be "awful," and the resulting buildings were deemed "not architecture."[23] The construction detail was (and for most architects remains) understood as the locus of disciplinary intensity, the moment at which mere building is transcended to become architecture. Honest, compelling details were embedded deeply in the ideology of the modern movement and aligned tightly with its ethical mission. Mies, recall, purportedly found God in them. Grappling with details was (and is) regarded as the truest test of one's architectural mettle, their successful solution key to a work's ability to compel conviction. Such attitudes find their roots deep in architecture's "operational lore" and may be traced back through eighteenth- and nineteenth-century theorists such as Marc-Antoine Laugier and Gottfried Semper to the field's mythical origins.[24] Details such as those developed by CLASP, which were procured "ex-catalog" and applied without effort, appeared to sidestep the activity that defined the architect as a professional and architecture as a discipline.[25] Trained to execute and appreciate complex, custom, and exacting solutions, Foster and Rogers were conditioned to be wary of shortcut solutions such as CLASP, and they were understandably astonished by the California architects' achievement, in contrast to Mies's spiritual and astringent "less is more," of a casual and relaxed delivery of more with less.

By combining *Klarheit, Ehrlichkeit,* and *Einfachkeit* with "Wit, Too," the title of Banham's essay on the Case Study architects captured the orthodox values of Foster's and Rogers's European training as well as the playful quality with which it had been tempered in America. It should be noted that much of that wit was, as Michael Brawne observed, "largely the result of the additive process, of the seemingly casual juxtaposition of different elements" in the Eames House.[26] While Banham (and Brawne) chose to link this combinatorial wit to American sources, the method's distinctly English characteristics should not pass unmentioned. Substantial wit, also derived from the juxtaposition of elements, was baldly on display in Stirling and Gowan's celebrated Leicester University Engineering Building (1959), which Foster and Rogers would have known well. A few years earlier, Nikolaus Pevsner had outlined similar compositional tendencies, if less overt wittiness, as endemic to the English national character. Discussing the idiosyncrasies of English Perpendicular Gothic, Pevsner noted the peculiar boxiness of its forms. Typical "square-ended chancels," he submitted, would be "very unusual in France and Germany. They prefer the rounded end with or without a passageway like an aisle around—what we call an ambulatory. This gives a sense of moulded space, of plasticity, of pulling together." Continuing, he pointed out the English alternative's lack of such integrated unity: "England prefers that the walls should meet at right angles and remain separate from each other and that the enclosed spaces should be a box, a cube, or a block.... Part is added to part instead of the sculptural pulling-together in France, where transepts get short and keep close to the unified composition of the center."[27] Thus, to embrace the Eameses' ad hoc Americanisms was unwittingly (pardon the pun) to realign oneself with exactly the provincial qualities of Englishness that Banham—and the young modernists he had influenced with his aggressive early writings—had rejected as complicit with the nostalgic propositions of Townscape and the Festival of Britain.[28] Whether or not they were fully aware of them, such were the disciplinary complexities at play when Foster and the Rogerses returned to London in 1963 to join with the sisters Georgie and Wendy Cheesman (the latter of whom Foster would later marry) and launch their independent practice, Team 4.

Team 4
Early Team 4 commissions included the house at Murray Mews (London, 1965) and the Creek Vean House (Cornwall, 1966), which were completed in traditional materials such as brick and concrete block. While their futuristic, cockpit-like Retreat at Pill Creek (Cornwall, 1964) foreshadowed the High Tech aesthetic the two architects would later pursue in earnest, none of these projects emulates the relaxed disposition and lightweight materials of the Case Study architects. The blank-faced Murray

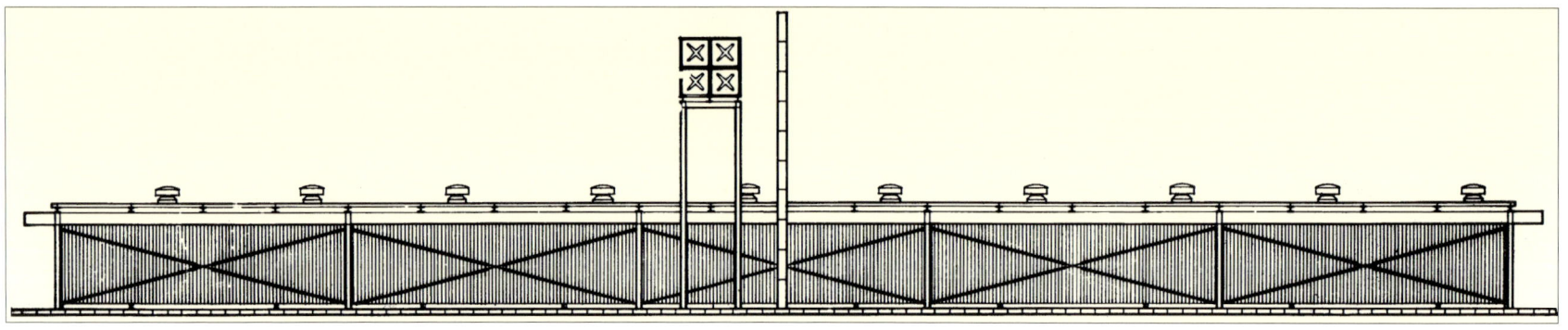

FIG. 4.3 | Team 4 (Norman Foster, British, b. 1935; Wendy Foster [née Cheesman], British, d. 1989; Richard Rogers, British, b. Italy, 1933; Su Rogers [née Brumwell], b. 1939).
Reliance Controls Building (Swindon, England, 1967). Elevation.

FIG. 4.4 | Team 4 (Norman Foster, British, b. 1935; Wendy Foster [née Cheesman], British, d. 1989; Richard Rogers, British, b. Italy, 1933; Su Rogers [née Brumwell], b. 1939).
Reliance Controls Building (Swindon, England, 1967). View of entry.

FIG. 4.5 | Anshen and Allen (Robert Anshen, American, 1910–64; William Steven Allen, American, 1912–92).
Eichler Homes Model E-111 (1959). General view.
Photo by Ernie Braun.

Mews recalled the austere early offerings of the Smithsons, and the Creek Vean House showed affinities to the domestic work of Frank Lloyd Wright.[29] Despite these differences, each project employed crisp angular geometries and generous expanses of glass. Glass roofs were detailed in the manner of greenhouse construction at Murray Mews and sealed with more expensive neoprene gaskets at the two Cornwall projects. Murray Mews was plagued with incessant leaks, and all three projects suffered from the difficulty of traditional construction techniques (and construction crews) to deliver the meticulous precision demanded by their architects.

With the Reliance Controls Building (figs. 4.3, 4.4; see figs. 4.6–4.9, pl. 11), the young architects abandoned the inherent crudeness of traditional materials and methods to embrace the lightweight steel construction and programmatic openness at which they had marveled in Southern California. The project, which came to Team 4 on the recommendation of James Stirling, called for 3,200 square meters of space to accommodate both the assembly and management facilities for an electronics manufacturer. Laid out on a twelve-meter-square grid, the project was enclosed on three sides with the same corrugated metal decking that formed the roof. The fourth side was fully glazed and intended to allow easy future expansion to the north.[30] All cladding was positioned inboard of the perimeter structure, foregrounding the stark white structural steel against subdued gray siding. A symmetrical street elevation comprised five windowless bays, each crossed by diagonal bracing. At the central bay, where a Yale-trained American modernist (or a

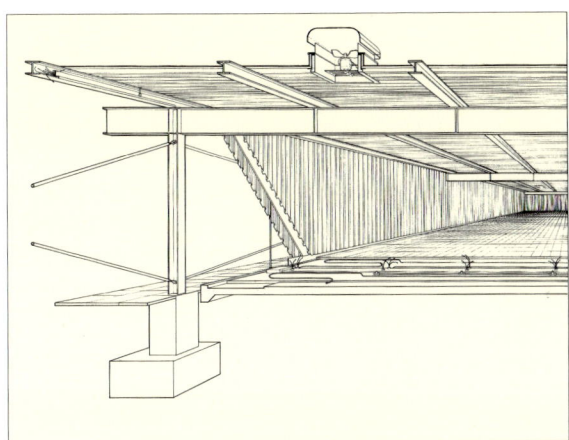
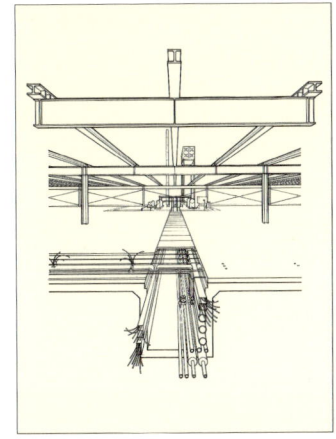
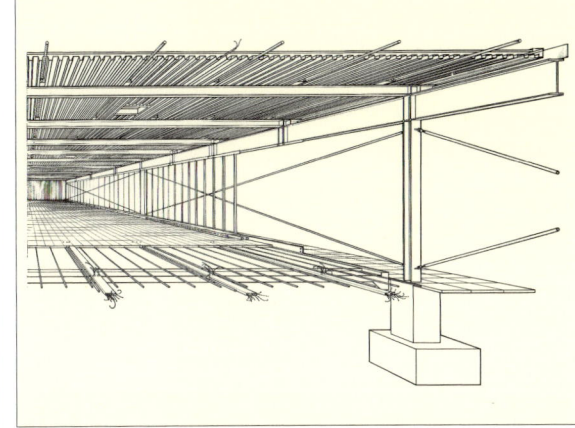

Wittkower-reading English one) might be expected to locate the main entrance, the young architects cheekily placed a mechanical exhaust flue and a cubic water tower as an "homage" to the Smithsons' Hunstanton School (see figs. 4.3, 1.10).[31] The main entry was located around the corner, the lone asymmetrical feature on an otherwise rigidly symmetrical west elevation. The subversion of convention at the entry would return in later projects by Rogers and Foster alike.[32]

The centralized exhaust flue marked the presence of an invisible yet crucial element to the scheme—a service passage running beneath the ground slab along the central north–south axis of the building. From here, mechanical and electrical services (including hot-water pipes to feed the radiant-heating system embedded in the slab) were distributed, while ample space was left for maintenance and the provision of additional service runs to accommodate future expansion. Organized in this manner, the project resonates with the Royal Victoria Hospital in Belfast (see figs. 3.6, 3.7), which Banham soon would celebrate in *The Architecture of the Well-Tempered Environment;* the "endless and indeterminate" projects of Albert Kahn and John Weeks, which Banham had presented in "A Clip-On Architecture"; and, more emphatically, with the California houses designed by Anshen and Allen for developer Joseph Eichler from the 1950s, which Foster undoubtedly would have encountered during his tenure with the firm. Reliance Controls' planned internal atria, opaque street facade, glazed rear facade, frankly exposed structure, curiously extended roof beams, and radiant heating all echo the vocabulary of Eichler homes (fig. 4.5). A. Quincy Jones's widely published steel-framed X-100 house, which Eichler commissioned and built near San Francisco in 1956, also appears to be an important precedent, particularly for its exposed steel framing and roof deck. Baldly emulating another California precedent, Ezra Ehrenkrantz's School Construction Systems Development (SCSD) school prototypes of 1961–63, Team 4 illustrated their integrated approach to structure and services in an oft-republished series of cutaway perspective sections (fig. 4.6).[33]

FIG. 4.6 | Team 4 (Norman Foster, British, b. 1935; Wendy Foster [née Cheesman], British, d. 1989; Richard Rogers, British, b. Italy, 1933; Su Rogers [née Brumwell], b. 1939).
Reliance Controls Building (Swindon, England, 1967). Section perspectives.

 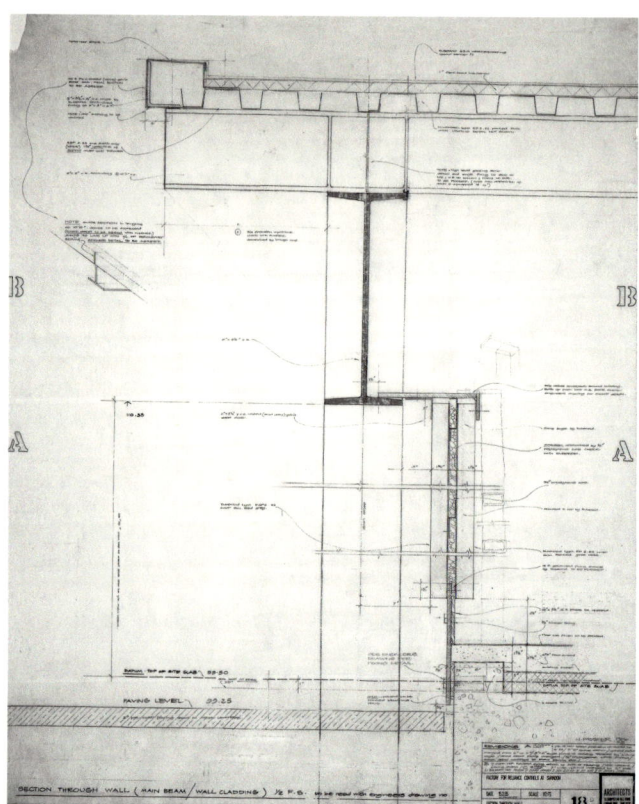

FIG. 4.7 | Team 4 (Norman Foster, British, b. 1935; Wendy Foster [née Cheesman], British, d. 1989; Richard Rogers, British, b. Italy, 1933; Su Rogers [née Brumwell], b. 1939).
Reliance Controls Building (Swindon, England, 1967). Corner detail.

FIG. 4.8 | Team 4 (Norman Foster, British, b. 1935; Wendy Foster [née Cheesman], British, d. 1989; Richard Rogers, British, b. Italy, 1933; Su Rogers [née Brumwell], b. 1939).
Reliance Controls Building (Swindon, England, 1967). Section detail.

Like its entry, the floor plan at Reliance Controls does not resonate with the building's rigid structural and mechanical organization. In keeping with the architects' interest in promoting a nonhierarchical "industrial democracy" in which blue- and white-collar workers were treated equally, programmatic elements were loosely organized within the regular grid.[34] Lightweight partitions were designed for easy reconfiguration, entry and dining facilities were shared by all workers, and liberal amounts of glass maintained visual continuity between office and assembly areas. Both architects would continue to advance such open, flexible planning in subsequent projects.

With these features, Reliance Controls not only swerved away from the "massy, sculptural east coast approach of Rudolph and Chermayeff"[35] but also diverged sharply from the rigid, classicized plans of Mies van der Rohe's midcentury projects in Chicago. Yet, in its fastidious detailing, the work did not quite achieve the fabled casualness of Southern California. At Reliance, twenty-one-inch-deep steel beams sit atop eight-by-eight-inch columns, with eight-by-eight-inch purlins resting on the beams. The symmetrical proportion of the purlins is conspicuously inefficient, but it exactly matched the width of both the columns and beams below (figs. 4.7, 4.8). Prior to delivery to the site, crosshead sections of the beams and purlins—the beams cantilevered one and a half meters beyond the column centerlines; the purlins, eighteen inches—were welded to the columns, with shop-welded gussets reinforcing their webs. Aligned with the flanges of the columns below, the gussets gave the impression that the columns continued uninterrupted through the beams above.[36] After these prewelded assemblies were erected on site, beams were temporarily bolted in place to fill the gaps between the crossheads and additional purlins arranged over the beams at three meters on center. As at the Farnsworth House, these connections were then field-welded, the temporary bolts were removed, and all surfaces were ground smooth.

Intimating that even the Case Study architects were in fact something less than casual, Banham noted that such details display "distinctly Ellwoodian" tendencies, which he illustrated with two large photographs of the mannered column-to-truss connections at Ellwood's Scientific Data Systems Plant in El Segundo, California (1966).[37] Ellwood's columns, cruciform in plan, were built up from standard W-sections; his trusses were assembled from custom-welded square steel tubes and angles. Steel gussets were added throughout to give rectilinear closure to standard steel shapes. In their fastidious combination of standard elements with labor-intensive handicraft, they foreshadow the built-up cruciform columns Mies van der Rohe would use at the New National Gallery in Berlin (1969), and they make the adjective *casual* somewhat difficult to pronounce. Each case demonstrated the familiar story of an architect's stubborn ambition to wring aesthetic sophistication from the limited vocabulary of industrial construction, even at the cost of significant additional complexity, material, and labor.

Contradictions such as these abounded at Reliance. Much has been made, for example, of the project's diagonal bracing on all four sides, even though it was required on only two. Like the redundant gusset plates and overly wide roof purlins deployed to maintain the continuous lines of the structural frame, the bracing betrayed Foster and Rogers's visual agenda.[38] Again, Banham noted that such embellishment of structural necessity for aesthetic reasons could be found in Southern California: "In [the diagonal bracing's] ultimate source, the Eames house, *all* the diagonal bracing were unnecessary in the opinion of the engineers and survived into the built design only because Charles Eames wanted to keep them!"[39]

Unlike his later imitators, Mies distilled the structure of the Farnsworth House to a spare minimalism. The plug-welded connections erased not only the traditional tectonic affiliations to handicraft at the interface between the exposed steel columns and beams but also, owing to the rigid connections throughout, the need for diagonal bracing. Such details, as Cadwell observed, cause the house to "approach the laconic splendor of a line drawing. Specifically, it is perspective drawing that erases any distraction from the persistent thrust of its projecting lines so that the play of house and landscape can unfold unfettered."[40]

Like the Farnsworth House, the Reliance Controls Building betrayed a desire by its architects to achieve the abstract quality of an architectural drawing. But here, the ambition was not Mies's confrontation of interior and landscape through the pervasive distillation of the architecture from physical form to abstract line. Instead, Team 4 amplified the tension between "the persistent thrust of its projecting lines" and the "distractions" caused by the details. Where Mies's details disappear in the act of construction, the complex connections at Reliance demanded expert scrutiny, a level of attentiveness typically instilled in architects as they master the painstaking act of preparing construction drawings.

Notice the overhanging beam-ends on the east and west facades (see fig. 4.4). These superfluous projections were the same cantilevered cross-heads deployed at every column in the building. They signaled the redundancy of standard components and implied the potential extensibility of the project as demanded by the program brief. Nonetheless, budget-conscious purists rightly have questioned their inclusion. Steel in building construction is purchased by weight, and eliminating them would have trimmed approximately 2,700 pounds of it from the project.[41] This represented an insignificant overall savings, but given that Foster later "had the temerity to answer Buckminster Fuller's non-rhetorical question 'But what does your house weigh?' with a detailed weight-breakdown of the Sainsbury Centre,"[42] the extensions have proven troublesome for later apologists. Rowan Moore, in an otherwise hagiographic treatment, admitted that the extensions were "self-conscious, even expressionist."[43] Bryan Appleyard offered the even more understated observation that "the detailing is evidently chosen for reasons other than merely functional."[44]

Whether or not they signaled a lapse in ideological rigor, the beam-ends sponsored a series of highly specific effects that rippled through the building. Observe that they project perpendicular to the axis of extension suggested by both the subgrade mechanical trunk and the north–south orientation of the property. At the north facade, in the direction in which extension was possible, the purlins were composed in a friezelike detail far more indicative of classical closure than indefinite extensibility (see pl. 11).[45] Given the symmetrical column grid of the building, it should not have been an issue to rotate the structure 90 degrees to make five of the offending beam-ends usable in a future extension, but this drastically would have altered the perspectival effects within. As constructed, the purlins were oriented in the extensible direction and are made visually discontinuous by the regular intersections of the larger, lower beams. The tight corrugations of the roof decking and the fluorescent lights seated in them also ran counter to the axis and worked with the primary beams subtly to compartmentalize the interior into layered cross-axial strips. Coupled with the emphatic X-patterns inscribed across the north-facing windows, the elements conspired to impede, rather than encourage, a smooth visual connection between interior and exterior. Where Mies's detailing collapsed landscape and interiors together at the expense of the structure's physicality, Team 4's

tectonic articulation placed their architecture emphatically in between. As the building was demolished in 1991, the effect is best seen in Foster's meticulous renderings, which, with one exception, represent the space in one-point perspective along the main axis (fig. 4.9). Photographers, as evidenced in nearly every published image of the project, routinely oriented their cameras perpendicular to this axis within the lateral slots of space, thus exaggerating the perspectival recession Team 4 apparently aimed to suppress.

Given Banham's indictments against the aesthetic preoccupations of the Smithsons and their allies (*The New Brutalism* had been published just one year previously), one might expect him to have had little patience for the similar pretensions on display at Reliance. And, indeed, he would not comment on the project or its architects for five years. For Banham, this was the era of "Flatscape with Containers" (1967), *The Architecture of the Well-Tempered Environment* (1969), and *Los Angeles: The Architecture of Four Ecologies* (1971)—works that sternly took issue with architecture's status quo. But as the 1970s unfolded, the disciplinary mainstream moved steadily away from modern movement values toward ecological, linguistic, and postmodern concerns. In response, Banham softened his dogged criticism of canonical modern architecture and turned his attention toward the work of a dwindling number of adherents—Foster, Rogers, and Renzo Piano among them—who operated not outside the ken of the modern movement but rather in what remained of its very core. Mainstream modern architecture, once the motivation to seek an "other" architecture, had become the most promising source of its eventual delivery.

FIG. 4.9 | Team 4 (Norman Foster, British, b. 1935; Wendy Foster [née Cheesman], British, d. 1989; Richard Rogers, British, b. Italy, 1933; Su Rogers [née Brumwell], b. 1939).
Reliance Controls Building (Swindon, England, 1967). Interior perspective of early scheme.

Appropriate Tech

Banham's polemical writings of the 1950s and '60s had been sharply critical of orthodox modern architecture. Many took his vociferous attacks on the movement's more damning contradictions (particularly those that kept an architecture of technologically enhanced performance hamstrung by an allegiance to outmoded compositional tropes) to be an indictment of modern architecture as a whole.[46] Yet Banham's texts operated consistently as a corrective to, rather than a condemnation of, modern architecture. Banham's earlier essays were written at a time when modern architecture and the disciplinary establishment were closely aligned and thus easily conflated. In later works, however, as the establishment began to shift away from modernist values, the distinctions came into sharper relief, and Banham's consistent support of modern architecture became clearer. At the same time, his desire for coherent imagery and his simultaneous commitment to technology that seemed to ensure invisibility remained intact, suffusing his late writings with a distinct tension with which he would grapple throughout his final years.

Banham's texts on Norman Foster, the first of which appeared in 1972, demonstrate both the establishment's changing attitudes toward modern architecture and Banham's consistently critical attitudes toward that establishment. In them, Banham focused on the persistent modernist tendencies on display in the work, in particular Foster's deft accommodation of complex programs with lightweight materials and his Miesian distillation of industrial materials into ephemeral, abstract forms. These qualities offered Banham ample opportunity not only to harden his position with respect to modern architecture but also to highlight, often with mischievous relish, damning contradictions in the positions advanced by establishment institutions, such as the Royal Academy of Art and the Royal Institute of British Architects (RIBA), and mainstream publications, such as the *RIBA Journal,* the *Architects' Journal,* and his former employer, the *Architectural Review.*

In 1972, Foster's IBM Pilot Head Office Building (Hampshire, 1971) received an award from the RIBA.[47] Contrasting Reliance Controls, where a meticulously detailed steel frame was monumentalized inside and out, here an uninflected glass envelope offered scant indication of the particularities of structure from outside, while a suspended ceiling discretely masked the structural and mechanical elements within (see pl. 12). In the same issue of the *RIBA Journal* that published Foster's winning scheme, RIBA president Alex Gordon announced the "long life/loose fit/low energy study," a new program aimed at engaging environmental issues.[48] Curiously, the study's ultimate model for environmentally sensitive construction was not an example from the modern canon but was instead the traditional Georgian terrace house.

At first glance, the IBM building does appear less than energy efficient. In the same month that the award was announced in the *RIBA Journal,* the project's minimal exterior details—neoprene gaskets and thin glazing bars between twelve-foot-tall glass panes and an equally spare cap flashing concealing the junction at the roof—were published in the *Architects' Journal*.[49] While many were taken in by the building's restrained elegance, one reader feared the lack of insulation at the coping would lead to condensation and the eventual degradation of the building envelope. Loren Butt, Foster's mechanical engineer and future partner, responded by noting that the circulation of conditioned air through the space eliminated the condensation problem.[50] This prompted Astragal, the anonymous critical pundit whose weekly column ran in the *Architects' Journal,* to attack the project for reliance on round-the-clock air conditioning. "The process," he opined, "can only be extremely wasteful. Foster might now turn his back on lightweights and try to design heavy buildings which have many advantages—including an inbuilt resistance to condensation."[51]

Banham entered the fray the following November. He countered Astragal and the RIBA's automatic embrace of heavy masonry construction by pointing out the propensity for condensation and mold in traditional "Glasgow tenements" and modern "tower blocks" alike.[52] And, as round-the-clock air conditioning was required at IBM to cool the computers it housed, why not, Banham challenged, "take better advantage of the energy that's got be used anyhow?" He went on to criticize each of the tenets of the LL/LF/LE approach. Long Life, he opined, seemed predisposed to litter the landscape with out-of-date buildings at exactly the time that land shortages seemed to call for more frequent building replacement. The Loose Fit of the Georgian terrace house, while mitigating some of the LL issues, appeared to him ill-equipped to accommodate many programs. And finally, LF seemed to undermine the Low Energy ambition, a condition he saw in the Architectural Association's lecture space, which required "a startling amount of electric lights and similar gadgetry" to be loosely fit into the Georgian terrace houses at Bedford Square.[53] Instead of the blunt partisanship of LL/LF/LE, Banham advocated a studied, case-by-case approach, which conveniently came down on the side of Short Life/Tight Fit/High Energy and indicated his own preferences even as he endeavored to give a fairer account of the problem at hand. For Banham, the RIBA's LL/LF/LE study was nothing more than a partisan retrenchment in traditional design; it was less concerned with the sober analysis of the problems of environmental management than with positioning a preselected, neo-Georgian solution. And the group's inherent contradictions, which foreclosed design tactics that might combine traditional and modern methods, were too damaging to be left unchallenged.

Foster would offer exactly such a combination of modern and traditional methods in his 1974 Willis Faber & Dumas Headquarters in Ipswich (fig. 4.10; see figs. 7.1–7.4, pls. 18–20). Clad in a glass skin even more minimal than IBM's, the project drew immediate comparisons to "generic modern" designs.[54] Yet, unlike the suburban

FIG. 4.10 | **Foster Associates (Norman Foster, British, b. 1935).** Willis Faber & Dumas Headquarters (Ipswich, England, 1974). Aerial view. Photo by Mike Page.

boxes at Reliance Controls and IBM, Willis Faber was set down in the heart of a vibrant urban context. In addition, the project eschewed the simple rectilinearity of the earlier works to offer an undulating plan that dutifully follows the irregular curves of the site. Further complicating matters, Foster capped the building with a turf roof. Banham's reaction is telling. Again, he challenged the opinions of the establishment (in this case, the editors of the *Architectural Review*). But rather than focus on details and performance, he made his case in terms of aesthetics. In using the uninflected glass skin, he claimed, the project seemed to adhere to familiar modern conventions. But with its irregular, site-derived massing, the project seems less beholden to the strictures of modern architecture than to the neopicturesque sequences of Townscape.[55]

According to the partisan logic of the day, Banham opined, abstract glass boxes were associated with an indifferent modern architecture that flagrantly consumed scarce energy resources, while looser shapes were associated with "the Contextual, 'herbivore' approach" that had come to be associated with energy conservation. But, as Banham pointed out, the deep floor plates at Willis Faber provided an energy-efficient ratio between enclosing glass and enclosed volume, while the turf roof offered ample insulation. He delighted in this incongruous combination of high modernism and low vernacular: "turf on top of a high-technology building full of air-conditioning, escalators, computers, and stuff? Once again, separate expectations, different architectural languages, have been shotgun-married without apology or regard for the niceties of academic discourse." Much of his pleasure stemmed from the inherent orthodoxy of this apparently ad hoc solution. It was none other than "the true and onlie begetter of the universal, damn-local-traditions, glass-skinned, pure rectangular office block, Le Corbusier himself," he explained, who had "reminded the present century of the roofing virtues of growing turf."[56]

Banham then turned his sights on his former employers at the *Architectural Review*, whose criticism of the building he found "contemptible." Finding little to fault in the building as designed, the editors proposed the possibility of two such buildings: "One Willis Faber and Dumas building may be a revelation, but two facing one another make a prison."[57] For Banham, this was too much. "Come off it!" he retorted, before delivering his stern conclusion:

> Two such facades facing one another would not (just) reflect a lack of craftsmanly detail on both sides of the street but also—as in all facing-mirror situations—the viewer repeated to infinity in both directions. Not only does this flatter the viewer, but it is a form of ego massage which the editors of the *Architectural Review* enjoy all over their editorial offices every day of the work week, for their premises are notoriously the most bemirrored in the business. Perhaps they're just jealous. Perhaps it is not flattering to see a bankrupt ideological position reflected to infinity. Perhaps they should put turf on their heads and see if that looks any better.[58]

Banham regularly combined such careful observation of architectural facts with cheeky criticism of establishment positions in his contributions to *New Society*.[59] A more serious tone can be found in a 1979 treatment of Foster's work in which Banham made a forceful case for the persistence of modern architecture. He opened with a succinct statement of the contemporary condition, which doubled as a tacit response to Charles Jencks, whose *Language of Post-Modern Architecture* was enjoying a successful reception at the time:

> The collapse of the Modern Movement, when it finally happened, proved not to be as much fun as had been anticipated. The brave new post-modern world of stylistic pluralism, popular participation, architecture for its own sake, and all the rest of it, coincided with an economic recession that left the new *avant/arrière-garde* impotent to build. Even so, the most galling aspect of their unrealized millennium must be that "that old modern architecture" survived as the dominant element in the new pluralism, is still producing the best buildings that are actually being built in Europe and North America, and is building them with its mythologies (social, economic, technological) still intact.[60]

FIG. 4.11 | **Foster Associates (Norman Foster, British, b. 1935).** The Sainsbury Centre for Visual Arts (Norwich, England, 1978). General view. Photo by John Donat.

FIG. 4.12 | **Piano + Rogers (Renzo Piano, Italian, b. 1937; Richard Rogers, British, b. Italy, 1933).** Centre Georges Pompidou (Paris, 1977). General view. Photo by Marco Covi.

The essay moves through themes already examined in his earlier treatments of IBM and Willis Faber, including environmental performance, lightweight materials, vernacular sources, the role of style, and relationships to vernacular traditions. Though he considered Foster's work "recognizably stylish," Banham found it was governed not by a particular style or ideology but rather by a consistent attitude toward details and a "series of master-concepts" deployed through lightweight materials. Neither high- nor low-tech, Foster employed what Banham refers to as "appropriate technology" fitted to the task at hand. This method set Foster apart from both "simple-mindedly low-tech" and "woolly-minded high-tech" architects and aligned him with the pragmatic ad hoc approach Banham so often championed. For where both low- and high-tech architects had developed discernible iconographic signals of their ideological allegiances ("windmills and pisé walls" for the former, "highly coloured exposed duct-work" for the latter), Foster's "'appropriate tech' must have whatever is usefully at hand, whatever it may be."[61] Thus, like Buckminster Fuller and Willis Carrier before him, Foster was presented as a boffin-designer who solved problems as they came by the best means available.

Banham went on to praise Foster's unexaggerated offerings at Willis Faber and the Sainsbury Centre for Visual Arts (fig. 4.11). And though Foster offered "everyday ubiquitous, nine-to-five proof that Modern Architecture Lives — and thrives," it was Foster's former partner Richard Rogers, in collaboration with Renzo Piano, who offered "the only monumental building of consequence to go up in Europe in the 1970s": the celebrated Centre Georges Pompidou in Paris.[62] Willis Faber and the Sainsbury Centre, like Foster's earlier IBM building, each advanced an astringent and ephemeral form of modern architecture that approached invisibility. And while these restrained buildings might stand as appropriate models for "nine-to-five" practice, it was Piano + Rogers's monumental work at the Plateau Beaubourg that, for Banham, best demonstrated the enduring efficacy of modern architecture.

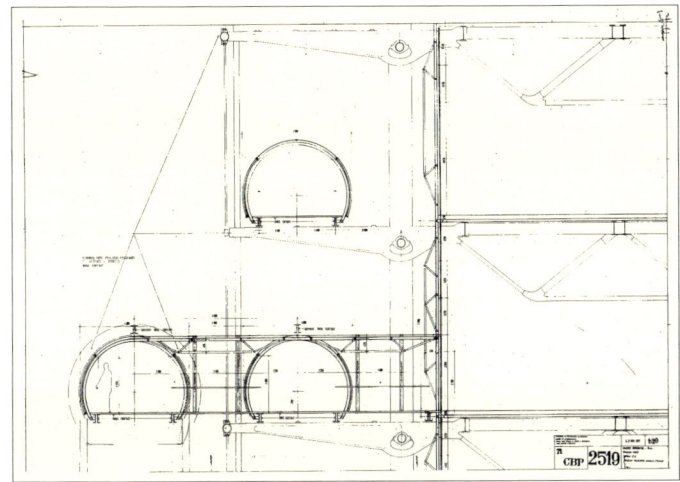

Monumental Tech

A year before the project's completion, Banham provided an important examination of Centre Pompidou (figs. 4.12–4.14; see pl. 13) in *Megastructure: Urban Futures of the Recent Past* (1976). In his assessment, the megastructure movement owed much to Archigram projects such as Peter Cook's Plug-In City, and, with many representative projects in the movement adopting an aesthetic of rough-concrete frames infilled with fine-grain and apparently (if not often actually) interchangeable pieces, it also seemed to absorb many of the qualities associated with the New Brutalism.[63] Banham's treatment of projects by the Archigram group and others in that book are dealt with in a later chapter. At this point in the narrative, it will suffice to point out that Centre Pompidou's boldly exposed structure and mechanical equipment were rendered in the bright hues typical of Archigram projects, and that the project bore a strong resemblance to the radical proposals of the 1960s.[64] Though Banham found it to be "a shade less adventurous than the Fun Palace" and "far less free-form and participatory" than Constant Nieuwenhuys's New Babylon,[65] it secured its place as the culmination of the megastructure movement through its remarkable visual imagery. As he put it, Centre Pompidou "will be perceived to be a megastructure [because] it answers the ultimate acid-test of looking like one."[66]

For Banham, such strong visual qualities were crucial to the megastructure movement. These were "mainly…architectural perceptions," and megastructure, in the end, was fundamentally an architectural problem. The movement's development and ultimate rejection in the wake of 1968, he surmised, did not result from outside forces (whether social, political, or economic) but rather from forces internal to the discipline. Indeed, it appeared to have succumbed to exactly the criticism George Baird had leveled at Eero Saarinen and Cedric Price in 1966.[67] Like Saarinen at CBS, megastructure offered a coherent body of imagery. At the same time, it promised personal freedom and functional flexibility on the order of Price's

FIG. 4.13 | Piano + Rogers (Renzo Piano, Italian, b. 1937; Richard Rogers, British, b. Italy, 1933). Centre Georges Pompidou (Paris, 1977). Section detail.

FIG. 4.14 | Piano + Rogers (Renzo Piano, Italian, b. 1937; Richard Rogers, British, b. Italy, 1933). Centre Georges Pompidou (Paris, 1977). View of gallery (opaque panels in the exterior envelope).

Potteries Thinkbelt Project (see fig. 3.2). This dual ambition laid bare a core paradox: To promise freedom, megastructure needed a legible image, which required a high degree of architectural control. To deliver that freedom, megastructure needed to relinquish control, which necessarily compromised the efficacy of its image. "Megastructure," Banham concluded, "proved to be a self-cancelling concept."[68]

Nonetheless, Banham predicted Centre Pompidou would be a "unique achievement…the only realized monument to some of the best aspirations and most cherished ambitions of the architectural generation to which Piano + Rogers belong—well serviced, adaptable, immensely stylish, an architecture whose main aesthetic virtues will be seen in its performance."[69] Of course, the values he described here were as much his own as anyone's. This fact surely accounts for the pathos that colors Banham's writings of the mid-1970s and '80s, which were published as those values saw decreasing efficacy in global architectural culture. It also helps to explain Banham's slow shift from aggressive critic of the modern establishment in the 1950s and '60s to one of modern architecture's most dependable apologist in the 1970s and '80s.

Centre Pompidou opened to the public on 31 January 1977. In May of that year, the *Architectural Review* dedicated its cover and twenty-four pages to the project, with Banham providing the critical commentary. In a short editorial, the *Review*'s editors described "a *menacing* building which stands like a man in full armour in a room full of civilians" before arriving at a familiar conclusion: "One Centre Pompidou (like one Faber Dumas in Ipswich) is an exhilarating sight; but only contemplate what the centers of our cities would be like if they were chiefly composed of buildings of this kind and you will see what a repellant fix we could be in." The text continued with a dismissal of exactly what Banham had celebrated in the design a year earlier:

> The Centre reflects the supreme moment of technological euphoria in Western society: the moment when we genuinely believed that "freedom" was to be got by providing ourselves with endless power-supplied facility: with servicing which would be so elaborate and so heavily duplicated that you could do anything you want, any where, at any time. We are wiser now; for we know that even if our resources allowed this sort of indulgence, the political machinery we would have to forge to operate it would be so offensive that it would remove true freedom from the face of the earth. This is why there is no reason to expect a multiplicity of Pompidou-like buildings; and why there is no call to agonize too much about the political implications of such a structure.[70]

The *Review*'s admonitions might as well have been directed at Banham himself. For over a decade, Banham had been advocating technologically assisted anywhere/anytime freedom, and had been heaping scorn on establishment pundits who had turned their backs on such ambitions. His *Review* essay holds true to form. Rather than characterize the building as the end of the line (as he had done in *Megastructure*'s melancholy conclusion), he read it as the basis of a resurgent modern architecture that "seems to have taken its revenge on two generations of academic doubters, intellectual Luddites, and all those energetic breast-beaters who nowadays contribute to the comic pages at the beginning of the AR."[71]

Banham's arguments were particularly cunning. Adhering to a pattern he would follow often in his late-career writing, he linked Pompidou tightly to the founding ambitions of the modern movement. But in tracing a genealogy somewhat different from the typical path trod by adherents of the International Style, Banham crafted a version of modern architecture that cleaved much more closely to the aspirations and ambitions of the radical works he had advocated in the 1960s. His argument turned around the question of monumentality, in particular the version of it advanced by Sigfried Giedion, Fernand Léger, and José Luis Sert in their influential essay "Nine Points on Monumentality." Though Giedion had been a stern critic of Archigram and their contemporaries,[72] his 1943 program for monumentality eerily resonated with Centre Pompidou: "Modern materials and new techniques are at hand: light metal structures; curved, laminated wood arches; panels of different textures, colors, and sizes; light elements like ceiling which can be suspended from big trusses covering practically unlimited spans."[73] This, Banham was quick to point out, was not the sort of monumentality that was typically associated with modern architecture in the 1970s, a situation he blamed on Le Corbusier's "increasingly geriatric understanding of monumentality as mere mass and impenetrable substance." While Banham provides a judicious caveat,[74] the point was clear: Piano + Rogers's was "a vision that is quintessential to the Modern Movement."

Turning his attention to Pompidou's relation to megastructure, Banham again distanced the facility's lightweight flexibility from the brooding concrete of other constructed megastructures such as Geoffrey Copcutt's Cumbernauld Town Center (1960). And, in a shotgun wedding that can only be seen as shocking, Banham joined Giedion and Archigram with a separatrix in support of 1960s ambitions: "What sets it [Centre Pompidou] apart from Cumbernauld, however, is its aesthetic—Geoffrey Copcutt's design, however brilliant, was lumbered (willingly, no doubt) with that ponderous Corbusian monumentality of mere mass, whereas Pompidou's Giedion/Archigram transparency and color seem even truer nowadays to the departed aspirations of 'the swinging '60s.'"[75] Having linked Pompidou and Archigram through Giedion to core modern movement values (and nudged Le Corbusier away from them in the process), Banham turned his sights toward more recent impediments to the resurgence of the movement. And like his enlisting of Giedion to his cause, his use of the Centre Pompidou's brash assemblage of mechanistic parts to take a critical swing at Charles Jencks's concept of adhocism is at first blush counterintuitive.

His point turned about the detailing of the Pompidou's glazed enclosure. In the original design, as in the constructed building, mechanical equipment and structural steel were held outside of the glass facades or above the ceilings to provide maximum interior flexibility (see fig. 4.13). While Banham appeared somewhat less than convinced by the complexity of the building's structure, he was blunt in his criticism of modifications to the glass skin required to meet city fire regulations. The original design called for a smooth envelope of curtain-wall glazing slipped behind the main exterior columns. In the final scheme, opaque panels of heat-resistant material were required to be added at each column as well as across the upper portion of the glazing at each floor level (see fig. 4.14). A battery of fire sprinklers and emergency shutters also were added. For Banham, these late additions conspired to ruin the pristine skin promised by the original design.[76] His disapproval was unequivocal: "I find myself stunned that a design team that had poured so much inventiveness into setting up that very pure concept in the first place, should allow it to be ad-hocked to pieces in the last resort." Banham pursued this admonition more broadly in the next section: "Ad-hocism, of course, is somewhat in fashion at present, and will always have a big place in the art of design, but its visible presence at Pompidou is curiously disturbing. It is conspicuously inappropriate to a design which otherwise has avoided manifest compromise."[77]

These are strange lines to come from the author of "A Clip-On Architecture." Indeed, the ad hoc assembly of elements also had been in fashion in the 1960s, and much of the most celebrated work of the period was characterized by the expedient combination of dissonant parts. Of course, Banham had an ambivalent relationship to such tactics even then, and he was always careful to differentiate between visual and programmatic dissonance. Observe his careful early description of Piano + Rogers's second scheme for Pompidou, which "comes closer to Plug-In City in its visible open frames, with communications etc. threaded through them, and even more so in the graphic detailing and the *ad hoc* transient-function implications of the very large presentation drawings that were made for it."[78] Notice that only the "transient-function implications" are described as ad hoc. The "graphic detailing," consistent with Archigram's own, proved to be fastidious, precise, and carefully coordinated.

Banham was quick to celebrate immersive milieus such as the Plateau Beaubourg. Recall, for example, his vivid descriptions of a near-future Paris, in which highway convenience and the urbanity of *Gigi* were combined on the Champs-Elysées;[79] the Fun Palace, in which a "mechanized shrine to *Homo Ludens*" accommodated "political rallies…Greco-Roman wrestling, table tennis, choral song, dervish-dancing, model drag-racing or just goofing and falling about";[80] Archigram's drawings, in which "dolly-girls" twist[ed] and "frug[ged]," families promenaded, children danced, and crowds surged;[81] and the un-house, in which Dionne Warwick sang, protein turned, and cocktails poured in the mechanically enhanced comfort of the great outdoors.[82] Banham delivered some of his most lyrical passages as vibrant carnivals of images and activities held in unlikely proximity by little more than serial commas. Of course, those commas were crucial. Though he often peppered his sentences with neologisms and custom-hyphenated constructions, Banham always respected the grammatical conventions of English usage. Consistently lucid and often exuberant, his writing, like the work he championed, is fastidious, precise, and carefully coordinated. And, as anyone who has attempted to paraphrase it can attest, it is also impressively efficient. Banham was hard on himself when it came to his prose,[83] and he was hard on the subjects of that prose when they failed to live up to the high standards he demanded. Above all, Banham praised precision, efficiency, and thorough coordination in the objects he examined. Adhocism offered an easy shortcut by which to bypass these requirements and thus could only be seen as an offense. While he once might have suggested the rejection of "the accepted rules of architecture—symmetry, unity, coherence, balance, and all of those,"[84] Banham would never relinquish his taste for efficiency, rigor, and conviction.

These qualities, for the most part, were what he found at Centre Pompidou. And it was these qualities that raised the enigmatic questions with which Banham concluded his essay. One question was operational. For if the facility had been commissioned and designed to accommodate adaptable flexibility, critics could no longer hold the architects solely responsible for the work's quality, "the question of management will qualify all attempts to judge whether the Centre is functionally adequate."[85] The other question was symbolic: "Centre Pompidou is clearly a monument, a very permanent monument presenting what is already a fixed image to outward view, and few of the routine modifications that might be adapted to its services and other externals is likely to have much effect on that fixed image of transparency and tracery, bright color and mechanical equipment. But can one have a permanent image of change?" The question encapsulated a central paradox of High Tech architecture as well as Banham's own writing—a contradictory drive to cleave to the monumental values of traditional architecture and simultaneously to advance an "other" set of values characterized by flexibility and change. On one hand, he sought a fixed and indelible image, on the other, the fleeting, ephemeral traces of incessant transformation. For Banham, "the problem is one that has fascinated philosophers and poets as long as language has been able to distinguish the two concepts, but it has troubled architectural theory only since the Futurists at the beginning of the present century decided to celebrate the impermanence of technology."[86] By driving adaptability so deeply into the fabric of the structure,

Piano + Rogers had unleashed a powerful new image on the Parisian milieu and had pressed the question into uncharted territory. Returning once more to the Centre Pompidou's persistent modernism, Banham concluded with what, depending on one's stylistic allegiances, can be taken as easily for a premonition as a hedge: "If that fixed image can retain its present power until, say, the century's end, Centre Pompidou will prove to have succeeded in one of the most teasing but central tasks that were in the unwritten (*pace* Giedion) programme of the Modern Movement."[87]

NOTES

1. Colin Davies cited the Reliance Controls Building as High Tech's first building, with the Bathroom Tower as a "close rival for the title." See Colin Davies, *High Tech Architecture* (New York: Rizzoli, 1988), 19. Peter Buchanan, another important early chronicler of the movement, credited the Bathroom Tower with inaugurating the movement. See Peter Buchanan, "High-Tech: Another British Thoroughbred," *Architectural Review* 174 (1983): 15–19.
2. See "Unconventional Combinations: A Clip-On Architecture," this volume.
3. Smithson and Price were members of the AA faculty through the late 1950s and into the 1960s, while Reyner Banham was a frequent presence as a studio jury critic. All three would prove influential to Rogers, Grimshaw, and company. Peter Cook began teaching at the AA shortly after his graduation in 1960, one year after Rogers finished but in time to instruct Grimshaw and Hopkins. For illuminating reflections on the culture of the AA from Banham, Cook, Price, Smithson, and other figures, including Warren Chalk, Charles Jencks, and Martin Pawley, see James Gowan, ed., *A Continuing Experiment: Learning and Teaching at the Architectural Association* (London: Architectural Press, 1975).
4. Foster's remarks on his Willis Faber and Dumas Headquarters building provide a typical example of such rhetoric: "The invitation to write about the philosophy/approach behind the Willis Faber building…provided an opportunity to set down the value judgements behind the design which are social—generated by people rather than the hardware of buildings.… Another vital part of the approach is a conscious attempt to put all those dry objective pieces of the jigsaw (research, statistics, cost plan, site analysis, structural options—the check list is endless) together with some very subjective joy. It certainly doesn't cost any more, so why not?" See Norman Foster, "The Design Philosophy of the Willis Faber + Dumas Building in Ipswich," *Architectural Design* 47 (1977): 614.
5. See "Savage Minds and the Well-Tempered Environment," this volume.
6. For the quintessential indictment of modern architecture for its complicity with capital, see Manfredo Tafuri, "Toward a Critique of Architectural Ideology" [1969], in *Architecture Theory since 1968*, ed. K. Michael Hays (Cambridge, MA: MIT Press, 1998), 6–35. For a more recent text in which High Tech architecture is criticized along these lines, see Ignasi de Solà-Morales, "High Tech: Functionalism or Rhetoric" [1992], in idem, *Differences: Topographies of Contemporary Architecture,* ed. Sarah Whiting (Cambridge, MA: MIT Press, 1997), 117–31.
7. See Charles Jencks, "Late-Modernism and Post-Modernism," in idem, *Late-Modern Architecture* (New York: Rizzoli, 1980), 10–30.
8. See Prince Charles's speech to the RIBA on 30 May 1984: http://www.princeofwales.gov.uk/media/speeches/speech-hrh-the-prince-of-wales-the-150th-anniversary-of-the-royal-institute-of.
9. Both buildings, though completed well before the term *High Tech* saw widespread application to architecture, would routinely be included in the High Tech canon, which historians and critics began to assemble in the early 1980s.
10. Rogers was awarded a Fulbright Scholarship, and Foster, the Henry Fellowship. Su Rogers was admitted to study urban planning at Yale University. For biographical treatments of Rogers's and Foster's early years, see Bryan Appleyard, *Richard Rogers—A Biography* (London: Faber & Faber, 1986); Deyan Sudjic, *Norman Foster: A Life in Architecture* (London: Weidenfeld & Nicolson, 2010); and Richard Rogers, "Team 4," in Norman Foster, *Norman Foster: Team 4 and Foster Associates; Buildings and Projects,* vol. 1, 1964–73, ed. Ian Lambot (Hong Kong: Watermark, 1989), 14–15.
11. See Sigfried Giedion, "The New Monumentality," in *New Architecture and City Planning,* ed. Paul Zucker (New York: Philosophical Library, 1944), reprinted as Sigfried Giedion, "The Need for a New Monumentality," in idem,

Architecture, You, and Me: The Diary of a Development (Cambridge, MA: Harvard University Press, 1958), 25–39.

12 Appleyard, *Richard Rogers,* 96.

13 Rogers, "Team 4," 14.

14 Chermayeff (1900–1996) was a Russian-born, English-educated architect and a member of the Modern Architectural Research (MARS) group, the British wing of the Congrès internationaux d'architecture moderne (CIAM). According to Rogers, Chermayeff "was as academic and European as Rudolph was visual and American." Rogers, "Team 4," 14.

15 Rogers, "Team 4," 14.

16 Reyner Banham, "Klarheit, Ehrlichkeit, Einfachkeit…and Wit, Too! The Case Study Houses in the World's Eyes," in *Blueprints for Modern Living: History and Legacy of the Case Study Houses,* ed. Elizabeth A. T. Smith (Cambridge, MA: MIT Press, 1989), 183–95.

17 Banham, "Klarheit, Ehrlichkeit, Einfachkeit," 185.

18 See "Apartmenthaus mit vier Wohnungen in Hollywood," *Bauen und Wohnen* 2 (April 1955): 91. Lohse (1902–88) had been an editor for the Swiss magazine from 1947 to 1956.

19 Banham, "Klarheit, Ehrlichkeit, Einfachkeit," 185–86.

20 Esther McCoy, *Modern California Houses: Case Study Houses, 1945–1962* (New York: Reinhold, 1962).

21 Banham, "Klarheit, Ehrlichkeit, Einfachkeit," 189.

22 Michael Cadwell, *Strange Details* (Cambridge, MA: MIT Press, 2007), 113.

23 Reyner Banham, "On Trial 4: CLASP: Ill-Met by Clip-Joint?," *Architectural Review* 131 (1962): 349. Banham disagreed with these assessments in the essay, and found most CLASP details to work well both functionally and visually.

24 Semper, for example, saw the essence of architecture in the joints between materials (an observation he gleaned from studying a model Caribbean dwelling at the 1851 Great Exhibition in London). Laugier saw it in the traces of assembly evident in trabeated construction that linked classical and contemporary works to the mythical primitive hut. See Gottfried Semper, "The Four Elements of Architecture" [1851], in idem, *The Four Elements of Architecture and Other Writings* (Cambridge: Cambridge University Press, 2010); and Marc-Antoine Laugier, *An Essay on Architecture* [1753] (Los Angeles: Hennessey & Ingalls, 1977).

25 On the other hand, CLASP represents an extreme instantiation of English architects' core pragmatism and capacity for boffinesque invention.

26 Banham quoted this passage from Michael Brawne, "The Wit of Technology," *Architectural Design* 36 (1966): 449–57, in Banham, "Klarheit, Ehrlichkeit, Einfachkeit," 186. Brawne's essay was part of "An Eames Celebration," a full issue of *Architectural Design* dedicated to the Eameses and spearheaded by the Smithsons.

27 Nikolaus Pevsner, "The Englishness of English Art" [1955], in idem, *Pevsner on Art and Architecture: The Radio Talks,* ed. Stephen Games (London: Methuen, 2002), 204–5.

28 See Reyner Banham, "Revenge of the Picturesque: English Architectural Polemics, 1945–1965," in *Concerning Architecture: Essays on Architectural Writers and Writing Presented to Nikolaus Pevsner,* ed. John Summerson (London: Penguin, 1968), 265–73; and Reyner Banham, "The Style: 'Flimsy…Effeminate'?," in *A Tonic to the Nation: The Festival of Britain 1951,* ed. Mary Banham and Bevis Hillier (London: Thames & Hudson, 1976), 190–98.

29 See Appleyard, *Richard Rogers,* 117–19; and Brian Hatton, "Creek Vean House," in Foster, *Norman Foster,* 1:40.

30 Note that while fig. 4.3 and pl. 11 depict the south facade of the Reliance Controls Building, the north facade is detailed similarly, with the exception that the vertical metal siding shown in the image would have been floor-to-ceiling glass.

31 Foster, *Norman Foster,* 1:77.

32 As outlined in "Unconventional Combinations: A Clip-On Architecture," this volume, Rogers's Zip-Up Enclosures similarly deployed symmetrical, axial arrangements with entries located seemingly arbitrarily on the side elevation. Foster would set up and then subvert classical expectations at, among other examples, the 1978 Sainsbury Centre in Norwich, England, where the entry also is punched through the side, and at the Hong Kong and Shanghai Bank Headquarters, which admits and disgorges visitors via splayed escalators that slice through the raised atrium's glazed underbelly.

33 Ezra Ehrenkrantz (1932–2001) was a strong influence on Foster and Rogers and routinely is cited in the literature on the two architects. For Banham's remarks, see Banham, "Klarheit, Ehrlichkeit, Einfachkeit," 193; and Reyner Banham, "Introduction," in *Foster Associates,* by Norman Foster (London: RIBA, 1979), 5. David Jenkins provides a useful treatment in "Factory Systems," in Foster, *Norman Foster,* 1:100–105. Notice that the right-hand portion of fig. 4.6 is oriented perpendicular to the main axis of the building.

34. Rowan Moore, "Reliance Controls," in Foster, *Norman Foster,* 1:77. Compare with Rogers's similar approach in the DRU Conversion discussed in "Unconventional Combinations: A Clip-On Architecture," this volume.
35. Moore, "Reliance Controls," 76.
36. The beam and purlin sections did in fact continue uninterrupted over the top of the columns. At the purlins, the double gussets changed direction to reinforce the purlins' webs but, given the matched widths of all elements, maintained the continuous line of the column flange through to the roof deck. *NB:* The double gussets occurred only at the beam lines. Where purlins rested on the beams between columns, only a single gusset plate was provided.
37. Banham, "Klarheit, Ehrlichkeit, Einfachkeit," 190–93.
38. The structural engineer describes the situation as follows: "Of course, the point that I always have to answer for now is the multiple cross-bracing.... I am still a little embarrassed: it is not a 'pure' structure, so the engineer in me can never be entirely satisfied. The designer in me, however, tends to agree it makes the building look better." He goes on to describe the simultaneous presence of an equal and opposite condition: "The real irony—and for me a far more difficult problem—was that Norman, who had used all his charm to persuade me to accept multiple cross-bracing for the building, then decided the water tower would be better without it. As a very tall, very slender portal frame, this really did present some problems." Tony Hunt, "In the Beginning," in Foster, *Norman Foster,* 1:146.
39. Banham, "Klarheit, Ehrlichkeit, Einfachkeit," 192, Banham's emphasis.
40. Cadwell, *Strange Details,* 115.
41. Ten beam-ends at 1.5 meters = 15 meters (49'-2") × 55 lb./ft. (the weight specified in the published construction details) = 2704.17 pounds.
42. Banham, "Introduction," 4. A recent documentary further accentuates Foster's attentiveness to quantitative efficiencies. See *How Much Does Your Building Weigh, Mr. Foster,* directed by Norberto López-Amado and Carlos Carcas (Spain: Aiete Ariane Films, 2010). Foster's biographer, Deyan Sudjic, similarly employs the phrase as a chapter title in *Norman Foster: A Life in Architecture* (London: Weidenfeld & Nicolson, 2010).
43. Moore, "Reliance Controls," 83.
44. Appleyard, *Richard Rogers,* 129–30. Banham also cites this passage, before noting the irony of Charles Eames's similarly superfluous cross bracing. See Banham, "Klarheit, Ehrlichkeit, Einfachkeit," 192.
45. Of course, these purlins could be spliced in a building extension in the same manner as the beam-ends on the east and west facades. While these members comprise approximately 2,200 pounds of steel (42 beam-ends at 18" = 63'-0" × 35 lb./ft. = 2,205 lb.), they also serve to carry the roof overhang and are therefore justified structurally in a way the longer beam-ends are not.
46. See, for example, reviews of *The Architecture of the Well-Tempered Environment* by James Marston Fitch, "Review of *The Architecture of the Well-Tempered Environment,*" *Journal of the Society of Architectural Historians* 29 (1970): 282–84; and John Kouwenhoven, "Architecture as Environmental Technology," *Technology and Culture* 11, no. 1 (1970): 85–93.
47. See "Architecture Awards 1972," *RIBA Journal* 79, no. 7 (1972): 276. The project was featured on the cover of the issue.
48. See "Forward to First Principles," *RIBA Journal* 79, no. 7 (1972): 268.
49. See "Working Detail no. 408," *Architects' Journal,* 12 July 1972, 97–98.
50. Loren Butt, "Insulation and Condensation," letter to the editor, *Architects' Journal,* 16 August 1972, 350–51. Butt wrote in response to John I. P. Bradfield, "Environmental Performance Data," letter to the editor, *Architects' Journal,* 9 August 1972, 297. Banham mistakenly cited the date of Bradfield's letter as 19 July 1972 in Banham, "LL/LF/LE v. Foster," *New Society* 22, no. 527 (1972): 344.
51. Astragal, "Yes Butt...," *Architects' Journal,* 23 August 1972, 409, quoted in Reyner Banham, "LL/LF/LE," 344.
52. Banham, "LL/LF/LE," 344.
53. Banham, "LL/LF/LE," 345.
54. "Ipswich Reflections," *Architectural Review* 158 (1975): 131.
55. Reyner Banham, "Grass Above, Glass Around," *New Society* 42, no. 783 (1977): 22–23, reprinted in Reyner Banham, *A Critic Writes: Essays by Reyner Banham,* ed. Mary Banham (Berkeley: University of California Press, 1996), 208.
56. Banham, "Grass Above," 210.
57. "Ipswich Reflections," 132, quoted in Banham, "Grass Above," 211.
58. Banham, "Grass Above," 211.
59. Again using Foster's work as a catalyst, Banham later would poke fun at the contradictory implications of the

conservative London Royal Academy's displaying a full-scale construction mock-up from the Hong Kong and Shanghai Bank Headquarters. See Reyner Banham, "The Thing in the Forecourt," *New Society* 65, no. 1080 (1983): 138–39.

60   Banham, "Introduction," 4.
61   Banham, "Introduction," 5.
62   Banham, "Introduction," 4.
63   For a solid treatment of the megastructure movement and Banham's interpretation of it, see Sarah Deyong, "The Creative Simulacrum in Architecture: Megastructure, 1953–1972" (PhD diss., Princeton University, 2008).
64   This was especially true of the drawings for the second version of the scheme, which were made largely by members of the Chrysalis group—former UCLA students who had studied under Peter Cook in the late 1960s and were recruited to staff Piano + Rogers's Paris office. As Simon Sadler noted, the original competition images had been prepared in a spare, reticent style more akin to the drawings of Cedric Price. See Simon Sadler, *Archigram: Architecture without Architecture* (Cambridge, MA: MIT Press, 2005), 162–67.
65   Reyner Banham, *Megastructure: Urban Futures of the Recent Past* (New York: Harper & Row, 1976), 211.
66   Banham, *Megastructure,* 212–14.
67   See "Savage Minds and the Well-Tempered Environment," this volume.
68   Banham, *Megastructure,* 216.
69   Reyner Banham, "Piano + Rogers' Architectural Method," *Architecture + Urbanism* 6, no. 6 (1976): 65.
70   "The Pompidolium," *Architectural Review* 161 (1977): 272, emphasis in the original.
71   Reyner Banham, "Enigma of the Rue du Renard," *Architectural Review* 161 (1977): 277.
72   See Sigfried Giedion, *Space, Time, and Architecture,* 5th ed. (Cambridge, MA: Harvard University Press, 1967), 586.
73   Sigfried Giedion, José Luis Sert, and Fernand Léger, "Nine Points on Monumentality" [1943], in Giedion, *Architecture, You, and Me,* 50. Banham quoted a portion of this passage (and cunningly edited around Giedion's mention on wooden arches) in Banham, "Enigma," 277.
74   "This is not to say that Giedion's vision of lightweight, highly coloured, mobile elements is necessarily more valid or valuable than Corb's latter-day Bismarckisms." Banham, "Enigma," 277.
75   Banham, "Enigma," 277.
76   To my eye, the heavy secondary structure and mullions that support the glass (especially the exterior trusses that brace the mullions) make it difficult to imagine a pristine glazed enclosure even without the heat-resistant panels. Nonetheless, they are the only opaque, vertical, planar elements in the building envelope, and do introduce a distracting patchwork quality to the interior of some of the galleries.
77   Banham, "Enigma," 278.
78   Banham, *Megastructure,* 212, Banham's emphasis.
79   Reyner Banham, "1960—Stocktaking," *Architectural Review* 127 (1960): 100.
80   Reyner Banham, "A Clip-On Architecture," *Design Quarterly* 63 (1965): 13.
81   Banham, *Megastructure,* 100–101. For a discussion, see "Architecture beyond Building," this volume.
82   Reyner Banham, "A Home Is Not a House," in *Meaning in Architecture,* ed. Charles Jencks and George Baird (New York: George Braziller, 1969), 133.
83   "The misery (and splendour) of such writing, when it is exactly on target, is to be incomprehensible by the time the next issue comes out—the splendour comes, if at all, years and years later, when some flip, throw-away, smarty-pants, look-at-me paragraph will prove to distill the essence of an epoch far better than subsequent scholarly studies ever can." Reyner Banham, "Foreword," in *Design by Choice,* ed. Penny Sparke (New York: Rizzoli, 1981), 7.
84   Banham, "A Clip-On Architecture," 7.
85   Banham, "Enigma," 278. Nine years later, Banham returned to Paris to weigh in on exactly this question, chastising commentators for leveling unwarranted criticism at the architects for problems that lay with the institution's management and curatorial staff. These last he went on to berate for their lax maintenance, for their timid engagement of the facility's flexibility, and for commissioning a particularly damaging permanent installation by Gae Aulenti, which, to Banham, seemed to undermine Piano + Rogers's modernist ambitions. See Reyner Banham, "Art Space Angst," *New Society* 75, no. 1204 (1986): 152–53.
86   Banham, "Enigma," 278.
87   Banham, "Enigma," 278.

CHAPTER 5

MAKING ARCHITECTURE
THE ETHICS OF HIGH TECH

With Centre Georges Pompidou, High Tech architecture had come into maturity. But while the Pompidou and other major High Tech buildings garnered extensive individual coverage in architectural periodicals and occasionally in the popular press, general literature on the movement is scarce. Attempts to provide an assessment of High Tech as a whole are limited to a single hardback account and a handful of articles dating to the 1980s. With unusual consistency, these texts tend to be structured around thematic oppositions that pit, among other pairings, visual style against functional performance, monumentality against flexibility, classical sources against Gothic precedents, even building against architecture. Thus organized, these texts rehearse dialectics at play in Centre Pompidou as they mirror the structure of many of Reyner Banham's own late writings, including *Making Architecture: The Paradoxes of High Tech*. A draft introduction to this unfinished book, along with project correspondence and notes, is kept with the Reyner Banham papers, held at the Getty Research Institute in Los Angeles. Read alongside previous publications on the architects and buildings he intended to examine as well as course notes and lecture transcripts from his final years, these archival materials offer a rough indication of the form and content Banham intended for that work as they elucidate the disciplinary stakes, tectonic preoccupations, theoretical complexities, and paradoxical implications that color High Tech architecture.

High Tech Literature
Though high-technology themes often were associated with the work of Norman Foster, Richard Rogers, Renzo Piano, and others throughout the 1970s, High Tech would not be deployed as a stylistic category until 1978, a year after Centre Pompidou opened.[1] That year saw the publication of Joan Kron and Suzanne Slesin's *High-Tech: The Industrial Style and Source Book for the Home*, the first book to use the

Richard Rogers Partnership (Richard Rogers, British, b. Italy, 1933).
Inmos Microprocessor Factory (Newport, Wales, 1982). General view (detail).
Photo by Ken Kirkwood.
See p. 156, fig. 5.7.

phrase in its title.² The book is largely a style catalog for interior design that favors industrial elements deployed ad hoc within domestic and corporate milieus.³ Peter Buchanan, an editor at the *Architectural Review* throughout the early 1980s, provided a series of useful interpretations.⁴ In an echo of Banham's assessment of the New Brutalism, he argued that High Tech began as a promising "anti-art" mode driven primarily by "process" toward "indeterminacy," and then it matured into a "high art" pursuit of elegant architectural assemblies. Rehearsing Banham's portrayal of the megastructure movement, he saw High Tech tending simultaneously toward operational freedom and stylistic control. The movement, he claimed, was heading either to an "arcadian" extreme in which "the building evaporates" (he offered Banham's musings in "A Home Is Not a House" as an example) or to a "utopian" one that, in its pursuit of ultimate flexibility in long-span structures, paradoxically results in little more than monumental rhetoric (as he read Centre Pompidou).⁵ In another assessment, he outlined a "vitalist" camp that used technology primarily as an alibi for formal elaboration (a line that begins with James Stirling and develops toward Foster and Rogers) and a "lifestyle" group extending from Archigram and Cedric Price that sought to deploy technology to enhance the social situation.⁶ Echoing George Baird's dismissal of "total architecture" and "life conditioning,"⁷ Buchanan rejected both approaches. His assessments were ultimately skeptical. High Tech, for him, was "a shallowly conceived and deeply alienating project."⁸

In 1978, Charles Jencks coined the term "Late-Modern architecture" to distinguish more orthodox contemporary practices from emerging postmodern positions, and he included "High-Tech" among a collection of subcategories he outlined within the idiom.⁹ Reacting against the polarized debate on High Tech in England in a 1988 text, Jencks dispassionately tallied the movement's formal characteristics.¹⁰ Though he ultimately favored the postmodern works he had championed throughout his career, Jencks supported the continued development of High Tech. A robust and multifaceted debate on style, he reasoned, signaled a vital, interesting, and ultimately democratic architectural culture.

Colin Davies's 1988 book, *High Tech Architecture,* stands as an emphatic punctuation mark to the literature. In his introductory essay, he provided both a long-range history, which stretches back to Abraham Darby III's Iron Bridge (1779) near Coalbrookdale, England, and a short-range one, which stemmed from the radical architects of the 1960s. Familiar long-range precedents such as the Crystal Palace, the Eiffel Tower, and various nineteenth-century halls were recounted, as were more recent works by the Archigram group, Pierre Chareau, Buckminster Fuller, Cedric Price, and Jean Prouvé. The short-range history divided neatly into an inaugural period marked by the Reliance Controls Building and the Bathroom Tower, a middle period around Centre Pompidou, and a waning phase signaled by Foster's

Hong Kong and Shanghai Bank Headquarters (fig. 5.1; see pl. 14) and Richard Rogers's Lloyd's of London building (fig. 5.2; see fig. 5.15). An important discussion turned about construction details, with Piano's complex bolted connections standing in stark contrast to Foster's minimal neoprene gaskets. Like previous commentators, he noted High Tech's particularly British inflections, as well as the movement's difficult tensions between technique and style, operative flexibility and formal legibility, revolution and continuity. Importantly, Davies treated High Tech as a completed project. In a Jencksian twist, he even provided a precise date for the "death of the High Tech style"—28 January 1986, the day the space shuttle Challenger, a significant symbol of contemporary culture's embrace of technology, exploded due to "the failure of a Neoprene gasket."[11]

FIG. 5.1 | Foster Associates (Norman Foster, British, b. 1935).
Hong Kong and Shanghai Bank Headquarters (Hong Kong, 1986).
General view.
Photo by Ian Lambot.

FIG. 5.2 | Richard Rogers Partnership (Richard Rogers, British, b. Italy, 1933).
Lloyd's of London (London, 1986).
General view.
Photo by Stephen Rogers.

Other writings on High Tech tend toward largely hagiographic monographs on the work of Foster, Piano, Rogers, and Nicholas Grimshaw, and occasional attacks by critics such as Prince Charles, Léon Krier, Joseph Rykwert, and others.[12] A few positive and negative gems exist, but in large part, High Tech passed from architectural conversation after 1988.[13] Despite the early posturing of Jencks and Banham, by the late 1980s, postmodern architecture's significant stylistic adversary was no longer High Tech but rather deconstructivist architecture.[14] Even throughout the 1970s, High Tech architects rarely entered the critical fray. While the Whites and the Grays sparred in the American architectural journals over theoretical projects and small-scale residential work,[15] High Tech architects in Europe quietly went about the business of putting up major buildings in cities around the world.

Making Architecture: The Paradoxes of High Tech
With extended treatments by Jencks and Davies, 1988 was the banner year for High Tech publication. In March of that year, Reyner Banham died of cancer. In the months leading up to his death, he had been at work on his own book-length assessment of the movement. Though the final form and specific content of the book remained unsettled, Banham offered his "current thinking on the subject" in a letter to his publisher and an attached summary, outline, and draft introductory chapter.[16]

In the summary, Banham established Centre Pompidou as "A Monument of Definition."[17] From it, he gleaned five "canonical characteristics," which he developed as the "Elements and Origins of the Canon." The first, wide-span construction connected High Tech to "the most central tradition of the modern movement, one which has the warrant of [Peter] Behrens, [Eugène] Freyssinet, Fuller, [Ludwig] Mies van der Rohe among designers, and [Sigfried] Giedion, [Nikolaus] Pevsner, and others among writers."[18] Next, he pointed out the necessity of a "high level of mechanical servicing," which, as he had argued in *The Architecture of the Well-Tempered Environment,* "has no such place in the explicit traditions of the modern movement, in spite of the fact that most modern buildings would be un-inhabitable without it." The third characteristic, "expressed structure," raised questions about the nature of architecture's interactions with engineering practice, while the fourth, "exhibiting the services," seemed to represent "a very different achievement, and one for which the architects are almost solely responsible." The culmination of these factors resulted in "the invention of a unified aesthetic for structure and services" with roots deep in the modern movement.[19]

Banham's intent to concentrate on visual style is apparent throughout. "The crucial stages in accommodating the art of architecture to advances in technology," he opined, "have always been *stylistic.*"[20] In the modern movement, it was Mies van der Rohe who "establishe[d] the kind of standard by which most other architectural excursions into higher technology are judged."[21] For while "[Auguste] Perret forced an old aesthetic on concrete, and Le Corbusier forced a new one on it, Mies discovered a new mode of expression within steel construction."[22] Working in the same manner but with different technologies, High Tech architects seemed to offer the possibility of once again discovering a new aesthetic in the expression of mechanical services. Yet, as he argued in a section on "An Opposite Case," such reasoning failed to account for a project such as Foster's Willis Faber & Dumas Headquarters, "which reveals nothing at all of its structure or workings, and yet tends to get classified as High Tech." Suggesting that recent computer-controlled "Smart Buildings" might indicate the terrain for architecture's next engagement with high technology, he suggested these projects "may prefigure an even higher form of High Tech."[23]

In a final section, on the "Scope of the Study," he outlined his intention to examine existing literature on High Tech, larger issues pertaining to modernism in general, and "hostile commentary by supporters of the Post-Modernist position." For Banham, High Tech and modernism were intertwined and require parallel exposition. High Tech, he concluded, "has raised questions that are fundamental both to Modernism and to Architecture."[24]

Thus, Banham planned a book sharply differentiated from the writings of previous commentators. Where Kron and Slesin saw the superficial trappings of a fashionable new decorative idiom, Banham saw profound implications for the history of modern architecture. Where Buchanan described a regional movement of primarily British extraction, Banham intended to portray a global phenomenon with important American, French, and German ancestors and significant practitioners at work around the globe. And where Jencks found a nostalgic maintenance of modernist stylistic tropes that paled in comparison to the broad semantic pluralism of postmodern architecture, Banham saw an important swerve away from orthodox habits that developed an "alternative Modernism" out of new technologies.[25] As the draft introduction Banham prepared for the book makes clear, he saw in High Tech an architecture that paradoxically maintained close ties to the ideologies of the modern movement yet diverged from certain of its principles to suggest a manner of working that might overcome modern architecture's deficiencies to stand in staunch resistance to postmodern architecture.

High Tech and Advanced Engineering

In his characteristic style, Banham outlined in his introduction the terminology, characteristics, and core complexities of High Tech architecture. His opening comparison between the skillfully styled but more or less conventional Salomon ski boot (fig. 5.3) and the Moulton AM 7 bicycle (fig. 5.4), which, he claimed, rejected

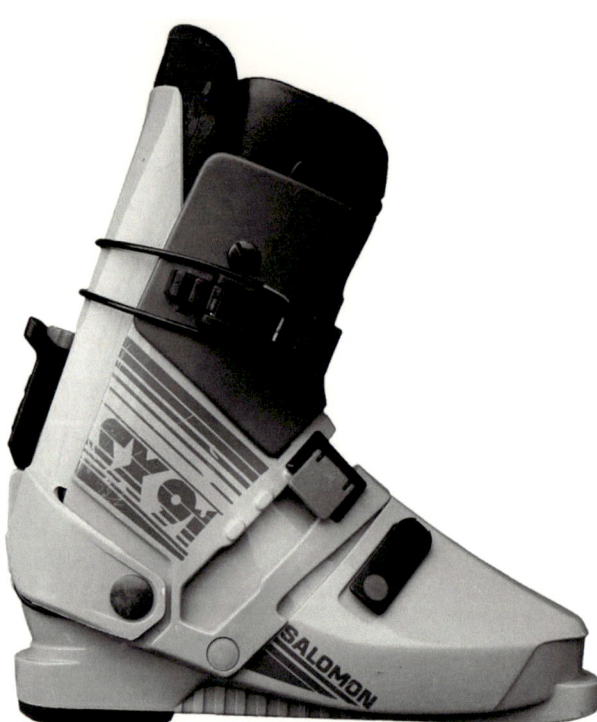

"self-conscious decision about what style to employ,"[26] baldly signaled his allegiance, as it is well known that Banham had been an avid cyclist and proud Moulton owner throughout his adult life.[27] Regardless of any bias implicit in the comparison, the complex interplay of visual style and actual performance was crucial to Banham's understanding of High Tech.

A lengthy comparison of two representative buildings, Dewhurst Haslam Partnership's United Kingdom headquarters for Porsche (Reading, 1986) (fig. 5.5) and Foster Associates' Warehouse and Distribution Center for Renault (Swindon, 1983) (fig. 5.6), demonstrated the wide range of stylistic possibilities in High Tech. Porsche, Banham noted, aligned neatly with established characteristics of what he termed "Modern architecture of the International Style."[28] This pivot from modern architecture in general toward the more specific International Style was crucial. Throughout his career, Banham was highly attentive to specific subcategories within modern architecture, such as futurism, expressionism, and constructivism, which he focused on in *Theory and Design in the First Machine Age,* and the New Brutalism, clip-on, megastructure, and High Tech, which were the focus of numerous texts from the 1950s to the '80s. Over the course of his career, Banham marshaled each of these minor modern movements into his cause of charting an alternative trajectory into the immediate future to the one outlined under the banner of International Style, which Banham saw as the modern movement's primary inflection. Distinguishing the International Style as something *less than* the modern movement as a whole gave Banham a way to continue his attack on certain aspects of modern architecture without

FIG. 5.3 | Salomon SX 91 ski boot (1987).

FIG. 5.4 | Moulton AM 7 (1983). Photo by Tom Taylor.

damning the modern movement outright. This bracketing of the International Style would prove crucial to his revisionist agenda with respect to modern architecture.

Curiously, Banham did not refer directly to the arguments of Henry-Russell Hitchcock and Philip Johnson to align the Porsche building with the International Style. Instead, he cited the three-part postulation of planar volumes, regular massing, and lack of applied ornamentation as the style's essential traits that Alfred Barr had laid out in his preface to Hitchcock and Johnson's book.[29] With its bright colors and filigreed silhouette, Banham argued, Renault adhered to a different set of characteristics: "the use of…bright, usually primary colors," "a conspicuous exhibition of structure," and "exposure of mechanical and environmental services."[30]

These, Banham continued, "may well be called the three distinguishing stylistic principles of High Tech,"[31] and they served to demarcate a stylistic boundary between that idiom and the International Style. Once again, Banham offered a tidy, three-part taxonomy of the visual qualities of an architectural movement. For the New Brutalism, it had been "Memorability as an Image," "Clear exhibition of Structure," and "Valuation of Materials 'as found.'"[32] In his 1961 text "Design by Choice," Banham refined these tenets to become a "convincing unity of the total effect," a frank exhibition of services, and standardized products used "off-the-peg," thus formulating several years avant la lettre an approximation of the visual characteristics of clip-on architecture.[33] In the context of High Tech, one finds a further development. A unified aesthetic was presumed and warranted no explicit mention; exposed structure and services were placed on an equal footing; and a bold

FIG. 5.5 | **Dewhurst Haslam Partnership (Derek Dewhurst, British, b. 1929; David Haslam, British, b. 1939).**
Porsche United Kingdom Headquarters (Reading, England, 1986). View of facade.
From Stephen Trombley, "The Architect at Work: Porsche Motoring," *RIBA* 92, no.12 (1985): 21.

FIG. 5.6 | **Foster Associates (Norman Foster, British, b. 1935).**
Renault Warehouse and Distribution Center (Swindon, England, 1983). General view.
Photo by Richard Davies.

TABLE 1

International Style	New Brutalism	Clip-On	High Tech
Planar Volumes	Memorable Images	Exposed Services	Exposed Services
Regular Massing	Exposed Structure	Unity of Effect	Exposed Structure
Blank Surfaces	As-Found Materials	Off-the-Peg Products	Bold Colors

use of color replaced both the honesty of "as-found" and the expediency of "off-the-peg." Taken together, these three formulas trace Banham's shifting position on the visual qualities he associated with "otherness" throughout his career. Reading them against Barr's International Style characteristics, one can tabulate Banham's alignments with and swerves from orthodox modern architecture (table 1).

Banham's encapsulations of the New Brutalism and clip-on emphatically stated the requirement of a coherent visual image (derived from exposed structure and exposed service elements, respectively); with respect to both the International Style and High Tech, he assumed its presence. The former derived its coherence from planar forms and "regular" massing, while the latter derived it from the inherent visual logic of structure and services. Significantly, none of the four stylistic categories sanctioned compositional strategies based on ad hoc juxtaposition or collage, just as none betrayed any overt allegiance to classical coherence.[34] Banham distanced his own position from both qualities throughout his career, which points to a fundamental agreement between certain modern movement values and his own. Each category also called for a distinct material effect: abstract blankness and concrete physicality in the older pair, and the artificiality of off-the-peg (often plastic) elements and applied color in the newer one. This marks a shift in Banham's material sensibility one might attribute to his well-known appetite for pop in both art and culture.

Paradoxically, neither of the examples Banham examined in his introductory comparison adhered to his stylistic criteria. Renault lacked any significant exposition of mechanical services, though its structural system was expressed with bold colors. Porsche lacked all three, and it aligned with exactly the International Style criteria High Tech works supposedly flouted. Here, one must keep in mind that, for Banham, visual style was only part of the equation. Just as the New Brutalism necessitated engagement with the movement's formal and ideological inflections, High Tech required the historian to consider both visual style *and* enhanced performance. Importantly, and in sharp contrast to his earlier argumentation in *Theory and Design in the First Machine Age*, "A Home Is Not a House," *The Architecture of the Well-Tempered Environment*, and elsewhere, Banham cautioned that this commitment to technologically enhanced performance did *not* imply a move away from architecture as a discipline. High Tech, he reminded his readers, was "still architecture, 'the mother of the arts,' with all that is implied in that traditional claim."[35]

Banham ended his essay by returning to the famous closing passage of *Theory and Design in the First Machine Age,* in which the technologically engaged architect may be required to "discard his whole cultural load including the professional garments by which he is recognized as an architect" in order to keep pace with technology.[36] In stark contrast to one of his most oft-quoted lines, Banham argued in his introduction that High Tech, the direct inheritor of the attitudes he had outlined nearly thirty years earlier, demonstrated "how far some architects were prepared to go, in defiance of a rising tide of historical revivalism, in order to keep up with advanced engineering, but without divesting themselves of those 'professional garments.'"[37] Positioning his work emphatically against both the International Style and postmodern architecture, he closed by defining High Tech as "an alternative Modernism that had arisen from what might be termed the 'disgrace' of the older Modernism of the International Style," which had, in his view, "surprised the world of architecture by becoming successful against the grain of expectations in the ostensibly Post-Modernist culture of the nineteen-seventies and eighties."[38]

Banham wrote these lines as he was recovering from the cancer surgery he had undergone in August 1987. Judging by other materials in the archive, the letter, summary, and outline of 15 December represent his final recorded thoughts on High Tech. And while *Making Architecture* would remain unfinished, Banham's earlier writings and teaching throughout the 1980s hint at his intentions for articulating "this alternative Modernism."[39] In them, Banham demonstrated an acute attention to the imagistic concerns of visual style as well as to the often invisible signals of enhanced performance. This two-pronged line of inquiry led him to engage projects as both autonomous objects and immersive environments, to celebrate them as often for carefully assembled construction details as for masterfully choreographed atmospheric effects, and to write from the contrasting vantage points of the attentive connoisseur and distracted flâneur. Although many of the writings examined in this study saw Banham leaning heavily to one or the other extreme (or shifting abruptly from one to the other), his late writings on High Tech demonstrate an attempt to accommodate these contrasting ambitions under the rubric of what he called "making architecture." With this "deceptively simple phrase," which, he admitted, "some may find…rather old-fashioned,"[40] Banham attempted to capture the elusive qualities that defined not just High Tech but also the fundamental essence of architecture itself.

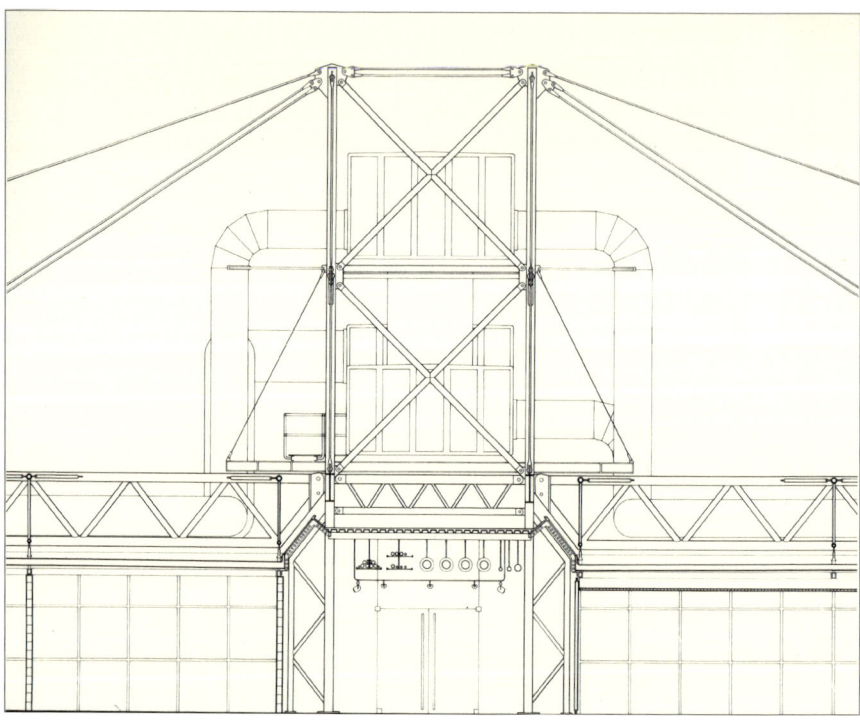

FIG. 5.7 | **Richard Rogers Partnership (Richard Rogers, British, b. Italy, 1933).**

Inmos Microprocessor Factory (Newport, Wales, 1982). General view. Photo by Ken Kirkwood.

FIG. 5.8 | **Richard Rogers Partnership (Richard Rogers, British, b. Italy, 1933).**

Inmos Microprocessor Factory (Newport, Wales, 1982). Detailed cross section through the circulation spine. Photo by Richard Rogers Partnership.

Making Architecture

Four major themes can be traced through Banham's late work on High Tech. Throughout it, one encounters a consistent appeal to functionalism and technology. This staunch commitment to core modernist values leads Banham explicitly to champion the continued relevance of the machine aesthetic as the ultimate source of High Tech's visual qualities. For Banham, the machine aesthetic implied a particular form of part-to-whole coherence, leading him to a keen attentiveness to construction details. This commitment to rational and legible building assemblies prompted repeated reflections on the canon of modern architecture, the clear genealogy of works extending back through innovative structures of the eighteenth and nineteenth centuries and projecting forward through High Tech into the immediate future. Taken together, these themes comprise the fundamental components of Banham's attempts to make sense of the varied output of High Tech architects and to articulate the task of "making architecture."

A 1982 treatment of Richard Rogers's Inmos Microprocessor Factory (Newport, Wales, 1982) (figs. 5.7, 5.8) demonstrates Banham's nuanced position regarding functionalism.[41] At Inmos, significant mechanical provisions were required to accommodate the facility's "clean room" for microchip assembly, resulting in an extensible, axial scheme with an array of air-handling equipment prominently displayed on the building's roof. In this, Rogers turned the organization of Henman and Cooper's Royal Victoria Hospital (1903) (see figs. 3.6, 3.7) on its head. Where in the older building an axial array of mechanical equipment was deployed invisibly beneath the building (as Team 4 would later do at Reliance Controls), at Inmos, Rogers placed the required equipment proudly in view. Yet, for Banham, the imagery at Inmos was less about legibly representing this equipment than about producing a palpable feeling of necessity that he likened to that of sailing ships: "The air of conviction that pervades almost every part of the design seems to derive, as in naval architecture, from a sense of necessity, a feeling that nothing could be other than it is."[42] Banham also noticed this link between function and necessity in Piano + Rogers's B&B Italia Office Building (1971–73) in Novedrate, Italy, where he found "nothing to be seen in, or on, this building beyond what is necessary *as architecture*." Importantly, this constituted "a little more than what might be necessary as engineering, but the purely engineering solution would not be anywhere near as rich. The difference between those two conceptions of 'necessary' is what makes architecture of B&B."[43] If architecture, as opposed to engineering practice, required an excess of necessity, so too did nautical works move beyond the strictly functional. Much of the necessity on display in sailing ships, Banham explained, was "rhetorical," even "superstitious."[44] In the end, it was not the *fact* but rather the *feeling* of necessity that was crucial to the inherent rightness of both sailing ships and High Tech architecture. And while this accommodation of rhetorical elements certainly represented a softening of the ruthless logic Banham had praised in the New Brutalism and elsewhere,[45] it maintained his consistent requirement of "apprehensibility and coherence of the building as a visual entity."[46] In addition, and notwithstanding his requirement that performance actually be delivered, it underlined Banham's insistence that the problem of functionalism was first and foremost aesthetic.

Linked to Banham's advocacy of functionalism was his faith in the enduring relevance of the machine aesthetic. "The concept of the Machine Age," he intoned in a 1976 lecture, "won't go away."[47] In an interview a decade later, he opined,

> I think the one continuing cultural significance is the desire to convince clients and passersby, visually, that this is a building that really works like a machine. The occasional passing quotation from the Crystal Palace, as for example at Lloyd's, is more a profession of faith in the tradition.... When the Rogers office or the Foster office does an apparent quote from a 19th-Century structure, it is a quite considered, deliberate statement that they belong to that grand old Rationalist tradition.[48]

That "grand old Rationalist tradition" of glazed, iron-framed construction had been outlined in canonical books by Nikolaus Pevsner and Sigfried Giedion.[49] Banham was unconvinced by the links these authors drew between nineteenth-century precedents and the canonical twentieth-century projects. In his eyes, the "International

Style work of Giedion's friends Le Corbusier, Mies van der Rohe, or Pevsner's hero, Gropius" did not resonate visually with the "open-work, transparent" frames of "the *Grand Constructeurs*" of the nineteenth century such as Joseph Paxton and Gustave Eiffel.[50] Here again, Banham nudged the label "the International Style" away from Hitchcock and Johnson, this time not toward Alfred Barr but rather toward more proximate adversaries in the fight to define modern architecture, namely Pevsner and Giedion. And if these historians were unconvincing in their association of Corbusier, Mies, and Gropius with the "Rationalist tradition" of the nineteenth century, Banham felt he was on surer footing, offering Foster, Piano, and Rogers as rightful heirs to that tradition. These younger architects' tendency to use open frames and exposed fasteners and to foreground the starkly mechanical over the Platonically abstract aligned them with "that 'Other' modernist tradition—that of Constructivism, Futurism, etc." to which Banham had devoted so much attention throughout his career.[51] Importantly, if High Tech rejected the refined abstractions of the International Style, it also seemed to move away from the jarring radicalism Banham had earlier sought under the banner of *une architecture autre*. For if, as he surmised in 1966, *une architecture autre* was "something the traditions of architecture could not absorb,"[52] then High Tech, the true inheritor of the "other" tradition, displayed "a desire for clarity and frugality in resolving functional problems within the canons of architecture."[53]

———

In his late writings, Banham repeatedly forged deliberate links between the work of the 1970s and '80s and the tradition of technological innovation dating to the nineteenth century. In his final years, one finds interspersed with these arguments broader speculation on the links between architecture and technology in general. High Tech was presented as the inheritor not just of the grand traditions of Victorian engineering and the machine aesthetic but also of a technological legacy stretching back to antiquity. This attitude pervades the seminar on High Tech he led at the University of California at Santa Cruz (UCSC) in 1987. He devoted three of the term's ten weeks to High Tech's historical pedigree, spending one week each on "Technology and Architecture," "History and Symbolism," and the "Ancestors of High Tech."[54] Though these lectures unfortunately were not recorded, lecture notes taken by student Janey Bennett offer a sense of the material Banham covered.[55]

In the course, Banham linked all architecture closely with technology, though his typical partisanship was clearly on display. Bennett recorded in her notes an early contrast of the Doric order (a "conservative technology") with the technical daring of the Gothic period ("not conservative"). Where Greek architects were mocked for their ornamental tendencies ("I know it fell down but the fluting on the columns was beautiful"[56]), the Gothic period won praise for bolder innovation (marked, ironically, by a high rate of structural failure) and for a culture in which "technicians were admired most."[57] A similar partitioning can be seen in Banham's discussion of the Crystal Palace ("conservative"[58]) and the Brooklyn Bridge ("cutting edge stuff"[59]). A text Banham often cited, Paul Valéry's *Eupalinos, ou l'architecte* (1921), also found its place in the seminar.[60] Banham had referenced Valéry's contrast of the architect Eupalinos and the shipwright Tridon years earlier in *The Architecture of the Well-Tempered Environment:* "The former was preoccupied with the right method for doing the allotted tasks, and deploying the accepted methods, of his calling, and seemed to find a philosophical problem in every practical decision. Tridon, on the other hand, applied the technology that came conveniently to hand, whether or not it was part of the shipbuilding tradition, and treated the sayings of philosophers as further instruction of the direct solution of practical problems."[61] At UCSC, Banham's praise of Tridon's boffinesque pragmatism and distaste for Eupalinos's intellectual proclivities was far blunter. "One loaded gun beats 4 aces," reads Bennett's notes, followed by "design defeats itself by being too good."[62] With these and other examples, Banham rehearsed some of his most well-known argumentation: praising aggressive technical innovation, damning overt theoretical speculation, and defining architecture as a field fundamentally linked to technology yet perennially hamstrung by both methodological convention and delusions of intellectual grandeur.

Though Banham directed significant attention to the visual qualities of High Tech buildings and their sources in the modern architecture of the late nineteenth and early twentieth centuries, he ultimately saw modernism as far more than a style. Rather, the concept represented an underlying ethos of rationality that held firm beneath visually diverse and chronologically distant buildings and continued to exert a vital influence on contemporary culture. Modernism, he argued, "made sense to the kind of practical-minded men who managed the building programs of major corporate and government clients."[63] Of course, making sense to such "practical-minded men" might mean little more than reinforcing their agendas, and thus close associations with corporate and government culture could as easily represent modernism's "triumph" as its "tragedy." The latter, he found, was the case of the MACE system for school construction,[64] which "could not protect its original social idealism and aesthetic vision against the erosions and corrosions of three decades of cost cutting and vote-chasing." The results were no "mere stylistic crisis," as many critics took them to be, but rather "a complicated civic and professional disaster." Where postmodern critics stepped in to articulate the faults of misfires such as MACE in stylistic terms (and also to offer alternatives in stylistic terms), Banham noticed that "Manfredo Tafuri, almost alone, with his concept of the inability of architecture as a profession to deliver the 'Utopia of Social Democracy' to which the Modern Movement had been committed, seems to have understood the magnitude of the problem." Implying that he was also to be counted among those who saw the writing on the wall, Banham continued, "but one may beg leave to differ from his diagnosis: the problem may have been less to do with social ideology than with the business of actually putting buildings together."

Banham would routinely sidestep ideological questions by pivoting to construction details, and doing so left him open to criticism that he was unconcerned with the ideological implications of architecture's technological servicing and iconographic symbolization of the status quo. Referring to Banham as a "paladin of technological orthodoxy," Tafuri suggested as much in otherwise respectful comments in 1976.[65] Indeed, for Banham, the central preoccupation of the resurgent modern architecture of High Tech was detailing—not ideology, materials, or style—and it was in their detailing that such works would demonstrate their efficacy and earn their status not only as modern but also as architecture. Consider his treatment of details at Rogers's Lloyd's of London building:

> Confront any single detail—the fixing of the uprights of the handrails of the external stairs, for instance—and one is looking at a design solution that would be virtually inconceivable in normal engineering practice. An engineer might, indeed, have done a handrail upright for half the price, but the result would not have been half as rewarding as a piece of architecture.... Engineering is one way of designing things, architecture is another. The triumph of Lloyd's is, paradoxically, that it is so often difficult to tell them apart.[66]

Or consider his careful description of the connections at Renzo Piano's IBM Traveling Pavilion (1982–86; figs. 5.9, 5.10; see pl. 15):

> A complex metal element sits in a trunnion that permits movement (shades of Behren's *Turbinfabrik!*)[. T]o its inner face is bolted the anchorage of a stay to hold the plastic glazing, while its top is split into four teeth which accept three matching teeth cut in the end of the laminated wooden rib which forms the first component of the half-arch above. This object is a work of architectural art in its own right, the complexity of its functions and connections is an architectural composition richer than many complete buildings, and the fanaticism that informs its conception suggests the kind of passion that Le Corbusier found in the *modenature* [sic] of Michelangelo.[67]

Examples of this deft combination of precise description, historical contextualization, and exuberant celebration of construction details can be found throughout Banham's writing on the work of Foster, Piano, Rogers, and elsewhere.[68] In these

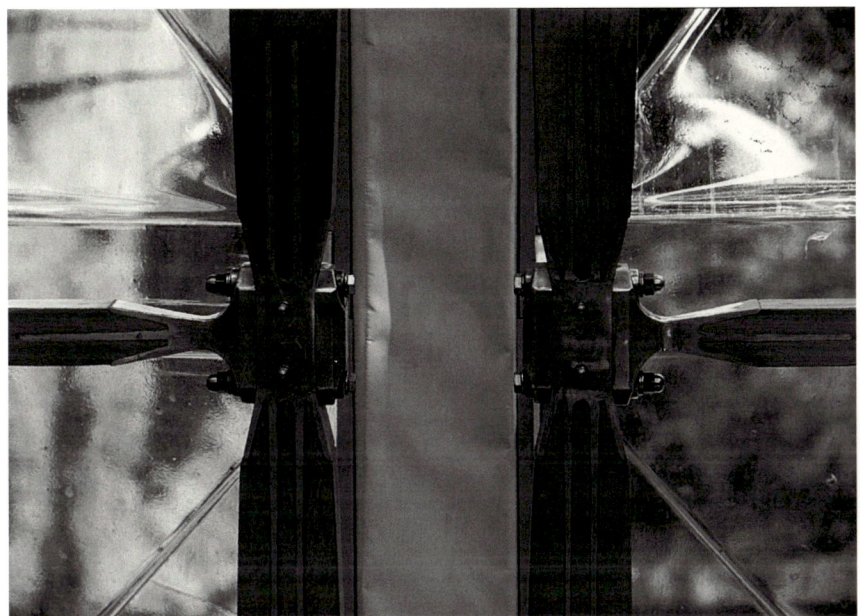

writings, as Nigel Whiteley noticed, Banham returned to many of the disciplinary values he first articulated in the context of the New Brutalism.[69] Whiteley did not comment, however, on Banham's reversal of his attitude toward details. In 1955, Banham advocated the Smithsons' "abstemious under-designing" of the details at Hunstanton. By the mid-1980s, he appeared fully to support "arty" details such as those he had chastised at Louis Kahn's Yale University Art Gallery.[70] And while Banham did endorse the minimal gasketed joints employed by Foster at the buildings for the IBM Pilot Head Office and Willis Faber & Dumas, in those writings one scarcely finds the glowing praise he lavished on Piano's complex connections.

"High-Tech," as Banham put it in the context of Rogers's work, "as epitomized by the elaborate and painstaking detailing of Lloyd's, was clearly preoccupied with putting buildings together properly."[71] Piano's work similarly was centered around the careful assembly of building components. And while Piano described his approach to architecture as "dealing with a language," Banham maintained that "the linguistic analogy does not quite explain the complete situation." In projects such as the IBM Pavilion, "the pieces do not form a simple hierarchical assembly, in which one piece supports another piece which supports another, etc., but the ribs and plexiglass [sic] pyramids work together to form a complex three-dimensional truss, whose 'whole is greater than its parts.' The pieces are usually perceived by Piano himself, and by anyone who looks at the finished work, as organic parts of the building as a whole."[72] Thus, Banham found in Piano's work an unapologetically classical form of part-to-whole coherence. A similar appeal to traditional notions of unity can be found in his discussion of Lloyd's: "The more unified image produced by the almost monochrome finishes, as opposed to the diverse colors of say, Centre

FIG. 5.9 | Renzo Piano Building Workshop (Renzo Piano, Italian, b. 1937).
IBM Traveling Pavilion (1982–86).
Construction detail.
Photo by Gianni Berengo Gardin.

FIG. 5.10 | Renzo Piano Building Workshop (Renzo Piano, Italian, b. 1937).
IBM Traveling Pavilion (1982–86).
General view.
Photo by Gianni Berengo Gardin.

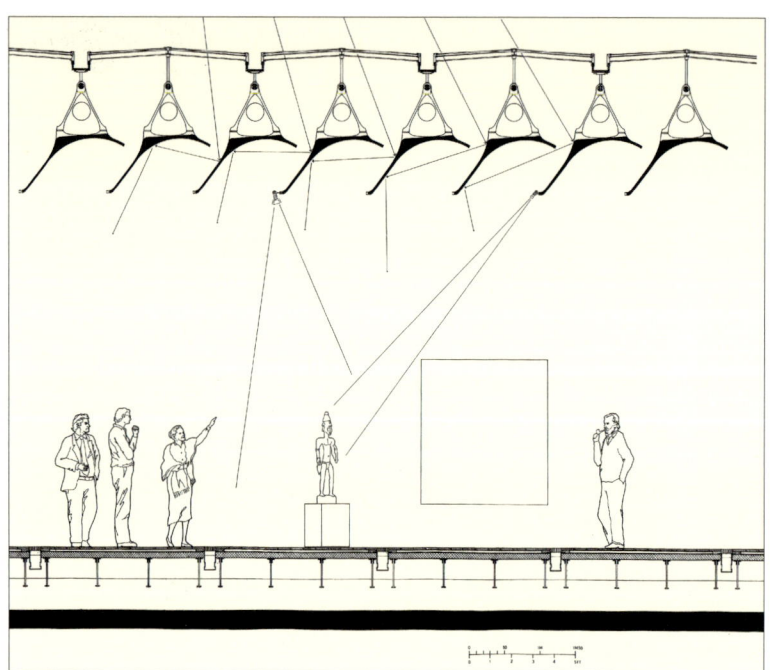

FIG. 5.11 | Renzo Piano Building Workshop (Renzo Piano, Italian, b. 1937).
The Menil Collection (Houston, 1982–87). Section through gallery.

FIG. 5.12 | Renzo Piano Building Workshop (Renzo Piano, Italian, b. 1937).
The Menil Collection (Houston, 1982–87). View from the street. Photo by Paul Hester Photography.

Pompidou, which tended to separate the parts, draws attention to the kind of unified general conception that is usually supposed to be the product of architectural designing."[73] While Banham had flirted with ad hoc composition and expendable construction throughout his career, he never fully endorsed them. In his late writings on High Tech, he emphatically rejected such tactics and instead championed traditional disciplinary values such as unity, permanence, and monumentality. In 1965, in the context of clip-on, Banham had written, "What was at stake in all these projects, concepts, and the rare completed buildings, was an architecture whose form was not defined by the accepted rules of architecture—symmetry, unity, coherence, balance, and all of those."[74] Two decades later, he appeared to be betting heavily on at least three of those four qualities as the bases of a technological architecture "appropriate to the times."[75]

The elegant assembly of architectural components into coherent unities Banham saw at the IBM Pavilion was at the core of "making architecture." In later works, such as Piano's museum for the Menil Collection in Houston (1986) (figs. 5.11, 5.12; see pl. 16) and his Lowara Office Building (Vicenza, Italy, 1984–85) (figs. 5.13, 5.14), Banham saw the concept developed "beyond joining neat pieces together organically...to involv[ing] the whole conception of the building."[76] Both projects are dominated by complex roof elements—a series of carefully sculpted concrete louvers in the former and a sweeping curved plane in the latter. In each case, these elements were carefully detailed and not only provided building form and structure but also, much to Banham's delight, contributed to "an elaborate program of environmental management."[77] In section, the high end of Lowara's roof peeks

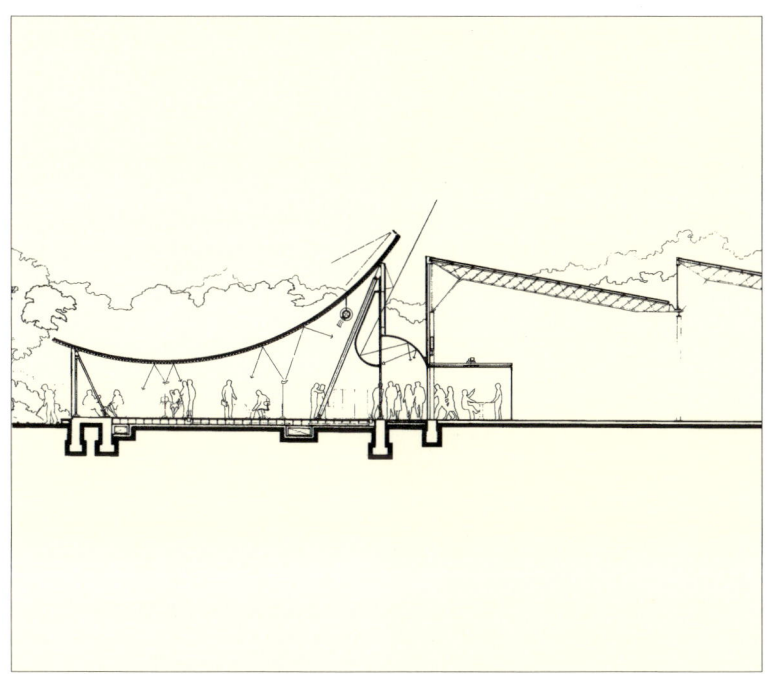

above an adjacent factory building to the south (see fig. 5.13). At first blush, lifting the roof to invite direct southern sunlight to the interior would seem counterintuitive. Yet rather than admit this glaring light directly, Piano nestled a curved reflector against the project's canted steel columns to bounce that light into the opposing curve of the adjacent corridor's roof, delivering tempered natural light to the space below. Freestanding light fixtures within the main office area were aimed vertically to reflect their light off the convex roof surface above similarly to provide indirect illumination throughout the facility. At Menil, Piano developed an intricate ceiling assembly comprised of triangulated roof trusses capped by shallowly sloped glass gables. A cast-concrete light reflector—its curved surfaces carefully calibrated to bathe the galleries in diffuse natural light while ensuring that damaging direct rays would never be admitted—was suspended from each truss (see fig. 5.11). Describing the space for *Art in America* in 1987, Banham was uncommonly poetic:

> The floors are stained almost black, so that the strips of bronze ventilation-grille are hardly visible; the walls are painted white, and over them spreads a light of—frankly—ethereal beauty. That is not the kind of language that I use very frequently, but the quality of light that enters the Menil through the sunshades is breathtaking. The only gallery light that I can compare it with is that in Louis Kahn's Kimbell [Art Museum] in Fort Worth, but whereas the light under the vaults there is mysterious and largely a matter of optical illusion—it looks natural but is heavily supplemented with artificial—the daylight in the Menil is honest, pellucid, and without additives.[78]

FIG. 5.13 | **Renzo Piano Building Workshop (Renzo Piano, Italian, b. 1937).**
Lowara Office Building (Vicenza, Italy, 1984–85). Section.

FIG. 5.14 | **Renzo Piano Building Workshop (Renzo Piano, Italian, b. 1937).**
Lowara Office Building (Vicenza, Italy, 1984–85). Interior view.
Photo by Gianluigi Trivellato.

FIG. 5.15 | **Richard Rogers Partnership (Richard Rogers, British, b. Italy, 1933).** Lloyd's of London (London, 1986). Interior view of central atrium. Photo by Richard Bryant.

Though the Menil was replete with Piano's signature details, Banham directed his comments primarily at Piano's integration of the building into its suburban context and to the atmospheric qualities of its gallery spaces (see fig. 5.12, pl. 16). While *Art in America*'s primarily nonarchitectural readership might account for this shift in emphasis, one finds a similar concentration on immersive environmental effects in Banham's earlier discussion of Lloyd's (fig. 5.15):

> When one looks down into the pit of the Room where the business of Lloyd's is actually done, one is suddenly struck by the recognition that its uncanny resemblance to a set piece from some old science-fiction movie is less due to the glittering finishes or the exposed structure or the illuminated criss-crossing escalators, than to the sheer numbers of grey- and brown-clad human beings (up to 5000 at a time, it is believed) moving about everywhere. It is like up-market Kafka, or T.S. Eliot's 'many' whom 'death had undone' re-choreographed by Busby Berkely [*sic*]. A great spectacle of financial power, but is it necessary?[79]

To answer his own question, Banham confronted the dissipative effects of contemporary technology with the traditional values of architectural place-making. "Surely," he argued, "in the High-Tech world of electronic communications and personal computers most of these people could stay home—stay in bed, even—and do their business without crowding on to this hopelessly overloaded site." That they do not, Banham surmised, was because "being there is what it is all about.… Every item of high technology at Lloyd's, structural, environmental, mechanical, or electrical, services a concept of business that still puts its ultimate faith in face-to-face contact and rumors whispered in passing ears." He concluded: "If one finds this an irony—and it is extremely difficult not to—then it seems to be an irony proper to our late-Modern times. Architecture may have abandoned its utopian dreams of changing the world, because the world is perfectly capable of changing itself without architecture's aid, but the compulsion to try and make sense of the resulting human dilemma is still the most essential quality of Modernism." In Banham's estimation, High Tech architects—when successful—enacted Horatio Greenough's definition of beauty as "the promise of function made sensuously pleasing."[80] And if the satisfaction of Greenough's proviso made High Tech buildings beautiful, for Banham, it was the solution of "the technical problems of creating fit environments for human activities" *within the accepted traditions of the discipline* that made them architecture.[81]

The Paradoxes of High Tech
In the concept of "making architecture," Banham's argumentation came full circle. Where earlier writings had placed tradition and technology in opposition, in his writings on High Tech, the latter was ultimately brought in line with the former. But rather than resulting in syntheses, the various themes that have been traced through this chapter each elicited something of a paradox. Earlier invocations of functionalism and technology had led Banham to predict the dissipation of architecture into invisibly serviced milieus (such as the un-house he had imagined in 1965).[82] But in the context of High Tech, they led him to sanction the visual presentation of functional necessity and to endorse functionally unnecessary rhetorical elements to assure architecture's legibility. With such tactics, Banham, who had criticized orthodox modern architecture throughout much of his career, closely aligned High Tech projects such as Inmos with the coherent imagery of canonical works such as Walter Gropius and Adolf Meyer's Fagus Factory (Alfeld an der Leine, Germany, 1911).

Yet Banham continued to take issue with the International Style, which, as noted above, he associated not only with Hitchcock and Johnson but also closely with Alfred Barr, Sigfried Giedion, and Nikolaus Pevsner. While he would espouse that style's derivation of the visual character of contemporary works from nineteenth-century precedents, he had little enthusiasm for the white-walled aesthetic so revered by the modern movement's first historians. He did, however, maintain a firm commitment to the machine aesthetic, and he offered mechanistic projects such as Centre Pompidou and Renault as alternatives to the International Style that more closely adhered to that movement's stated ambitions to legibly exhibit functional performance.

Reading High Tech's exuberant compositions against the restrained offerings of the International Style, one might have expected Banham to finally embrace the brash juxtapositions he had flirted with in "A Clip-On Architecture" and periodically throughout his career. But as has been shown in his repeated admonitions of ad hoc compositional techniques, High Tech inspired him to reject the expedient accretion of elements in favor of elegant, unified compositions reinforced by meticulously crafted construction details. In his careful explication of connective elements, Banham took on the role of attentive and learned connoisseur, engaging High Tech works as discrete aesthetic objects in the manner of his mentor, Nikolaus Pevsner. Yet, as in his treatment of James Stirling's Olivetti Training Center over a decade earlier,[83] Banham's attention had a tendency to wander from the object of inquiry. The details at Lloyd's, recall, in the end collapsed into a cacophonous social milieu, while those at Menil vanished into a near-spiritual atmosphere dedicated to the physical experience of art. In neither building was the contemplation of architectural details the ultimate goal, even if the specific character of the details that composed each space was crucial to the overall effect. Thus, while Banham himself remained a learned connoisseur, he ultimately found High Tech's most potent effects in the production of immersive spaces populated by distracted flâneurs.

Perhaps strangest of all, Banham, who demonstrated a knack for capturing a movement's iconographic qualities in tidy tripartite phrases throughout his career, set out to organize a book on High Tech around a set of concepts he admitted were underequipped to fully characterize the movement.[84] Banham's work on *Making Architecture* began as High Tech architects moved their work resolutely away from adherence to his triple definition of exposed structure, exposed services, and bold colors. Indeed, like Dewhurst Haslam's Porsche building, discussed in the previous chapter, significant late projects such as Menil and Lowara bore little resemblance to the criteria.[85] Yet, as Foster, Piano, and Rogers distanced themselves from the visible iconography of High Tech as a style, they appeared more firmly to embrace the moral imperatives of modernism as a technique for "making architecture." In the pursuit of clearly integrated building technologies, honest and appropriate visual expression, and a unified discipline that governed "the whole conception of the building,"[86] the task of making architecture adhered to a different triple set of criteria Banham outlined toward the end of his career—not structure, services, and color but rather clarity, honesty, and unity.[87]

Barr's Aesthetic Modernism	Pevsner's Stylistic Modernism	Giedion's Tectonic Modernism	Banham's Ethical Modernism
Planar Volumes	Victorian Engineering	Iron and Steel	Clarity
Regular Massing	Arts and Crafts	Reinforced Concrete	Honesty
Blank Surfaces	Art Nouveau	Glass	Unity

TABLE 2

These, Banham pointed out, were central "dogmas" of "the modernist establishment in Europe" in the interwar years just as they were primary motivating principles for the Eameses, the Smithsons, and other major adherents to modernist doctrine of the immediate postwar period.[88] With them in hand, we can differentiate Banham's position on modern architecture from that of the more orthodox predecessors he had studied at the outset of his career (table 2). The triple formula of planar volumes, regular massing, and blank surfaces Alfred Barr invoked in *The International Style* outlined a version of modern architecture understood primarily in terms of aesthetics, a vision that bore out in Hitchcock and Johnson's explication of the approach in the same book. Pevsner, in *Pioneers of the Modern Movement* (1936), defined modern architecture primarily in terms of period styles, seeing it as the inheritor of three traditions: Victorian engineering, the arts and crafts movement, and art nouveau. Giedion, by contrast, laid out a fundamentally tectonic modern architecture in *Bauen in Frankreich, Bauen in Eisen, Bauen in Eisenbeton* (1928), in which he posited the use of iron and steel, reinforced concrete, and (though he did not include it in his title) glass as central characteristics. Though Banham would grapple with the aesthetic, tectonic, and stylistic implications of modern architecture throughout his career, ultimately, his position came down to the ethical imperatives of clarity, honesty, and unity. These values also featured strongly in the writings of nineteenth-century thinkers such as Augustus Pugin, John Ruskin, Gottfried Semper, and Eugène-Emmanuel Viollet-le-Duc; and they colored classical conceptions of architecture dating to antiquity.[89] Indeed, more traditional values in architecture scarcely could be found. Though Banham considered abandoning many of architecture's traditional values in his writings,[90] his commitment to clarity, honesty, and unity—tenets meant to outline architecture's ethics as well as to govern its aesthetics—never wavered. These qualities capture the essence of the modern architecture Banham saw in High Tech and advocated throughout his career, and their centrality to his notion of "making architecture" makes clear that for Banham, technique was the primary determinant of style.

NOTES

1. The *Oxford English Dictionary* puts the first use of the term at 1972, in Stuart Brand's *Last Whole Earth Catalog*, no. 1160, which in fact was published in June 1971. Banham argues that "no buildings were actually labeled as 'High Tech' until 1979, and the main currency of the term really dates to 1983." See Reyner Banham, "High Tech and Advanced Engineering," ca. 1987, p. 1, Reyner Banham papers, acc. no. 910009, box 8, folder 3, Getty Research Institute, Los Angeles; and "High Tech and Advanced Engineering," this volume, p. 233.

2. Joan Kron and Suzanne Slesin, *High-Tech: The Industrial Style and Source Book for the Home* (New York: Clarkson N. Potter, 1978). Banham provides a brief discussion of the book in Banham, "High Tech and Advanced Engineering," 2–4, Reyner Banham papers; and this volume, pp. 234–35.

3. The book contains a useful foreword by Emilio Ambasz. See Emilio Ambasz, "The Alternative Artifact," in Kron and Slesin, *High-Tech*, x.

4. See Peter Buchanan, "Foster/Rogers: High-Tech; Classical/Gothic," *Architectural Review* 169 (1981): 265–67; Peter Buchanan, "High-Tech: Another British Thoroughbred," *Architectural Review* 174 (1983): 15–19; Peter Buchanan, "Romantic High-Tech," *Architectural Review* 174 (1983): 32–39; and Peter Buchanan, "Nostalgic Utopia," *Architects' Journal*, 4 September 1985, 60–69.

5. Buchanan, "High-Tech," 17–19.

6. Buchanan, "Nostalgic Utopia."

7. See "Savage Minds and the Well-Tempered Environment," this volume.

8. Buchanan, "High-Tech," 19.

9. Charles Jencks, "Late-Modern and Post-Modern Architecture," *Architectural Design* 48 (1978): 592, reprinted as "Late-Modernism and Post-Modernism," in Charles Jencks, *Late-Modern Architecture and Other Essays* (New York: Rizzoli, 1980), 10.

10. Charles Jencks, "The Battle of High-Tech: Great Buildings with Great Faults," *Architectural Design* 58, nos. 11–12 (1988): 19–39. On English debates, see Charles Jencks, ed., *The Prince, the Architects, and New Wave Monarchy* (New York: Rizzoli, 1988).

11. Colin Davies, *High Tech Architecture* (New York: Rizzoli, 1988), 21.

12. See Charles, Prince of Wales, *A Vision of Britain: A Personal View of Architecture* (London: Doubleday, 1989); Léon Krier, "God Save the Prince!," *Modern Painters* 2 (1988): 23–25; and Joseph Rykwert, "On the High-Tech Style," *Wolkenkuckucksheim: International Journal of Architectural Theory* 12, no. 7, Heaven and Earth: Festschrift to Honor Karsten Harries (2007), http://www.cloud-cuckoo.net/openarchive/wolke/eng/Subjects/071/Rykwert/rykwert.htm.

13. For a useful positive treatment, see Peter Cook, "Richard Rogers + Architects," in *Richard Rogers + Architects*, ed. Frank Russell (London: Academy Editions, 1985), 4–5. For a worthwhile negative opinion, see Ignasi de Solà-Morales, "High Tech: Functionalism or Rhetoric" [1992], in idem, *Differences: Topographies of Contemporary Architecture*, ed. Sarah Whiting (Cambridge, MA: MIT Press, 1997), 117–31. Tellingly, Cook, choosing to highlight the resonance between Rogers's work and modern architecture, did not use the phrase "High Tech" (a tactic employed in most other monographs on Foster, Piano, and Rogers); Solà-Morales, criticizing both modern architecture and High Tech, emphasized the term. A late entry into the literature on High Tech is Martin Pawley's *Theory and Design in the Second Machine Age* (London: Blackwell, 1990), in which he lamented the state of British architecture in the 1980s and, opposing the nostalgic position of Prince Charles and other neohistoricists, presented the possibility of a "Gothic Solution" of information and "technology transfer."

14. See Philip Johnson and Mark Wigley, eds., *Deconstructivist Architecture* (New York: Museum of Modern Art, 1988).

15. The White/Gray debate between neomodernist and early postmodernist American architects emerged from a 1969 discussion at the Museum of Modern Art in New York among the "New York Five" (Peter Eisenman, Michael Graves, Charles Gwathmey, John Hejduk, and Richard Meier). The White position was galvanized in the Museum of Modern Art's influential catalog *Five Architects: Eisenman, Graves, Gwathmey, Hejduk, Meier* (New York: Oxford University Press, 1972). A collection of critical responses from Romaldo Giurgola, Allan Greenberg, Charles Moore, Jaquelin Robertson, and Robert A. M. Stern appeared in "Five on Five," *Architectural Forum* 137 (1973): 46–57. With a slightly altered cast of characters, a development of the debate was published in "White and Gray: Eleven Modern Architects," *Architecture + Urbanism* 52 (1975): entire issue. K. Michael Hays offered a brief summary of the debate in *Architecture Theory since 1968* (Cambridge, MA: MIT Press, 1998), 240–41. A more developed treatment can be found in Nadia Watson, "The Whites vs the Greys: Re-Examining the 1970s Avant-Garde," *Fabrications: The Journal of the Society of Architectural Historians, Australia and New Zealand* 26, no. 2 (2005): 55–69.

16 Reyner Banham to Axel Menges, 15 December 1987, p. 1, Reyner Banham papers, acc. no. 910009, box 8, folder 3, Getty Research Institute, Los Angeles. Banham's correspondence with Menges began with a 1985 suggestion by the publisher that Banham write a book on High Tech. See Axel Menges to Reyner Banham, 7 December 1985, Reyner Banham papers, acc. no. 910009, box 8, folder 3. Their correspondence continued through December 1987, when Banham provided a detailed outline and a draft of the first chapter.

17 See Reyner Banham, "High Tech Architecture: The Beginning of an Argument," 15 December 1987, Reyner Banham papers, acc. no. 910009, box 8, folder 3, Getty Research Institute, Los Angeles.

18 Banham, "High Tech Architecture," 1–2, Reyner Banham papers.

19 Banham, "High Tech Architecture," 3, Reyner Banham papers.

20 Banham, "High Tech Architecture," 4, Reyner Banham papers, Banham's emphasis.

21 Banham, "High Tech Architecture," 4, Reyner Banham papers.

22 Banham, "High Tech Architecture," 4, Reyner Banham papers. *NB:* Here Banham again dismisses Le Corbusier, whom he included as evidence of "the failure of the French contribution." Boffinesque French designers fare better: "Chareau and Bijvoet came close to discovering a new aesthetic, and Jean Prouvé came even closer." Banham, "High Tech Architecture," 4.

23 Banham, "High Tech Architecture," 4, Reyner Banham papers.

24 Banham, "High Tech Architecture," 5, Reyner Banham papers.

25 Banham, "High Tech and Advanced Engineering," 20, Reyner Banham papers; and this volume, p. 245.

26 Banham, "High Tech and Advanced Engineering," 2, Reyner Banham papers; and this volume, p. 234.

27 See Banham, "The Atavism of the Short-Distance Mini-Cyclist," *Living Arts* 3 (1964): 91–97, as well as the iconic photographs of Banham on his Moulton that grace the cover of Nigel Whiteley's *Reyner Banham: Historian of the Immediate Future* (Cambridge, MA: MIT Press, 2002) and pepper the literature surrounding his life and work.

28 Banham, "High Tech and Advanced Engineering," 12, Reyner Banham papers; and this volume, p. 240.

29 See Alfred Barr, "Preface," in *The International Style,* Henry-Russell Hitchcock and Philip Johnson (New York: W. W. Norton, 1932), 13. Barr's tenets align closely with Hitchcock and Johnson's devotion of three chapters of *The International Style* to "Architecture as Volume," "Concerning Regularity," and "The Avoidance of Applied Decoration." For further discussion of Barr's role in defining the International Style, see "Architecture Beyond Building," this volume.

30 Banham, "High Tech and Advanced Engineering," 15–16, Reyner Banham papers; and this volume, p. 242.

31 Banham, "High Tech and Advanced Engineering," 16, Reyner Banham papers; and this volume, p. 242.

32 Reyner Banham, "The New Brutalism," *Architectural Review* 118 (1955): 361.

33 Reyner Banham, "Design by Choice: 1951–1961," *Architectural Review* 130 (1961): 43–48.

34 Where Barr rejected symmetry, he maintained "fine proportions" as an inherent characteristic, leaving a whiff of classicism in his formulation. See Barr, "Introduction," 9.

35 Banham, "High Tech and Advanced Engineering," 18, Reyner Banham papers; and this volume, p. 244.

36 Reyner Banham, *Theory and Design in the First Machine Age* (London: Architectural Press, 1960), 329–30, quoted in Banham, "High Tech and Advanced Engineering," 19–20, Reyner Banham papers; and this volume, p. 245.

37 Banham, "High Tech and Advanced Engineering," 20, Reyner Banham papers; and this volume, p. 245.

38 Banham, "High Tech and Advanced Engineering," 20, Reyner Banham papers; and this volume, p. 245.

39 In addition to several articles published on Foster, Piano, and Rogers throughout the 1970s and '80s, Banham led a seminar on High Tech at the University of California, Santa Cruz, in the winter of 1987. See Reyner Banham, "The Rise of High Tech Architecture," course syllabus for "Art History 186" at the University of California, Santa Cruz, 1987, Reyner Banham papers, acc. no. 910009, box 13, folder 4, Getty Research Institute, Los Angeles. He also delivered a "pair of lectures on High Tech" in New York in late 1985, which are discussed in Daralice Boles and Susan Doubilet, "Interview with Reyner Banham," *Progressive Architecture* 67, no. 3 (1986): 75–77. Though Banham mentions lectures given at Princeton and Rockefeller Universities around that time "which engage some aspects of the general topic," I have been unable to locate any documentation of them. See Reyner Banham to Axel Menges, 5 January 1986, p. 1, Reyner Banham papers, acc. no. 910009, box 8, folder 3, Getty Research Institute, Los Angeles.

40 Reyner Banham, "Making Architecture: The High Craft of Renzo Piano," *Architecture + Urbanism,* extra edition, no. 3 (March 1989): 158, 153.

41 Reyner Banham, "Art and Necessity: Inmos and the Persistence of Functionalism," *Architectural Review* 172 (1982): 34–38.

42   Banham, "Art and Necessity," 37.
43   Banham, "Making Architecture," 154, Banham's emphasis.
44   Banham, "Art and Necessity," 37.
45   It also moved Banham toward the rhetorical biases of certain postmodern practitioners, including Peter Eisenman and his insistence that architecture operate on both physical and rhetorical registers.
46   Banham, "The New Brutalism," 358.
47   Reyner Banham, untitled lecture given at the Southern California Institute of Architecture, Los Angeles, 26 March 1976.
48   Boles and Doubilet, "Interview with Reyner Banham," 75.
49   See Sigfried Giedion, *Bauen in Frankreich, Bauen in Eisen, Bauen in Eisenbeton* (Leipzig, Germany: Klinkhardt & Biermann, 1928); and Nikolaus Pevsner, *Pioneers of the Modern Movement from William Morris to Walter Gropius* (London: Faber & Faber, 1936).
50   Banham, "High Tech and Advanced Engineering," 17, Reyner Banham papers; and this volume, p. 243.
51   Banham, "Making Architecture," 152.
52   Reyner Banham, *The New Brutalism: Ethic or Aesthetic?* (New York: Reinhold, 1966), 68.
53   Reyner Banham, "Making Architecture," 154.
54   See Reyner Banham, "The Rise of High Tech Architecture," course syllabus for "Art History 186" at the University of California, Santa Cruz, 1987, Reyner Banham papers, acc. no. 910009, box 13, folder 4, Getty Research Institute, Los Angeles.
55   See Janey Bennet, course notes for "The Rise of High Tech Architecture," Reyner Banham papers, acc. no. 910009, box 13, folder 4, Getty Research Institute, Los Angeles.
56   Bennet, course notes, 11.
57   Bennet, course notes, 12.
58   Bennet, course notes, 16.
59   Bennet, course notes, 18.
60   See Paul Valéry, *Eupalinos; or, the Architect* [1921], trans. William MacCausland Stewart (London: Oxford University Press, 1932).
61   Reyner Banham, *The Architecture of the Well-Tempered Environment* (London: Architectural Press, 1969), 266. A decade earlier, Banham had discussed this work in "Tridon," *Architectural Review* 123 (1958): 229–31.
62   Bennett, course notes, 19.
63   Banham, "The Quality of Modernism," *Architectural Review* 186 (1986): 55. Subsequent quotations in this paragraph were taken from the same source.
64   MACE (Metropolitan Architectural Consortium for Education) was developed out of the earlier CLASP system discussed in "High Tech and the Persistence of Modernism," this volume.
65   See Manfredo Tafuri, *Theories and History of Architecture* [1976] (New York: Harper & Row, 1980), 14.
66   Banham, "The Quality of Modernism," 56.
67   Banham, "Making Architecture," 152.
68   The third of seven "Commentaries" that structure Banham's book on Ron Herron, for example, is titled "Articulations." It provides an important historical gloss on detailing. See Reyner Banham, *The Visions of Ron Herron* (London: Academy, 1994), 62–65.
69   Whiteley, *Reyner Banham*, 299.
70   Banham, "The New Brutalism," 357. For a discussion, see "In Search of Alternatives: Banham, Britain, and the New Brutalism," this volume.
71   Banham, "The Quality of Modernism," 55.
72   Banham, "Making Architecture," 153.
73   Banham, "The Quality of Modernism," 56.
74   Reyner Banham, "A Clip-On Architecture," *Design Quarterly* 63 (1965): 7.
75   Banham, "The Quality of Modernism," 55.
76   Banham, "Making Architecture," 155.
77   Banham, "Making Architecture," 157.
78   Reyner Banham, "In the Neighborhood of Art," *Art in America* 75, no. 6 (1987): 128.
79   Banham, "The Quality of Modernism," 56. All remaining quotations in this paragraph are from the same source.
80   See Horatio Greenough, "American Architecture" [1853], in *Form and Function: Remarks on Art by Horatio Greenough*, ed. Harold Small (Berkeley: University of California Press, 1947), 71–72. Banham discussed Greenough's remarks in "Art and Necessity," 38.

81 Banham, "Making Architecture," 154.
82 See Reyner Banham, "A Home Is Not a House," *Art in America* 53, no. 2 (1965): 70–79; and "High Tech and the Persistence of Modernism," this volume.
83 See Reyner Banham, "Problem x 3 = Olivetti," *Architectural Review* 155 (1974): 197–200; and "Unconventional Combinations: A Clip-On Architecture," this volume.
84 "Structure, Services, and Color—these may well be called the three distinguishing stylistic principles of High Tech, but only *in opposition* to Barr's three principles of the International Style." Banham, "High Tech and Advanced Engineering," 16, Reyner Banham papers; and this volume, p. 244, Banham's emphasis.
85 The structure and services at these buildings are often but not always exposed, and more accurately might be described as "integrated." And as both Banham and Jencks noticed, High Tech architects seemed to have abandoned the bold colors of Centre Pompidou and Renault for the monochromatic "silver aesthetic" of Lloyd's and Hong Kong or the anachronistic white at Menil. See Jencks, "The Battle of High-Tech," 23–25.
86 Banham, "Making Architecture," 155.
87 See Reyner Banham, "Klarheit, Ehrlichkeit, Einfachkeit…and Wit, Too! The Case Study Houses in the World's Eyes," in *Blueprints for Modern Living: History and Legacy of the Case Study Houses,* ed. Elizabeth A. T. Smith (Cambridge, MA: MIT Press, 1989), 183–95. For a discussion of Banham's mistranslation of *Einfachkeit* as "unity," see "High Tech and the Persistence of Modernism," this volume.
88 Banham, "Klarheit, Ehrlichkeit, Einfachkeit," 185.
89 See A. W. N. Pugin, *The True Principles of Pointed or Christian Architecture* [1841] (Reading, UK: Spire, 2003); John Ruskin, *The Seven Lamps of Architecture* [1849] (New York: Dover, 1989); Eugène-Emmanuel Viollet-le-Duc, *The Foundations of Architecture: Selections from the "Dictionaire raisonné"* [1854–68], ed. Barry Bergdoll (New York: George Braziller, 1990); and Gottfried Semper, *The Four Elements of Architecture* [1851] *and Other Writings* (London: Cambridge University Press, 2010).
90 See his expectation that the New Brutalism "could be expected to abandon the concepts of composition, symmetry, order, module, proportion" or that clip-on arose from a rejection of "the accepted rules of architecture—symmetry, unity, coherence, balance, and all of those." See Banham, *The New Brutalism,* 68; and Banham, "A Clip-On Architecture," 7, respectively.

A SET OF ACTUAL MONUMENTS

an inaugural lecture which was not delivered on Monday, February 8, 1988

at the

Institute of Fine Arts, New York University

by

Reyner Banham

First Sheldon H. Solow Professor of the History of Architecture

---

The time is 1952, the place Stokesay Court, the occasion a visit by the Second Attingham Park Summer School on the Great Houses of England. The house deserved visitation for any number of reasons — as the Victorian counterpart of the famous mediaeval Stokesay Castle in the valley below, as a characteristic design by Thomas "Victorian" Harris who first applied "Victorian" to architecture, and as the first house in England to be specifically designed for electric lighting, as we know from the construction photographs in the album which Harris presented to the RIBA.

But at this moment, none of the above is at issue. Together with the rest of the party, I am standing in the middle of the great flying landing halfway up the <u>opulently</u> carved and carpeted main staircase, a space that seems to be about twenty feet by eighteen, and hung about with <u>ancestral</u> portraits and tapestries which seem to cause some of the visitors to start doing detective-novel routines. Feeling that some kind of ambiguously smart-ass observation is called for, I launch one "Hey, I wonder if <u>Hitchcock</u>

CHAPTER 6

ARCHITECTURE BEYOND BUILDING

In 1987, Reyner Banham was named Sheldon H. Solow Professor of the History of Architecture at New York University's Institute of Fine Arts. Though his illness would prevent him from assuming the post, he prepared an inaugural lecture that was published posthumously in *Art in America*.[1] In it, Banham saluted his predecessor at NYU, Henry-Russell Hitchcock, primarily through an analysis of *The International Style,* the famous 1932 book Hitchcock coauthored with Philip Johnson. Hitchcock, he argued, "viewed buildings as 'discrete aesthetic objects,' and tended to avoid theory and ideology."[2] While this attitude brought serious drawbacks to the book (particularly an occlusion of the political and social implications of modern architecture), its authors' unashamed concentration on matters of style was, for Banham, a laudable achievement.

Banham also was impressed by Alfred Barr's provision in the preface to the book of a tidy three-part formula "distinguishing [the] aesthetic principles of the International Style" as planar volumes, regular massing, and blank surfaces.[3] "The propositions," he claimed, "curl back on one another until in the end we realize that we are confronted with a kind of minimal—but definitive, integrated, and irreducible—description of building in the modern style."[4] In concentrating on the discernible qualities of objects themselves, Banham surmised, Barr's formulations—as well as Hitchcock and Johnson's book as a whole—offered a rigorous portrait of modern architecture relatively free of the ideological mystifications that had colored so many other accounts of the movement.

Banham often treated his objects of inquiry as "discrete aesthetic objects," and he attempted throughout his career to affect the laconic efficiency of Barr's triple tenets in his own stylistic formulations of the New Brutalism, clip-on architecture, and High Tech. But for Banham, defensible visual criteria were never enough. In his NYU address, for example, he teased out crucial tectonic affiliations (steel or

Reyner Banham (English, 1922–88). "A Set of Actual Monuments," 1988, handwritten manuscript for an inaugural lecture at the Institute of Fine Arts, New York University, that was never delivered.
Los Angeles, Getty Research Institute.

173

concrete construction), economic factors (which necessitated mass production and precluded ornamentation), and extradisciplinary affiliations (such as compositional "help" drawn from "the current state of abstract art") from Barr's formulas before arriving at a careful statement of the implications of working in a similarly objective manner: "The sort of blanket definition of a Great International Style that one would derive from the Rationalist attitude could be formulated as: the immanence of a coherent set of structural procedures and esthetic ambitions in an orderly sequence of monuments."[5] Banham's shift in emphasis was subtle but important. *The International Style,* in both Barr's formulation and Hitchcock and Johnson's "rigorous description,"[6] offered visual, organizational, and material criteria as a test of stylistic orthodoxy. Banham, by contrast, looked to the immanence not of formal properties but rather of "procedures" and "ambitions" in modern architecture. Where each author might be guilty of subscribing to "a good, old-fashioned 'materials and methods' view of architectural development,"[7] the older generation focused on the "materials" that determined a *style,* while Banham gravitated toward the "methods" that characterized a *technique.*

A Black Box

This valorization of technique over style was implicit in Banham's early championing of ethics over aesthetics in *The New Brutalism,* just as it had been in his move away from structure, services, and color toward clarity, honesty, and unity in the context of High Tech. Though meticulously attentive to the formal and organizational characteristics of the building designs he examined, Banham ultimately was less concerned with categorizing aesthetic objects than with understanding (and, often, influencing) the thinking subjects that occupied and executed them. With his final essay, "A Black Box: The Secret Profession of Architecture," he offered a case in point.[8] In this poignant text, written during the terminal phase of his illness and characterized by Peter Hall as his "swan song,"[9] Banham reinforced his belief that architecture ultimately was determined not by objects but rather by actions.

The text opens with the polemical claim that "[Nicholas] Hawksmoor was an architect and [Christopher] Wren was not," with the distinction between the two coming down to a difference between "fundamental modes of designing."[10] Banham was at pains to determine the characteristics of the architectural mode, but lacking a clear definition, he proceeded negatively through a series of sharp-witted anecdotes to draw increasingly close boundaries around the field. If Wren's output was not to be mistaken for architecture, neither should the works of "programmatic postmodernism." He took a caustic parting shot at that idiom: "Reliance on erudition alone leaves postmodernism in the same relation to architecture as female impersonation to femininity. It is not architecture, but building in drag."[11] Banham's distinction between architects and engineers was similarly exclusive, if decidedly less derisive toward the outsiders. He characterized engineers as "problem solvers," while architects appeared to subscribe to "some secret value system" that had little to do with the solution of environmental or constructional challenges.[12] Indeed, he warned that architecture should not be seen as "synonymous with 'good design'" or even with the design of buildings.[13] This series of exclusions led Banham to his central thesis: "What distinguishes architecture is not *what* is done—since on their good days, all the world and his wife can apparently do it better—but *how* it is done."[14] Attempting to glean something of the field's working method, Banham then turned to Christopher Alexander's notion of a "pattern language."[15] These patterns, Banham explained, contained "knowledge of the form and how to make it."[16] In addition, he continued, these patterns "will have moral force, will be the only right way of doing that particular piece of designing—at least in the eyes of those who have been correctly socialized into the profession." For Banham, "such patterns—perhaps even a finite set of patterns—and their imperatives seem to be shared by all architects, and are, in some sense, what we recognize in Hawksmoor but do not find in Wren."

In this, Banham was rehearsing arguments he had made twenty-two years earlier in *The New Brutalism*. In the conclusion of that book, he ruminated on the tightly circumscribed and ultimately traditional boundaries of the discipline and the consolidation of "moral force" into a professional ethics by its adherents.

> The ethic of Brutalism was a campaign of "mens sana in corpore sano," but no-one should have doubted that the mind and the body would prove, ultimately, to be the mind and body which had always belonged to architecture....I make no pretense that I was not seduced by the aesthetic of Brutalism, but the lingering tradition of its ethical stand, the persistence of an ideal that the relationships of the parts and materials of a building are a working morality—this, for me, is the continuing validity of the New Brutalism.[17]

Thus, Banham linked architecture's ethics to its aesthetics through a specific form of coherence between a building's formal composition, its material instantiation, and an underlying sense of morality. This link had been forged and remained intact, he surmised, through the persistence of a specific disciplinary technique, drawing, which Banham saw as "a kind of meta-pattern that subsumes all other patterns and shelters them from rational scrutiny."[18] Produced through drawing, architecture's patterns emerged as images, just as New Brutalist buildings had been seen to do in 1955. The persistence of drawing in architecture appeared to Banham ultimately to signify an adherence to "a set of rules of thumb derived from, and entirely proper to, the building arts of the Mediterranean basin alone, and whose master-discipline, design, is simply *disegno,* a style of draughtsmanship once practiced only in central Italy."[19] Reinforcing the field's classical roots, Banham hazarded a final three-part categorization, this time aiming to encompass the totality of architectural production: "architecture is from masonry, held together by gravity, and its volumes effectively closed."[20]

"To a certain kind of old-timer," Banham continued, "this could be good news: confirmation that they were right all along and that we should have stuck to the orders and the theory of composition and ignored all that technology and modern stuff."[21] Indeed, in Banham's final, restrictive definition, the more technological exponents of both historical and contemporary building practice were threatened with exclusion from the disciplinary ken:

> I am increasingly doubtful that the timber buildings of northern Europe, for instance, or the triumphs of Gothic construction, really belong under the rubric of architecture at all. Le Corbusier felt that Gothic cathedrals were "not very beautiful," not architecture even, because they were not made of the pure geometrical forms that he found in the buildings of classical Greece and imperial Rome. Current misgivings about high-tech, with its exposed structures and services, seem to derive from a similar classicist sentiment.[22]

What is one to make of Banham's final deathbed testament? Anthony Vidler has argued that the text represents "an admission of defeat in changing 'architecture' at all during his polemical career, and an expression of respect for such a tenacious tradition."[23] In postulating an architectural object as the projection of a compressive, closed, masonry work by means of a specific drawing technique and an architectural subject as one properly socialized according to an "arcane and privileged aesthetic code,"[24] Banham's final definitions are strict and traditional, and they bear scant evidence of the field having been affected by his famous overtures to innovation and technology. The exchange of *une architecture autre* for an "other" tradition within modern architecture he performed in his late work on High Tech only reinforces Vidler's assessment, as do the melancholy conclusions of *Theory and Design in the First Machine Age, The New Brutalism, The Architecture of the Well-Tempered Environment,* and *Megastructure: Urban Futures of the Recent Past,* each of which finishes with a recounting of the triumph of tradition and convention over technology and innovation.

Nonetheless, glimmers of Banham's radicalism shine through "A Black Box." Architecture, while perhaps a tenacious tradition, remained in the essay under threat from both the emergence of computer-aided drawing techniques and impending anthropological scrutiny. In addition, Banham's suggested excision of so much material from architecture's "intellectual portfolio"—not just northern vernaculars, Gothic cathedrals, and High Tech but also the "Zulu kraals, grain-elevators, hogans, lunar excursion modules, cruck-houses, Farman biplanes and so forth" that had been "co-opted" into the architectural canon during the twentieth century[25]—certainly signaled an act of aggression against proponents of the field's hegemony over the totality of the building arts. By drawing disciplinary boundaries as tightly as he did—tightly enough to liberate the design of buildings from the purview of architecture—Banham appears not so much to have capitulated to a "tenacious tradition" as to have offered a way out from under the "crippling limitation" adherence to the field's "parochial rule book" had imposed upon "building's power to serve humanity."[26] This too was a consistent refrain throughout his writing. In *Theory and Design*, Banham famously suggested that an architect hoping to keep up with technology might have to "discard his whole cultural load, including the professional garments by which he is recognized as an architect."[27] In the closing paragraphs of *The New Brutalism,* he opined that "architects who genuinely see how narrow and restricting are the traditions of their profession, normally get out of it, and become industrial designers, real-eastate [sic] agents, systems-engineers and any other discipline that enables them to tangle with the 'realities of the situation,' in a less inhibited manner."[28] Relieving building from responsibilities to architecture and architecture from responsibilities to building, Banham attempted to free the one to better serve the needs of "a world increasingly desperate for better buildings" while allowing the other to "be recognized as something that belongs as valuably at the heart of western culture as do the Latin language, Christian liturgy, Magna Carta, or—precisely—the Masonic mysteries of *Die Zauberflöte*."[29] Banham's final writings thus echo his persistent call for two alternative trajectories for the field. The first enacted an unapologetic embrace of architecture's "operational lore," while the second offered a liberated approach to building committed not to disciplinary tradition but rather to the application of "apparent intelligence" to the design and construction of "fit environments for human activities."[30]

Radical Convention: Archigram

Banham made these themes a central concern of his last completed book, *The Visions of Ron Herron,* written in 1987–88 and published posthumously in 1994. In it, Banham drew significant attention to the work of this influential member of the Archigram group and, importantly, to the specific disciplinary techniques—drawing foremost among them—through which Herron produced his work. Projects by Herron and other Archigram members figured strongly in Banham's writing from the mid-1960s to the end of his career. "A Clip-On Architecture" (1965) foregrounded themes that would become central to Banham's writings on High Tech in the 1970s and '80s. Later treatments in *Megastructure: Urban Futures of the Recent Past* (1976) and in his 1994 monograph drew these tensions into sharp relief. Both books are examined below, but before turning to them, a brief review of the group's activities and Banham's earlier treatments of them is in order. As in Banham's writing, one finds in Archigram a distinct tension between celebrating and lamenting architecture's dissipation in the face of alternative technological possibilities. And while Archigram's trajectory suggested an eventual triumph of invisibility over the image, the legacy and impact of the group, as well as the material fact of their output, suggests a different outcome. Many commentators have noticed that Archigram's seminal imagery of dissipated objects and distracted subjects offered a radical vision of a fundamentally altered architectural milieu. Few, however, have recognized that those very images, executed with a virtuosic command of the field's standard representational techniques, simultaneously advanced discrete objects and attentive subjects to reinforce, rather than to resist, conventional notions of architectural disciplinarity.

Archigram burst onto the international scene in the mid-1960s. The series of radical projects, polemics, publications, and protests generated independently by and through various collaborations between Warren Chalk, Peter Cook, Dennis Crompton, David Greene, Ron Herron, and Mike "Spider" Webb has since been published widely and has received voluminous commentary.[31] Whether praising or panning the group, most commentators have gravitated toward two key themes that resonate throughout the Archigram oeuvre: the emancipation of the leisure subject and the eradication of the architectural object. In 1999, Mike Webb offered a prototypical instance of the approach:

> Let us now enter the world depicted in one of these drawings: figures suggestive of young, healthy, and hard-bodied men and women—mostly women I have to say—have been cut out of magazines and pasted on the surface. There is a bovine quality to them. They remind one somewhat of the Eloi in H. G. Wells' *The Time Machine*. They are all happy, healthy, and have health insurance bestowed upon them by a beneficent Labour government although they are beginning to look—how shall I put it—a bit faded, even jaundiced, over the last few years. They probably work no more than a three-day week and are undoubtedly "with it"; a quaint phrase from the sixties that when used today shows the speaker to be anything but.

To provide "a backdrop for the activities for [their] bovine friends," Archigram would pilfer architectural elements from leading figures of the day (Webb cited

Buckminster Fuller and Konrad Wachsmann as dependable sources), combine them with their own graphic and verbal musings, and assemble the fragments to "show how things would look if only planners, governments, and architects were magically able to discard the mental impedimenta of the previous age and embrace the newly developed technologies and their attendant attitudes."[32] Unencumbered by the shackles of convention and the habits of experience, these young architects advanced all manner of technological gadgetry to solve problems previously addressed with buildings. Suitaloon (1967), a wearable membrane designed by Webb, offered a sartorial alternative to traditional brick-and-mortar construction; Info-Gonks (1968), Peter Cook's premonition of today's augmented-reality glasses, dazzled the eye with supercharged spectacles; and LogPlug and RokPlug (both 1969), by David Greene, smuggled electronic convenience into the great outdoors. Theirs was "a world free of heavy and ponderous buildings that 'just get in the way,'" a world in which "architecture gets smaller and smaller." As Webb pointed out, Greene even proposed a "moratorium on all new building" in 1969.[33]

In seemingly countless drawings and proposals,[34] the Archigram group celebrated swinging youth culture and advocated the dissolution of buildings. Yet the group started out with very different ambitions. The first two issues of their eponymous magazine focused on monumental buildings (mostly student projects) by London's younger generation. The premier broadsheet emphatically demanded (twice in two pages) that a "new generation of architecture must arise."[35] Infatuated with the burgeoning space age, the group expressed (with a deliberate nod to Alison and Peter Smithson) a desire "to drag into building some of the poetry of countdown, orbital helmets."[36] Monumental building proposals remained the focus through issue 2, but with the third issue, the group's interests began to move beyond architectural form toward themes of expendability and global communication, among others.[37] By issue 7, Peter Cook famously would proclaim, "There may be no buildings at all in *Archigram* 8."[38] And while building proposals would continue to appear in later issues of the pamphlet, their right to be the sole recipient of an architect's attention and advocacy was challenged (often with tongue firmly in cheek) by increasingly ephemeral events (such as the various Instant City proposals by Cook and Herron, 1968–71) and distributed networks (such as Crompton's Computor City, 1964) better suited to accommodate and entertain the stylish representatives of youth culture that populated the group's imagery from the mid-1960s forward.[39] Thus, Archigram's (and *Archigram*'s) trajectory arcs in a three-part transformation from eagle-eyed experts rallying a like-minded audience in support of a specific vision of monumental architecture to increasingly snarky pundits postulating distracted "bovines" efficiently serviced by their technologically enhanced pastures.

Banham's "A Clip-On Architecture"[40] is the earliest serious study of the Archigram group and remains a seminal resource. In it, Banham built on the revisionist arguments of his influential *Theory and Design in the First Machine Age* to provide Archigram with a coherent genealogy of "anti-formal," "indeterminate," and "endless" precedents while using the group to take obvious if sotto voce potshots at the monumental figures and tendencies of orthodox modern architecture.[41] Countering a dismissive treatment in *Arena*,[42] Banham next offered "Zoom Wave Hits Architecture" in 1966.[43] Here, in a widely read national magazine, he praised independent magazines produced at English architecture schools such as *Polygon* (Regent Street Polytechnic), *Megascope* (Bristol University), and *Clip-Kit* (Architectural Association), as well as *Archigram,* for advancing "up-to-the-minute" proposals that countered the "dreary solutions" demanded by the aging faculties at those same institutions.[44] *Clip-Kit* drew special applause for its tidy encapsulation of the spirit of the contemporary scene, but, for Banham, "the reigning champion of protest mags"[45] and the standard bearer of the "Movement" was *Archigram.*

While his tone remained panegyric throughout, Banham subtly nudged the young architects toward more aggressive experimentation.

> If you design right up to the minute, it will be many millions of minutes later before the human race can move in, and the buildings will be out of date by just that time period. Hence the constant preoccupation of the Movement with far-out figures like Buckminster Fuller, Yona Friedman or (in Britain) Cedric Price, men who propose not only a more up-to-the-minute environment, but wild technological methods for getting it built quicker and in quantities more nearly commensurate with human needs.[46]

For Banham, these concerns, combined with an "insistence on relevance" to contemporary culture, provided the cornerstones of the little magazine project. Aimed at individual human needs rather than at idealistic general solutions, the ideology of the "Movement" offered a means to avoid the leaden profundities that undermined the efforts of more established theoreticians. As he put it, "We architectural pedagogues are prone to build architecture up into a higher discipline of abstractly ordering the masses about for their own good." Once again, Banham subtly jibed the humanist tradition and hinted at a means to project alternative subjectivities through architecture. Rather than advancing geometric harnesses that stretch Vitruvian and Modulor Men alike into idealized configurations, Archigram and other young architects offered loose, flexible, and indeterminate environmental appurtenances that fostered "the other kind of humanism" in contemporary culture.[47] Banham went on to link these ambitions directly to visual imagery: "Admittedly, the level of relevance is often only that of form-fondling, round-corner styling, art-work and paint-jobs. It is more than that, but even if it *were* purely visual and superficial, that would not in itself be contemptible. It does still matter to people what buildings look like. Indeed it matters more than it did."[48]

These passages reveal once more a contradictory tension in Banham's thinking. On one hand, buildings (or at least "environments") needed to adopt "up-to-the-minute" technology to address as fully as possible contemporary human needs. On the other hand, a deep engagement in the "purely visual and superficial" had to be maintained to guarantee relevance to contemporary culture. A balance, then, apparently was required to avoid the tendency of such new works of "going invisible on us," of "form follow[ing] function into oblivion."[49] For Banham, Archigram's balance of expressive imagery and expedient accommodation offered a provocative model for the discipline.

Megastructure: Urban Futures of the Recent Past

This tension between visual coherence and functional performance also colors Banham's 1976 book on the megastructure movement. Beyond providing an informative treatment of a body of work that had significant influence on the development of High Tech architecture, Banham provided an extended discussion on the Archigram group in which he gathered important precedents for their activities, traced the history and impact of the *Archigram* pamphlets, and outlined the group's imbrications in the short-lived megastructure movement.

Banham also provided an important account of Constant Nieuwenhuys's evolving project for New Babylon in which Banham closely aligned *Homo Ludens*, Johan Huizinga's ideal ludic subject, with the activities of the Situationist International, of which Constant was a member.[50] Constant's proposal illustrated an environment he saw as more conducive to the emergent possibilities the situationists sought through their famous *dérives* and thus more appropriate for the ludic subjects who incited them. New Babylon, he argued, was "the environment the homo ludens is supposed to live in."[51] Constant's situationist compatriots were not convinced, and Banham's explanation of their opposition to Constant's architectural proposals echoes nearly to-the-letter criticisms that later would be leveled at Archigram: "[Constant's] building of actual models only served to excuse the *techniciens de la forme architecturale,* while the attempt to propose actual mechanisms for *la vie ludique* merely played into the hands of a consumer economy."[52]

In a later chapter, "Fun and Flexibility," Banham developed arguments he first made in "A Clip-On Architecture." He addressed the question of the ludic subject in Price's and Archigram's work, ultimately distancing the English architects from the strict ideological positions of their situationist counterparts on the Continent, and he highlighted the English contribution to the megastructure movement as the introduction of issues specific to building construction, a move that resulted in a subtle and important conflation of drawing and detailing. Repeating a device he would deploy throughout his career, Banham began by shifting the focus from theory to practice: "Looking back over the first half of the sixties and the characteristic megastructures of the period, it is noticeable—alarming even—how few of them offer any nut-and-bolt proposals as to how the transient elements should be secured to the megaform, or what precise devices and services are required for the playful activities of *Homo ludens*." Price's Fun Palace (see pl. 2), by contrast, had been worked out sufficiently to satisfy English building and planning regulations, while Archigram "seemed to be motivated by sheer manic pleasure in proliferating drawings." Yet both practices seemed somehow devoid of a specific ideological position. As Banham explained, "The absence of any explicit ideology was found disturbing, or at least baffling, outside Britain; on the other hand, the presence of detailing was almost universally welcomed, especially in the stunning graphic forms in which Archigram would present it."[53] Banham again left the ideological question hanging and returned to the question of the ludic subject, noting that the Fun Palace was unlikely to offer fully self-directed pleasure and thus would not have lived up to Constant's or the situationists' radical ambitions. The scale and complexity of the project's components would have necessitated the participation of an expert staff of operators to coordinate the varied activities pursued by the Palace's occupants and to manipulate the complex array of cranes and equipment that supported the work's indeterminate activities. "The whole proposition," he argued, "would probably have been unacceptable to Constant, and anathema to the hard-line Situationists—but not unacceptable to someone raised in the tradition of the theatre, nor to English progressive professionals of the Left; neither group would see anything wrong with a little professional backstage assistance to the people's participatory pleasure out front."[54] Banham noted Buckminster Fuller's similar willingness to allow individual participation to be mediated by an "expert staff" in his contemporaneous World Game project before offering his own synopsis of the political situation: "The Fun Palace team, pragmatists to a man, were not minded to wait for the Revolution to make a perfect *palais ludique* possible; they would have a practicable Fun Palace here and now, as a way of raising public consciousness to the level where a Revolution might be found to have happened."[55]

Like Price's Fun Palace, Peter Cook's Plug-In City (see pl. 3) undoubtedly would have required a team of trained experts to manage and operate the cranes, trains, and other infrastructural appurtenances that accommodated its inhabitants' ludic wishes. Indeed, these limitations were noticed by the Archigram members, and throughout the late 1960s, the group began to distance themselves from the megastructure movement. The move was crystallized in a cut-out megastructure model kit included in *Archigram* 7. For Banham, the kit was presented unequivocally as "a joke, a self-satire, on the grounds that 'everyone can do megastructures now, make your own.'" The message was clear: "megastructure was now a bore."[56]

Moving forward, Archigram turned their attention away from monumental construction toward diminutively scaled individual living units and personal gadgets. In these later works, the immediate satisfaction of "individual wishes" reigned supreme. Alongside this shift in attention from collective monumentality to individual stimulation—that is, from problems of the image to the promise of increasing invisibility—came a much more emphatic presentation of human figures in Archigram's drawings. It is only to works dating after about 1966 that Mike Webb's formulation that "these figures probably occupy about a quarter of the given surface area of any given page" can be applied accurately.[57] As noted above, "these figures" represented a specific sort of ludic subject. While Webb was to see them as distracted "bovines" in 1999, Banham in 1976 noticed significantly more energy: "It seemed to be nothing but dolly-girls of every race and hue twisting or frugging in their modish miniskirts or striped mini-dresses, exclaiming their delight at visiphone messages, relaxing in capsules, while smiling families promenaded the deck spaces, children danced ring-a-roses, crowds surged before giant images of pop stars on vast eidophore screens; everywhere were sunglasses, freaky hair, wild clothes."[58] Banham went on finally to address Archigram's deliberate postulation of a ludic subject head-on. In a move aiming to insulate Archigram from any specific ideology, he wrote, "I must lay down a firm *caveat* against making too much of this fun-imagery.... The presence of all these leisure people in Archigram's permissive cities is as much an empirical solution to the problem of finding someone—anyone!—to populate them as it is a theoretical proposal for who *should* populate them."[59] Few would agree with Banham's assessment, as he himself noted.[60] Nigel Whiteley put it bluntly: "This...is Banham at his least convincing.... The incorporation of a specific type of person did indicate the particular type of environment Archigram wished to create: Archigram were designing a Pop environment for the urban young." To underline his point, Whiteley appended a quotation from Warren Chalk: "You don't have to live in Plug-In City.... Retired people probably won't."[61]

These passages mark another strange maneuver in Banham's argumentation. Two years before *Megastructure,* Banham had turned against attentive appreciation of James Stirling's clip-on visual imagery at the Olivetti Training Center to champion instead a form of distracted subjectivity.[62] In the closing paragraphs of "Problem × 3 = Olivetti," Banham described a disinterested flâneur gliding across Stirling's ramps blissfully inattentive to the architectural composition and details that surround her (see pl. 8).[63] Throughout their later work, Archigram advanced exactly such a subject. Whether "twisting," "frugging," or just relaxing in "bovine" contentment, the inhabitants of Archigram's technological environments appear to perform in a manner exactly aligned with Banham's own vision of an ideal ludic subject; they pay scant attention to the increasingly ephemeral architectures that surround them as they move happily about their business. Indeed, by *Archigram* 9, architectural construction had dissipated almost completely into the natural landscape or dreamlike virtuality, and the inhabitants of these new spaces were encouraged to pursue new forms of architectural stimulation beyond their material confines. Yet, though Archigram's late projects and pamphlets leave little doubt about their reconfigured views of architecture and the new forms of subjectivity they might engender, Banham distanced the group from their own rhetoric.

At Olivetti, Stirling crafted carefully composed forms and materials to produce an architecture of visual effects steeped in mannerist references and subversions. His was an architecture aimed at attentive and knowing connoisseurs of architectural form every bit as intentionally as the Smithsons' Hunstanton School had been (see pl. 1).[64] Banham responded with annoyance and argued instead that the strongest effects at Olivetti were felt when the visitor's attention to detail lapsed into immersive experience. Strangely, when Archigram's projects much more emphatically encouraged just such a distracted mode of engagement, Banham drew attention not just to the group's images but specifically toward their concept of "jointing."[65] Where Stirling's *actual* details had been a source of irritation, Archigram's *images of them* were a potent source of architectural interest. Further praising the group for qualities he had disdained in Stirling's work, Banham went on to align Archigram with a disciplinary tendency to quote and comment. Certain projects, Banham pointed out, were "arabesqued with in-group jokes about Cedric Price and Buckminster Fuller."[66] Where Archigram's critics from the mainstream seized the opportunity to cast them as radical reformers, Banham's comments undercut the radicalism of their propositions and aligned with the charges of traditionalism leveled at them—and at Banham himself—in the same year by Peter Eisenman. Foreclosing the possibility of an "English Revisionist Functionalist" return to bygone modern tendencies, Eisenman argued that modernism in architecture had not yet even occurred. He wrote, "Deriving from a non-humanistic attitude toward the relationship of an individual to his physical environment, it [modernism] breaks with the historical past, both with the ways of viewing man as a subject and...with the ethical positivism of form and function. Thus, it cannot be related to functionalism. It is probably for this reason that modernism up to now has not been elaborated in architecture."[67] While modernism had been successfully adopted in painting, literature, and music, it had not developed in architecture because the discipline had yet to engage the "non-objective," "non-narrative," and "a-temporal" qualities that signaled the movement's fundamental condition: "a displacement of man away from the center of his world."⁶⁸ To finally bring about architectural modernism, Eisenman argued for the abandonment of the form/function dialectic (and its outmoded humanism) in favor of a "new, modern dialectic" of "transformation" and "decomposition" located "within the evolution of form itself."⁶⁹

Such radicalism, more appropriate to the postmodern discourse of the 1970s and '80s, was not to be found in the Archigram oeuvre. Peter Cook affirmed the group's interest in core disciplinary values in a 2008 interview:

> Q: A common opinion of Archigram is that the group was trying to dissolve architecture or break it down.
> Peter Cook: I never felt that. I always felt that we were trying to revive architecture via a pruning process, to extend the vocabulary by showing that architecture could be more than this. It could be that, it could appropriate.... It can very easily be argued that in the twentieth century, and probably before that, architecture was always appropriating stuff from the art world.
> Q: The work seems much more interested in the center of the discipline than in the periphery. It is mining the periphery for raw materials to bring back to the center.
> PC: To bring back to the center. That's my view. Now, if you talk to somebody else, you might get a slightly different view of it.⁷⁰

Mike Webb offered similar sentiments in 1999: "An architectural drawing is without doubt what its author, the young master, understood himself to be making.... The drawing was never intended to be a window through which the world of tomorrow could be viewed but rather as a representation of a hypothetical physical environment made manifest simultaneously with its two-dimensional paper proxy."⁷¹ Banham, then, offered an accurate portrayal of the group's own ambitions and ideological stance. Archigram unequivocally directed their work at their peers within the field of architecture, an audience steeped in disciplinary convention and conditioned to pay attention not just to a drawing's content but also to the technical processes involved in its production. While their images may have *depicted* leisure subjects in varying states of distracted contentment, in presenting meticulously crafted and pun-laden artifacts specifically to architects, Archigram *encouraged* the deep attention and focus of knowledgeable connoisseurs, a move that ultimately reinforced rather than resisted conventional disciplinarity. Theirs was not a project of radical subversion but rather one of mischievous prodding, the work of precocious masters deeply committed to their field but dismayed by a state of pervasive lassitude among their elders. Ultimately and unequivocally, Archigram saw their work as a continuation of the field's core activities — activities, it is often forgotten, that only *sometimes* play out on the construction site but *always* and more fundamentally unfold on the drafting table and, more recently, on the computer screen. Though they undoubtedly altered the cut and color with a stylish infusion of pop materials and methods, each member of Archigram was, throughout the 1960s and the ensuing decades, proudly clad in "the professional garments by which he is identified as an architect."[72]

The Visions of Ron Herron

Banham reinforced this assessment of Archigram's commitment to conventional disciplinarity in *The Visions of Ron Herron*. As with "A Black Box" and "Actual Monuments," Banham completed the text during the final stages of his illness. Like the two late essays, this little-examined text focuses on core disciplinary questions. In contrast to many commentators, who place work by Archigram members at the fringes of the field, Banham located Herron's output at its very center. According to Banham, Herron was engaged in a perennial task of the discipline: "to transmute the stuff of technology into the matter of architecture."[73] This engagement took place not so much through building, though Herron's practice had authored several impressive ones, but rather through architectural drawings, which Banham saw as bona fide works of architecture in their own right. Coupled with descriptions of key projects by the Herron office that undermine the stable architectural subjects and objects Banham had articulated in "A Black Box," this attitude toward drawing suggested the possibility of works that, while produced through distinctly conventional methods, moved resolutely away from the traditionalism in evidence in his other late writings.

Banham began by articulating the strange conventionality of Herron's supposedly iconoclastic work.

> [Herron's sketches] rarely seem to imply anything more than conventional current technologies of equipment and construction, bricolated together with off-the-shelf componentry — though not always from the world of regular architecture. And that too should come as no great surprise, since Herron's whole output is somewhat at variance with the world of regular architecture.
>
> Paradoxically though, there can be no nonsense about him *not* being an architect. He is not a structural nor a systems engineer; in spite of his knowledge of both areas; he is not a computer whizz [sic], nor even a hacker, though few living architects are quite so computer-friendly. He is in himself, and in his generation entirely at home in the world of current technology, yet always and entirely an architect. He knows exactly what he is after when he goes round invading the

professional turfs of adjacent specializations (or even remote ones), but when he returns from these forays of design-piracy he does not appear bent over and burdened down, as were the Machine Aesthetes of the 1920s, with the weight and importance of the loot he has acquired. He still occupies his usual professional posture.

He never ceases to think and design like an architect, so that if his projects appear strange, they are no more than strange, rather than alien or threatening, to other architects, and the excitement he derives from these forays is communicable to other architects by purely architectural means—or drawings, as they are more usually called.[74]

Banham was relentless in his alignment of Herron's working method with conventional disciplinary techniques. He continued: "The techniques of capture and domestication for architectural purposes, are entirely conventional, not to say traditional—a Pentel R50 ballpen, Magic Markers, all that kind of familiar stuff. Only a little material is collaged in as found; the historical method of architectural recording—*disegno, dessin, tekening, zeichnung* [sic], drawing—is employed, and even his electronic outputs are computer graphics, right?"[75] These extended passages are set down here verbatim not just in submission to the stubborn resistance of Banham's prose to adequate paraphrase but also to demonstrate their author's emphatic explication of traditional disciplinary values and techniques at the base of Herron's output. In moving on to trace specific trends in the architect's approach, Banham further linked seemingly extradisciplinary tactics to venerated canonical precedents. Herron's Lyric Theater at Hammersmith (1982) and British Telecom Mobile Exhibition Structure (also known as the Telecom Slug, 1985–89) (figs. 6.1, 6.2), for example, both feature brash juxtapositions of rigid frames and pneumatic

FIG. 6.1 | **Ron Herron (British, 1930–94).**
British Telecom Mobile Exhibition Structure (1985–89). Sketch.

FIG. 6.2 | **Ron Herron (British, 1930–94).**
British Telecom Mobile Exhibition Structure (1985–89). Sketches.

FIG. 6.3 | Ron Herron (British, 1930–94).
Walking City (1964). Sketch.

membranes reminiscent of clip-on. Nonetheless, Banham highlighted their formal affiliation to modern movement icons such as Le Corbusier and Charlotte Perriand's Grand Confort armchair and a genealogy of antecedents stretching back to Auguste Perret, Ludwig Mies van der Rohe, and Eugène-Emmanuel Viollet-le-Duc.[76]

At the same time, Banham was careful not simply to rehearse established opinions. Discussing Herron's Walking City (see pl. 17), Banham attempted to diffuse fearful condemnations that appeared in its wake as he encapsulated the work's distance from orthodox modern architecture, its disregard for outmoded conventions, its simultaneous adherence to modernist principles, and its alignment with the renovated humanism he had championed throughout his career:

> What got crushed under the mighty feet of this stalking vision was not "humanity" but the empty claims of the "functionalism" that had once been the driving energy of modern architecture, but had since become a paralyzing inertia in the hands of academics and the establishments.
>
> The old libidinous mechanical kraken of Modernism had re-awakened and raised itself from the placid waters of the dead sea of current architecture, and the panic was on. Had the panicked hung around a bit, they would also have seen that marvelous, witty and life-enhancing later drawing of four or five walking cities gathered together in friendly interlinked discourse (fig. 6.3).[77]

Banham found a similar set of seemingly contradictory affiliations in Herron's Suburban Sets, elaborated, in collaboration with his son, Andrew, from Archigram's Monaco Underground project in a series of iterations throughout the 1970s and '80s

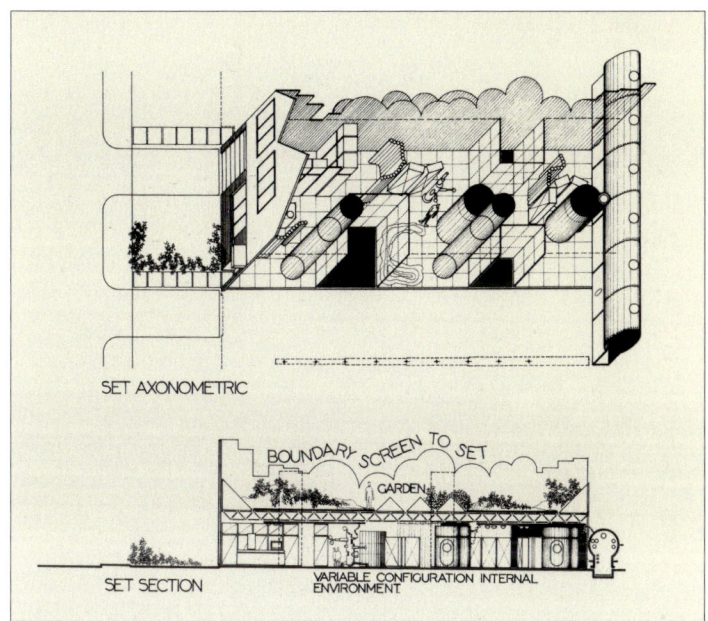 

(figs. 6.4, 6.5). In them, Herron combined anonymous vernacular street facades with customized domestic and entertainment elements to support—from telltale Archigram space frames—any number of lifestyle possibilities, as well as individual occupants ranging from typically "with-it" ludic subjects to the Queen of England. To Banham, the situation was perplexing: "How can one explain, even to the Brits, that—yes—it is possible for a supposedly radical architect to accept at face value the 'Castles on the Ground' of bourgeois suburbia, and their presiding genius, the irretrievably bourgeois House of Windsor, with its polo-ponies and corgis."[78] To answer his own question, Banham pointed to a deconstructive ambition lurking at the heart of Herron's playful musings: "One valid (but never exclusive nor exhaustive) reading of his Suburban Sets is the undermining of suburbia from within and by its own implicit value system." True to his pragmatist leanings, Banham found the fulcrum of Herron's critique not in theoretical concepts but rather in practical tectonics: "The inner contradiction that will destroy suburbia-as-we-know-it has nothing to do with Marxist theory and a great deal to do with, e.g., picture windows." Where conventional wisdom has it that picture windows existed so that occupants may see out, Herron (and Banham) understood that their more important function was to allow others to see in, to reveal the individual subjects lurking behind the anonymous suburban facades. The situation was taken to an extreme in the Suburban Sets: "All those backyard secrets, all that illusionistic gismology, all those gazebos and grounded 747s, floodlit fountains and electronic tomatoes must, sooner or later, come bursting through the façade into public view…and their flaunting will blow the cover off all the latter-day Mr Pooters (who may include Mr Herron) who thought they could have your secret and eat it, so to speak."[79]

FIG. 6.4 | **Ron and Andrew Herron (Ron Herron, British, 1930–94; Andrew Herron, British).** Suburban Sets (1974). Isometric and section.

FIG. 6.5 | **Ron and Andrew Herron (Ron Herron, British, 1930–94; Andrew Herron, British).** Suburban Sets (1974). Interior collage.

If Herron's suburban visions threatened to "blow the cover off" conventional suburban subjectivity, his Telecom Slug (see figs. 6.1, 6.2) appeared to Banham poised to undermine the stable formations that constituted a conventional architectural object. Herron's unrealized project was designed to house a traveling exhibition for British Telecom. As in the Suburban Sets, Herron exploited a set of contradictory affiliations with varied building technologies. The Slug's structural system—a cavernous PVC-coated fabric inflatable lashed with steel cables within a grid of space-frame towers—wore its redundancy on its sleeve, with tensile supports visually (and only sometimes actually) pulling at a fabric structure that, due to internal air pressure, was already in tension.[80] The visual contradiction in structure was compounded by the building's similarly expedient solution to the problem of demountable and transportable construction. The Slug was designed to sit on a cast-in-place concrete slab—a new slab was to be poured at each installation in preparation for the arrival on site of the rest of the Slug's components. Redundant building elements and installation crews would leapfrog from site to site; each iteration of the Slug would involve a different combination of new and reused elements. Herron thus proposed an architecture that could not be defined fully with reference to a specific location or a finite collection of material components. In this, one may notice a curious parallel with Peter Eisenman's elevation of "process" in concurrent writings: "The order or nature of the object now resides in that process which constitutes its differences…it is a nature now grounded in process, not in being; it is no longer based on the substance of the object…the object is no longer identical with its substance."[81] But where Eisenman developed a new architectural ontology in the collapse of the formal aspects of an object into the conceptual processes of design, Herron did so by conflating the material and temporal aspects of building construction.

The Slug would have been articulated as much by specific material assemblies as by the designation of an event—as with the fleet of aircraft that trade components and the appellation "Air Force One" based on the presence of a specific occupant, or the Grateful Dead's "Wall of Sound," a collection of redundant sound-stage equipment that leapfrogged from venue to venue during the band's tours in the mid-1970s. Along a similar vein, while one Telecom Slug was up and running, other components would be in varying states of assembly, disassembly, reconfiguration, and transportation in anticipation of a future deployment. Banham described the complex ontology of such an object:

> At the level where one begins to visualize the logistics of managing and moving such an object as the Slug—the size of a small cathedral, remember—systems-thinking begins to have a curiously solvent effect on established architectural

concepts like "a building." The Slug may well have to be *two* Slugs, or two-and-some-vulgar-fraction Slugs, if it is to satisfy the programmed requirements of actually having one Slug on site for all of the times per annum that its operational calendar stipulates.[82]

Yet, in characteristic fashion, Banham quickly reinscribed the Slug's bold challenge to traditional understandings of architectural objects into the core workings of the field: "Whether Ron Herron stops any longer to make distinctions between designing buildings, or near-buildings, or kits that periodically add up to quasi-buildings, or whatever; I very much doubt, but every so often he comes up with something like the Slug which seems light-years away from what one commonly considers to be a building—and, dammit! the thing is still architecture."[83]

Complicating the Slug's relation to core disciplinary values was the fact that Herron developed the work with the aid of computers, which placed the subversive object at odds with traditional drawing. Herron's use of computer-aided design—at the time a technology still in its infancy—prompted Banham to offer a final commentary on "Digital Design." This short section is a valuable rumination of the pressures applied by digital techniques to both architectural objects as well as the subjects that produce those objects. Tallying the advantages of computer-aided techniques, Banham noted the now obvious fact that they allow architects to "monitor the effects of re-design almost instantaneously, and can go on accumulating revision without sweating blood. More importantly, they can do it without generating labour-intensive works of art that are too hard-won to discard; the basic image in the computer program is always there somewhere in digital storage, and can be summoned back at the clack of a couple of keys."[84] Its author's naive faith in undo buffers notwithstanding, the passage marks yet another important dissipation of architecture. If the Suburban Sets worked to undermine stable forms of suburban domesticity and the Telecom Slug's inherent multiplicity challenged the stable ontology of the architectural object, here, the architectural drawing itself, the very element with which Banham began the book, was threatened by a new technology. No longer bound to the physical artifacts produced through painstaking drawing, the act of designing was now recorded in ephemeral traces on the computer monitor. In another passage eerily resonant with contemporary digital design discourse and production, Banham praised Herron and his office for having "the sort of audacity to think in terms of presenting one of their projects as the architectural equivalent of a music-video."[85] Like the Sets and the Slug, the video, exhibited at the 1986 exhibition *Vision der Moderne,* pushed architectural thinking well beyond the traditional artifacts generated through drawing and building.[86] At the same time, it challenged the received notions of the subjectivity of the architect. For Banham:

It's all jolly Post-Modern, not in the routine "Look-Mum-I-can-do-Palladian-Windows" architectural manner, but in the "Modes-of-Discourse-about-Discourse" manner that had lately engaged the minds of heavier-than-architectural thinkers in academe. Like a Post-Modern novelist abandoning the Almighty Author stance of traditional writers in favour of the modest Untrustworthy Narrator posture of the writer who is part of his own fiction, Ron Herron presents himself in the video as part of his own design project, far more convincingly than does, say, James Stirling in the famous perspectives of his own Olivetti Milton Keynes project.

For, where the draftsmanly convention of Rob Krier's [sic][87] drawings of-and-for Stirling cannot but present Big Jim as the Almighty Architect of tradition, Ron Herron, speaking *in propria voce* from the overgrown private garden behind his own computer simulation, presents himself as a user-friendly illusion just like you or me (only without making a big deal out of it, like some novelist hung up on "narratology"). The architect who has always been metaphorically at home *with* technology, here—thanks to his personal computer—appears as a mean-sensual man who is literally at home in technology. And, perhaps, in that flourishing backyard that is real despite the graphic illusions of robot domesticity by which we have come at it, he can begin to discern for us that elusive essence of technology that technologists cannot elucidate—without ever ceasing to be the architect he has always been.[88]

In the end, Banham offered a vision of architecture dissipated into the flux of digital design and the architect absorbed into the virtual ether of his illusory animations. And while such iconoclastic work tore at the heart of received conventions—indeed it had "little to do with the ancient vocabularies of *disegno*"—and distinctly intertwined the subjectivity of the architect with the objective (if virtual) realities he or she created, the architecture remained undeniably real, and its designer remained unequivocally an architect. For while "the software names will mostly fade from importance, the endeavor that bends them to the architectural will can never fade, however—not while architecture persists, not while architects like Ron Herron persist in making architecture."[89] Expanding on his important late-career concept,[90] Banham explained that making architecture did not necessarily involve the act of building but rather the "revelation of truth," an idea he gleaned from Martin Heidegger's essay "The Question Concerning Technology."[91] As Banham put it, "All the breakthroughs toward an architecture of technology have been, in a literal sense, revelations—of how to make architecture, that pure creation of the human spirit, out of concrete, or steel, or glass, or whatever. And each revelation that has comprehended or uncovered an essence—the Villa Savoye, the Farnsworth House, just as much as the Pantheon or La Sainte Chapelle—has been a truth out of which architects can make architecture." Further, "Not all such revelations have to be buildings. They could be a paragraph from Ruskin's *Stones of Venice,* or Geoffrey Scott's *Architecture of Humanism,* or even Asimov's *Caves of Steel.*" Banham continued:

> But, then, the work of the architect as he bends over the paper, pencil in hand, is all illusion. He produces simulacra of reality, diagrams which, by some form of sympathetic magic, are supposed to cause real buildings to happen out in the instrumental world. We all know that it is not sympathetic magic but a vast and frequently fallible industrial complex that will turn the illusory vision into real construction but, for architects, the moment of magic, the revelation of truth, is when pencil marks the paper, and the process of making architecture begins.[92]

Even the title of the chapter from which these lines are quoted, "Outlines of Real Illusions," reinforced Banham's claim that all of architecture's artifacts, whether drawn, animated, written, or built, are each equally and undeniably real. Herron's drawings, though perhaps "simulacra of reality," fundamentally are *not* mere representations of buildings. Rather, they are instantiations of Banham's earlier concept of "architecture as 'an image.'"[93] Herron's images demonstrate that, for Banham, architecture is less a matter of constructed buildings than of applied technique, and the sense of conviction they convey, as Banham made clear in his late writings, confirms that some of the field's most important achievements have been realized not in the realm of building construction but rather in the production of architecture beyond building.

NOTES

1. See Reyner Banham, "Actual Monuments," *Art in America* 76 (October 1988): 173–77, 213, 215, reprinted in Reyner Banham, *A Critic Writes: Essays by Reyner Banham,* ed. Mary Banham (Berkeley: University of California Press, 1996), 281–91.
2. Banham, "Actual Monuments," 284.
3. Alfred Barr, "Preface," in *The International Style,* by Henry-Russell Hitchcock and Philip Johnson (New York: W. W. Norton, 1932:13), 29, quoted in Banham, *A Critic Writes,* 284. For a discussion of Barr's postulation of the defining qualities of the style, see "Making Architecture: The Ethics of High Tech," this volume.
4. Banham, "Actual Monuments," 289.
5. Banham, "Actual Monuments," 289.
6. Banham, "Actual Monuments," 288.
7. Banham, "Actual Monuments," 285.
8. Reyner Banham, "A Black Box: The Secret Profession of Architecture," *New Statesman and Society,* 12 October 1990, 22–25, reprinted in Banham, *A Critic Writes,* 292–99.
9. "The posthumous 1990 piece is particularly significant, not simply because it was his swan song, but because he knew it and wrote it that way." Peter Hall, "Foreword," in Banham, *A Critic Writes,* xv.
10. Banham, "A Black Box," 292. Sir Christopher Wren (1632–1723) was educated at Oxford University and was a founding member of the Royal Society. An accomplished polymath and self-trained architect, he designed

St. Paul's Cathedral in London (completed in 1711) and oversaw the reconstruction of over fifty London parish churches after the Great Fire of 1666. Nicholas Hawksmoor (1661–1736) began his career as Wren's personal clerk, worked as an assistant on St. Paul's, and authored some of the most celebrated of the London parish churches, including St. Mary Woolnoth (completed in 1727), Christ Church Spitalfields (1729), and St. George's, Bloomsbury (1730).

11 Banham, "A Black Box," 293.
12 Banham, "A Black Box," 295.
13 Banham, "A Black Box," 293. He continued, "To separate architecture from good design in this way may unsettle those who do not question the mythologies by which architecture has operated for some six centuries now, but it does not imply that the two are incompatible; simply that one can have either without the other."
14 Banham, "A Black Box," 294, Banham's emphases.
15 See Christopher Alexander et al., *A Pattern Language: Towns, Buildings, Construction* (New York: Oxford University Press, 1977), in which he outlined 253 patterns intended to ensure "good" design decisions; Christopher Alexander, *The Timeless Way of Building* (New York: Oxford University Press, 1979), in which he elaborated on the motivations, objectives, and values that underlie his method; and Christopher Alexander et al., *The Oregon Experiment* (New York: Oxford University Press, 1975), which documents Alexander and company's initial development of participatory, pattern-based methods for the planning of the University of Oregon campus in the mid-1970s.
16 See Banham, "A Black Box," 296–97, for this and all subsequent quotations in the paragraph.
17 Reyner Banham, *The New Brutalism: Ethic or Aesthetic?* (New York: Reinhold, 1966), 135.
18 Banham, "A Black Box," 298.
19 Banham, "A Black Box," 297.
20 Banham, "A Black Box," 297.
21 Banham, "A Black Box," 298.
22 Banham, "A Black Box," 297.
23 Anthony Vidler, *Histories of the Immediate Present: Inventing Architectural Modernism* (Cambridge, MA: MIT Press, 2008), 220n1.
24 Banham, "A Black Box," 297.
25 Banham, "A Black Box," 294.
26 Banham, "A Black Box," 298.
27 Reyner Banham, *Theory and Design in the First Machine Age* (London: Architectural Press, 1960), 330.
28 Banham, *The New Brutalism*, 135.
29 Banham, "A Black Box," 298.
30 Reyner Banham, "1960—Stocktaking," *Architectural Review* 127 (1960): 93.
31 The early literature on Archigram is dominated by the group's own writings. Their first monograph, Peter Cook, ed., *Archigram* (London: Studio Vista, 1970, reissued by Princeton Architectural Press, 1999), republished much of the written and graphic material from the original *Archigram* pamphlets as well as extended presentations of projects by group members. Other important presentations include Priscilla Chapman, "The Plug-In City," *The Sunday Times Colour Supplement,* 20 September 1964, 28–33; Peter Cook, "Archigram Group, London, A Chronological Survey," *Architectural Design* 35 (1965): 559–73; and "Amazing Archigram: A Supplement," *Perspecta* 11 (1967): 131–54. In the 1990s, group members participated in the design and execution of the traveling exhibition *Archigram: Experimental Architecture, 1961–74* and its attendant catalogs. See Alain Guiheux, ed., *Archigram* (Paris: Editions du Centre Georges Pompidou, 1994); Dennis Crompton, ed., *A Guide to Archigram: 1961–74* (London: Academy, 1994); Dennis Crompton, ed., *Concerning Archigram* (London: Archigram Archives, 1998); and Dennis Crompton, ed., *Archigram: Experimental Architecture, 1961–1974* (Tokyo: PIE, 2005). The latter reproduces selected pages of the original *Archigram* pamphlets as inserts within the catalog. Editorial pieces by group members were regular occurrences in the pages of *Architectural Design, Arena, AA Quarterly,* and elsewhere from 1965 onward. More recently, two excellent monographic studies have appeared. See Simon Sadler, *Archigram: Architecture without Architecture* (Cambridge, MA: MIT Press, 2005); and Hadas Steiner, *Archigram: The Structure of Circulation* (London: Routledge, 2008).

   Curiously, the *Archigram* pamphlets, which the group published at irregular intervals from 1961 to 1974, have received scant attention. Steiner's book is among a growing number of recent texts that have attempted a sustained treatment of the pamphlets. Sarah Deyong gives a useful summary of them (concentrating on the Archigram group's affiliations with the megastructure movement) in "The Creative Simulacrum in

Architecture: Megastructure, 1953–1972" (PhD diss., Princeton University, 2008), 49–60. My own writings on the *Archigrams* include Todd Gannon, "Return of the Living Dead: *Archigram* and Architecture's Monstrous Media," *Log* 13/14 (2008), 171–80; and Todd Gannon and N. Katherine Hayles, "Virtual, Actual, Ineffable: Architecture and Media in the Age of Computation," in *Ineffable: Architecture, Computation, and the Inexpressible,* ed. Bradley Horn (Barcelona: Loft, 2010), 58–71. Several ideas in the present chapter first appeared, in a different form, in these two essays.

32 Mike Webb, "Boys at Heart," in Cook, *Archigram,* 2.

33 Webb, "Boys at Heart," 3.

34 In fact, the drawings have been counted, as well as cataloged, systematically archived, and made available in digital facsimile by researchers at the University of Westminster. See the Archigram Archival Project (AAP), launched in April 2010: http://www.interactivearchitecture.org/the-archigram-archival-project.html.

35 *Archigram Paper One* (1961): cover sheet and main page.

36 *Archigram Paper One,* cover sheet. The lines were written by David Greene.

37 This shift in editorial focus immediately followed a 1962 lecture by John McHale at the London Institute of Contemporary Arts (ICA). "The Plastic Parthenon" outlined nearly all of the major themes to be taken up in subsequent issues of *Archigram.* Given their close ties to the ICA at the time, it is likely that at least some of the members of the Archigram group were in attendance. Regardless of their presence, the period immediately following McHale's lecture marked a notable shift in the *Archigram* pamphlets, as their concern migrated from the promotion of projects by the younger generation to the elaboration of specific themes—all of them developed in McHale's talk—such as expendability (issue 3, 1963), science fiction (issue 4, 1964), individual living pods (issue 7, 1966), and nomads (issue 8, 1968).

McHale developed the lecture from his 1959 essay "The Expendable Ikon 1," *Architectural Design* 22, no. 2 (1959): 82–83; and "The Expendable Ikon 2," *Architectural Design* 22, no. 3 (1959): 116–17. A text version of McHale's "The Plastic Parthenon" appeared in Gillo Dorfles, ed., *Kitsch: The World of Bad Taste* (New York: Bell, 1969), 98–110. In "Recycling Recycling," Mark Wigley provides an important commentary on McHale: see Amerigo Marras, ed., *Eco-Tec: Architecture of the In-Between* (New York: Princeton Architectural, 1999), 38–49. Sarah Deyong attributes *Archigram*'s shift in editorial focus to the influence of Banham, who had opined on expendability in "A Throw-Away Aesthetic" [written 1955, originally published as "Industrial Design and Popular Art," *Industrial Design* 7 (March 1960): 45–58] in Reyner Banham, *Design by Choice,* ed. Penny Sparke (New York: Rizzoli, 1981), 90–93. See Deyong, "The Creative Simulacrum," 53. Given the group's commitment to monumentality in the issues that appeared immediately after Banham's essay, McHale's talk seems the more likely instigator of the shift.

38 Peter Cook, "A Very Straight Description," *Archigram* 7 (1966): n.p. (Archigram Archival Project, Insert 9/2).

39 The human figures that became a fixture in later Archigram images are rare in the pamphlets themselves. The inability economically to reproduce images cut from color magazines undoubtedly influenced their absence. The group's telltale female figures first appear hand drawn in Warren Chalk's 1964 Capsule Homes project. The earliest collaged female figure (black-and-white) appears in Peter Cook's Plug-In Mews scheme of 1965. After 1966, the technique became increasingly common in Archigram projects. The technique was not unprecedented. The Smithsons had included collaged images of celebrities, including James Dean, Joe DiMaggio, and Marilyn Monroe in their well-known 1952 perspectives of Golden Lane (see fig. 1.14).

40 See Reyner Banham, "A Clip-On Architecture," *Design Quarterly* 63 (1965): entire issue.

41 For a discussion, see "Unconventional Combinations: A Clip-On Architecture," this volume.

42 See Francis Duffy, ed., "Some Notes on Archigram," *Arena: The Architectural Association Journal* 82 (June 1966): 171–72.

43 Reyner Banham, "Zoom Wave Hits Architecture," *New Society* 7, no. 179 (1966): 21, reprinted in Banham, *Design by Choice,* 64–65.

44 For an excellent study of the independent magazines of the period, see Beatriz Colomina and Craig Buckley, eds., *Clip/Stamp/Fold: The Radical Architecture of Little Magazines, 196x to 197x* (Barcelona: Actar, 2010).

45 Banham, "Zoom Wave," 64.

46 For this quote and the subsequent one, see Banham, "Zoom Wave," 65.

47 Reyner Banham, "The History of the Immediate Future," *RIBA Journal* 68, no. 7 (1961): 256.

48 Banham, "Zoom Wave," 65, emphasis in the original.

49 Banham, "A Clip-On Architecture," 30.

50 On New Babylon, see Constant [Nieuwenhuys], "New Babylon: An Urbanism for the Future," *Architectural Design* 34 (1964): 304–5; and Mark Wigley, *Constant's New Babylon: The Hyper-Architecture of Desire*

(Rotterdam: 010, 1999). On the situationists, see Simon Sadler, *The Situationist City* (Cambridge, MA: MIT Press, 1998); and Martin van Schaik and Otakar Máčel, eds., *Exit Utopia: Architectural Provocations, 1956–76* (Munich: Prestel, 2005).

51   Constant, "New Babylon," 304, quoted in Reyner Banham, *Megastructure: Urban Futures of the Recent Past* (New York: Harper & Row, 1976), 81.

52   Banham, *Megastructure,* 83.

53   Banham, *Megastructure,* 84.

54   Banham, *Megastructure,* 86.

55   Banham, *Megastructure,* 88.

56   Banham, *Megastructure,* 98.

57   Webb, "Boys at Heart," 2.

58   Banham, *Megastructure,* 99–100.

59   Banham, *Megastructure,* 100–101, emphasis in the original.

60   Banham cited criticism from Mechthild Schumpp, Argentine students, the French Utopie group, and "other left-wing critics." Banham, *Megastructure,* 101.

61   Nigel Whiteley, *Reyner Banham: Historian of the Immediate Future* (Berkeley: University of California Press, 2002), 178. Chalk's quote is from Priscilla Chapman, "The Plug-In City," 33.

62   For a discussion, see "Unconventional Combinations: A Clip-On Architecture," this volume.

63   Reyner Banham, "Problem × 3 = Olivetti," *Architectural Review* 155 (1974): 197–200.

64   For a discussion of the Hunstanton School, see "In Search of Alternatives: Banham, Britain, and the New Brutalism," this volume.

65   Banham, *Megastructure,* 93. Jointing, as Banham used it here, signified an attentiveness to part-to-part connections as central to a building's coherence, even if those connections were not worked out to the level of plausibly constructible details.

66   Banham, *Megastructure,* 98.

67   Peter Eisenman, "Post-Functionalism," *Oppositions* 6 (1976): i–ii, reprinted in Peter Eisenman, *Eisenman Inside Out: Selected Writings, 1963–1988* (New Haven, CT: Yale University Press, 2004), 86.

68   Eisenman, "Post-Functionalism," 86.

69   Eisenman, "Post-Functionalism," 87.

70   Peter Cook, personal communication, Santa Monica, CA, 10 May 2008.

71   Webb, "Boys at Heart," 2.

72   Banham, *Theory and Design,* 330.

73   Reyner Banham, *The Visions of Ron Herron* (London: Academy, 1994), 12.

74   Banham, *Visions of Ron Herron,* 8.

75   Banham, *Visions of Ron Herron,* 8.

76   Banham, *Visions of Ron Herron,* 40.

77   Banham, *Visions of Ron Herron,* 76–77.

78   Banham, *Visions of Ron Herron,* 82. Banham invokes here the conservative writings of *Architectural Review* editor J. M. Richards. See J. M. Richards, *The Castles on the Ground: The Anatomy of Suburbia* (London: J. Murray, 1946). For Banham's earlier indictment of this book, see Reyner Banham, "Revenge of the Picturesque: English Architectural Polemics, 1945–65," in *Concerning Architecture: Essays on Architectural Writers and Writing Presented to Nikolaus Pevsner,* ed. John Summerson (London: Allen Lane, 1968), 265–73.

79   Banham, *Visions of Ron Herron,* 83.

80   Herron intimated that the steel structure was unnecessary and was included simply to "meet by-laws." Banham, *Visions of Ron Herron,* 106. While this may be, the steel is crucial to the project's dissonant visual effects.

81   Peter Eisenman, "The Futility of Objects: Decomposition and the Processes of Differentiation," *Harvard Architecture Review* 3 (1984), reprinted in Peter Eisenman, *Eisenman Inside Out,* 186.

82   Banham, *Visions of Ron Herron,* 105, Banham's emphasis.

83   Banham, *Visions of Ron Herron,* 106.

84   Banham, *Visions of Ron Herron,* 112.

85   Banham, *Visions of Ron Herron,* 112.

86   Herron's description of the project sheds light on a parallel reliance on analog techniques to make the video:
      With Dennis Crompton, who did some trickery with the backcloths, we made a video that was eventually shown at the German Architecture Museum in the 1986 exhibition, *Vision der Moderne.* The video starts with an animated walk into the Studio Strip. Then you see me sitting in the computer model with

moving images on the video wall behind me — I'm in real space talking about real images. In the end sequence the screen opens and I'm sitting in my own garden finishing the conversation.

Banham, *Visions of Ron Herron,* 118. For more on the exhibition, see Heinrich Klotz, ed., *Vision der Moderne: Das Prinzip Konstruktion* (Munich: Prestel, 1986).

87 The drawings, in fact, were made by Léon Krier.
88 Banham, *Visions of Ron Herron,* 118, Banham's emphasis.
89 Banham, *Visions of Ron Herron,* 119.
90 See Reyner Banham, "Making Architecture: The High Craft of Renzo Piano," *Architecture + Urbanism,* extra edition, no. 3 (March 1989): 151–58; and "Making Architecture: The Ethics of High Tech," this volume.
91 Banham, *Visions of Ron Herron,* 14. For Martin Heidegger's text, see "The Question Concerning Technology [1955]," in idem, *The Question Concerning Technology and Other Essays* (New York: Harper Torchbooks, 1977), 3–35.
92 Banham, *Visions of Ron Herron,* 15–16.
93 Banham, "The New Brutalism," *Architectural Review* 118 (1955): 358. For a discussion, see "In Search of Alternatives: Banham, Britain, and the New Brutalism," this volume.

CONCLUSION
BUILDING BEYOND ARCHITECTURE

In spite of his late-career decoupling of architecture from building, throughout his career, Banham often railed against what he saw as the field's inadequate attentiveness to architecture's role in the production of the built environment. In 1977, for example, he wrote: "The pity of it is that so much of this academic debate is about matters which are marginal and trivial to the important business of seeing the world better housed, better serviced, better symbolized—but are matters suitable for academic debate."[1]

This admonition, a typical example of his opinion and manner of expressing it, came in an article on Norman Foster's Willis Faber & Dumas Headquarters (Ipswich, 1974) (figs. 7.1–7.4; see fig. 4.10, pls. 18–20). In his unfinished book on High Tech, Banham located the project in the category of "The Opposite Case," works that did not subscribe to High Tech's distinctive monumentality of exposed structure, exposed services, and bold colors; rather, they were conceived as subdued glass boxes reticent of their structural and functional workings.[2] Banham often treated such works with hostility. Recall, for example, his dismissive remarks on modified "smart sheds" in "Art and Necessity" and *The Architecture of the Well-Tempered Environment*.[3] Yet his position was markedly ambivalent. "The Opposite Case" not only signaled an allegiance to what Banham saw as the outmoded visual traits of the International Style but also appeared to "prefigure an even higher form of High Tech."[4] In 1981, writing of the recent crop of corporate facilities constructed to house the burgeoning computer culture of Silicon Valley, Banham labeled the group a "better than respectable body of architecture" and applauded corporate firms such as Gensler Associates and Hawley & Peterson Architects for coupling pleasant, well-serviced, open-plan work environments with coherent visual imagery.[5]

While Banham's visit to Silicon Valley appears to have softened his normally aggressive stance on anachronistic affiliations with the International Style, in "Silicon

Foster Associates (Norman Foster, British, b. 1935).
Willis Faber & Dumas Headquarters (Ipswich, England, 1974). Facade (detail).
Photo by Ken Kirkwood.
See p. 229, pl. 19.

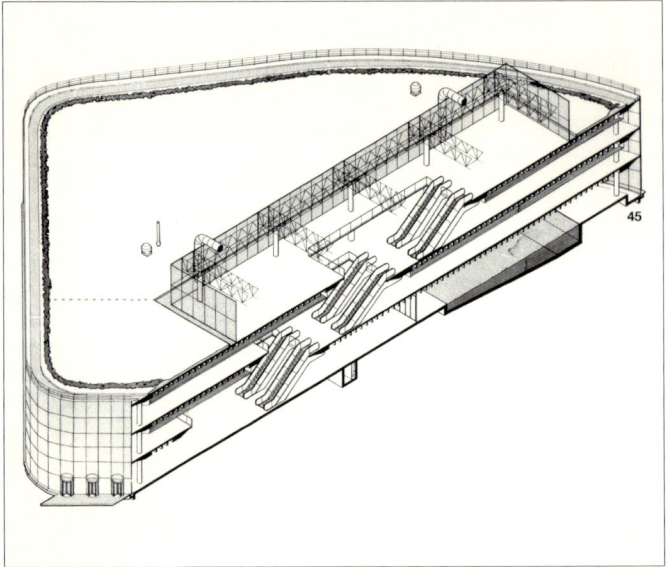

FIG. 7.1 | **Foster Associates (Norman Foster, British, b. 1935).** Willis Faber & Dumas Headquarters (Ipswich, England, 1974). General view. Photo by Ken Kirkwood.

FIG. 7.2 | **Foster Associates (Norman Foster, British, b. 1935).** Willis Faber & Dumas Headquarters (Ipswich, England, 1974). Cutaway axonometric.

FIG. 7.3 | **Foster Associates (Norman Foster, British, b. 1935).** Willis Faber & Dumas Headquarters (Ipswich, England, 1974). Cutaway axonometric showing construction system.

FIG. 7.4 | **Foster Associates (Norman Foster, British, b. 1935).** Willis Faber & Dumas Headquarters (Ipswich, England, 1974). Turf roof. Photo by Tim Street-Porter.

Style," it was not to the buildings themselves but rather to their distinctive landscaping that Banham devoted the bulk of his attention. "By their bush work shall ye know them," he churlishly intoned. "From the start, the historical development of the valley's corporate vision has been measured in shrubs and trees."[6] Many of these projects pushed landscape design well beyond the fastidious cultivation of planted areas adjacent to the building proper. At Hawley & Peterson's Qume Headquarters (San Jose, California, 1980), for example, planting was internalized to become a major element of the interior milieu, while at the Dysan Corporation Headquarters (Santa Clara, California, 1980), the building was nestled into the earth to engender a more thorough conflation of interior and exterior. Banham expressed a measure of dismay at this occlusion of architectural objects with planting and earthwork, and he closed by suggesting the possibility of a renewed appreciation of the corporate glass box shorn of its verdant disguise: "Whatever the present preoccupation with external imagery and cosmetic shrubbery, it will need only a slight shift of corporate vision for the basic box to be found admirable for its simplicity and for Digital and IBM Santa Teresa to be praised for their naked honesty. For the moment, though, fig leaves are in, full frontal industrial nudity is out, and…how green is our Silicon Valley!"[7]

Working in close collaboration with corporate leaders, Norman Foster had offered a potent example of just such a shift in vision seven years earlier at Willis Faber. But where Banham, in the passage quoted above and throughout the 1970s and '80s, had praised works that aligned with his late-career valuation of clarity, honesty, and unity, Foster's project systematically flouted the historian's categorizations and stubbornly resisted affiliation with any of the stylistic idioms Banham had advanced during his career. Refusing the New Brutalism's coherent imagery

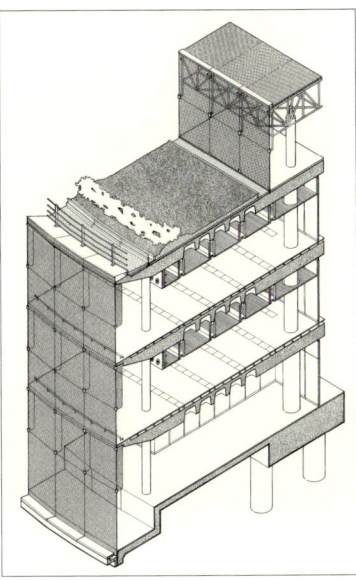

and clip-on's "unity of effect," at Willis Faber, Foster offered a dizzying mélange of reflected architectural incident on the building's mirror-glass facade (see pls. 18, 19). Where exposed services and structure signaled clear and honest expression for New Brutalist, clip-on, and High Tech works, Foster answered with an exterior that effaced tectonic expression and interior spaces that betrayed nothing of the environmental and communication technologies at work beyond their raised floors and suspended ceilings (see fig. 7.3). As-found materials and off-the-peg components similarly were avoided. Foster's team developed custom-fabricated building assemblies such as the work's unprecedented glass skin,[8] one-off interior ceiling system, and fenestrated escalators. Of the nine architectural qualities Banham articulated for the New Brutalism, clip-on, and High Tech (see table 1, p. 154), Foster's work exhibited just one—bold colors—but even this was limited to interior finish systems such as floor coverings. Further, and unlike other "smart sheds" Banham used to indicate High Tech's "Opposite Case," Willis Faber did not offer much in the way of enhanced environmental performance,[9] nor did it align with Alfred Barr's triple formula for the International Style. Its volumes are not planar but bulbous, its massing is far from regular, and its glass surfaces, while unadorned, are replete with fragmented contextual reflections by day and revealed interior incident by night—a far cry from Barr's canonical blankness. Banham's modern traits of clarity, honesty, and unity are likewise in short supply, with obscurity, dissimulation, and what Banham termed "a nicely judged eclecticism" much more readily at hand.[10] While these latter qualities soon would be associated with flagship examples of architectural postmodernism, it would be difficult, given the building's earnest functionality and lack of overt referentiality, to argue convincingly for alignment with that style. Rather, Willis Faber stands as a defiant catalog of exclusions: neither New Brutalist nor clip-on nor High Tech; neither International Style nor modern nor postmodern. Further, boasting as it does a suspended glass facade, cantilevered floor slabs, and vast open-plan interiors, Willis Faber flaunted the final set of criteria Banham offered in "A Black Box": the building is neither masonry nor compressive nor closed. By Banham's final definition, Foster's building is *not even architecture* at all.

If Ron Herron's career heralded the possibility of architecture beyond building, with Willis Faber, Foster took the opposite approach to deliver a mode of building beyond architecture. Though there is ample evidence of architectural intelligence on display, there is little celebration of architecture as such at Willis Faber. Writing in the *Architectural Review,* Christopher Woodward pointed out that the designers were unwilling "formally to monumentalize any one of the main elements of the building, neither structure, services, nor the usual paraphernalia of modules."[11] Banham, for his part, described how the secondary structure of the exterior glazing "has been refined away almost, but not quite, to nothing, a clamp bar to hang the glass from at the top, and a patch plate at each corner where the four plates meet. Otherwise, there is nothing except a translucent line of sealant between each sheet [of glass] and the next, optically lost in the inevitable refractions and reflections that occur at any cut edge of glass."[12] And as architectural interest was effaced at the level of the details, so too did it dissipate as one moved through the building. Banham explained: "The rising plane of the escalator through the generous central light well makes one look at, and think about other matters. It is a building to be explored before it is understood, and for this reason its levels of technology, servicing, and energy consumption are not to be read by snap-judgment or any single viewpoint."[13] As was the case at James Stirling's Olivetti Training Center and Richard Rogers's building for Lloyd's of London, Banham the detail connoisseur gave way here to Banham the flâneur. Moving around the facility's undulating perimeter, one does not encounter an emphatic architectural object but rather a reflected and refracted re-presentation of its immediate context (see pls. 18, 19). And if the exterior morphs into a cinematic display of virtual images animated by the roving eye of the mobile observer, moving within only amplifies the project's promiscuous slide toward adjacent fields of disciplinary expertise. For the "other matters" one is compelled to look at and think about on the "rising plane of the escalator" are not architectural in the least. Rather, one glides through two expansive levels of interior furnishings before being deposited at the top upon a fastidiously clipped and seemingly limitless lawn (see fig. 7.4, pl. 20). The effect is at once disarmingly pleasant and shocking. At no point along this sequence from urban street through corporate interior to bucolic park does one find anything even remotely monumental in the conventional architectural sense. Instead, the building effectively melts away, and a visitor encounters no architecture at all. Willis Faber & Dumas is nothing but interior and landscape.

The Opposite Case

This slouch into adjacent design fields betrays an unlikely allegiance at the heart of the building's conception. For while Willis Faber's unsettling effects spurn affiliation with progressive architectural movements from the 1930s to the '70s, they distinctly resonate with a body of English architectural thought that had been disdained by forward-thinking young architects from the 1950s to the '70s—that is, Townscape.[14]

If Sigfried Giedion's "Nine Points on Monumentality" provided Banham with an unlikely template for the design of Centre Georges Pompidou,[15] Gordon Cullen provided an eerie premonition of the design tactics Foster employed at Willis Faber with his "Townscape Casebook" (1949).[16] In the building, Foster evaded Banham's nine stylistic traits for the New Brutalism, clip-on, and High Tech as well as the nine additional qualities Banham associated with the International Style, modern architecture, and architecture as such. By contrast, he neatly aligned Willis Faber with all forty qualities Cullen advocated in the "Casebook." "Screened Vistas" abound along the building's perimeter, while a "Grandiose Vista" is delivered as instructed "from the air" at the culmination of the escalator trip to the upper lawn. Here, a minimal guardrail, low parapet, and slight mounding of the outlying turf conspire to transform the building edge into a picturesque ha-ha. Uninterrupted by a visual boundary, the rooftop expanse of turf collapses seamlessly into the aggressively flat landscape of surrounding Suffolk (see figs. 7.3, 7.4). "Netted Sky" is provided to the lower floors through the open atrium, while the drama of "Enclosure" and "Exposure" plays out through the entry sequence. In an uncanny resonance with Cullen's sketches (fig. 7.5), Willis Faber perfectly choreographs a "Free Development" of juxtaposed historical elements on its undulating perimeter.[17] "Incident," "Undulation," and "Flowing Lines" all amply are employed, and directives toward "Multiple Use," "Roofscape," "Change of Level," "Significant Objects," and "Floorscape" dutifully are followed. Even "Nostalgia," the final element advocated in the "Casebook," is represented in the building's fragmentary reflection of adjacent historical buildings. And if, at Willis Faber, Foster evacuated architecture into the adjacent fields of interior and landscape design, he arrived at exactly the fields that had sparked the Townscape movement three decades earlier.

The ideas that would harden into Townscape first were advanced in the *Architectural Review* in a 1944 editorial. "Exterior Furnishing or Sharawaggi: The Art of Making Urban Landscape" is an unabashed manifesto for a new form of town planning that took its cues from the English picturesque movement as well as from broader tendencies the author saw as endemic to the English national character.[18] Contrasting prevailing trends of the Garden City movement, modernist planning, and British neoclassicism, "Exterior Furnishing" signaled a form of coherence in town planning based on dissonance and juxtaposition. Such coherence often was found *inside*

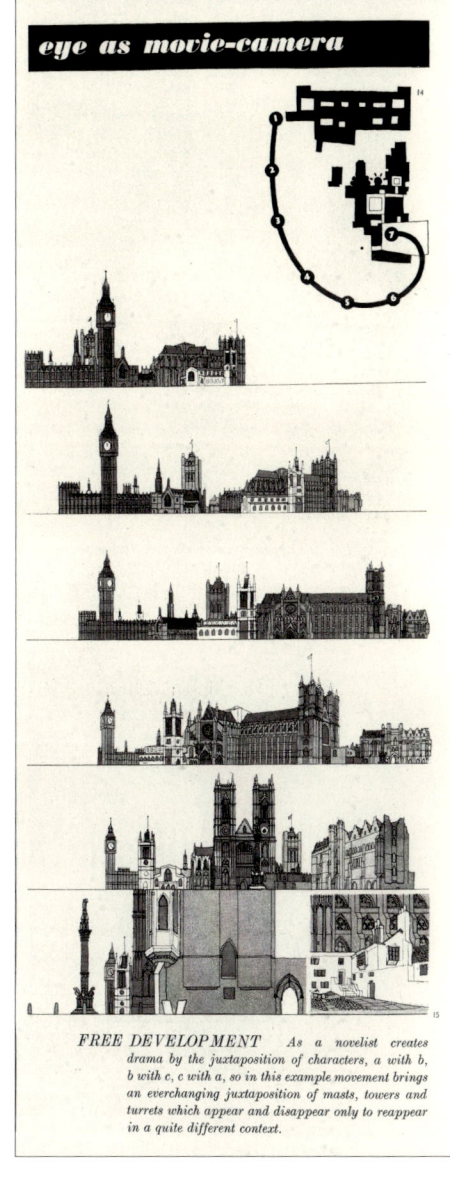

FIG. 7.5 | Gordon Cullen (British, 1914–94).
"Eye as Movie-Camera."
From Gordon Cullen, "Townscape Casebook," *Architectural Review* 106 (1949): 366.

England's homes but rarely was seen in its cities and towns: "An interior to be successful should be the result of growth, of attachments formed over years to things old and new. The fear of one's modern cupboard clashing with the Victorian atmosphere of a room, or one's Victorian chandelier looking out of place in an Aalto environment is wholly unjustified."[19] Five years later, the exotic label "Sharawaggi" was exchanged for the more pedestrian "Townscape" in a lengthy development of the earlier article signed by I. de Wolfe, nom de plume of Review editor Hugh de Cronin Hastings.[20] Here, Hastings found a more recent analogy for dissonant coherence in English middle-class decoration in the capricious combination of mismatched furniture, accessories, and chintz in everyday domestic interiors. Townscape marked a concerted attempt to transfer this potent visual sensibility to the urban landscape. To assist in the translation, Hastings's article was followed by Cullen's eleven-page "Casebook" of principles to be adopted by the would-be Townscape planner.

Among the many critics of Townscape was the architect Basil Taylor, who in a 1954 BBC Radio talk attempted to draw sharp distinctions between modern architecture and these renovated picturesque principles.[21] Nikolaus Pevsner's response to Taylor—in which he remarked, "The modern revolution of the early twentieth century and the picturesque revolution of one hundred years before had all their fundamentals in common"[22]—sparked an intense partisan debate on the topic. "Had Pevsner deliberately set out to infuriate the young," Banham opined, "he could hardly have done better."[23] Alan Colquhoun issued a stern rebuke of Pevsner's position,[24] and later, following Pevsner's "Englishness of English Art" radio addresses on the BBC, a flurry of critical reactions appeared, including Colin Rowe's condemnation of "the insufferable tedium of Townscape."[25] As outlined at the outset of the present book, many of the younger generation reacted against the Review by embracing a geometrically disciplined modern classicism introduced via Le Corbusier and Rudolf Wittkower.[26] But as Banham pointed out, these attempts were undermined by a growing distance between the rigid geometries of classical form and advances in technology, mathematics, and other influences during the 1950s and '60s. In moving away from classical forms, many architects inadvertently moved their work directly toward the neopicturesque tendencies they proclaimed to resist. As Banham put it, "Such 'scientific' concepts as open-endedness, the promulgation of growth and change as qualities to be incorporated in building designs, and the acceptance of expendability and impermanence, all combined to bring on a kind of architecture, and architectural philosophy, that must have looked reassuringly familiar to the editors of the Architectural Review."[27]

In his articulation of Uvedale Price's theory of the picturesque, De Wolfe [Hastings] outlined an "English Revolt" against the "Grand Manner" of French classical planning. The "radical" English approach contrasted the "rational" French method by advancing independence over equality, the particular over the universal, parts over wholes, the real over the ideal, and increasing complexity over increasing conformity.[28] Banham prized exactly these values, not least among them radicalism, throughout his career. He and his colleagues at the *Review* also shared an unabashed commitment to functional accommodation, a pragmatic approach that addressed each problem on its own merits, a tendency to foreground architecture's visual aspects, and a soft spot for disciplinary outsiders.

These associations point to a final paradox in Banham's late writings. On one hand, Banham left behind a near-classical definition of architecture as achieved through closed, compressive, masonry works. On the other, he cleaved to the distinctly modern values of clarity, honesty, and unity. Canonical High Tech works such as Centre Pompidou rejected the former values but retained the latter, suggesting either the possibility of an architecture that eschewed traditional "materials and methods" while espousing modern values or the possibility that High Tech represented a mode of building that operated somewhere outside the disciplinary ken.[29] The "Opposite Case" at Willis Faber went even further toward the possibility of building beyond architecture by eluding all six of Banham's categories and dissolving into an experiential milieu constructed primarily of interiors and landscape. Whether or not one chooses to label it architecture, Centre Pompidou rightfully inherited Banham's "other" tradition extending from Victorian engineering via Giedion through constructivism and clip-on into canonical High Tech. Willis Faber and other examples of Banham's "Opposite Case," however, suggested an altogether different historical lineage with claims to the parentage of High Tech—another "other" that moves back via Pevsner through Townscape, the International Style, and nineteenth-century eclecticism to the picturesque.

In accommodating these contrasting affiliations, Banham's late writings on High Tech hold in paradoxical suspension dichotomies with which he had wrestled throughout his career: on one hand, an architecture of rigorous formal coherence and memorable visual images; on the other, an architecture of dissonant juxtaposition with a tendency to dissipate into adjacent fields of cultural production. In High Tech, Banham found both a progressive aesthetic suffused with "operational lore" and a responsible ethic charged with "apparent intelligence." He also found a method of working suitable for the construction of monumental symbols of contemporary culture and equipped to handle the quotidian challenges of "nine-to-five" practice. In High Tech buildings, he found compellingly articulated details to satisfy learned connoisseurs dispersed within immersive experiential milieus that accommodated distracted flâneurs; and, in its architects, he found a staunch commitment to architecture's most storied traditions coupled with a firm resolve, when necessary, to militate against unproductive habits and conventions. Tragically, Banham's life was cut short before he could marshal these dichotomies into the chapters of *Making Architecture: The Paradoxes of High Tech.* In this unfinished chronicle of both a visual style and an operative technique, Banham was poised not to resolve High Tech's paradoxes but rather to instrumentalize them to explain a mode of "making architecture" suffused, like his own writing, with clarity, honesty, and unity as well as with complexity, invention, diversity… and, of course, with wit, too!

NOTES

1. Reyner Banham, "Grass Above, Glass Around," *New Society* 42, no. 783 (1977): 22–23, reprinted in Reyner Banham, *A Critic Writes: Essays by Reyner Banham,* ed. Mary Banham (Berkeley: University of California Press, 1996), 210.
2. Reyner Banham, "High Tech Architecture: The Beginning of an Argument," ca. 1987, p. 4, Reyner Banham papers, acc. no. 910009, box 8, folder 3, Getty Research Institute, Los Angeles.
3. Reyner Banham, "Art and Necessity: Inmos and the Persistence of Functionalism," *Architectural Review* 172 (1982): 35, 38; and Reyner Banham, *The Architecture of the Well-Tempered Environment* [1969], 2nd ed. (Chicago: University of Chicago Press, 1984), 297. For a discussion, see "Making Architecture: The Ethics of High Tech," this volume.
4. Banham, "High Tech Architecture," 4.
5. Reyner Banham, "Silicon Style," *Architectural Review* 169 (1981): 285.
6. Banham, "Silicon Style," 288.
7. Banham, "Silicon Style," 288, Banham's ellipsis.
8. The frameless glass facade, hung from the building parapet and stabilized with minimal patch fittings and perpendicular glass stiffeners in lieu of steel secondary structure, was the first of its kind. Its manufacturer, Pilkington Industries, later added the system to its standard product line. For an informative treatment, see Ian Lambot, "The Glass Wall," in Norman Foster, *Foster Associates: Buildings and Projects,* vol. 2, 1971–73, ed. Ian Lambot (Hong Kong: Watermark, 1989), 34–35.
9. "Its energy consumption is neither sensationally low, nor sensationally high…. The level of servicing is not sensational, nor the provision over-elaborate—just appropriate." Reyner Banham, "Introduction," in *Foster Associates,* by Norman Foster (London: RIBA, 1979), 6.
10. Banham, *Well-Tempered Environment,* 2nd ed., 292.
11. Christopher Woodward, "Head Office, Ipswich, Suffolk," *Architectural Review* 158 (1975): 150.
12. Banham, "Introduction," *Foster Associates,* 6.
13. Banham, "Introduction," *Foster Associates,* 6.
14. As was noted in "High Tech and the Persistence of Modernism," this volume, Banham made this connection between Willis Faber and the Townscape movement in 1977. See Banham, "Grass Above."
15. See Sigfried Giedion, José Luis Sert, and Fernand Léger, "Nine Points on Monumentality" [1943], in *Architecture, You, and Me: The Diary of a Development,* by Sigfried Giedion (Cambridge, MA: Harvard University Press, 1958), 48–51; and "Making Architecture: The Ethics of High Tech," this volume.
16. Gordon Cullen, "Townscape Casebook," *Architectural Review* 106 (1949): 363–74.
17. Compare Cullen's "free development of styles" with pls. 19 and 20.
18. The editor, "Exterior Furnishing or Sharawaggi: The Art of Making Urban Landscape," *Architectural Review* 95 (1944): 3–8. Authorship is generally credited to Hugh de Cronin Hastings, though recent scholars have suggested that Nikolaus Pevsner was an important collaborator on this text, and others on Townscape signed with Hastings's pseudonym, Ivor de Wolfe. See John Macarthur and Mathew Aitchison, "Ivor de Wolfe's Picturesque; or, Who or What Was Townscape?," in *Limits: Proceedings of the 21st Annual Conference of the Society of Architectural Historians, Australia and New Zealand,* ed. Harriet Edquist and Hélène Frichot (Melbourne: SAHANZ, 2004), 301–6.
19. The editor, "Exterior Furnishing," 6.
20. See I. de Wolfe, "Townscape: A Plea for an English Visual Philosophy Founded on the True Rock of Sir Uvedale Price," *Architectural Review* 106 (1949): 354–62.

21 See Basil Taylor's "English Art and the Picturesque," a series of unpublished 1954 talks on BBC Radio's Third Programme.

22 Nikolaus Pevsner, "C20 Picturesque," *Architectural Review* 115 (1954): 229.

23 Reyner Banham, "Revenge of the Picturesque: English Architectural Polemics, 1945–1965," in *Concerning Architecture: Essays on Architectural Writers and Writing Presented to Nikolaus Pevsner,* ed. John Summerson (London: Allen Lane, 1968), 267.

24 See Alan Colquhoun, "Twentieth Century Picturesque: Letter to the Editors," *Architectural Review* 116 (1954): 2, as well as Pevsner's measured response that was appended to Colquhoun's letter in the same issue.

25 See Nikolaus Pevsner, *The Englishness of English Art* (London: Penguin, 1956). Rowe's attack appeared in Rowe, "Connell, Ward, and Lucas," letter to the editor, *Architectural Association Journal* 72 (1957): 163, and is quoted by Banham, along with citations of other critical responses, in "Revenge of the Picturesque," 269.

26 See Le Corbusier, *Towards a New Architecture* [1923] (London: John Rodker, 1931); Le Corbusier, *The Modulor: A Harmonious Measure to the Human Scale Universally Applicable to Architecture and Mechanics* [1948] (Cambridge, MA: Harvard University Press, 1954); Rudolf Wittkower, *Architectural Principles in the Age of Humanism* [1949], 4th ed. (New York: W. W. Norton, 1972); and "In Search of Alternatives: Banham, Britain, and the New Brutalism," this volume.

27 Banham, "Revenge of the Picturesque," 272.

28 De Wolfe [Hastings], "Townscape," 358.

29 The latter possibility, as well as a characterization of architecture markedly similar to Banham's, was suggested by Sigfried Giedion in 1928. His chapter on "Architecture" in *Bauen in Frankreich* begins as follows: "The concept of architecture is linked to the material of stone. Heaviness and monumentality belong to the nature of the material, just as the clear division between supporting and supported parts does." Owing to the influence of new materials, he continued, "It seems doubtful whether the limited concept of 'architecture' will indeed endure." See Sigfried Giedion, *Building in France, Building in Iron, Building in Ferro-Concrete* [1928] (Santa Monica, CA: Getty Center, 1995), 90. Importantly, Giedion intended the chapter title to include a question mark—"*Architektur?*"—but the editors failed to include it in the book as published. For a discussion of the omission, see Sokratis Giorgiadis's critical introduction to the English edition, Giedion, *Building in France,* 49. This line of argumentation, of course, resonates deeply with the tendency among German architects of the 1920s and '30s to use the term *Baukunst* in lieu of *Architektur*. See, for example, Hans Hildebrand's translation of Le Corbusier's *Vers une architecture* as *Kommende Baukunst* (Stuttgart: Deutsche Verlags-Ansalt, 1926). If the English title, *Towards a New Architecture,* exaggerated the French original's claims to novelty, the German one downplayed its endorsement of traditional disciplinarity.

PLATES

◄ **PL. 1** | **Alison Smithson (British, 1938–93) and Peter Smithson (British, 1923–2003).**
Hunstanton Secondary Modern School (Hunstanton, England, 1954). Interior view. Photo by John Maltby.

▲ **PL. 2** | **Cedric Price (British, 1934–2003).**
Fun Palace for Joan Littlewood Project (1963–66). Perspective. New York, The Museum of Modern Art.

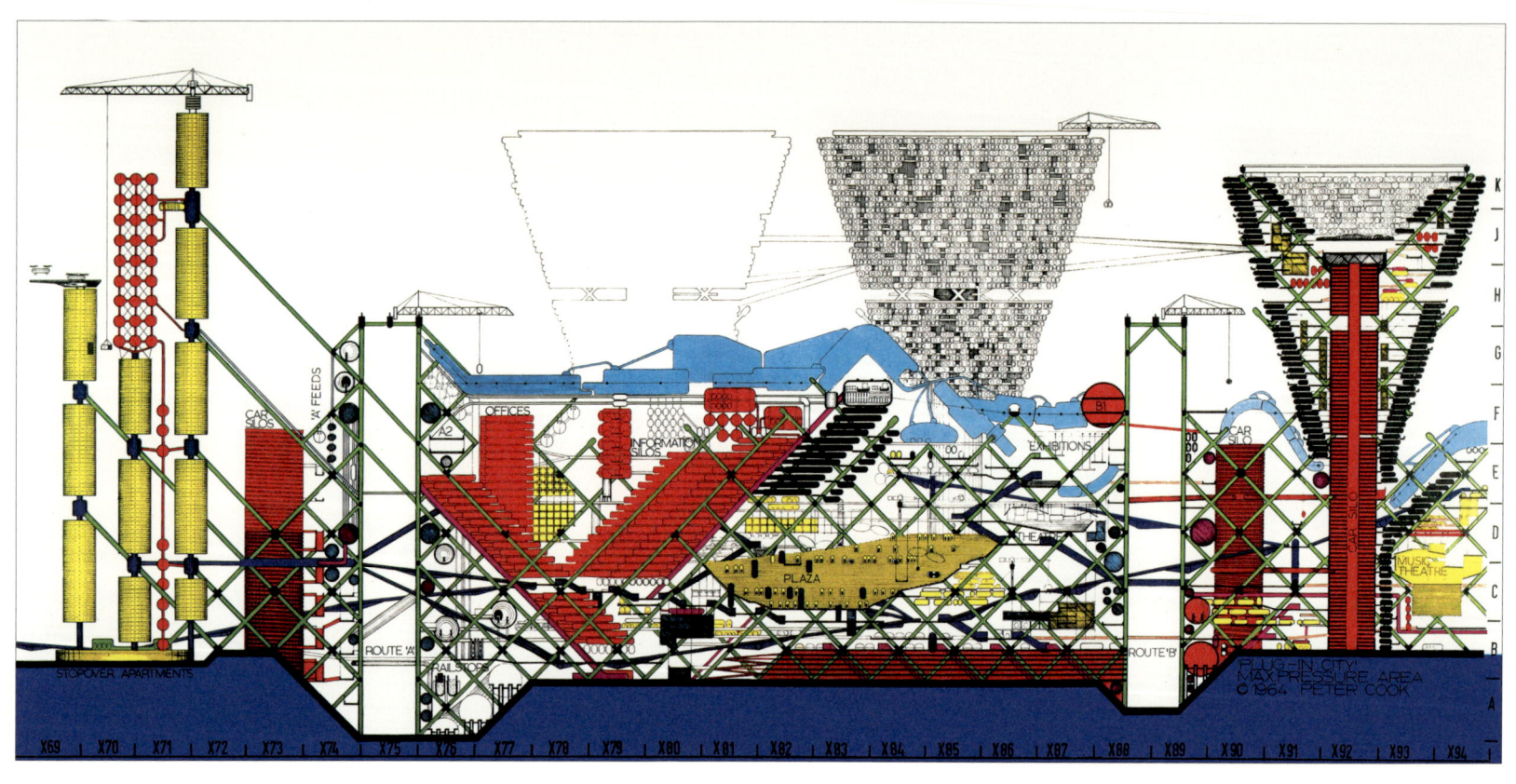

▲ PL. 3 | **Peter Cook (British, b. 1936).**
Plug-In City, Max Pressure Area (1964).

▶ PL. 4 | **Farrell/Grimshaw Partnership (Terry Farrell, British, b. 1938; Nicholas Grimshaw, British, b. 1939).**
Service Tower and Dormitory Conversion (London, 1967).
View from rear.
Photo by Tim Street-Porter.

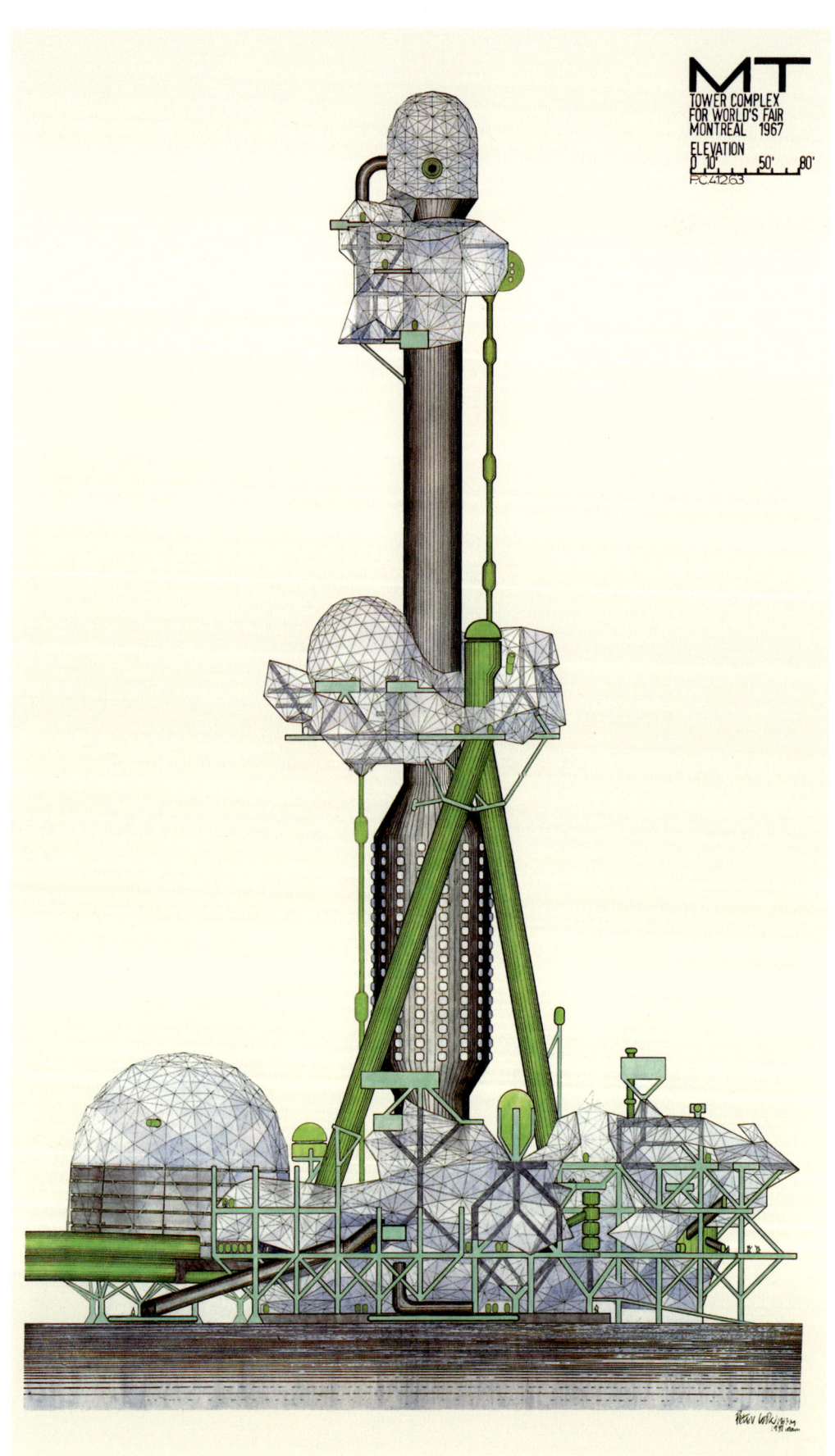

◄ PL. 5 | **Peter Cook (British, b. 1936) for Taylor Woodrow Design Group.**
Entertainments Tower for Expo '67 in Montreal (1963).

▲ PL. 6 | **Richard + Su Rogers (Richard Rogers, British, b. Italy, 1933; Su Rogers [née Brumwell], British, b. 1939).**
Jan Kaplický concept collage for the Extension to the Design Research Unit (London, 1969–71).

◄ PL. 7 | **Edward Cullinan (British, b. 1931).**
Olivetti Training Center residential wing
(Haslemere, England, 1969–74). View of lobby.

▲ PL. 8 | **James Stirling (British, 1926–92).**
Olivetti Training Center (Haslemere, England, 1969–74). Interior view.
Photo by Richard Einzig.

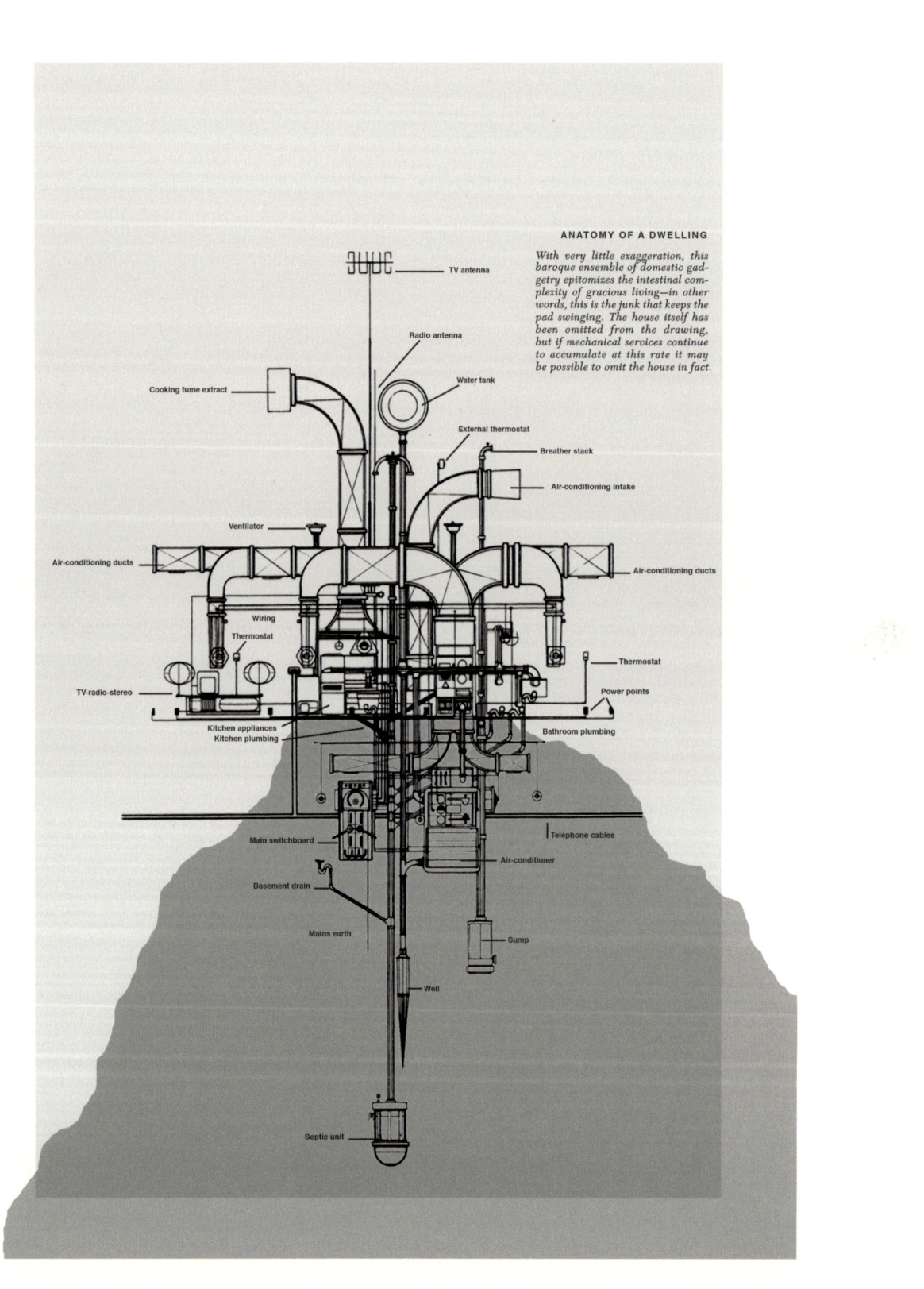

◀ **PL. 9** | **François Dallegret (French, b. 1937).**
Anatomy of a Dwelling.
From Reyner Banham, "A Home Is Not a House,"
Art in America 53, no. 2 (1965): 71.

▲ **PL. 10** | **Philip Johnson (American, 1906–2005).**
Glass House (New Canaan, Connecticut, 1949). General view.
Photo by Steven Brooke.

◀ PL. 11 | Team 4 (Norman Foster, British, b. 1935; Wendy Foster [née Cheesman], British, d. 1989; Richard Rogers, British, b. Italy, 1933; Su Rogers [née Brumwell], b. 1939).
Reliance Controls Building (Swindon, England, 1967).
View of street (south) facade.
Photo by Norman Foster.

▲ PL. 12 | Foster Associates (Norman Foster, British, b. 1935).
IBM Pilot Head Office Building (Hampshire, England, 1971).
General view.
Photo by Ken Kirkwood.

▲ **PL. 13** | **Piano + Rogers (Renzo Piano, Italian, b. 1937; Richard Rogers, British, b. Italy, 1933).**
Centre Georges Pompidou (Paris, 1977). General view.
Photo by Michel Denancé.

▶ **PL. 14** | **Foster Associates (Norman Foster, British, b. 1935).**
Hong Kong and Shanghai Bank Headquarters (Hong Kong, 1986). General view.
Photo by Ian Lambot.

▲ **PL. 15** | **Renzo Piano Building Workshop (Renzo Piano, Italian, b. 1937).**
IBM Traveling Pavilion (1982–86). Detail view of structure.
Photo by Fulvio Roiter.

▶ **PL. 16** | **Renzo Piano Building Workshop (Renzo Piano, Italian, b. 1937).**
The Menil Collection (Houston, 1982–87). View of gallery.
Photo by Richard T. Bryant.

EACH WALKING UNIT HOUSES NOT ONLY A KEY ELEMENT OF THE CAPITAL, BUT ALSO A LARGE POPULATION OF WORLD TRAVELLER-WORKERS.

A WALKIN

PL. 17 | **Ron Herron (British, 1930–94).**
Walking City (1964). General view.

▲ **PL. 18** | **Foster Associates (Norman Foster, British, b. 1935).**
Willis Faber & Dumas Headquarters (Ipswich, England, 1974).
Street view.
Photo by Ken Kirkwood.

▶ **PL. 19** | **Foster Associates (Norman Foster, British, b. 1935).**
Willis Faber & Dumas Headquarters (Ipswich, England, 1974). Facade.
Photo by Ken Kirkwood.

PL. 20 | **Foster Associates (Norman Foster, British, b. 1935).**
Willis Faber & Dumas Headquarters (Ipswich, England, 1974).
Interior view.
Photo by Tim Street-Porter.

HIGH TECH AND ADVANCED ENGINEERING

REYNER BANHAM

High Tech was the only real novelty to emerge in the architecture of the 1980s, though some of the most characteristic buildings exemplifying this trend were designed, or even built, during the seventies. However, none were actually labelled "High Tech" until 1979, and the main currency of the term really dates from 1983, by which time it had become a common label for many things besides buildings, and was rapidly passing into general usage in journalism and conversation. Any stylistic label that gains such wide and rapid public acceptance as did "High Tech" in the 1980s is not likely to be well-defined or precise. Popular usage, especially in journalism and advertising copy, applied the term to everything that was new and fashionable from proprietary medicines to running shoes and skiing equipment, to almost anything controlled by a microprocessor chip, and as a visual or stylistic label it seems to mean everything from round-cornered (portable radios, or if made of white wire-mesh, cosmetic trays) to horizontally ribbed (travel goods), from matte black (light fittings) to "industrial blue" (also light fittings) to dead white (certain sports cars) or black and perforated (furniture) and almost anything at all that even faintly resembles a space vehicle or a toy robot from Japan.

If we may make a preliminary but important distinction at this point, it is necessary to make a clear differentiation between "High Tech," which seems to be most often used as a label for the visual aspects of the design of whatever object is so called, and such terms as "Advanced Engineering" and "State of the Art Technology," both of which refer to the actual level of technological innovation in a design. This text will avoid the phrase "State-of-the-Art Technology" because of grave ambiguities in its everyday usage and will normally distinguish between High Tech and Advanced Engineering.

To illustrate this distinction from outside the field of architecture, we may instance the Salomon downhill ski boot and the Moulton AM7 bicycle. The Salomon ski boot, which has been called High Tech by some writers, appears not to contain many significantly "higher" technologies than have been available in other downhill boots, but its visual presentation has been very skillfully styled to emphasize whatever claims to technical superiority it may possess. The Moulton cycle, described as "advanced engineering" by its manufacturer, on the other hand, derives its appearance almost entirely from the engineering techniques involved in its design and construction, which are indeed unique to this type of bicycle, rather than from any self-conscious decision about what style to employ. And one may admit that neither of these two statements is necessarily one hundred percent absolutely true; the styling of the Salomon boot probably does derive in part from innovations in its materials and mode of fabrication, and the apparent absence of self-conscious styling from the Moulton may itself derive from some barely formulated aesthetic preferences on the part of Alex Moulton, the *patron* of the company that makes them.

As applied to architecture, which is our main (but not exclusive) business here, the term High Tech often seems to partake of the sense of Advanced Engineering as well as that of visual style and therefore can mean anything from "slickly mechanistic presentation" to "at the cutting edge of environmental technology"—and it can mean either or both of them in any ratio of admixture and at any level from the purely factual to the strictly visual to the clearly mythological. In their book *High-Tech: The Industrial Style and Source Book for the Home,* which was the first to use the phrase in its title, and popularized the term among general readers interested in design, the authors, Joan Kron and Suzanne Slesin, derive the phrase itself from "High Style" and seem to be unaware that, in architectural circles at least, the phrase "High Technology" had been in use since the very late 1960s. Furthermore, they seem to use and interpret the term as no more than the label for a particular fashion for using industrial (or industrial-looking) products in home furnishing and interior decorating, though most of the designs and *produits trouvés* which they illustrate are probably better described as merely "Functional" since few are advanced in their engineering, and equally few exhibit self-conscious styling beyond choice of paint colors.

This basically Functionalist quality may be the reason they felt justified in invoking in their introduction the whole mythology of the Modern Movement in architecture—the opening words of their first chapter claim (with the utmost historical insouciance) that "the industrial aesthetic was born in 1851 when Sir Joseph Paxton, an engineer and gardener, designed and built the vast Crystal Palace."[1]

Whether or not this statement is accurate or historically useful, it represents a version of a proposition that every member of the Modern Movement in architecture has accepted as something like religious dogma since the beginning of the present century and was taught to all the architects of the High Tech generation while they were still at architecture school. This almost un-thought phrase of Kron and Slesin should alert us to the kind of deep and diffuse underpinnings on which High Tech as an attitude and as a body of design practice claims to be founded. One cannot understand High Tech, nor the accusations of "nostalgia" that are often levelled at it, without understanding the nature of this mythology of "Les Grands Constructeurs du XIX Siècle," founded on the works of Sigfried Giedion and Nikolaus Pevsner, and its permeation throughout the ideology of Modernist design in the present century.

There are, however, other kinds of mythologies at work in the general understandings of High Tech, and of those who have taken a stand in opposition to it. Chief of these is the Mythology of Technical Ignorance. Thus the one thing that "everybody knows" about the Centre Pompidou in Paris, the building designed by Renzo Piano and Richard Rogers, which serves as the High Tech "monument of definition" for Kron and Slesin (and most other writers) is that it is supposed to "look like an oil refinery!" In fact, it looks like nothing of the sort, this mythology depends on a general ignorance of engineering among the "culturati," and if Pompidou resembles any other class of building at all, it is a particular type of steam-powered electrical generating station that is favored in California. Yet this strikingly clear resemblance to the California power stations has never entered into the general body of discourse about either the *Centre* or about High Tech in general. Such anecdotal mythologies of ignorance, based upon the technical unawareness of humanists, have encumbered critical and historical writing about Modern Architecture since its beginnings but have been made worse in recent years by that recrudescence of hostility to all forms of technology among Western intellectuals, which is discussed later in this chapter.

A more suggestive and extremely instructive type of mythologizing appears in a very strange observation on aeronautical design by the Italian industrial designer and proponent of "Bio-design," Luigi Colani:

> The Battle of Britain fought in 1940 revealed very interesting examples of bio-design as seen in aircraft. The two adversaries in this decisive air battle were the German Messerschmitt 109 and the British Spitfire. The former was a hi-tech squarish looking plane, while the Spitfire looked more like a fish than a plane, with its oval shaped fluke-like wings and soft aero-design. Messerschmitt was a stubborn man and he ignored the advice of his aerodynamic expert Edgar Schmued who was better aware of what a high-speed fighter should look like. Schmued quit Messerschmitt and went to America. There he designed for North American Aviation the P-51 Mustang—a bio-look Messerschmitt with softer lines and better aerodynamics. The fact that both the bio-Spitfire and the bio-derivative of the Messerschmitt, the P-51 Mustang, were both superior to

the hard-headed, hi-tech design of the German plane makes a very funny bio-design inside story. For one could say that bio-design won the Battle of Britain![2]

Whatever else may be wrong with this passage, in terms of military history or aeronautics, its main offense must surely be that it goes against common sense—if the Spitfires were so superior as a fighting machine, then surely it must have been *more* "High Tech" than the Bf109, rather than the other way about. Clearly, Colani is not talking about technology but is exercising a private system of aesthetics or iconography—except that the system is not so private; much conversation and critical writing on these topics uses the term "High-Tech" to mean something like what Colani appears to mean here: "resembling the appearance of machines as they were understood in the classic literature of Modernism of the Twenties and Thirties." Most alert and currently well-informed readers, confronted with these remarks of Colani's, would know exactly what he intended, even if they knew that the words would be nonsense in any other context.

Almost all discourse employing the term "High Tech" tends to vacillate between a purely stylistic reading at one extreme and a genuine appreciation of technological matters at the other, and any study of the topic which intends to do justice to it must recognize and incorporate this variability, even at the risk of some confusion. And since this study will be discussing architecture, not simply engineering, the symbolic elements and other traditional aspects of architecture as a civic art—"style," that is—are an essential part of the cultural pretensions and rewards of the High Tech adventure.

Again, the rise of High Tech must be seen in the context of a number of hostile counter-mythologies, quite apart from the accusations of technical nostalgia, and/or ineradicable suspicions about the actual technical qualities of the buildings themselves. Of these counter-mythologies, the most significant was, obviously, the general hostility to Technology that has already been mentioned. The period of the rise of High Tech is conveniently bracketed by two books that expressed the profoundest misgivings about Technology as a force in design and in the world at large. The first was *La Speranza Progettuale (Design, Nature, and Revolution)* by Tomás Maldonado, which had first appeared in 1970. Since Maldonado had been head of the immensely influential *Hochschule für Gestaltung* at Ulm in Germany, where he had seemed bent on revivifying Functionalism by injections of Information Theory, Cybernetics, and Systems Analysis, his apparent defection from Technological Modernism was the more provocative and, as will be observed below in the case of Porsche Design, the more paradoxical.

This was, however, something of an "inside" affair, a designer turning against technological enthusiasms in design; the second book was more general and encyclopedic in its scope and, published in 1977, appeared in the year that Centre Pompidou was opened. This was *Autonomous Technology* by the MIT sociologist Langdon Winner; not a work of noisy polemic like so many of the Anti-Tech tracts of the earlier 1970s, it was more of a grand survey of all the doubts about technology's place in society that had been expressed by major thinkers like H. G. Wells, Lewis Mumford, Jacques Ellul, Paul Goodman, Herbert Marcuse, and Henri Lefebvre down to Alvin Toffler. Nevertheless, Winner's introduction does include a prime quotation of early 1960s Techno-paranoia, from Mario Savio's famous speech at the very beginning of the student disturbances at Berkeley: "There is a time when the operation of the machine becomes so odious, makes you so sick at the heart that you can't take part; you can't even passively take part, and you've got to put your bodies upon the gears and upon the wheels, upon the levers, upon all the apparatus and you've got to make it stop."[3] Though it will be clear that Savio's "Machine" is a metaphor for a whole social and political system, the very use of such a metaphor of hostility is a fair indication of the kind of disrepute that Technology—understood or misunderstood—was about to enter in academic circles. *Autonomous Technology*, for all its carefully academic tone of voice, presents an intellectual prospect so bleak that it remains almost incredible that, in the year of its publication, there should also be a celebration of the apparent pleasures of technology as exuberant as Renzo Piano and Richard Rogers's colorful culture-machine on the Plateau Beaubourg. The subsequent rise and consolidation of the High Tech "movement" thus took place in a doubly hostile intellectual environment, caught between extreme pessimism about Autonomous Technology on the one hand, and the return of Revivalist architecture, in the guise of Post-Modernism, on the other. It is clear, therefore, that High Tech must have been securely rooted in a powerful sense of self-confidence (or moral self-justification) among its architects and a knowing (or indifferent) resistance to current intellectual fashions among the clients who commissioned [it.]

The architectural and historical-critical complexities that must be faced in considering High Tech architecture are therefore profound but rewarding, wide-ranging but ultimately even more instructive about the nature of architecture than about technology. For let it be emphasized here, as it will be throughout this study, High Tech has far more to do with architecture than it does with Technology, even though it would be inconceivable without the availability of certain materials and techniques and the example and vital contributions of certain engineers.

The kind of architectural and technological issues that are at stake will be demonstrated here in a "first approximation" argument by comparing two buildings that both answer to most of the commonly held views of High Tech architecture. Between them they display most of the characteristics of the "style" however it be defined; both are in England, barely thirty miles apart, and designed by British architectural offices, but they serve two continental European automobile manufacturers with strong claims to be at the cutting edge of automotive technology because of their successes in competition: Porsche and Renault. They also serve substantially similar functions involving customer relations and the storage and distribution of spare parts.

In architectural terms they could hardly be more different, however, yet both have been confidently identified as "High Tech," albeit with qualifications. The Porsche building of 1986, designed by the Dewhurst Haslam Partnership, probably comes closer to the general public's idea of what High Tech should be like, and this is not surprising since the architects clearly gave attention to the creation of imagery sympathetic to the company's products: "Having decided that one elevational treatment must convey the company's image, the architects felt that it should somehow relate to the company's product, perhaps the most highly engineered production-car on the road," wrote Stephen Trombley,[4] in his extended account of the building's design—but without observing that "the company's product," in the eyes of many of the public, would tend to include not only cars but also the various items of non-automotive luxury consumer merchandise, such as watches and sunglasses, that are marketed under the brand *Porsche Design* and enjoy a prestige that derives in part from the competition successes of the cars and in part from their styling, which corresponds well to what style-conscious members of the public in the 1980s supposed High Tech to be.

And it is not only the non-architectural public who read Porsche Design as "High Tech"—the first example of *der High-tech Asthetik* cited in a polemical article of 1986 by the German architectural historian Volcker Fisher, "Technologie als Fetisch: High-tech in Architektur und Design," is Porsche Design's celebrated *Feuerzeug* (cigarette lighter) of 1984,[5] a typically and conventionally reticent/elegant product that acquires "esteem by association" by having the Porsche name on it, regardless of functional merit or technical qualities (which in this case are both high, as is the price!). Among well-informed, affluent, fashion-conscious consumers, Porsche was thus a name with distinct stylistic, as well as technical, connotations.

Dewhurst Haslam thus had the conspicuous advantage, not often enjoyed by even High Tech architects, of working with a corporate imagery that was understood by a wide public, but it was also directly applicable to buildings, since it employed an imagery born of the same modernist tradition as their architecture. Ferdinand Alexander Porsche III, chief of the car company and later of Porsche Design, had received a crucial part of his design training at the Hochschule für Gestaltung at Ulm, one of the focal institutions of technical/aesthetic Modernism in the 1950s when its dominant teacher was Tomás Maldonado. The Porsche 911, which he designed shortly after leaving the HfG, may well be the first example of "High Tech" in the sense which is being discussed here, because it has also been (together with the products of Mercedes Benz and BMW) one of the sacred objects of the mythology of German technological mastery, the legend of *Vorsprung durch Technik*.

This anchorage in the older traditions of Modernism is underlined by the architects' own definition of the Porsche building's style as being "high tech…but high tech classic. Not high tech innovatory."[6] The outcome of this attitude, as it is seen by drivers approaching the Porsche building from the motorway, is a long, twenty-two-bay two-story facade of brushed aluminum cladding panels of "hard, grey metallic appearance" and dark glass strip windows. Each letter of the Porsche company's famous logo occupies almost the full width of one 4.5-meter panel on the upper facade, and the elevation finishes as a flat, straight, and uninterrupted cornice line. The roof, in fact, is not absolutely flat but is interrupted by the thirty-six glazed pyramids that cover the internal atrium, but none of this can be perceived from ground level at normal viewing distances. The architectural image is an uninflected square box; a classic—not to say conventional—Modernist package, neat and smooth and as reticently elegant as the non-automotive products of Porsche Design.

This tightly packaged image not only conceals the facts about the roof layout, but it also fails to acknowledge the functional differentiations of the interior of the building. As the Porsche company's operational base in Britain, it has to provide reception areas for customer relations, administrative offices, a large service bay where newly delivered cars are made ready for delivery, and an even larger area for receiving, storing, and dispatching spare parts (engine testing and other "dirty" functions are in a separate structure). Only some changes in the fenestration of the upper story of the facade give any clue that there might be internal functional differences, and these cannot be made to yield any specific information about which function is where.

The style of the exterior is marked by precisely that "anonymity" that has always been one of the more mythological characteristics of Modern Architecture—but also one of the prized qualities of the "Black Box" approach to the case-work for high-technology equipment (though one should observe that the most admired boxes, from Max Braun to Saxpy computers, have been grey or beige).

One should also pause to observe that there is no necessary connection between architecture that is in any of the styles that have been termed "High Tech" and the presence of "high technology" or even advanced engineering in the building, either as a function to be housed or as an aid to the better structural or environmental performance of the building shell. Of all the buildings known to the author, the one which contains the very highest technology, the most advanced engineering must be the Stanford Linear Accelerator Facility in California. The contents of the building are, chiefly, a two-mile-long evacuated steel tube in which super-conducted electromagnets produce 20 billion electron volts of energy to accelerate a beam of sub-atomic particles to almost the speed of light. The building that houses this wonder-machine is a simple and almost character-less corrugated metal shed that extends over two miles of territory but is otherwise totally unremarkable in any sense relevant to architecture as an art. Contrariwise, some of the most visually elaborate and highly finished works of High-Tech architecture have, in fact, no more than rhetorical or mythological connection with any advanced technology or engineering.

At Porsche, however, there seems to be a good correlation between the claims to quality and performance implicit in the style of architecture and the actual quality and performance of the building. Not only do the external cladding systems, for instance, give the total building envelope excellent thermal characteristics, balancing heat gains and losses so that heating is needed for only the coldest eight weeks of the year, but this is also, in the current phrase, a "Smart Building"—it uses its own computer and installed circuitry not only for the customary business purposes but also to monitor and control its environmental installations as a self-regulating system.

The concept of the Smart Building is only one of the ramifications of the impact of the use of computers or buildings in architecture. Computerization already affects all aspects of design from the initial feasibility studies and cost analysis to the final production drawings, the management of the construction site, and the building itself when completed. It is one of the ironies of the High Tech period that the ready availability of computerization, one of the higher technologies now within the reach of all but the most modest architectural offices, has had almost no effect on the style or appearance of buildings, nor is there any reason why it should—so that any purported references to computer technologies in the appearance of buildings are therefore purely symbolic.

Smart systems aside, however, Porsche may indeed be judged "Classic" and "Not innovatory" as its architects claimed. Its view of architecture and design, both inside and outside, holds closely to the three distinguishing principles of Modern architecture of the International Style in the version set out by Alfred H. Barr as long ago as 1932: "The distinguishing aesthetic principles of the International Style…are three: emphasis upon volume—space enclosed by thin planes or surfaces as opposed to the suggestion of mass or solidity; regularity as opposed to symmetry or other kinds of obvious balance; and, lastly, dependence upon the intrinsic elegance of materials, technical perfection, and fine proportions as opposed to applied ornament."[7]

Although the brushed metal surfaces around the central atrium inside the Porsche building, the lavish planting, the fountains, and the programmed lighting that complements the play of water may represent a very extreme "Late Modern" version of the International Style, everything is still reassuringly familiar to the visitor. If the design of the Porsche building had been described as "Off-the-shelf components and off-the-shelf thinking," this in no way derogates the quality of its construction, the immense competence of its resolutely conventional design, its functional serviceability, or the satisfaction that it clearly affords to the company and the customers—both owners and agents—who come to use it…

But if it is compared to the 1983 Renault building at Swindon, which serves almost exactly the same purposes, it can only appear less inspired, however stylish, and (apparently) less innovatory. Against Porsche's sleek exterior "without rhetoric" (to revive Peter Smithson's phrase to characterize the *grau-im-grau* boxwork of Braun radio, another manifestation of the HfG at Ulm), Renault flourishes its expressed and articulated structural system on the exterior, outside the enclosed envelope that forms its functional volume.

This system is a tracery of tensile rods stabilizing a regular grid of yellow upright columns joined by braced bridging girders that support the roofing membrane, all in striking contrast with both the greenfield site on which it sits in splendid isolation and the matte grey metallic panels of the enclosing walls, set back a full meter behind the external skeleton and across which the structure casts elegant shadows even in the misty British sunlight.

In striking contrast to Porsche, again, the roof line is not flat, but acknowledges the fact that each 25-meter-square bay of the structure is roofed by a kind of stiff tent formed by the bridging girders and suspended by more tensile rods from the tops of the upright columns that form its corners like tent poles. Nor is the plan a neat rectangle, as at Porsche. Although the main spare-parts store is indeed a rectangle, four bays by nine bays, there are six other bays added at the "public" end of the building that destroy any visual sense of that rectangle—the most visible of them, indeed, being an open-sided canopy over a parking space for visitors. This not only destroys any sense of the enclosing walls as a substantial part of the building but puts the emphasis instead on the skeletal system of uprights and tension rods and bridging girders that support the roof-tents, and thus serves to explain, as it were, the whole generating system of the design.

Similar as its functions may be to those of Porsche, physically and commercially, there are clearly a range of other considerations that serve to set the two operations apart conceptually, and—aside from differences of architectural temperament—the most important of these is concerned with company imagery. Success in competition, and the kind of engineering resourcefulness that is needed to win races and rallies have played a large part in the public relations of the *Régie Renault,* but since these matters were manifested in specialized competition vehicles remote from the Renault models the public can actually buy (whereas all Porsches are sports cars), they are not integrated into the public's view of the company's everyday products.

Nor is there a parallel high-style product brand like Porsche Design to reinforce an imagery of high performance and high technology. Foster Associates therefore had neither the help nor the limitations of an architecturally relevant company image when they came to design the building, and the only connection one may perceive is that the yellow color of the exposed structure is more or less the same as the livery that was used on Renault's Formula One Racing cars—but, then, such a yellow is also notoriously one of the favorite colors of Norman Foster, whose office designed the building, for his own personal vehicles, from bicycles to helicopters.

Furthermore, yellow is also one of the preferred colors of High Tech as a "movement." It—and a variety of related greens, as well as reds and blues—appears frequently in the work of Rogers and other practitioners of the style, and it thus makes it easier to see Foster's work of this kind as part of a coherent and deliberated tendency in recent architecture. Indeed, it was the publication of Renault that provided the occasion for the *Architectural Review* to produce, in July 1983, what appears to be the first special issue of any professional magazine to be devoted specifically to High Tech as an architectural movement in being, rather than a putative tendency, and to an attempted assessment of the movement's background and value systems.

The use of such bright, usually primary colors—in opposition to the "canonical white" (and occasional earth tones) of the International Style—together with a conspicuous exhibition of structure, might speculatively be taken as two of a set of three "distinguishing principles" of High Tech architecture as a style, to match Barr's three principles of the International Style. In that case, the third principle would probably be something like "exposure of mechanical and environmental services," as exemplified by the exterior of Centre Pompidou and the interiors of works such as the University Medical Center at Calgary, Alberta, by Eb Zeidler and Associates.

Yet, if this were a test of orthodoxy, so to speak, it is one that Foster's work would normally fail. Since the Renault building was not deemed to need heavy servicing, there was not originally much ductwork or trunking that could be exposed. Certainly it can be seen if one knows where to look, but not to the same explicit and dramatic effect as in the work of Rogers, for instance. Indeed, it is the spectacular servicing of Centre Pompidou, together with its exhibitionistic structure and its brilliant coloring (though the yellow is missing for once!) that make it the monument of reference by which High Tech Architecture is usually defined.

Structure, Services, and Color—these may well be called the three distinguishing stylistic principles of High Tech, but only *in opposition* to Barr's three principles of the International Style. For between High Tech and the International Style, there is one of the most notable and instructive oppositions (or, at least, distinctions) that has appeared in the history of Modern architecture *as a fine art,* and it is a distinction that throws an interesting light on the way that Modernism in architecture has construed (or misconstrued) its own history.

The main issue can be summarized thus: the major historical accounts of the sources of Modern architecture in the immediately pre-Modern phase, most notably Pevsner's *Pioneers of Modern Design* and Giedion's *Bauen in Frankreich, Bauen in Eisen, Bauen in Eisenbeton,* tend to present views of the architecture of the nineteenth century which did not connect, visually, with the kind of twentieth-century architecture that these historian-apologists supported and claimed to be descended from them.

Briefly, the buildings of the *Grands Constructeurs,* like Paxton and Eiffel, who were so admired by historians of that generation, tended to be open-work, transparent, with clearly expressed structural skeletons, whereas the International Style work of Giedion's friends Le Corbusier, Mies van der Rohe, or Pevsner's hero, Gropius, tended to consist of closed volumes whose structural skeletons were not easily perceived nor—indeed—part of the visual design of the building. Thus, in order to provide a respectable nineteenth-century parentage for Mies van der Rohe's Weissenhof apartment block of 1927 by comparing it to the pioneering metal-framed structure of the famous *Chocolat Menier* factory, for instance, Giedion has to illustrate the Mies building in the unfinished condition, with its steel frame still visible,[8] which clearly was not how Mies intended his building to be seen.

Nevertheless, there has for a long time been another tradition within architectural Modernism, often visionary and unbuilt, which—unlike the International Style—has seemed more directly affiliated to the work of *Les Grands Constructeurs:* Constructivism and its derivatives. This was the kind of architecture which was celebrated in the Frankfurt Museum's exhibition *Vision der Moderne* in 1986, and seems to have been regarded by many (including the exhibition's organizers) as a kind of "revenge of the *other* modern architecture." It might be better to regard the works of this tradition simply as the realization of some unused possibilities of the Modern tradition, but however the case is interpreted, it is clear that—a few works like the Porsche building aside—nearly all of what passes as High Tech in architecture belongs in that part of the Modern Movement, and not that which later became the orthodox International Style.

What then of Porsche, which clearly does not belong on that Constructivist side, yet is widely (and convincingly) regarded as being of the High Tech persuasion? It is clear that High Tech is not simply a subdivision of "Constructivist Architecture" as the Frankfurt team have tended to maintain but has other roots and allegiances. It will be argued in this book that what constitutes the crucial novelty and difference between High Tech and the more generalized "Constructive" tradition is that High

Tech takes a more-than-constructive view of architecture; [High Tech] does not see buildings simply as passive shelters against the elements, but rather as complete and active environmental systems, dispensing energy and information to maintain a well-regulated ambiance for the building's functions. The appearance of a High Tech building normally offers the explicit promise, and hopefully the physical delivery, of superior environmental performance. Hence, therefore, the important part played by exposed service ducting and visible environmental machinery—conspicuously absent from Constructivist projects—in High Tech as a style. But even without such three-dimensional symbolism, the high finish and the understood technological product affiliations of Porsche do at least offer an allegory of superior performance—which, fortunately, is made real by the observable facts of the building's interior environment.

In general, then, the argument of this book will be that High Tech, however variable its visual manifestations may be, along the scale from Porsche to Centre Pompidou, contains an implicit or explicit promise of higher performance than was the case in earlier architectures. This elevated performance might be structural, environmental, functional, but preferably all three, and it is understood to be obtained by recourse to the most advanced engineering technologies—"cutting edge" as opposed to merely "state of the art"—available in all the relevant fields.

And it is also, let us remind ourselves, still architecture, "the mother of the arts," with all that is implied in that traditional claim. Lay observers, however elevated their social rank, may perhaps be excused for superficially supposing otherwise, and the fact that they do suppose otherwise is, in a sense, a striking tribute to the symbolic power of the architectural forms they have employed. "Well, Mr. Rogers," said the Prince of Wales at the opening of the Inmos factory in South Wales, "it looks as though the engineers got their own way this time!"[9]

The engineer in question, Tony Hunt, is universally accepted as having made crucial contributions to the structure, but closer study will show that architecture is still at work, still in ultimate control of design, most notably in the disposition of the ventilating ductwork, which is disposed as the architects wanted it, not as the servicing consultants had proposed. High Tech, it seems, is another step in the long struggle to bring innovative engineering techniques within the traditional disciplines of architecture, or to stretch those disciplines until the technologies can be accommodated within them. If I had to produce a first approximation definition of High Tech, one that would embrace the whole range from Porsche to Pompidou, I would be tempted to say that it was the most recent way of bringing advanced engineering within the discipline of architecture, comparable with the achievements of Peter Behrens and Auguste Perret in the first fifteen years of the present century.

At the end of my first extended study of the history of Modern Architecture, I wrote:

> It may well be that what we have hitherto understood as architecture, and what we are beginning to understand of technology are incompatible disciplines. The architect who proposes to run with technology knows now that he will be in fast company, and that, in order to keep up, he may have to emulate the Futurists and discard his whole cultural load including the professional garments by which he is recognized as an architect. If, on the other hand, he decides not to do this, he may find that a technological culture has decided to go on without him.[10]

These words caused some offense at the time, but the subsequent twenty-five years of architecture seem to have revealed a grain of truth in them; this challenge is, it now appears, one of the fundamentals of Modernist architecture. What I did not appreciate at the time, however, was how far some architects were prepared to go, in defiance of a rising tide of historical revivalism, in order to keep up with advanced engineering, but without divesting themselves of those "professional garments." The achievement of architects of that particular persuasion is High Tech, an alternative Modernism that has arisen from what might be termed the "disgrace" of the older Modernism of the International Style. What follows is an attempt to define, chronicle, and understand this alternative Modernism, which surprised the world of architecture by becoming successful against the grain of expectations in the ostensibly Post-Modernist culture of the 1970s and '80s.

NOTES

Note to the reader: Reyner Banham's manuscript was clearly a draft; as such, minor changes have been made to bring consistency to the style, to correct minor spelling errors (including the addition of accents), and to improve readability through small changes to punctuation. For the most part, Banham's capitalization, British spellings, emphases, and use of quotation marks were retained. The citations below appear in the original; however, additional information has been supplied.

Reyner Banham, "High Tech and Advanced Engineering," ca. 1987, Reyner Banham papers, acc. no. 910009, box 8, folder 3, Getty Research Institute, Los Angeles.

1   Joan Kron and Suzanne Slesin, *High-Tech: The Industrial Style and Source Book for the Home* (New York: C. N. Potter, 1978), 9.
2   Luigi Colani, "Bio-Design Victorious over Hi-Tech in WWII," *Car Styling* 46 1/2 (1984): 28. As one who observed the Battle of Britain from within the aircraft industry itself, I find Colani's reading of the subject very dubious. In terms of straight-line speed and maneuverability, the Bf109's used in the Battle of Britain were regarded as superior to the Spitfires of that epoch, and in any case, more than half the British combat missions were flown by other aircraft, such as Hawker Hurricanes and Boulton Paul Defiants. The margins of victory seem not to have been aerodynamics, but the heavier armament of the British machines and hesitation by the *Luftwaffe* in exploiting the numerical advantage they had acquired over the RAF in the first weeks of the battle.

3   Langdon Winner, *Autonomous Technology: Technics-Out-of-Control as a Theme in Political Thought* (Cambridge, MA: MIT Press, 1977), x.
4   Stephen Trombley, "Reflecting the Porsche Image," *RIBA Journal* 92, no. 3 (1985): 34.
5   In the catalog of the exhibition, Heinrich Klotz, ed., *Vision der Moderne: Das Prinzip Konstruktion,* exh. cat. (Frankfurt am Main: Prestel, 1986), 66–67.
6   Stephen Trombley, "Porsche's Fast Track at Theale," *RIBA Journal* 92, no. 1 (1985): 34.
7   Alfred Barr, "Preface," in *The International Style*, by Henry-Russell Hitchcock and Philip Johnson (New York: W. W. Norton, 1932), 13.
8   Sigfried Giedion, *Bauen in Frankreich, Bauen in Eisen, Bauen in Eisenbeton* (Leipzig, Germany: Klinkhardt & Biermann, 1928). See the English edition, where the project is erroneously labeled as part of the Werkbundsiedlung: *Building in France, Building in Iron, Building in Ferro-Concrete,* trans. J. Duncan Berry (Los Angeles: Getty, 1995), 131.
9   As reported in Bryan Appleyard, *Richard Rogers: A Biography* (Boston: Faber & Faber, 1986), 193.
10 Reyner Banham, *Theory and Design in the First Machine Age* (London: Architectural Press, 1960), 329–30.

ACKNOWLEDGMENTS

The research that led to this book began nearly a decade ago. In that time, I have enjoyed the help, support, and encouragement of more people than I could possibly account for here. So, in addition to the individuals named below, I offer a hearty thank-you to the countless friends, colleagues, teachers, and students who lent me a hand, knowingly or not, as I nudged these pages toward completion. I owe each of you a cocktail.

That I undertook this project at all owes primarily to Joe Day, whose enthusiasm for my earlier work on Reyner Banham convinced me to reopen a body of research I thought I had completed years ago. I thank him for maintaining that enthusiasm as I flooded his inbox with drafts of the present book over the last three years.

I am honored by the wealth of support I have received from the staff at the Getty Research Institute. I extend my sincere thanks to Gail Feigenbaum for initially entertaining the possibility of this project; Thomas Gaehtgens and the senior staff for approving it; Michele Ciaccio and Janelle Gatchalian for providing cheerful stewardship through its early phases; Karen Ehrmann for conscientious work on the illustrations; Catherine Lorenz for thoughtful graphic design; Victoria Gallina for her careful eye through production; and Lauren Edson, whose editorial acumen down the home stretch brought my arguments into much sharper focus than I could have mustered on my own. I also wish to thank my anonymous reviewers, whose generous criticism of the initial draft was crucial in shaping the final form of the book.

Much of this book was first formulated during my doctoral studies at University of California, Los Angeles. Sylvia Lavin supervised my research and provided sound advice, razor-sharp criticism, and staunch advocacy, for which I will always be grateful. I am also indebted to the other members of my committee: Dana Cuff, Diane Favro, and in particular N. Katherine Hayles, who provided substantial assistance. Further afield, I thank Kristy Balliet at The Ohio State University and Stephen Phillips at California Polytechnic State University, San Luis Obispo. Their invitations to lecture at those institutions brought welcome opportunities to hone my arguments. Cynthia Davidson provided a platform for me to develop my early interest in the Archigram group in the pages of *Log*, and Peter Cook cordially endured my interrogations. I am grateful to the many students with whom I have worked through this material at Ohio State, Otis College of Art and Design, UCLA, and SCI-Arc. A special thank-you to Duane McLemore, Zaid Kashef Alghata, and Alex

Maymind for their assistance tracking down hard-to-find journal articles in London and Los Angeles, and to David Haslam for last-minute help with the images.

This project could not possibly have come together as it did without the mentorship and friendship of Jeffrey Kipnis. His unflinching support of my work over the last two decades has been essential, and his influence has left its mark on every page. In addition, I wish to recognize Hitoshi Abe, George Acock, Hernan Diaz Alonso, John Bohn, Ewan Branda, Mike Cadwell, Mark Danielewski, Thomas Daniell, Dave DiMaria, John Enright, Hsinming Fung, Tracy Gannon, Margaret Griffin, Marcelyn Gow, Carolyn Hank, Thomas Hines, Craig Hodgetts, Mike Hunter, Dora Epstein Jones, Jason Kerwin, Michael Kovac, Tali Krakowsky, Gustavo Leclerc, Rob Livesey, Elena Manferdini, Kevin McMahon, Mike Meehan, Eric Owen Moss, Michael Osman, José Oubrerie, Linda Pollari, Jonah Rowen, David Ruy, Mohamed Sharif, Bob Somol, Katrin Terstegen, Anthony Vidler, Jennifer Volland, Tate Wilson, Tom Wiscombe, Amit Wolf, Jon Yoder, Andrew Zago, and Claudia Ziegler Acemyan, as well as my parents, siblings, and extended family, who each provided some combination of criticism, encouragement, support, and much-needed diversion along the way.

Finally, my heartfelt thanks go to Yumna Siddiqi, who made it possible for me to work on this book, and to our children, Tycho and Zarina, who made it worthwhile.

—Todd Gannon

ABOUT THE AUTHOR

Todd Gannon is Head of the Architecture Section at The Ohio State University's Knowlton School. His previous books include *The Light Construction Reader* (2002), *Et in Suburbia Ego: José Oubrerie's Miller House* (2013), and *A Confederacy of Heretics* (2013, coedited with Ewan Branda). He is the author of monographs on the work of Peter Eisenman, Zaha Hadid, Steven Holl, Mack Scogin Merrill Elam Architects, Morphosis, Eric Owen Moss, Oyler Wu Collaborative, Bernard Tschumi, and UN Studio.

ILLUSTRATION CREDITS

Photographs of items in the holdings of the Research Library at the Getty Research Institute are courtesy the Research Library.

Chapter 1: In Search of Alternatives
FIG. 1.3. From Reyner Banham, *The New Brutalism: Ethic or Aesthetic?* (New York: Reinhold, 1966), 12.
FIG. 1.7. Photo © Tate, London 2016. © Nigel Henderson Estate.
FIGS. 1.9, 1.10, 1.11, 1.12, 1.15, 1.17, 1.18, 1.20, 1.21. Alison and Peter Smithson Archive. Courtesy of the Frances Loeb Library.
FIG. 1.13. Louis I. Kahn Collection, University of Pennsylvania and Pennsylvania Historical and Museum Commission. Photo by Lionel Freedman.
FIG. 1.16. Digital Image © The Museum of Modern Art / Licensed by SCALA / Art Resource, NY.
FIG. 1.22. Photo by Paolo Monti. European Library of Information Culture Foundation.

Chapter 2: Unconventional Combinations
FIGS. 2.1, 2.2, 2.5. Alison and Peter Smithson Archive. Courtesy of the Frances Loeb Library.
FIG. 2.3. Image © General Motors Technical Center, Warren, Michigan.
FIG. 2.6. © Archigram 1964.
FIG. 2.7. Cedric Price fonds. Collection Centre Canadien d'Architecture / Canadian Centre for Architecture, Montréal.
FIGS. 2.8, 2.9, 2.10. Image © Grimshaw.
FIG. 2.11. © Archigram 1964.
FIG. 2.13. Richard + Su Rogers.
FIG. 2.14. Richard Einzig / Arcaid.co.uk.
FIG. 2.15. Image © Eamonn O'Mahony.
FIGS. 2.16, 2.19, 2.21. James Stirling / Michael Wilford fonds. Collection Centre Canadien d'Architecture / Canadian Centre for Architecture, Montréal.
FIGS. 2.20a, 2.20b. Courtesy of the Canadian Centre for Architecture, Montréal.
FIG. 2.22. Richard Einzig / arcaidimages.com.

Chapter 3: Savage Minds and the Well-Tempered Environment
FIG. 3.1. From Jayne Merkel, *Eero Saarinen* (London: Phaidon, 2005), 172.
FIG. 3.2. Digital Image © The Museum of Modern Art / Licensed by SCALA / Art Resource, NY.
FIG. 3.3. © 1965 François Dallegret.
FIGS. 3.9, 3.10. Drawings by and courtesy of Todd Gannon.
FIG. 3.12. Library of Congress Prints and Photographs Division. Carol M. Highsmith Archive. LC-DIG-highsm-14066.

Chapter 4: High Tech and the Persistence of Modernism
FIG. 4.1. © J. Paul Getty Trust. Getty Research Institute, Los Angeles (2004.R.10).
FIG. 4.2. Wikipedia / Victor Grigas.
FIG. 4.3. Image © Foster + Partners.
FIG. 4.4. Image © Norman Foster.
FIGS. 4.6a, 4.6b, 4.6c. Image © Foster + Partners.
FIG. 4.7. Image © Foster + Partners.
FIGS. 4.8, 4.9. Image © Norman Foster.
FIG. 4.10. Image © Mike Page.
FIG. 4.11. John Donat / RIBA Library Photographs Collection.
FIG. 4.12. Mondadori Portfolio / Art Resource, NY.
FIGS. 4.13, 4.14. Image © Studio Piano & Rogers © Fondazione Renzo Piano.

Chapter 5: Making Architecture
FIG. 5.1. Image © Ian Lambot.
FIG. 5.2. Image by Stephen Rogers.
FIG. 5.3. RPK4.com.
FIG. 5.4. Image by Tom Taylor.
FIG. 5.6. Image by Richard Davies.
FIG. 5.7. Image © Ken Kirkwood.
FIG. 5.8. Image © Rogers Stirk Harbour + Partners.
FIG. 5.9. Photo by Gianni Berengo Gardin / contrasto.
FIG. 5.10. Photo by Gianni Berengo Gardin / contrasto.
FIG. 5.11. Image © Piano & Fitzgerald © Fondazione Renzo Piano.
FIG. 5.12. Photograph by Paul Hester Photography. © Piano & Fitzgerald © Fondazione Renzo Piano.
FIG. 5.13. © RPBW - Renzo Piano Building Workshop Architects © Fondazione Renzo Piano.
FIG. 5.14. © Fondazione Renzo Piano. Photograph by Gianluigi Trivellato.
FIG. 5.15. Richard Bryant / arcaidimages.com.

Chapter 6: Architecture beyond Building
PAGE 174. Reprinted by kind permission of Mrs. Mary Banham. Reyner Banham papers, 1930–1990, bulk 1970–1988, acc. no. 910009, box 12, folder 1, Getty Research Institute, Los Angeles.
FIGS. 6.1, 6.2, 6.3, 6.4, 6.5. Art © 2016 Artists Rights Society (ARS), New York.

Conclusion: Building beyond Architecture
FIG. 7.1. Image © Ken Kirkwood.
FIGS. 7.2, 7.3. Image © Foster + Partners.
FIG. 7.4. Tim Street-Porter.

Plates
PL. 1. Alison and Peter Smithson Archive. Courtesy of the Frances Loeb Library.
PL. 2. Digital Image © The Museum of Modern Art / Licensed by SCALA / Art Resource, NY.
PL. 3. © Archigram 1964.
PLS. 4, 20. Tim Street-Porter.
PL. 5. © Archigram 1963.
PL. 6. © Rogers Stirk Harbour + Partners.
PL. 8. Richard Einzig / arcaidimages.com.
PL. 9. © 1965 François Dallegret.
pl. 10 © Steven Brooke Studios.
PL. 11. Image © Norman Foster.
PL. 12. Image © Ken Kirkwood.
PL. 13. Image © Michel Denancé.
PL. 14. Image © Ian Lambot.
PL. 15. © Fondazione Renzo Piano. Photograph by Fulvio Roiter.
PL. 16. Image © Piano & Fitzgerald © Fondazione Renzo Piano.
PL. 17. Art © 2016 Artists Rights Society (ARS), New York. Image © Ron Herron Archive. All Rights Reserved, DACS 2016.
PLS. 18, 19. Image © Ken Kirkwood.

INDEX

Note: page numbers in italics refer to figures; those followed by n refer to notes, with note number.

Aalto, Alvar, 56–57
adhocism, 140–41, 154, 162, 166
Adhocism (Jencks), 97, 99, 100, 140–41
Alberti, Leon Battista, 66–67, 68, 85n56
Allen, William Steven. *See* Eichler Homes Models
Alton East Housing (LCC Architect's Department), *20*
American architecture, 103, 112, 114n11, 121–25. *See also* California architecture
Anshen, Robert. *See* Eichler Homes Models
antimonumental landscapes, 92–94
Archigram Architects
    and architectural object, eradication of, 109, 178
    and architecture as discipline, 178
    Banham on, 53, 140–41, 177–78, 180–86
    and boffin subculture, 100
    buildings by, 120
    and clip-on architecture, 61, 62–63
    eclectic style of, 178–79
    focus on drawings vs. construction, 182, 186
    and High Tech architecture, 120, 148
    and *Homo Ludens*, 60, 178, 181–82, 183–84, 195n39
    humanism and, 180
    influence of, 64–65
    influences on, 65–66, 67
    and megastructures, 137, 139, 182–83
    members of, 178
    Monaco Underground project, 188
    program of, 179, 182, 183
    scholarship on, 178, 194n31
    situationists and, 181–82
    striking imagery of, 62
    stylistic labels used by, 120
    and technology as replacement for buildings, 179
    as traditional architects, 184–88, 191, 192
    turn from monumentalism, 179, 183
Archigram magazine, 179–80, 183–84, 194–95n31, 195n37
Architectural Association School of Architecture (AA), 119–20, 121, 123, 142n3
Architectural Review, 15, 17–21, 29, 30–31, 40–41, 65, 70, 72, 123, 132, 134, 134n51, 135, 138–42, 202–4, 242
architecture. *See also* making architecture
    academic debate on, 199
    antimonies in, 8, 9
    and architectural object, eradication of, 109, 148, 178
    avenues of escape from constraints of, 176–77
    Banham's definition of, 176–77, 202, 205
    computer-based design and, 191–92
    as defined by actions not objects, 174–75, 199
    disappearance of, 6
    vs. engineering, 174–75
    history of, 158–59
    and pattern language, 175
    potential incompatibility with technology, 155, 177, 244
    professional ethics of, 175
    revelation of truth as primary function of, 192–93
    and utopianism, 95, 148, 159–60, 165

"Architecture after 1960" series (Banham), 29
une architecture autre, 3, 10, 12n13, 16, 27, 33–40, 44–45, 54, 83, 121, 131, 158, 176
The Architecture of the Well-Tempered Environment (Banham), 4, 7, 89, 93, 102–12, *105*, 127, 141, 150, 159, 165, 176
Asplund, Erik Gunnar, *19*, 19–20
Association of Collegiate Schools of Architecture (ACSA), Banham lecture for (1964), 8, 9
at-hand/off-the-shelf materials, 43, 69, 95, 98, 123, 133–36, 153–54, 159, 186, 240–41

Baird, George, 89–91, 95, 99, 113n8, 120, 137–38, 148
Baker House (Aalto), 56–57
Banfi, Gianluigi, 42, *42*
Banham, Mary, 1, 15–16, 17, 104, *105*
Banham, Reyner
    antiestablishment stance of, 2–3, 16, 41, 98–99, 132–36
    background and education, 16–18
    cancer and final illness, 1, 150, 155, 173, 174, 186
    move to United States, 112
    range of interpretations of, 2–3
    writing style of, 141, 145n83
Banham's analysis
    contradictions underlying, 3–4, 6–8, 141–42, 180, 205
    criteria in, 173–74, 199
    linking of ethics and aesthetics in, 175
    as observational history, 9
    overview of, 4
Barbiano di Belgiojoso, Lodovico, 42, *42*
Barr, Alfred J., 4, 5, 153, *154*, 167, *167*, 173–74, 240
Bathroom Tower. *See* Student Hostel Service Tower
B&B Italia Office Building (Piano + Rogers), 157
BBPR, 42, *42*
"A Black Box" (Banham), 174–77
boffins, 100–103, 136, 159
bricolage, 94–100
British Telecom Mobile Exhibition Structure. *See* Telecom Slug
building
    concept of, Herron's Telecom Slug and, 190–91
    as image, 32, 193
Bunshaft, Gordon, 106–7, *107*

California architecture, 122–24, 126–29, 199–200
Capsule Homes Tower (Chalk), 64–65, *65*, 66, 195n39
Case Study architects, 122, 123, *123*, 125, 129
Casson, Hugh, *20*, 20–21
CBS Building (Saarinen), *90*, 90–91, 137–38
Centre Georges Pompidou (Piano + Rogers), 10, 110, 119, *136*, *137*, 137–42, 139, 145n64, 145n85, 150, *222*
    and High Tech, 147, 148, 150, 166, 205, 235, 242
    as megastructure, 137, 139–40
    and modern movement, 136, 139, 142
Chalk, Warren, 64–65, *65*, 66, 195n39
Chareau, Pierre, 101, 103, 148
city planning, and dissonant accretion, 40–41
CLASP (Consortium of Local Authorities Special Programme), 124

clip-on architecture
    and additive approaches, 58–60
    Banham on, 53–55, 57–60, 67, 97–98
    Banham's turn to, 44, 53
    and *bricolage*, 97
    characteristics of, 153, 154, *154*
    and construction permits, 71
    examples of, 63–83
    extradisciplinary influences on, 53
    flexible indeterminacy in, 57, 58, 59, 61–62
    High Tech architecture and, 119, 120
    and *Homo Ludens*, 60–63
    humanism and, 60, 66
    and mechanical services, 59–60, 61, 62
    and New Brutalism, 78
    as term, 53
    and visual unity, 53, 60, 154
"A Clip-On Architecture" (Banham), 53, 57–60, 63, 67, 75, 82, 127, 166, 177–78, 180
Collage City (Rowe and Koetter), 95, 96–97
Colquhoun, Alan, 17, 21, 95, 204
constructivism, High Tech architecture and, 243–44
contemporary style, in Great Britain, 15–16, 19–21, 30
Continental academic thought, Banham on, 100, 112
Conversion and Roof Extension for Design Research Unit (Richard + Su Rogers), 63, 68–71, *69*, *70*, 215
Cook, Peter, 64, 66, 100–101, 145n64, 179, 185. *See also* Entertainments Tower for Expo '67; Plug-In City
Cooper, Thomas. *See* Royal Victoria Hospital
Cullen, Gordon, 203, *203*, 204
Cullinan, Edward. *See* Olivetti Training Center

Dallegret, François, *93*, 93–94, 110, 116n65, *218*
deconstructionist architecture, 95–96, 150
Derrida, Jacques, 95–96, 98
"Design by Choice" (Banham), 42–43, 153
details
    and architecture as discipline, 124
    Banham's later focus on, 159–61, 166
    High Tech architecture and, 159–61
Dewhurst Haslam Partnership. *See* Porsche UK Headquarters
drawing, architecture and, 175–76, 186–87, 191–93

Eames, Charles and Ray, 56, 122, 123, *123*, 125, 129
École des Beaux-Arts, 18, 36
Economist building (Smithson and Smithson), 54, *54*, 57
Eichler Homes Models (Anshen and Allen), *126*, 127
Eisenman, Peter, 184–85, 190
Ellwood, Craig, 122, 123, 129
endless and indeterminate architecture, 36, 57–60, 75, 119, 127, 180
Endless House project (Kiesler), 36, *36*
Entertainments Tower for Expo '67 (Cook), 65, *214*
environmental issues, RIBA study on, 132–33
environments, controlled
    vs. aesthetics, 104–9
    Piano and, 162–63
    vs. traditional architecture, Banham on, 92–94, 102–4
"Exterior Furnishing or Sharawaggi," 203–4

251

Farnsworth House (Mies van der Rohe), 123, 123–24, 129
Farrell, Terry, 54, 68, 120. *See also* Student Hostel Service Tower
Festival of Britain, South Bank Exhibition, 20, 20–21
"Flatscape with Containers" (Banham), 92
formalism
    Banham on, 26–27, 41–43
    New Brutalism and, 25–26
    Smithsons and, 34–35
Foster, Norman, 1, 10, 67, 68, 101, 112–13, 120–25, 131–36, 147, 148, 150, 158, 166. *See also* Hong Kong and Shanghai Bank Headquarters; IBM Pilot Head Office Building; Renault Warehouse and Distribution Center; Sainsbury Center for Visual Arts
freedom, technologically assisted, Banham on, 138–39
Fuller, R. Buckminster, 44, 53, 65, 65–68, 70, 92, 94, 100–102, 101, 120, 148, 180, 182
functionalism. *See also* mechanical services
    vs. aesthetics, 6, 8–9, 41–45, 89, 98, 111, 122, 132, 147, 157, 181
    Banham's support for, 205
    clip-on and, 54–55, 63, 78, 80, 83
    Herron, 188
    High Tech and, 156–57, 166, 234
    vs. meaning, debate on, 89–94
    modern movement and, 18, 188
    New Brutalism and, 27
Fun Palace (Price), 44, 52, 53, 55, 60–61, 61, 62, 63, 137, 140, 182, 211

General Motors Technical Center (Saarinen), 57, 57, 60
Giedion, Sigfried, 5, 17, 29, 46n16, 121, 139, 150, 157–58, 167, 207n29, 235, 243
Glass House (Johnson), 88, 88, 108, 109, 219
Golden Lane Estate (Smithson and Smithson), 34, 34, 58
Grimshaw, Nicholas, 54, 64, 68, 119, 120, 142n3, 150. *See also* Student Hostel Service Tower
Gropius, Walter, 5, 17–18, 103, 165
Growth and Form exhibition (ICA, 1951), 21–22, 32

Hamilton, Richard, 17, 21–22
Harrison, Wallace, 106, 106–7
Hastings, Hugh de Cronin [Ivor de Wolfe, pseud.], 19, 47n28, 204–5
Henderson, Nigel, 17, 22, 22–23, 23, 33
Henman, William. *See* Royal Victoria Hospital
Herron, Ron, 60, 179, 186–88, 191–92, 196–97n86. *See also* Suburban Sets; Telecom Slug; Walking City
High Tech, as term, 4, 168n1, 233–34, 235–36
High-Tech (Kron and Slesin), 147–48, 151, 234–35
High Tech architecture
    and advanced engineering, 154–55, 234, 239–40, 244
    American architecture and, 121–25
    and *une architecture autre*, 131, 158
    Banham and, 119–20, 121, 150–51, 158–59, 205
    boffins and, 100–101
    characteristics of, 150, 152, 153, 165, 166, 242
    clients of, 121
    and constructivism, 243–44
    criticisms of, 2, 121, 236–37
    definition of, 244
    and definition of architecture, 205, 207n29
    ethical stance of, 120, 167
    examples of, 119, 152–53, 153, 238–42, 244
    focus on detail rather than ideology, 159–61
    focus on making architecture, 161
    foremost practitioners of, 119
    functionalism and, 156–57, 166, 234
    history of, 119–25, 149, 150, 233
    as inheritor of ancient technological tradition, 158
    vs. International Style, 2, 5, 152–54, 154, 155, 158, 166, 242–44
    literature on, 2, 147–50
    and machine aesthetic, 156, 157–58, 166
    and modern movement, 2, 5, 10, 151
    mythology surrounding history of, 234–36
    paradoxes inherent in, 2, 3, 7, 119, 120, 141, 147, 148, 149, 151, 165–67, 205–6
    vs. postmodern style, 112–13, 120–21, 150, 155
    scholarship on, 1–2
    success of, 120–21
    as term, 120, 147, 233
    unification of structure and technology/services in, 150, 151–52, 153–54, 154, 154–55, 165, 244, 245
    as visual style, 234, 239–40
Hitchcock, Henry-Russell, 5, 17, 153, 173, 174
"A Home Is Not a House" (Banham), 92–94, 93, 102, 103, 110, 116n65, 218
Homo Ludens, 6–7, 60–63, 178, 181–82, 183–84, 195n39
honesty in architecture, Banham on, 107, 110–11, 122, 167, 174, 199, 201, 205, 206
Hong Kong and Shanghai Bank Headquarters (Foster Associates), 118, 119, 143n32, 148–49, 149, 223
House at Colville Place (Smithson and Smithson), 27–29, 28, 31, 48nn73–74
House of the Future (Smithson and Smithson), 36–37, 37, 50n124, 58, 58–59
humanism. *See also* New Humanism
    Archigram group and, 180
    Banham on, 6–7, 40, 59, 103, 180, 188
    and clip-on architecture, 60, 66
    contemporary style and, 15
    modern movement and, 20, 165
    New Brutalism and, 21, 24, 30–32, 41–42, 66–67
Hunstanton Secondary Modern School (Smithson and Smithson), 14, 24, 25, 25–27, 34, 35, 42, 55–57, 210

IBM Pilot Head Office Building (Foster Associates), 132–33, 161, 221
IBM Traveling Pavilion, 160, 161, 161, 224
Ideal Home exhibition (1956), 37
Illinois Institute of Technology (Mies van der Rohe), 21, 55, 58
image
    building as, 32, 193
    dissociation from physical reality, Langer on, 33
    effect on emotions, 24, 31–34
    memorability of, Banham on, 31, 34–35, 44, 205
    in New Brutalism, Banham on, 34, 153, 154
Independent Group, 15–17, 21–27, 29, 30, 32–33, 46n14, 65
Info-Gonks (Cook), 179
Inmos Microprocessor Factory (Richard Rogers Partnership), 146, 156, 156–57, 165
Institute of Contemporary Arts (ICA), 21–24, 46n14
Institute of Fine Arts (NYU) Banham lecture, 172, 173–74
interior design, aesthetics vs. functionalism in, 42–43
International Style
    and aesthetic of pure form, 26
    and *une architecture autre*, 36
    Banham's critique of, 165–66, 199
    canonical works associated with, 17–18
    characteristics of, 154, 173, 174, 240, 243
    as dominant modern style, Banham on, 4
    Foster and, 201
    High Tech as alternative to, 2, 4, 152–54, 154, 155, 158, 166, 242–44

modern movement and, 5, 152–53
and rationalist tradition, 157–58
technological developments and, 104
as term, 4–5
The International Style exhibition (1932), 17
invisibility of architecture
    Archigram and, 178
    Foster's Willis Faber & Dumas Headquarters and, 202
    mechanical services and, 55–89, 109–13, 120, 165, 181
    tension between visual unity and, 132

Jencks, Charles, 78, 97–100, 112, 115–16nn40–41, 115n37, 135, 140–41, 148, 151. *See also* Adhocism; *Language of Post-Modern Architecture*; *Meaning in Architecture*
Johnson, Philip, 5, 17, 58, 67, 108–9, 112, 116nn70–71, 153, 173–74. *See also* Glass House

Kahn, Louis, 32, 32, 121. *See also* Yale University Art Gallery
Kallman, Gerhard, 57–58, 62
Kaplický, Jan, 71, 215
Kiesler, Frederick, 36, 36
Koetter, Fred, 95–97
Kron, Joan, 147–48, 151, 234–35

Langer, Susanne K., 8, 33, 34
Language of Post-Modern Architecture (Jencks), 97, 99, 115–16nn40–41, 135
Larkin Building (Wright), 104, 105, 110, 116n66
Le Corbusier, 5, 17–18, 21, 23, 31, 43, 89, 97, 103, 111–12, 151, 159, 204
Lever House (Bunshaft), 106–7, 107
Lévi-Strauss, Claude, 90, 91, 92, 94–95, 96, 114n25
Lloyd's of London building (Richard Rogers Partnership), 148–49, 149, 160, 161–62, 164–65, 166
London County Council Architects, 15, 20, 20
Los Angeles: The Architecture of Four Ecologies (Banham), 3, 7, 112
Lowara Office Building (Piano), 162–63, 163, 166
Lynn, Jack, 55, 56, 57, 58

MACE system for school construction, 159–60
making architecture, Banham on, 3–4, 155, 156, 161–63, 165–67, 192–93, 206
Making Architecture: The Paradoxes of High Tech (Banham), 1, 4, 7, 16, 147, 150–58, 154, 166, 205–6
    draft introduction to, 233–45
Maldonado, Tomás, 236, 238
McHale, John, 65, 67, 195n37
Meaning in Architecture (Jencks and Baird, eds.), 89–95
mechanical services. *See also* environments, controlled
    Banham's late definition of architecture and, 176
    and invisibility of architecture, 55–89, 109–13, 120, 165, 181
    as objects of architectural expression, 43–44, 61, 62
    unification of structure and, in High Tech architecture, 150–55, 154, 165, 244, 245
megastructure movement, 137–40, 181–83
Megastructure: Urban Futures of the Recent Past (Banham), 7, 137, 176, 181–86
The Menil Collection (Piano), 162, 162–64, 166, 225
Middleton, Robin, 55–57, 67, 83–84n6, 95
Mies van der Rohe, Ludwig, 5, 17–18, 21, 55, 56, 58, 122–24, 123, 129, 150–51, 158, 243
modern movement
    Banham on, 18, 89, 104, 112, 132–36, 138, 152–53, 159–60, 167, 167

Barr's definition of, 173
Eisenman on, 184–85
establishment shift from, 132, 138
High Tech architecture and, 2, 5, 10, 112–13, 120, 121, 150, 151, 243–44, 245
and human dilemma, 20, 165
moral imperatives of, 166–67, *167*
mythological history of, 234–35, 243
1950s debate on, 15–18
as term, 4–6
monumentalism, 121, 139, 179, 183, 202
Morgan, Emslie, 107–8, 112

New Brutalism
and *une architecture autre*, 35–36, 44–45, 54
as architecture beyond classical ideals, 25–26, 34–35
Banham's turn from, 44–45
characteristics of, 26, 30–31, 34–35, 39, 43–44, 154, *154*
clip-on architecture and, 78
decline into classicism, 44–45, 53, 54, 57, 62, 131
development of, 16, 24–27
discordant elements in, 6, 13n34, 16, 42, 54–56
examples of, 27, 34–40
High Tech architecture and, 119, 120
humanism and, 21, 24, 30–32, 41–42, 66–67
megastructure movement and, 137
Middleton on origins of, 55–57
modern movement and, 5, 26–27
vs. picturesque, 38–39
scholarship on, 16, 26
as search for holistic approach, 30
and standards from outside architecture, 41–42
and visual unity, 154
"The New Brutalism" (Banham), *23*, 26–27, 30–36, *38*, 40, 54
The New Brutalism (Banham), 7, 16, 34–36, 38, 44–45, 54, 174–77
New Humanism, 20, 41–42, 47n35, 188
Nieuwenhuys, Constant, 137, 181, 182
"1960—Stocktaking" (Banham), 40–41, 42, 101

Olivetti Training Center (James Stirling), 63,
72–83, *73*, 166, 183, 184, *217*
Cullinan's residential wing, 72–75, *73, 74*, 80, *216*
Stirling's education facilities wings, 75–77, 75–78, *79*, 80–81, *81*, 184

Paolozzi, Eduardo, 16, 17, 22, 22–23, *23*, 26, 33
Parallel of Life and Art exhibition (ICA, 1953), *22*, 22–24, *23*, 26, 32, 35–36
Park Hill Flats (Lynn), 55, *56*, 57, 58
Peressutti, Enrico, 42, *42*
Perret, Auguste, 150–51, 244
Pevsner, Nikolaus, 3, 5, 15, 17, 18, 30, 46n16, 83n6, 98, 104, 125, 150, 157–58, 167, 204, 235, 243
Piano, Renzo, 1, 10, 112–13, 120, 131, 147, 150, 158, 161, 166. *See also* Centre Georges Pompidou; IBM Traveling Pavilion; Lowara Office Building; The Menil Collection
picturesque style, 18–19, 21, 30–31, 38–39, 54, 58, 97, 134, 203, 204
Pirelli Tower (BBPR), 42, *42*
plug-in architecture, 60, 63, 120
Plug-In City (Cook), 53, 60, *61*, 63, 137, 182–83, *212*
Pollock, Jackson, *23*, 33, 58, 68
Porsche UK Headquarters (Dewhurst Haslam Partnership), 152–53, *153*, 154, 166, 238–41, 244
postmodern architecture
Banham on, 112–13, 174
and *bricolage*, 97
deconstructionist architecture and, 150

definition of, 115–16nn40–41
High Tech and, 2, 5, 112–13, 120, 121, 150, 155, 237
Jencks and, 99
Potteries Thinkbelt Project (Price), *90*, 90–91, 137–38
Price, Cedric, 44, 53, 101, 119–21, 142n3, 148, 180. *See also* Fun Palace; Potteries Thinkbelt Project
"Problem x 3 = Olivetti" (Banham), 183

rationalist tradition, International Style and,
157–58
Read, Herbert, 21, 22, 34, 69
Reliance Controls Building (Team 4), 119, *126–28*, 126–31, *131*, 144n36, 144n38, 148, 220
Renault Warehouse and Distribution Center (Foster Associates), 152, *153*, 154, 166, 241–42
Rogers, Ernesto Nathan, 42, *42*
Rogers, Richard, 1, 10, 112–13, 119–25, 131, 142n3, 147, 148, 150, 158, 166. *See also* Centre Georges Pompidou; Inmos Microprocessor Factory; Lloyd's of London building
Rogers, Richard + Su, 54, 68, 101, 121–23. *See also* Conversion and Roof Extension for Design Research Unit; Zip-Up enclosures
Rowe, Colin, 29, 95–97, 204
Royal Institute of British Architects (RIBA), 41–42, 58, 60, 132–33
Royal Victoria Hospital (Henman and Cooper), 104, *105*, 127, 156–57

Saarinen, Eero, 53, 57, 121. *See also* CBS Building; General Motors Technical Center
Sainsbury Center for Visual Arts (Foster Associates), 136, *136*, 143n32
Scenes in America Deserta (Banham), 3, 7, 112
"A Set of Actual Monuments" (Banham), *172*, 173–74
Sheffield University Extension (Smithson and Smithson), 27, 34, *35, 38*, 38–40, *39*, 42, 50n133, 53, 54, 55
Silicon Valley architecture, 199–200
situationists, 181–82
Slesin, Suzanne, 147–48, 151, 234–35
smart buildings/sheds, 151, 199, 240
Smith, Ivor, 55, *56*, 57, 58
Smithson, Alison and Peter. *See also Economist* building; Golden Lane Estate; House at Colville Place; House of the Future; Hunstanton Secondary Modern School; Sheffield University Extension
architectural principles, 23, 30, 56–57
and *une architecture autre*, 27, 34–35, 36–40
and automobile design, 37
Banham on, 31–32, 39–40, 41, 44
Banham's association with, 17
as boffins, 101
and *bricolage*, 95
buildings after 1970, 120
and clip-on architecture, 54, 58–59
and contemporary style, 21, 30
figures in plans by, 195n39
and formalism, 34–35
and High Tech architecture, 119–20, 121, 142n3
influence of, 127
influences on, 29, 56, 123
and New Brutalism, 16, 25–26, 30, 55–56, 57, 120
Parallel of Life and Art exhibition (1953), *22*, 22–24, *23*
and standards from outside architecture, 41
Sugden House, 36, *36*
Upper Lawn Pavilion, Fonthill Estate, 54, *54*
Wayland Young Pavilion, 54
standard-of-living packages, Banham on, *93*, 93–94
Stirling, James, 17, 21, 54, 72, 122, 125, 126, 148, 192. *See also* Olivetti Training Center

Stockholmsutställningen Entrance Pavilion (Asplund), 19, *19*, 20
Student Hostel Service Tower (Farrell/Grimshaw Partnership), 63–68, *64*, 119, 121, 142n9, 148, *213*
Suburban Sets (Herron), 188–89, *189*
Summer House at Stennäs (Asplund), 19, *19*
Swedish architecture, influence in Great Britain, 19–21

Tafuri, Manfredo, 66–67, 68, 85n56, 159–60
Team 4, 68, 125–26. *See also* Reliance Controls Building technology. *See also* High Tech architecture; mechanical services
and neopicturesque style, 204
potential incompatibility with architecture, 155, 177, 244
Telecom Slug (British Telecom Mobile Exhibition Structure), *187*, 187–88, 190–91
terminology in Banham, 4–6, 38
Thacher and Thompson, 109–11, *110*, 112
Theory and Design in the First Machine Age (Banham), 3, 4, 7, 10, 18, 65, 101, 102, 152, 155, 176, 177
Townscape, 19, 20, 30, 31, 39, 97, 203, 203–4
"Townscape Casebook" (Cullen), 203, *203*
Turnbull, William, 16, 17, 26

United Nations Headquarters (Harrison), *106*, 106–7
University of California, Santa Cruz, 158–59

Vidler, Anthony, 3, 16, 26, 33, 176
Viganò, Vittoriano, 42, *42*, 55
Vision der Moderne exhibition (1986), 191–92, 196–97n86, 243
The Visions of Ron Herron (Banham), 7, 177–81, 186–93
visual unity
Banham's insistence on, 6, 7, 54–55, 63, 79–83, 89, 107, 122, 132, 153–54, 157, 161–63, 166, 167, 174, 181, 199–201, 205, 206
clip-on architecture and, 57–58, 60, 68
Smithsons' New Brutalism and, 39–40, 50n133

Walking City (Herron), 188, *188*, 226–27
Webb, Mike, 178–79, 183, 185
Whiteley, Nigel, 3, 16, 99, 115n37, 160–61
Willis Faber & Dumas Headquarters (Foster Associates), 10, 133–36, *134*, 142n4, 151, 161, *198*, 199 200–205, 200–201, *203*, 206n8, *228, 229*, 230–31
Wittkower, Rudolf, 15, 29–32, 66, 81, 82, 204
Woodland Cemetery buildings (Asplund), 19–20
Wright, Frank Lloyd, 103, 122. *See also* Larkin Building

Yale University, High Tech architects and, 121–22
Yale University Art Gallery (Kahn), 32, *32*, 61, 121, 161

Zip-Up Enclosures (Richard + Su Rogers), 69–71, *70*, 75, 86n73, 143n32
"Zoom Wave Hits Architecture" (Banham), 180